A Cooperative Species

A Cooperative Species

HUMAN RECIPROCITY AND ITS EVOLUTION

Samuel Bowles and Herbert Gintis

Princeton University Press
Princeton and Oxford

Published by Princeton University Press, 41 William Street, Princeton, New Jersey
08540
In the United Kingdom: Princeton University Press, 6 Oxford Street, Woodstock,
Oxfordshire OX20 1TW
press.princeton.edu

Jacket art: The Zamenkomst Panel, discovered in the Maclear district in the southern
Drakensberg Mountains. Image provided by Iziko Museums of Cape Town, Iziko Social
History Collections.

Library of Congress Cataloging-in-Publication Data

Bowles, Samuel.
 A cooperative species: human reciprocity and its evolution / Samuel Bowles, Herbert
Gintis. p. cm.
 Includes bibliographical references and index.
 ISBN 978-0-691-15125-0 (hbk. : alk. paper) 1 . Cooperation. 2. Cooperativeness. 3.
Behavior evolution. I . Gintis, Herbert. II. Title.
 HD2961.B687 2011
 302.1'4-dc22

2 0 1 0 0 4 6 8 6 1

British Library Cataloging-in-Publication Data is available

The publisher would like to acknowledge the authors of this volume for providing the
camera-ready copy from which this book was printed

This book has been composed in Times and Mathtime

Printed on acid-free paper. ∞

Printed in the United States of America

10 9 8 7 6 5 4 3 2

For James Chaney (1943–1964), Andrew Goodman (1943–1964),
and Michael Schwerner (1939–1964)

Contents

Preface

I wish you would let an old man, who has had his share of fighting, remind you that battles, like hypotheses, are not to be multiplied beyond necessity.

T. H. Huxley, *Letter to F. Ray Lankester* (December 6, 1888)

Is self-interest a natural disposition of our species, other than generosity toward members of one's immediate family? For well over a century the sociobiology of human behavior, and especially this question, has been a minefield of heated debate and fiery rhetoric. Huxley was an avid participant, as the moniker "Darwin's bulldog" suggests.

We have attempted to follow Huxley's advice rather than his example (the quote is from Gould (2002), p. 120). We have been aided by a remarkable group of scholars, many of whom have offered sustained criticism of our work, in print and in person, as it progressed, and to all of whom we are most grateful: Christopher Boehm, Robert Boyd, Colin Camerer, Armin Falk, Ernst Fehr, Marcus Feldman, Urs Fischbacher, Simon Gächter, Peter Hammerstein, Joe Henrich, Kim Hill, Hillard Kaplan, Richard McElreath, Ugo Pagano, Peter Richerson, Eric Alden Smith, and Polly Wiessner, among others. Robert Boyd, Tanya Elliot, Alejandro Fajardo, Marcus Feldman, Laura Fortunado, Simon Gächter, Laurent Keller, Laurent Lehmann, Robert Rowthorn, and Jeremy Van Cleve read the entire manuscript and their suggestions improved it immeasurably.

For their contributions to the development of our ideas, and critiques of earlier versions of the material to follow, we would also like to thank Margaret Alexander, Kenneth Arrow, Carl Bergstrom, Bruce Bertram, Ken Binmore, Stephen Burks, Jeffrey Carpenter, Luigi Luca Cavalli-Sforza, Jung-Kyoo Choi, Timothy Clutton-Brock, George Cowan, Molly Daniell, Emma Einhorn, Steven Frank, Drew Fudenberg, Stefany Moreno Gamez, Daniel Gintis, Alan Grafen, Avner Greif, Henry Harpending, Kristin Hawkes, Kristin Howard, Keith Huntley, Sung-Ha Hwang, Kenneth Kennedy, Patricia Lambert, Kevin Langergraber, Steven LeBlanc, Olof Leimar, Iren Levina, Amara Levy-Moore, Bridget Longridge, Eric Maskin, John Mitani, Suresh Naidu, Molly O'Grady, John Pepper, Alan Rogers, Paul Seabright, Rajiv Sethi, Carlos Rodriquez Sickert, E. Somanathan, Eors Szathmáry, Robert Trivers, Alina Vereshchagina, Linda Vigilant, Jon Wilkins, David Sloan Wilson, Elisabeth Wood, Richard Wrangham, and Peyton Young,

We have drawn upon material from several journal articles, some written with coauthors Robert Boyd, Jung-Kyoo Choi and Astrid Hopfensitz, including the following articles: "Group Competition, Reproductive Leveling and the Evolution of Human Altruism." *Science* 314 (2006):1569–1572; "Did Warfare among Ancestral Hunter-Gatherer Groups Affect the Evolution of Human Social Behaviors?" *Science* 324 (2009):1293–98; "Strong Reciprocity and Human Sociality," *Journal of Theoretical Biology* 206 (2000):169–179; "The Hitchhiker's Guide to Altruism: Genes, Culture, and the Internalization of Norm," *Journal of Theoretical Biology* 220,4 (2003):407-418; "Solving the Puzzle of Human Prosociality," *Rationality and Society* 15,2 (2003):155-187; "The Coevolution of Individual Behaviors and Social Institutions," *Journal of Theoretical Biology* 223 (2003):135–147 (with Jung-Kyoo Choi and Astrid Hopfensitz); "The Evolution of Strong Reciprocity: Cooperation in Heterogeneous Populations," *Theoretical Population Biology* 65 (2004):17–28; "The Coevolution of Parochial Altruism and War," *Science* 318,26 (2007):636–640 with Jung-Kyoo Choi; and "Coordinated Punishment of Defectors Sustains Cooperation and Can Proliferate When Rare," *Science* 328 (2010): 617–620 (with Robert Boyd).

We have presented technical material in verbal as well as mathematical form wherever possible, and avoided mathematical formulations entirely where that was possible without sacrificing clarity. The appendix includes brief description of several techniques that we employ throughout the book. When a technical term is first used, the term appears in italics and is defined. The page number in which a definition will be found appears in boldface in the index. Further uses of technical terms refer back to the definition, or to an explanation in the appendix, using the symbol § followed by chapter number (if not in the current chapter) and section number. More complete statements of some of the technical aspects of our models and simulations are found in the works cited in the previous paragraph. Readers interested in the overall argument of the book may wish to read Chapters 1 and 12, and §2.4. The reader may skip §3.1 to §3.10, on the experimental evidence concerning social preferences, and §5.1 to §5.4, on economic models of cooperation based on repeated game theory, without losing the main themes of the book.

We are grateful to the Iziko Museums of Cape Town for permission to use the Zamenkomst Panel from Maclear district in the southern Drakensberg Mountains. Thanks also to Margaret Alexander, Joy Lecuyer, Timothy Taylor, and Della Ulibarri at the Santa Fe Institute, and the hospitality of the Certosa di Pontignano and the Scuola Superiore Santa Chiara of the University of Siena. Finally, we gratefully acknowledge the John D. and Catherine T. MacArthur Foundation, University of Siena, Central European University, the Hungarian Scientific Research Fund (OTKA), the U.S. National Science Foundation, and the Behavioral Science Program at the Santa Fe Institute for providing research support.

Santa Fe, NM USA
Budapest, Hungary
March 2011

1

A Cooperative Species

> How selfish soever man may be supposed, there are evidently some principles
> in his nature, which interest him in the fortune of others, and render their happi-
> ness necessary to him, though he derives nothing from it, except the pleasure of
> seeing it.
>
> Adam Smith, *The Theory of Moral
> Sentiments* (2000[1759]) Chapter 1, p. 3

Is our conscience nothing but "the inner voice that tells us that somebody might be looking," as the jaundiced H. L. Mencken (1949) put it? Or did the 20th century American essayist overlook humanity's penchant genuinely to care for others, including total strangers, and to act morally, even when nobody is looking? And if Adam Smith's affirmation of humanity's moral sentiments is more nearly correct than Mencken's skepticism, how could this oddly cooperative animal, *Homo sapiens*, ever have come to be?

In the pages that follow we advance two propositions.

First, people cooperate not only for self-interested reasons but also because they are genuinely concerned about the well-being of others, try to uphold social norms, and value behaving ethically for its own sake. People punish those who exploit the cooperative behavior of others for the same reasons. Contributing to the success of a joint project for the benefit of one's group, even at a personal cost, evokes feelings of satisfaction, pride, even elation. Failing to do so is often a source of shame or guilt.

Second, we came to have these "moral sentiments" because our ancestors lived in environments, both natural and socially constructed, in which groups of individuals who were predisposed to cooperate and uphold ethical norms tended to survive and expand relative to other groups, thereby allowing these prosocial motivations to proliferate. The first proposition concerns proximate motivations for prosocial behavior, the second addresses the distant evolutionary origins and ongoing perpetuation of these cooperative dispositions.

Cooperation was prominent among the suite of behaviors that marked the emergence of behaviorally modern humans in Africa. Those living 75,000–90,000 years ago at the mouth of what is now the Klasies River near Port Elizabeth, South Africa, for example, consumed eland, hippopotamus, and other large game (Singer and Wymer 1982). The image of hunters and their prey on the jacket of this book is from the nearby Drakensberg Mountains. Among the slaughtered remains found there is a now-extinct giant buffalo *Pelovoris antiquus*, which weighed almost 2000 kilograms and whose modern-day (smaller) descendant is one of the most dangerous game animals in Africa (Milo 1998). The Klasies River inhabitants, and their contemporaries in other parts of Africa, almost certainly cooperated in the hunt and shared the prey among the members of their group. Even earlier evidence of trade in exotic obsidians extending over 300 kilometers in East Africa is another unmistakable footprint of early human cooperation.

Like those living at Klasies River mouth, other "hunting apes" quite likely cooperated in the common projects of pursuing large game, sharing the prey, and maintaining group defense. Both *Homo neanderthalensis* and the recently discovered *Homo floresiensis* survived well into the *Late Pleistocene* (meaning the period from between about 126 and 12 thousand years before the present) and hunted large game, the latter targeting the pygmy (but nonetheless substantial) elephants that had evolved on the island environment of Flores, off the coast of Indonesia.

Other primates engage in common projects. Chimpanzees, for example, join boundary patrols and some hunt cooperatively. Male Hamadryas baboons respect proximity-based property rights in food and mates. Many species breed cooperatively, with helpers and babysitters devoting substantial energetic costs to the feeding, protection and other care of non-kin (Hrdy 2009). Social insects, including many species of bees and termites, maintain high levels of cooperation, often among very large numbers of individuals. Other common forms of cooperation among non-human animals, summarized by Kappeler and van Schaik (2006), are "grooming and other forms of body care, alarm calling, predator inspection, protection against attacks by predators or conspecifics, supporting injured group members. . . [and] egg-trading among hermaphrodites."

While cooperation is common in many species, *Homo sapiens* is exceptional in that in humans cooperation extends beyond close genealogical kin to include even total strangers, and occurs on a much larger scale than other species except for the social insects.

In the pages that follow we will examine the cultural, biological and other processes that explain how humans became this exceptionally cooperative species.

By *cooperation* we mean engaging with others in a mutually beneficial activity. Examples include the joint pursuit of political and military objectives as well as the more prosaic foundations of everyday life: collaboration among employees in a firm, exchanges between buyers and sellers, and the maintenance of local amenities among neighbors.

Cooperative behavior may confer benefits net of costs on the individual cooperator, and thus could be motivated entirely by self-interest. Market exchange is an example. In this case, cooperation is a form of *mutualism*, namely an activity that confers net benefits both on the actor and on others. But cooperation may also impose net costs upon individuals in the sense that not cooperating would increase their fitness or other material payoffs. In this case cooperative behavior constitutes a form of *altruism* (see §A1).

The evolution of cooperation that is mutualistic or that involves only close family relatives is easily explained. Cooperation among close family members could have evolved by natural selection because the benefits of cooperative actions are conferred on the close genetic relatives of the cooperator, thereby helping to proliferate alleles ("genes") associated with the cooperative behavior. Cooperation could also have evolved because one individual's costly contribution to the welfare of another individual is reliably reciprocated at a future date, thereby making cooperation mutualistic. Models of altruism toward close family members and reciprocal altruism (which really should be called "enlightened self-interest") are popular among biologists and economists alike and explain many forms of human cooperation, particularly those occurring in families or in frequently repeated dyadic (two-person) or other very small group interactions.

But these models fail to explain two facts about human cooperation: that it takes place in groups far larger than the immediate family, and that both in real life and in laboratory experiments, it occurs in interactions that are unlikely to be repeated, and where it is impossible to obtain reputational gains from cooperating.

The most parsimonious proximal explanation of cooperation, one that is supported by extensive experimental and other evidence, is that people gain pleasure from or feel morally obligated to cooperate with like-minded people. People also enjoy punishing those who exploit the cooperation of others, or feel morally obligated to do so. Free-riders frequently feel guilty, and if they are sanctioned by others, they may feel ashamed. We term these feelings *social preferences*. Social preferences include a concern, positive or negative, for the well being of others, as well as a desire to uphold ethical norms.

In many human groups, these motives are sufficiently common to sustain social norms that support contributions to projects of common benefit, even when cooperators bear costs in order to benefit others. The forms of cooperation and the behaviors that elicit punishment by peers differ from society to society, but the critical role of social preferences in sustaining altruistic cooperation is ubiquitous.

Because we are convinced that most people enjoy cooperating at least in some situations and dislike people who do not, the task we will set for ourselves is not that typically addressed by biologists and economists, namely to explain why people cooperate despite being selfish. Rather, we seek to explain why we are not purely selfish—why the social preferences that sustain altruistic cooperation are so common. Proximate answers to this question are to be found in the way that our brains process information and induce the behavioral responses that we term cooperation. But how did we come to have brains that function in this manner?

Early human environments are part of our answer. Our Late Pleistocene ancestors inhabited the large-mammal-rich African savannah and other environments in which cooperation in acquiring and sharing food yielded substantial benefits at relatively low cost. The slow human life-history with prolonged periods of dependency of the young also made the cooperation of non-kin in child rearing and provisioning beneficial. As a result, members of groups that sustained cooperative strategies for provisioning, child-rearing, sanctioning non-cooperators, defending against hostile neighbors, and truthfully sharing information had significant advantages over members of non-cooperative groups.

In the course of our subsequent history we created novel social and physical environments exhibiting similar, or even greater, benefits of cooperation, among them the division of labor coordinated by market exchange and respect of rights of property, systems of production characterized by increasing returns to scale (irrigated agriculture, modern industry, information systems with network externalities), and warfare. The impressive scope of these modern forms of cooperation was facilitated by the emergence in the last seven millennia of governments capable of enforcing property rights and providing incentives for the self-interested to contribute to common projects.

But prior to the emergence of governments and since, cooperation has been sustained also by motives that led some people to bear costs on behalf of others, contributing to common projects, punishing transgressors, and excluding outsiders. In the pages that follow we will advance three reasons why these altruistic social preferences supporting cooperation outcompeted unmitigated and amoral self-interest.

First, human groups have devised ways to protect their altruistic members from exploitation by the self-interested. Prominent among these is the public-spirited shunning, ostracism, and even execution of free-riders and others who violate cooperative norms. Other group activities protecting altruists from exploitation are leveling practices that limit hierarchy and inequality, including sharing food and information.

Second, humans adopted prolonged and elaborate systems of socialization that led individuals to internalize the norms that induce cooperation, so that contributing to common projects and punishing defectors became objectives in their own right rather than constraints on behavior. Together, the internalization of norms and the protection of the altruists from exploitation served to offset, at least partially, the competitive handicaps born by those who were motivated to bear personal costs to benefit others.

Third, between-group competition for resources and survival was and remains a decisive force in human evolutionary dynamics. Groups with many cooperative members tended to survive these challenges and to encroach upon the territory of the less cooperative groups, thereby both gaining reproductive advantages and proliferating cooperative behaviors through cultural transmission. The extraordinarily high stakes of intergroup competition and the contribution of altruistic cooperators to success in these contests meant that sacrifice on behalf of others, extending beyond the immediate family and even to virtual strangers, could proliferate. Modern-day nationalism is an example.

This is part of the reason why humans became extraordinarily group-minded, favoring cooperation with insiders and often expressing hostility toward outsiders. Boundary-maintenance supported within-group cooperation and exchange by limiting group size and within-group linguistic, normative and other forms of heterogeneity. Insider favoritism also sustained the between-group conflicts and differences in behavior that made group competition a powerful evolutionary force.

In short, humans became the cooperative species that we are because cooperation was highly beneficial to the members of groups that practiced it, and we were able to construct social institutions that minimized the disadvantages of those with social preferences in competition with fellow group members, while heightening the group-level advantages associated with the high levels of cooperation that these social preferences allowed. These institutions proliferated because the groups that adopted them secured high levels of within-group cooperation, which in turn favored the groups' survival as a biological and cultural entity in the face of environmental, military and other challenges.

Early humans were not alone in occupying territory and a feeding niche that made cooperation among group members highly advantageous. Indeed our ancestors competed with lions, hyenas, wild dogs and possibly other hominid cooperative hunters for the very same ungulates and other large mammals. Nor were our ancestors exceptional in the kinds of group competition for territory and other valued resources that made cooperation so essential to survival. Chimpanzees, too, engage in lethal contests between troops where winners gain territory and reproductive advantages. The same is true of species as diverse as meerkats and fire ants. Nor are humans exceptional in constructing our own physical and social environments. Beavers build dams, birds build nests, and burrowing animals build underground catacombs. Why then did humans, rather than chimps, lions, or meerkats, develop such exceptional forms of cooperation?

Central to our reply are the human cognitive, linguistic and physical capacities that made us especially good at all of the above, and more. These capacities allow us to formulate general norms of social conduct, to erect social institutions regulating this conduct, to communicate these rules and what they entail in particular situations, to alert others to their violation and to organize coalitions to punish the violators. No less important is the psychological capacity to internalize norms, to experience such social emotions as shame and moral outrage, and to base group membership on such non-kin characteristics as ethnicity and language, which in turn facilitates costly conflicts among groups. Equally essential was the developmental plasticity of humans and our long period of maturation, the latter initially a result of the particular feeding niche that early humans occupied. Also important is the unique human capacity to use projectile weapons, a consequence of which is to lower the cost of coordinated punishment of norm violators within a group, to reduce the costs of hunting large animals, with concomitant benefits accruing to groups with widely endorsed sharing norms, and to render intergroup conflicts more lethal. A result was to elevate group-level competition to a more powerful evolutionary force.

These exceptional aspects of human livelihoods and social interactions, we will show, have favored the evolution of an individual predisposition to cooperate with others and to punish those who exploit the cooperation of others. But more than individual-level motivation is involved. The regulation of social interactions by group-level institutions plays no less a role than altruistic individual motives in understanding how this cooperative species came to be. Institutions affect the rewards and penalties associated with particular behaviors, often favoring the adoption of cooperative actions over others, so that even the self-regarding are often induced to act in the interest of the group. Of course it will not do to posit these institutions *a priori*. Rather, we will show that they could have coevolved with other human traits in the relevant ancestral ecologies and social environments.

Had we chosen *A Colluding Species* as our title, it would not be necessary to point out that cooperation is not an end, but rather a means. In some settings, competition, the antithesis of cooperation, is the more effective means to a given end. Similarly, the individual motives and group-level institutions that account for cooperation among humans include not only the most elevated, including a concern for others, fair-mindedness, and democratic accountability of leaders, but also the most wicked, such as vengeance, racism, religious bigotry, and hostility toward outsiders.

Price-fixing by cartels and other baleful economic effects of collusion motivated Adam Smith to advocate a competitive economic system under which such forms of antisocial collusion would unravel. In its stead he advocated "an invisible hand" that would guide the efforts of countless self-interested producers to coordinate a modern division of labor in the interest of all, a stunning example of mutualistic cooperation.

But if the late 18th century gave us this evocative metaphor for the beneficial effects of the pursuit of individual gain, the mid-20th century invented two no less riveting metaphors for the dark side of self-interest: the prisoner's dilemma and the tragedy of the commons. Their logic inverted Adam Smith's invisible hand, showing that even where cooperation was essential to the pursuit of common ends, it would falter in the face of self-interest. Garrett Hardin's tragedy of the commons was rapidly assimilated by scholars, as it embraced a model of self-interest already well established in both economics and the neo-Darwinian synthesis in biology. Social preferences, Hardin made clear, were powerless to counter the "remorseless" degradation of the environment:

> The tragedy cannot be solved by an appeal to conscience, for those who heeded the appeal would have fewer children, and by the heritability of capacity of conscience, this would lead to a less moral population. (p. 1246)

Because "freedom in a commons means ruin for all," he advocated a modern version of Thomas Hobbes' *Leviathan*, which he termed "mutual coercion mutually agreed upon." Hardin termed his contribution a "rebuttal to the invisible hand." In like manner, Mancur Olson's no less ineluctable "logic of collective action" in n-person prisoner's dilemmas demonstrated the inevitability of a passive citizenry and the impossibility of cooperation, due to ubiquitous free-riders (Olson 1965).

But as the prisoner's dilemma and the tragedy of the commons were becoming staples of undergraduate instruction, field evidence from anthropologists and microhistorical studies of social movements pointed in an entirely different direction. Herders in high Alpine and Andean common summer pastures had averted tragedy without government regulation for centuries, possibly millennia (Netting 1989). Workers and democrats had for centuries risked their lives in collective actions that plainly defied Olson's logic (Moore, Jr. 1978, Hobsbawm 1983). The work of Elinor Ostrom and her collaborators documented literally hundreds of decentralized tragedy-averting commons governance systems around the world, bringing to a head this collision of empirical observation and the logic of self-interest (Ostrom 1990).

The tension between the relentless logic of self-interest and the ubiquity of collective action in real-world settings was eventually resolved by a series of experiments by psychologists and economists, most notably by Ernst Fehr and his colleagues (Fehr and Gächter 2000a, Herrmann et al. 2008). The experiments confirmed that self-interest is indeed a powerful motive, but also that other motives are no less important. Even when substantial sums of money are at stake, many, perhaps most, experimental subjects were found to be fair-minded, generous toward those similarly inclined, and nasty toward those who violate these prosocial precepts. In light of these results, the evidence that the tragedy of the commons is sometimes averted and that collective action is a motor of human history is considerably less puzzling. The puzzle, instead, is how humans came to be like this.

The growing interest in generous and civic-minded predispositions in the social sciences has been paralleled in biology, where the evolution of cooperative behavior, in the opinion of the editors of *Science*, is one of the top 25 questions facing scientists today (Kennedy et al. 2005). Biological classics such as Konrad Lorenz' (1963) *On Aggression* and Richard Dawkins' (1976) *The Selfish Gene* have now been joined by works whose titles signal the shift in attention: *Good Natured*, by Frans de Waal (1997), *Mother Nature*, by Sarah Hrdy (2000), *The Moral Animal*, by Robert Wright (1995), *Origin of Virtue*, by Matt Ridley (1998), *Unto Others*, by Elliot Sober and David Sloan Wilson (1998), *Altruistically Inclined?* by Alexander Field (2004), *The Genial Gene: Deconstructing Darwinian Selfishness*, by Joan Roughgarden (2009), and *Moral Origins: Social Selection and the Evolution of Virtue, Altruism, and Shame*, by Christopher Boehm (2011).

These recent works are reminiscent of Pyotr Kropotkin's *Mutual Aid* a century earlier, a book that had advanced a kinder, gentler view of the evolutionary process in opposition to the then popular dog-eat-dog Social Darwinist claims about what natural selection entails for human behavior. The moral, generous, and civic-minded predispositions documented in these works and in the pages that follow show that evolution can not only foster self-interest but also promote the generous and ethical behaviors that help us escape the prisoner's dilemma and avert the tragedy of the commons, and that permit us to sustain the hope for a society committed to freedom and justice for all. However, we will see that this is true not despite, but in important measure because, evolutionary processes are "red in tooth and claw," in Alfred, Lord Tennyson's famous words.

2

The Evolution of Altruism in Humans

> The Americans...are fond of explaining almost all the actions of their lives by the principle of self-interest rightly understood, how an enlightened regard for themselves constantly prompts them to assist one another...In this respect I think they frequently fail to do themselves justice; in the United States as well as elsewhere people are sometimes seen to give way to those disinterested and spontaneous impulses that are natural to man; but the Americans seldom admit that they yield to emotions of this kind.
>
> Alexis de Tocqueville, *Democracy in America*
> (1958[1835]) Vol. 2, chapter VIII

Like Alexis de Tocqueville's Americans, a distinguished tradition in biology and the social sciences has sought to explain cooperative behavior "by the principle of self-interest, rightly understood." Richard Dawkins (1976), in *The Selfish Gene*, writes "Let us try to teach generosity and altruism, because we are born selfish." Similarly, drawing out the philosophical implications of the evolutionary analysis of human behavior, Richard Alexander (1987) writes, "ethics, morality, human conduct, and the human psyche are to be understood only if societies are seen as collections of individuals seeking their own self-interest" (p. 3). From J. B. S. Haldane's quip that he would risk his life to save eight drowning cousins (but not fewer) to the folk theorem of modern game theory (§5.1–§5.3), this tradition has clarified the ways that helping close family members, repeated interactions and reputation-building might confer fitness advantages and other benefits on those engaging in seemingly unselfish behaviors.

Our approach, however, favors Tocqueville, not Tocqueville's Americans. Explaining why will take us through disciplines as diverse as population genetics, experimental economics, evolutionary game theory, and archaeology and across semantic minefields of heavily freighted terms, such as altruism, and controversial scientific questions, such as the relationship between genetic inheritance and cultural transmission. In this chapter we explain our conceptual strategy and define terms.

Following William Hamilton, we use the term *helping* to describe behaviors that confer benefits on others, reserving the term *altruism* for helping in situations where the helper would benefit in fitness or other material ways by withholding help. This is the standard biological definition adopted by Hamilton (1975), Grafen (1984), Kerr et al. (2004), Matessi and Karlin (1984) and others. A more complete definition is given in §A1. Our models and simulations in subsequent chapters show that these altruistic helping behaviors may proliferate under conditions similar to the natural and social environments of ancestral humans.

2.1 Preferences, Beliefs, and Constraints

We explore the proximal influences on an individual action such as helping using the *beliefs, preferences, and constraints* approach common to economics and decision theory. According to this approach, what individuals do when restricted to a specific set of feasible actions depends on their desires and goals on the one hand, and their beliefs on the other. The term *constraints* represent the limitations placed on the feasible actions an individual may take in a given situation. *Beliefs* are an individual's representation of the causal structure of the world, including the relationship between the individual's actions and the probabilities of the various possible resulting outcomes. *Preferences* are the pro or con sentiments that make up the individual's valuation of the various possible outcomes of taking an action.

Preferences may be described as an ordering (technically, a preference function) of the states of the world that may result from one's actions. We assume preferences satisfy two conditions: they are complete (any two states can be compared) and transitive; that is, consistent, so that if one prefers A to B and B to C, one then prefers A to C. Preferences are the results of a variety of influences: tastes (food likes and dislikes, for example), habits, emotions (such as shame or anger) and other visceral reactions (such as fear), the manner in which individuals construe situations (or more narrowly, the way they frame decisions), commitments (like promises), internalized norms of ethical behavior, psychological propensities (for aggression, extroversion and the like), and affective relationships with others.

We can succinctly and analytically summarize the individual's behavior as maximization of a preference function, even though this by no means describes the underlying psychological processes (Savage 1954). To say that individuals act on their preferences means that knowledge of these preferences provides a concise and accurate account of their actions, given their beliefs and constraints . Of course, this analytical account will not generally coincide with the account that individuals would give of their own behavior.

The preferences, beliefs, and constraints approach is silent on the cognitive and other processes determining individual action. In some situations, buying a car, for example, individuals may deliberately optimize, while in others, diet or ethical behavior, for example, they may follow rules of thumb that have been adopted without conscious optimization. Optimizing models are commonly used to describe behavior not because they mimic the cognitive processes of the actors, which they rarely do, but because they capture important influences on individual behavior in a succinct and analytically tractable way.

A version of the beliefs, preferences, and constraints model, incorporating the behavioral assumptions sometimes summarized as *Homo economicus*, has become standard not only in economics but throughout the human behavioral sciences. F. Y. Edgeworth, a founder of neoclassical economics, expressed this view in his *Mathematical Psychics*: "The first principle of economics is that every agent is actuated only by self-interest" (1881 p. 104). But self-interest need not be part of the preferences, beliefs, and constraints approach. Preferences could be altruistic or even masochistic. Nevertheless, while self-interest is not formally implied by the conventional approach, it is generally assumed in practice. The assumption allows precise predictions in strategic situations, where it takes the form of what we term the *self-interest axiom*, namely that people seek to maximize their expected payoffs and believe that others do the same.

But predictions based on Edgeworth's self-interest axiom often fail to describe the actions people take. Indeed, the axiom was never intended to be taken literally. Edgeworth followed the statement above with the caveat that the axiom was strictly true only in "contract and war." But even in these areas, exceptions to the canon are glaring and increasingly well documented, as is shown by Truman Bewley's (2000) finding that firms do not cut wages during recessions because wage cuts demoralize workers, who consider them unfair. Similarly, Jessica Stern's (2003) finding that terrorist violence is motivated as a reaction against perceived injustice, and the case of kamikaze pilots (Hagoromo Society 1973), who volunteer to sacrifice their lives out of a sense of honor and duty, are dramatic indications that people are often motivated by non-selfish principles.

The economist's usual defense of the self-interest axiom is that it is self-evident, with the fallback assertion being that natural selection could not have produced any other kind of preferences. But, as the evidence to follow suggests, the assertion is far from self-evident, and in fact is simply false.

The importance of fairness considerations in wage setting and other exchanges just noted is an example (see also Blinder and Choi, 2000). Equally at variance with self-evident self-interest is the fact that individuals bother to vote, given that the likelihood that their vote is decisive is vanishingly small, as well as their extensive support, when they do vote, for tax-financed income transfers to the poor even among those sufficiently rich and upwardly mobile to be very unlikely ever to benefit directly from these transfers (Gilens 1999, Fong 2001, Fong et al. 2005). Also telling against the self-evident status of the self-interest axiom are studies at Continental Airlines, Nucor Steel, and other companies that have found group incentives to be effective even where gain-sharing is distributed among such a large number that the additional income resulting from one's own effort is negligible (Hansen 1997, Knez and Simester 2001). Other examples include volunteering for dangerous military and other tasks, tax compliance far in excess of that which would maximize expected incomes (Andreoni et al. 1998), participating in various forms of collective action with little expectation of personal benefit (Moore 1978, Wood 2003), and conforming to norms and laws in cases where one's transgression would be personally advantageous and would not be detected or, as H. L. Mencken would say, when no one is looking.

2.2   Social Preferences and Social Dilemmas

Recall that *social preferences* are a concern for the well-being of others and a desire to uphold ethical norms. By contrast with *self-regarding* preferences, which are based on states concerning oneself alone, we stress *other-regarding* and *ethical* preferences, the former defined as valuations based at least in part on states that occur to others. Social preferences include not only generosity toward others and a preference for "fair" outcomes, but also what Thomas Hobbes called the desire for "eminence," Thorstein Veblen's "pecuniary emulation" exemplified by a desire to "keep up with the Joneses" (Veblen 1899), Charles Horton Cooley's "looking-glass self," according to which our self-esteem is dependent in part upon what others think of us, so we attempt to favorably impress others as a means of raising our subjective self-esteem (Cooley 1902, Brennan and Pettit 2004), and Aristotle's *character virtues*, such as honesty and courage, which are personal values that promote prosocial behavior (Aristotle 2002[350 BC]).

Social preferences may be self-regarding. Ethical commitments may reflect a concern for the states experienced by others, but need not. One can be honest because one seeks to avoid imposing costs on others by deceiving them. But honesty could be entirely self-regarding, practiced in order to be the kind of person one wants to be. Thus the textbook "economic man" would be described not only as self-regarding, but as amoral as well, though we will frequently use the simpler description—self-regarding—when the meaning is clear.

We prefer the term "social preferences" to the more common but ambiguous "unselfish" or "non-self-interested." "Unselfish" behaviors are, like "selfish" behaviors, motivated by the individual's preferences. If I get pleasure from helping others, or if I help others because I would feel guilty if I did not, I am no less motivated by my own preferences than if I enjoy eating a fine meal, or help another because I will be punished if I do not. Moreover, such other-regarding emotions as spite and envy would not generally be termed "unselfish" in any sense. Nevertheless, like empathy, they are social preferences. The distinction between other-regarding and self-regarding preferences is not that other-regarding behaviors are counter-preferential, but rather that they are motivated at least in part by a concern about the effects of one's actions on others.

Social preferences assume special importance in interactions termed *social dilemmas*, that is, interactions in which the uncoordinated actions of individuals result in an outcome that is *Pareto inefficient*, meaning that there exists some other feasible outcome such that at least one member could be better off while no member would be worse off. Examples of social dilemmas modeled by game theorists are the prisoner's dilemma, the public goods game, sometimes termed an *n*-person prisoner's dilemma, the so-called war of attrition and other so-called arms race interactions, the tragedy of the commons and the common pool resource game in which contributing to the common project takes the form of forgoing the overexploitation of a jointly utilized resource such as a fishery, water supply, or forest. We say a person *free rides* if he benefits from the contributions of other group members while himself contributing less or nothing at all.

Here is an example. The most famous of all experimental games (§A3) is the *prisoner's dilemma*, with payoffs (the row player's first) shown in Figure 2.1. In this game, Alice and Bob will interact only once and cannot make any binding agreements about how they will play the game. This is an example of an anonymous, non-repeated *noncooperative game* (the latter term refers to the no-binding-agreements condition, not to the interests of the party or the outcomes of the game). The experimenter explains to Alice and Bob that each can take one of two actions without knowing the action taken by the other: cooperate (C) or defect (D). If both choose to cooperate, each receives $10 (the intersection of the C row and the C column in the figure), and if both defect, each receives $5 (the intersection of the D row and the D column). Moreover, if one cooperates and the other defects, the defector gets $15 and the cooperator gets nothing (the off-main-diagonal payoffs in the figure).

Bob

	C	D
C	10,10	0,15
D	15,0	5,5

Alice

Figure 2.1. The prisoners' dilemma game. Here and in other payoff matrices, the row player's payoff is first (Alice in this case), and the column player's payoff is second.

We assume both Alice and Bob do not have social preferences, and hence only care about their own payoffs. Alice reasons as follows. "If Bob cooperates, I get $15 by defecting and $10 by cooperating, so I should defect. If Bob defects, I get $5 by defecting and nothing by cooperating, so I should still defect. Thus I should defect no matter what Bob does." Bob of course comes to the same conclusion. Thus both defect, and each gets $5, which is half of what each could have gotten by cooperating. Thus, for Bob and Alice, defecting is a *dominant strategy*; that is, it is a *best response* (i.e., a payoff-maximizing strategy) regardless of what the other does. Because this is true for both Alice and Bob, mutually defecting is a *dominant strategy equilibrium* and is the predicted outcome for players without social preferences.

An other-regarding player cares about not only his own payoff, but that of his partner as well. Such a player might reason as follows. "I feel sufficiently positive toward a partner who cooperates that I would rather cooperate even if by doing so I forgo the larger payoff ($15) I could have had by defecting. If my partner defects, I of course prefer to defect as well, both to increase my earnings, and to decrease the earnings of a person who has behaved uncharitably toward me." If Bob and Alice reason in this manner, and if each believes the other is sufficiently likely to cooperate, both will cooperate. Thus, both mutual cooperate and mutual defect are equilibria in this new game, transformed from the old by augmenting the material payoffs with the players' concerns about one another.

A choice of strategies by players is a *Nash equilibrium* if each player's choice is a best response to the choice of the others. Note that a dominant strategy is always a Nash equilibrium because it is a best response whatever the other players do, but the reverse is not true. Social preferences may thus convert a prisoner's dilemma material payoff structure into what is called an *assurance game* payoff structure—each player will cooperate if assured that the other will cooperate as well, and will not if not. Thus mutual cooperation and mutual defection are both Nash equilibria. Which of the two Nash equilibria will obtain depends on the players' beliefs about what the other will do.

Despite the strong temptation to defect out of either selfishness or fear of being exploited by the other player, many experiments have found that a considerable fraction of subjects prefer to cooperate rather than defect in the prisoner's dilemma (Sally 1995). One famous real-life, high stakes example is the popular TV show *Friend or Foe*, where contestants play a prisoner's dilemma with stakes varying between $200 and $22,000. About half the contestants choose to cooperate even though they are guaranteed to earn more money by defecting, no matter what their partner does. Even more striking, contestants are no more likely to defect when the stakes are higher (List 2006, Oberholzer-Gee et al. 2010).

Similar behavior is observed in the laboratory. Kiyonari et al. (2000) had Japanese university students play the prisoner's dilemma with real monetary payoffs. The experimenters ran three distinct treatments. The first treatment was a standard simultaneous prisoner's dilemma in which both players choose whether to cooperate or defect without knowing the partner's choice. The second was a sequential "second player" prisoner's dilemma in which one player had to choose between cooperating and defecting after being informed that the partner had already chosen to cooperate. The third was again a prisoner's dilemma, which we will call a "first player" prisoner's dilemma, in which a player was told that he would choose first, but his decision to cooperate or defect would be transmitted to his partner before the latter made his own choice. The experimenters found that 38% of the subjects cooperated in the standard simultaneous treatment, 62% cooperated in the second player treatment, and 59% cooperated in the first player treatment. The decision to cooperate in each treatment cost the subject about $5 (600 yen). This shows unambiguously that a majority of subjects (62%) were conditional altruistic cooperators. Almost as many (59%) were not only cooperators, but were also willing to bet that their partners would be, provided the latter were assured of not being defected upon, although under standard conditions, without this assurance, only 38% would in fact cooperate. Experiments conducted by Watabe et al. (1996), Morris et al. (1998), Hayashi et al. (1999), McCabe et al. (2000) and Clark and Sefton (2001) found similar subject behavior.

Chapter 3 presents experimental and other evidence that social preferences are common in the cultures for which we have evidence. The same evidence shows that the fraction of most populations motivated solely by amoral self-regarding preferences is quite modest.

2.3   Genes, Culture, Groups, and Institutions

We define *culture* as the ensemble of preferences and beliefs that are acquired by means other than genetic transmission. Culture is an evolutionary force in its own right, not simply an effect of the interaction of genes and natural environments.

An alternative but we think incorrect approach holds that while preferences and beliefs that are transmitted culturally may constitute the proximate causes of behavior, they in turn are entirely explained by the interaction of our genetic makeup and the natural environment. According to this view, for example, the Lamalera whale hunters we discuss in Chapter 3 would be said to share valued resources because they have social preferences, but they have social preferences because they live in a place where hunting whales is the best way to make a living, and those who hunt large game do better if they learn how to share.

It is of course true that natural environments and genes affect the evolution of culture. But it is also true that culture affects the relative fitness of genetically transmitted behavioral traits. C. J. Lumsden and Edward O. Wilson (1981), Luigi Luca Cavalli-Sforza and Marcus Feldman (1981), Robert Boyd and Peter Richerson (1985), William

Durham (1991), Richerson and Boyd (2004) and others have provided compelling instances of these cultural effects on genetic evolution.

Recognizing the intimate interactions between genes and culture in humans, Edward Wilson, Charles Lumsden, Robert Boyd, Peter Richerson, Luigi Luca Cavalli-Sforza and Marcus Feldman began working in the 1970's on the parallels between genetic and cultural evolution and their interactions, their work initiating the modeling of *gene-culture coevolution*, the second concept underpinning our explanation of the origins and distinctive nature of cooperation among humans. According to gene-culture coevolution, human preferences and beliefs are the product of a dynamic whereby genes affect cultural evolution and culture affects genetic evolution, the two being tightly intertwined in the evolution of our species.

To see how gene-culture coevolution works, think about the ways that an organism may acquire information. The genome encodes information that is used to construct a new organism, to instruct the new organism how to transform sensory inputs into decision outputs (i.e., to endow the new organism with a specific preference structure), and to transmit this coded information virtually intact to the new organism. Since learning about one's environment is costly and error-prone, efficient information transmission is likely to ensure that the genome encode information relevant not to ephemeral aspects of the organism's environment but rather those that are constant, or that change only very slowly through time and space. Environmental conditions that vary more rapidly can be dealt with by providing the organism with the capacity to learn from one's environment, and hence phenotypically adapt to specific conditions.

For most animals, genetic transmission and individual learning are about all there is as far as information acquisition is concerned. Humans, by contrast, also acquire information from one another through a process of social learning. To see just how inadequate individual learning and genetically transmitted information would be in supporting human life in the absence of social learning, consider this sad story. Four hapless Europeans in 1860 attempted to cross the Australian continent from south to north and back, armed only with their ability to devise ways of living in an unfamiliar environment with the help of then-sophisticated equipment and ample stocks of food, carried on imported camels (Henrich and McElreath 2003). After a series of reverses, and having eaten the unfortunate camels, they resorted to foraging, attempting vainly to learn how to trap rats and birds and to catch fish in the occasional well-watered spot. Despite the generous gifts of food from the aboriginal groups who they encountered as they struggled on, three perished and the last was saved by a community of Yantruwanta people living in the desert, where he fully recovered and was eventually found by a European search party.

Thus there is a distinctively human intermediate case that is not well-handled by either genetic encoding or learning from one's environment *de novo* in each generation. When environmental conditions are positively but imperfectly correlated across generations, each generation acquires valuable information through learning that it cannot transmit genetically to the succeeding generation, because such information is not encoded in the germ line. In such environments, an animal could benefit from the transmission of information concerning the current state of the environment through some non-genetic information channel. Such information, called epigenetic by biologists, is quite common (Jablonka and Lamb 1995) and achieves its highest and most flexible form in cultural transmission in humans and to a considerably lesser extent in other primates (Bonner 1984, Richerson and Boyd 1998). *Cultural transmission*, also called *social learning* as opposed to *individual learning*, takes the form of vertical (parents to children), horizontal (peer to peer), and oblique (non-parental elder to younger) transfer of information.

The parallel between cultural and biological evolution goes back to William James (1880) and Julian Huxley (1955). The idea of treating culture as a form of epigenetic transmission was pioneered by Cavalli-Sforza and Feldman (1973), Karl Popper (1979), and Richard Dawkins, who coined the term "meme" in *The Selfish Gene* (1976) to represent an integral unit of information that could be transmitted phenotypically. There quickly followed several major contributions to a biological approach to culture, all based on the notion that culture, like genes, could evolve through replication (intergenerational transmission), mutation, and selection (Lumsden and Wilson 1981, Cavalli-Sforza and Feldman 1982, Boyd and Richerson 1985).

Richard Dawkins added a second fundamental mechanism of epigenetic information transmission in *The Extended Phenotype* (1982), noting that organisms can directly transmit environmental artifacts to the next generation, in the form of such constructs as beaver dams, bee hives, and even social structures (e.g., mating and hunting practices). Creating a fitness-relevant aspect of an environment and stably transmitting this environment across generations, known as *niche construction*, is a widespread form of epigenetic transmission (Odling-Smee et al. 2003). Moreover, niche construction gives rise to what might be called a gene-environment coevolutionary process, since a genetically induced environmental regularity becomes the basis for genetic selection, and genetic mutations that give rise to mutant niches will tend to survive if they are fitness enhancing for their constructors.

Our own models of the coevolution of genetically transmitted individual behaviors and culturally transmitted group-level institutions provide additional examples of the same process. We will see (Chapter 7) that the presence of a culturally transmitted convention, resource sharing, is essential to the evolution of a genetically transmitted altruistic trait governed by natural selection. In Chapter 10 we show that the possibility of acquiring advantageous behaviors by social learning could generate the conditions under which a genetically transmitted capacity to internalize norms could evolve. Human cultures, along with the institutional structures they support, are instances of niche construction (Laland et al. 2000, Bowles 2000, Laland and Feldman 2004).

In our gene-culture coevolution model of group-structured populations, the process of differential replication affects the frequency of both individual traits, generosity toward fellow group members, say, and group traits, a system of consensus decision making or property rights. Though inspired by biological approaches, especially those of Cavalli-Sforza and Feldman (1981), Boyd and Richerson (1985), and Durham (1991), like these authors, we do not privilege biological explanation. Our approach may be summarized as follows.

First, while genetic transmission of information plays a central role in our account, the genetics of non-pathological social behavior is for the most part unknown. Knowledge of the genetic basis of the human cognitive and linguistic capacities that make cooperation on a human scale possible has expanded greatly in recent years, but virtually nothing is known about genes that may be expressed in cooperative behavior, should these exist. No "gene for cooperation" has been discovered. Nor is it likely that one will ever be found, for the idea of a one-to-one mapping between genes and behavior is unlikely given what is now known about gene expression, and is implausible in light of the complexity and cultural variation of cooperative behaviors. Thus, when we introduce genetic transmission in our models, our reasoning operates at the phenotypic level. The "A allele" that accounts for altruistic behavior in Chapter 7 is just a phenotypic character that is transmitted exclusively from parent to child, thus abstracting from diploid reproduction, complex gene interactions, the vagaries of development and other aspects of real human genetic transmission, development and phenotypic expression. Similarly, the strategies studied in Chapter 9 are just bi-parentally inherited haploid genotypes; that is, each gene has a single copy, inherited with equal probability from either parent. In Chapter 10, where we study the evolution of the human capacity to internalize norms, the "internalization allele" is just a behavior acquired from parents.

This phenotype-based approach is a standard tool for the study of the evolution of social behavior in humans and other animals, and has a cogent justification as a device for abstracting from inconsequential complications surrounding the mechanics of genetic inheritance (Eshel and Feldman 1984, Grafen 1991, Hammerstein 1996, Eshel et al. 1998, Frank 1998). Moreover, because it uses observable phenotypes rather than unknown genotypes and developmental processes as the basis for analysis, the approach is readily applied to the kinds of empirical questions we address here.

Second, as is conventional in all models of selection, relative payoffs, whether in terms of fitness, material reward, social standing or some other metric, influence the evolution of the population shares of various behavioral types, higher payoff behaviors tending to increase their frequency in a population. The resulting so-called *payoff monotonic dynamic* is often implemented using "as if" optimization algorithms, though in doing this we do not attribute conscious optimization to individuals. Nor do we conclude that the resulting outcomes are in any sense optimal. In general they are not. The aggregation of individually optimal choices is universally suboptimal, except under highly unrealistic conditions.

Individuals with higher payoffs may produce more copies of their behaviors in subsequent periods either through the contribution of their greater resources to differential reproductive success or because individuals disproportionately adopt the behaviors of the more successful members of their group. The latter may occur voluntarily, as when youngsters copy stars, or coercively, as when dominant ethnic groups, classes, or nations impose their cultures on subjugated peoples. Of course, cultural transmission may also favor lower payoff behaviors (think of smoking or fast food). We will introduce just such a process when we study socialization and the internalization of norms in Chapter 10.

Third, because positive feedbacks are common in the processes of behavioral and institutional change we study, otherwise identical populations may exhibit quite different trajectories, reflecting the multiplicity of equilibria that is typical of models with positive feedbacks. The outcome that occurs need not be that with the higher average payoff. The process of selection among equilibria may be on such a long time scale that two populations described by exactly the same model may exhibit dramatically different distributions of behaviors for thousands of generations. The process of determining which of many possible equilibria will occur, termed *equilibrium selection*, thus assumes major importance.

Fourth, the emergence, proliferation and biological or cultural extinction of collections of individuals such as foraging bands, ethno-linguistic units, and nations, and the consequent evolutionary success and failure of distinct group-level institutions such as systems of property rights, marital practices, and socialization of the young, is an essential, sometimes the preeminent, influence on human evolutionary processes. The maintenance of group boundaries (through hostility toward "outsiders," for example) and lethal conflict among groups are essential aspects of this process. Within-group nonrandom pairing of individuals for mating, learning and other activities also plays an important part.

Fifth, chance, in the form of mutation, recombination, developmental accidents, behavioral experimentation, deliberate deviance from social rules, perturbation of the structure of social interactions and its payoffs and other stochastic influences, plays an important role in human evolution.

Finally, an explanation of the evolution of human cooperation must hinge on the empirical evidence. The question is not "Which model works?" They all work, if mathematical coherence is the bar. The question we are asking is about something that actually happened in the human past. Thus we measure the empirical plausibility of alternative explanations against the conditions under which early humans lived during the *Pleistocene*, roughly 1.6 million years before the present, until the advent of agriculture beginning about 12,000 years ago, and especially the last 100 or so millennia of this period. Here is Christopher Boehm's (2007) summary, based on the common characteristics of the 154 foraging societies (about half of those in the ethnographic record) thought to approximate ancestral "highly mobile... storage-free economic systems":

> These highly cooperative nomadic multi-family bands typically contain some unrelated families, and band size, while seasonably variable, seems to be around 20–30 individuals with families often moving from one band to another. Band social life is politically egalitarian in that there is always a low tolerance by a group's mature males for one of their number dominating, bossing, or denigrating the others... economic life also tends to be quite egalitarian because of nomadism and a strong sharing ethic which damps selfish and nepotistic tendencies... regional social networks exist... [and] socially or militarily facilitated group defense of resources is far from infrequent... Drastic resource unpredictability, another likely factor [contributing to group conflict] could have been especially important in the changeable Pleistocene.

We will consider the relevant archaeological, climatic, genetic, ethnographic and historical evidence in detail in Chapter 6. Of course, models of the emergence, proliferation and persistence of modern human behaviors must apply to the whole sweep of human history and prehistory as well, including the past 12,000 years.

2.4   Preview

In the next chapter, we consider experimental and other evidence showing that even in *one-shot* (meaning non-repeated) interactions many individuals, most in some settings, willingly cooperate with strangers even at a cost to themselves. Moreover, they enthusiastically punish shirkers who seek to exploit the cooperation of others. These findings pose the evolutionary puzzle to which the remainder of the book is addressed: how did humans come to have these social preferences?

In Chapter 4 we review approaches commonly used by biologists to explain cooperation, including inclusive fitness models based on family- or group-structured populations in which cooperative individuals are more likely to interact with other cooperators than would occur by chance. We also study a quite different set of models in which because interactions are repeated and reputations can be built, helping others may confer indirect benefits on the actor such that apparently altruistic acts could be motivated by self interest with a long time horizon, consistent with the reasoning of Tocqueville's Americans.

While all of the approaches capture important aspects of human cooperation, none, at least in the simplified forms presented in Chapter 4, is entirely adequate. In Chapter 5 we ask if recent advances in the theory of repeated games, as exemplified by the so-called folk theorem and related models, address the shortcomings of the self-interest based models, finding that they do not.

The remaining chapters provide our explanation. In Chapter 6 we show that prehistoric human society was a social and natural environment in which group competition could have worked with great force to proliferate altruistic behaviors, by conferring fitness benefits on cooperators. Chapter 7 explains how group competition favored the coevolution of the distinctive institutions of hunter-gatherer society along with a predisposition for altruistic behavior. In Chapter 8 we study the process by which hostility toward outsiders and a warlike disposition could have proliferated, and how it strengthened the group competition processes essential to the evolution of altruistic cooperation. Chapter 9 explains how the punishment of individuals who exploit the cooperation of their fellow group members could have initially emerged and proliferated.

In Chapters 10 and 11 we move from the evolutionary processes accounting for human cooperation to the proximate motives for cooperation. In Chapter 10 we study deliberate socialization to internalize group norms, how this capacity for internalization could have evolved, and why the norms internalized tend to be group-beneficial. In Chapter 11 we study the role of social emotions such as guilt and shame in supporting cooperation, and how these could have evolved. Our final chapter reviews our explanation and considers the future of cooperation.

3

Social Preferences

"Is there one word which may serve as a rule of practice all one's life?" The Master said, "Is not reciprocity such a word?"

Confucius, *The Analects*, Book 15, Chapter 23. (4th C. BP)

A man ought to be a friend to his friend and repay gift with gift. People should meet smiles with smiles and lies with treachery. A man ought to be a friend to his friend and also to his friend's friend. But no one should be friendly with a friend of his foe.

The Edda (1923[13th C.]) verses 42, 43

Cooperation is common in humans in large part because people are motivated by social preferences: they care about the well-being of others and value fairness and other norms of decent behavior. Our explanation is that these social preferences are the proximate cause of altruistic cooperation. In this chapter we establish that these preferences are indeed ubiquitous.

Consider the *ultimatum game* (Güth et al. 1982). This is a one-shot, anonymous game in which one subject, called the "proposer," is allocated a sum of money, say $10, and is instructed to offer any number of dollars, from $0 to $10, to a second subject, called the "responder." The responder, who knows how much the proposer was given, can either accept the offer or reject it. If the responder accepts the offer, the money is shared according to the offer. If the responder rejects the offer, both players receive nothing, and the game ends. The self-interest axiom introduced in Chapter 2 provides a clear prediction of how the game will be played. Because the game is one-shot and anonymous, the responder will accept any positive amount of money. Knowing this, a self-regarding proposer will offer $1, and this will be accepted.

However, when actually played, the predicted outcome is almost never observed and rarely even approximated. In many replications of this experiment in more than 30 countries, under varying conditions and in some cases with substantial amounts of money at stake, proposers routinely offer responders very generous shares, 50% of the total generally being the modal offer. Responders frequently reject offers below 25% (Roth et al. 1991, Camerer and Thaler 1995, Camerer 2003, Oosterbeek et al. 2004).

In post game de-briefings, responders who have rejected low offers often express anger at the proposer's greed and a desire to penalize unfair behavior. The fact that positive offers are commonly rejected shows that responders have social preferences, and the fact that most proposers offer between 40% and 50% of the pie shows that proposers too have social preferences, or at least believe responders do, which would motivate them to reject lower offers. Of special interest are those who reject positive offers. The explanation most consistent with the data is that they are motivated by a desire to punish the proposer for being unfair, even though it means giving up some money to do so. While initially considered odd, these and other experimental results violating the self-interest axiom are now commonplace.

Here we survey ten key findings from recent experiments and also ask (in §3.10) if people act in natural settings the same way they behave as subjects in behavioral experiments. Laboratory experiments add critical information to our understanding of human behavior because, as we will see presently, controlled environments and the experimenter's ability to manipulate the relevant incentives allow us to distinguish between subtly different hypotheses about preferences. Colin Camerer (2003) and Armin Falk and James Heckman (2009) provide overviews of the field. Table 3.1 lists the experimental games reviewed here and the pages on which the game is described.

Game	Page	Reference
Ultimatum	p. 19	Güth et al. (1962), Henrich (2000)
Prisoner's dilemma	p. 20	Dawes(1980), Axelrod (1984)
Gift exchange	p. 21	Akerlof (1982), Fehr et al. (1993)
Public goods	p. 22	Yamagishi (1986), Ostrom et al. (1992)
Public goods with punishment	p. 24	Fehr and Gächter (2000a,2002)
Third-party punishment	p. 31	Fehr and Fishbacher (2004)
Dictator	p. 32	Kahneman et al. (1986), List (2007)
Trust	p. 36	Berg et al. (1995), Burks et al. (2003)

Table 3.1. Experimental games.

3.1   Strong Reciprocity Is Common

In experiments we commonly observe that people sacrifice their own payoffs in order to cooperate with others, to reward the cooperation of others, and to punish free-riding, even when they cannot expect to gain from acting this way. We call the preferences motivating this behavior *strong reciprocity*, the term "strong" intended to distinguish this set of preferences from entirely amoral and self-regarding reciprocation that would not be undertaken in the absence of some payback. Because the strong reciprocator would increase his game payoffs by not cooperating, the motives for behaving this way are, by the standard biological definitions, (see §A1) an altruistic preference and an important proximate cause of altruistic cooperation.

We have already described the one-shot prisoner's dilemma game, the key feature of which is that mutual cooperation maximizes the sum of the players' payoffs, but defecting on one's partner maximizes a player's payoffs independently of what the partner does. This is illustrated in Figure 3.1, where each player contributes $b > 0$ to the other player by helping, at a cost $c > 0$ to himself. If $b > c$, then both players benefit by mutual helping. However, among amoral individuals with self-regarding preferences, knowledge of the partner's strategic choice will make no difference in the outcome—the result should be mutual defection. The fact, as we saw in the previous chapter, that a high level of cooperation results when subjects are assured that their partner has already cooperated or that their own decision to cooperate would be transmitted to their partners prior to the latter choosing what to do is an indication that subjects are motivated by strong reciprocity. Knowing that your partner has cooperated changes the subjectively relevant payoffs in the game. One could still make more money by defecting, but the cooperativeness of the partner motivates reciprocation rather than exploitation.

	H	D
H	$b - c, b - c$	$-c, b$
D	$b, -c$	$0, 0$

Figure 3.1. A Prisoner's Dilemma: Single-period payoff to help (H) and don't help (D). We assume $b > c > 0$. Helping contributes b to the other player at a cost of c to the contributor.

Another experiment suggesting that strong reciprocity is common is the *gift exchange game*, modeled as the "experimental labor market" investigated by Fehr et al. (1997). The authors divided a group of 141 subjects into a set of "employers" and a set of "employees." If an employer hires an employee and pays wage w, with $0 \leq w \leq 100$, his profit is $\pi = 100e - w$, where $0.1 \leq e \leq 1$ is the amount of "effort" exerted by the employee. The payoff to the employee is then $u = w - c(e)$, where $c(e)$ is the employee's "cost of effort" function that is increasing at an increasing rate (i.e., $c', c'' > 0$). All payoffs involve real money that the subjects are paid at the end of the experimental session.

The employer then offers a "contract" specifying a wage w and a desired amount of effort e^*. A contract is made with the first employee who agrees to these terms. An employer can make a contract (w, e^*) with at most one employee. The employee who agrees to these terms receives the wage w and supplies an effort level e, which need not be the contracted effort, e^*. In effect, there is no penalty if the employee does not keep his promise, so the employee can choose any effort level with impunity. Although subjects may play this game several times, each employer-employee interaction in a given game is a one-shot (non-repeated) event.

If employees were self-regarding, they would choose the zero-cost effort level, $e = 0.1$, no matter what contract they have agreed to. Knowing this, self-regarding employers would never pay more than the minimum necessary to get the employee to accept a contract, which is 1. The self-regarding employee would accept this offer, and would set $e = 0.1$, giving him payoff $u = 1$. The resulting employer's payoff would then be $\pi = 0.1 \times 100 - 1 = 9$.

In fact, however, this outcome rarely occurred in this experiment. Indeed, the higher the employer's choice of demanded effort, the more both employers and employees earned. In effect, employers presumed the strong reciprocity predispositions of the employees, making more generous wage offers and receiving higher effort.

The above evidence does not, however, contradict the notion that the employers were purely self-regarding, because their seemingly generous behavior vis-à-vis their employees was effective in increasing employer profits. To see if employers were also strong reciprocators, following this round of experiments, the experimenters extended the game by allowing the employers to respond to the actual effort choices of their workers: at a cost of 1, an employer could increase or decrease his employee's payoff by 2.5. If employers were entirely self-regarding, they would of course do neither, because they do not interact with the same worker a second time, so a self-regarding employer would know that punishing a shirker or rewarding a hard worker to be just throwing away money. However, 68% of the time, employers punished employees that did not fulfill their contracts, and 70% of the time, employers rewarded employees who overfulfilled their contracts. Indeed, employers rewarded 44% of employees who exactly fulfilled their contracts. Moreover, employees expected this behavior on the part of their employers, as shown by the fact that their effort levels increased significantly when their bosses gained the power to punish and reward them. Underfulfilled contracts dropped from 86% to 26% of the exchanges, and overfulfilled contracts rose from 3% to 38% of the total.

We conclude from this study that the subjects who assume the role of "employee" reciprocate seemingly generous offers by employers, even when they are certain there are no material repercussions from behaving in a self-regarding manner. Moreover, subjects who assume the role of "employer" expect this behavior and make higher payoffs because they take this into account. "Employers" reward good and punish bad behavior when they are permitted to punish, even when their payoffs would be maximized by refraining from rewards and punishment. Finally, "employees" expect employer rewards and punishments, and adjust their own effort levels accordingly.

A large number of additional experiments with the game have replicated these results (Fehr et al. 2009, Gächter et al. 2011).

3.2   Free-Riders Undermine Cooperation

In a social dilemma that is repeated for a number of periods, subjects tend to start with a positive and significant level of cooperation, but unless there are very few free-riders in the group, cooperation subsequently decays to a very low level.

The experimental *public goods game* is designed to illuminate such problems as the voluntary payment of taxes and contribution to team and community goals (Ledyard 1995). The following is a common variant of the game. Ten subjects are told that $1 will be deposited in each of their "private accounts" as a reward for participating in each of the 10 rounds of the experiment. For every $1 that a subject moves from his "private account" to the "public account" on a given round, the experimenter will add one half dollar to the final payoffs to each of the subjects. At the end of 10 rounds, the subjects will be given the total of their final payoffs, and the experiment is terminated.

The sum of individual payoffs will be maximized if, in each round, each puts the entire $1 in the public account, generating a public pool of $10. In this case, the experimenter adds $5 to the final payoff of each subject. At the end of the game, 10 rounds having been played, each subject would be paid $50—in each round $1 contributed minus the $0.50 returned by the experimenter. However, every $1 a player contributes to the public account, while benefiting the 9 others by a total of $4.50, costs the contributor $0.50. Therefore the dominant strategy for a self-regarding player is to contribute nothing to the pool, and if all subjects do this, each then earns just $10. The experimental public goods game is thus an n-person prisoner's dilemma (§4.5).

In fact, as in prisoner's dilemma experiments (Fehr and Fischbacher 2002, Fischbacher and Gächter 2010), in public goods experiments, only a fraction of subjects conform to the self-interest axiom, contributing nothing to the public account. Rather, subjects contribute on average about half their private account in round one, but in later rounds, contributions decay to a level close to zero.

This decay is significant for the following reason. A supporter of the self-interest axiom is inclined to interpret other-regarding behavior in experiments as confusion on the part of the subjects, who are not accustomed to anonymous interactions. Their behavior therefore reflects their beliefs, that is, their understandings of the effect of their actions on the probability of achieving various outcomes, not their preferences, namely their assessment of the value of these various outcomes. In everyday life, one's actions are normally seen by others, so even if not contributing is the dominant strategy in the game, a failure to contribute would entail a loss of reputation, and hence a loss of future profitable exchanges. The anonymity of the laboratory may be sufficiently extraordinary that subjects simply play by these prudent and self-regarding rules of everyday life. Accordingly, the initially substantiated and later decline in contributions in the public goods game might be seen as a confirmation of this belief-based interpretation: subjects are not altruistic; rather, they are simply learning how to maximize their payoffs through game repetition.

However, were this explanation correct, if the same subjects were permitted to play a second multi-round public goods game identical to the first, they should refuse to contribute on the very first round. Andreoni (1988) and Cookson (2000) tested this prediction and found it to be wrong. When the public goods game is played with several groups and after every series of rounds group membership is reshuffled and the game is restarted, subjects begin each new series by contributing about half, but each time cooperation decays in the later rounds. If one believes that the decay in contributions within a game is due to learning how to maximize payoffs in the context of anonymity, one would also have to believe that subjects unlearn the money-maximizing behavior between series! In fact, the only reasonable explanation for the decay of cooperation is that public-spirited contributors want to retaliate against free-riders, and the only way available to them in the game is by not contributing themselves. Subjects often report this reason for the unraveling of cooperation retrospectively.

Another indication that free-riding and the retaliation against free-riders is the cause of the unraveling of cooperation comes from an experiment by Page et al. (2005). The experimenters compared four baseline sessions, each of which included 16 subjects in a 20-round public goods game, with four sessions in which, after three 20-round games, subjects were given a list of the average contributions of the other players in all four groups, and were permitted to rank their preference for playing with one or more of these subjects. Subjects who ranked each other highly were assigned to the same group, and subjects who were not ranked highly by others were also assigned to the same group.

In baseline treatments with random assignment to groups, contributions began at an average of 60% of the maximum possible and declined to 9% in the last round, for an average contribution rate of 38% of the endowment over the 20 rounds. Where subjects could choose their partners, cooperation did not decay over time, and the average contribution rate was 70% of the endowment. Note that this high average cooperation rate includes the performance of low contributors, who were obliged to play with one another.

To understand this result, note that when subjects could choose their partners, there was a strong tendency for subjects to play with others who approximately share their level of contribution. This is because the experimenters would always satisfy the request of two players who preferred to be together before the request of a pair only one of whose members preferred to associate with the other. Thus the top of the four elective groups maintained an average contribution rate of over 90% with no tendency to decay, except for an end-game effect in the last three rounds that brought contributions down to about 60%. The second most preferred group maintained an 80% average, with a similar end-round effect, while the third group averaged about 65%, with a relatively weak tendency to decay, from about 75% in the first rounds to 60% in rounds 12 to 16, and then to about 50% in the final three rounds. The lowest group showed the usual decay from 75% contribution in the first three rounds to 10% in the final round, for an average of 45%. These results are consistent with the idea that the decay of cooperation is due to relatively high contributors reacting to low contributors by lowering their own contribution. When subjects in the same group are relatively uniform in their contributing behavior, this decay mechanism is attenuated.

These experiment show that when those predisposed to cooperate can associate preferentially with like-minded people, cooperation is not difficult to sustain. We return to this basic rule in the next and subsequent chapters.

3.3   Altruistic Punishment Sustains Cooperation

In social dilemmas, strong reciprocators, by punishing free-riders, induce their cooperation in subsequent play, thereby allowing cooperation to be sustained over time. Experiments by Orbell, Dawes, and van de Kragt (1986), Sato (1987), Yamagishi (1988a, 1988b, 1992), and Ostrom, Walker, and Gardner (1992) and many experiments since show that when subjects are given a direct way of retaliating against free-riders rather than simply withholding their own cooperation, they use it in a way that helps sustain cooperation. A particularly clear example of this was given by Fehr and Gächter (2000, 2002), who designed a repeated public goods game with an option of costly retaliation against low contributors in some treatments, called the *public goods with punishment* game.

Ernst Fehr and Simon Gächter used four-person groups, employing three different methods of assigning members to groups. Under the *partner treatment*, the four subjects remained in the same group for all 10 periods. Under the *Stranger treatment*, the subjects were randomly reassigned after each round. Finally, under the *perfect stranger treatment* the subjects were randomly reassigned in such a way that they would never meet the same subject more than once, so subjects knew that costly retaliation against low contributors could not possibly confer any pecuniary benefit to those who punish. Subjects were informed which treatment would obtain for their experiment.

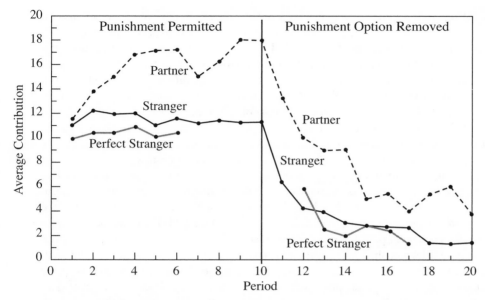

Figure 3.2. Public goods game with punishment, average contributions over time. Part-ner, Stranger, and Perfect Stranger treatments are shown when the punishment condi-tion is played first (Fehr and Gächter 2000a). Results are similar when the punishment condition is played second.

Fehr and Gächter ran the experiment for 10 rounds with punishment and 10 rounds without. Their results are illustrated in Figure 3.2. The experimenters found that sub-jects were more heavily punished, the more their contributions fell below the average for the group. As a result, when costly punishment was permitted, cooperation did not deteriorate, and in the Partner treatment, despite strict anonymity, cooperation increased to almost full cooperation, even on the final round (top line, left panel). When punish-ment was not permitted, however, the same subjects experienced the deterioration of cooperation found in previous public goods games.

This result is telling because in the stranger and perfect stranger treatment, punish-ing free-riders is itself a public good, and is no different from contributing to the public good itself; both confer benefits on others at a cost to oneself. In both treatments, not contributing and not punishing are dominant strategies (they maximize payoffs regard-less of the actions of the others). We term punishment in this setting altruistic for this reason. Yet as we saw subjects treat contribution and punishment differently. After the initial rounds in the standard public goods without punishment game, experimen-tal subjects decline to contribute altruistically but once punishment is permitted they avidly engage in the altruistic activity of punishing low contributors.

Part of the reason for the difference is that people have an intrinsic motivation to punish shirkers, not simply an instrumental desire to alter their behavior or to affect the distribution of payoffs to either reduce unfairness or enhance one's own relative payoffs. This intrinsic desire to punish miscreants is similar to what Boyd and Richerson (1992) call retribution punishment and the negative analogue of Andreoni's (1990) warm glow altruism. That subjects view punishment of shirkers also as retribution rather than simply as instrumental toward affecting behavior is consistent with the recent public goods with punishment experiment of Falk et al. (2005). The game was one shot, ruling out behavior modification as a motive for punishing low contributors, and the punishment technology was such that punishment could not alter the difference in payoff between the punisher and the target (the cost to the punisher was the same as that inflicted on the target). Nonetheless, 60% of cooperators punished defectors.

Further evidence for our assumption that punishment is in part non-strategic comes from the public goods experiment of Drew Fudenberg and Parag Pathak (2010). As in the standard game, following each round of contributions subjects were given information on the contributions of fellow group members and had the opportunity to deduct some of their own payoffs in order to lower the payoffs of another in the group. But unlike the usual treatment, in which the targets of punishment were informed of the level of punishment they received after each round, in the Fudenberg and Pathak experiment the levels of punishment were not to be revealed until the experiment was over, and those who punished others knew this. Thus the experimental design ruled out modifying the behavior of shirkers as a motive for punishment. Consistent with what the authors term a "pure preference" motivation for punishment, subjects nonetheless punished shirkers, leading the authors to conclude that "agents enjoy punishment, where 'enjoyment' includes anger and a desire for retribution." There is considerable further evidence for our non-strategic modeling of punishment (de Quervain et al. 2004).

3.4   Effective Punishment Depends on Legitimacy

Another public goods with punishment experiment confirms that altruistic punishment enhances cooperation among members of a group. But it raises a new question: do groups that punish free-riders actually benefit or do the costs of punishing outweigh the benefits to cooperation that result? Benedikt Herrmann, Christian Thöni and Gächter (2008) chose an unusually diverse set of subject pools from 15 populations ranging from familiar experimental sites such as Boston and Zurich to the less frequently studied Riyadh, Muscat, and Chengdu (China) to implement a 10-period public goods game similar to that in the Fehr and Gächter experiment. As expected, cultural differences among the subject pools were significant, but in all of them subjects contributed substantial amounts in the first period and, in the absence of the punishment option, in subsequent periods cooperation unraveled. As in earlier experiments, when the punishment option was available it was widely used, especially in the early periods, and as a result the unraveling of contributions did not occur.

What surprised the experimenters was the fact that, averaging over the 10 periods, most of the subject pools had higher average payoffs when the punishment option was precluded. They readily identified the problem: in many societies a significant amount of punishment was directed at high contributors, possibly as a retaliation against punishment received in earlier rounds by subjects who believed that it was the high contributors who were doing most of the punishment (Figure 3.3). The result was vendetta-like retaliation against punishment leading to costly arms-race dynamics of wasteful

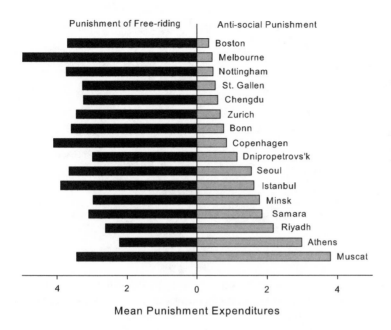

Figure 3.3. Free-riding and antisocial punishment in the public goods game with punishment around the world. The gray bars refer to punishment of those contributing the same or more than the punisher. The black bars indicate punishment of those contributing less than the punisher. Source: Herrmann, Thöni and Gächter (2008).

punishment expenditures. The authors termed this "antisocial punishment." Other experiments have found the same patterns (Cinyabuguma et al. 2006, Ertan et al. 2009).

A closer look at the data reveals that all but two of the subject pools improved their net payoffs over time, with about half gaining net benefits by the penultimate period. In most subject pools subjects took advantage of the last round to free ride on the contribution stage, expecting, in most cases falsely, it turns out, that their fellow group members would also free ride and not punish in the last period. In most subject pools, it appears, there was an initial learning period in which those predisposed to free ride by not contributing were heavily punished. The result was both low net benefits in early rounds and more cooperative behavior in contributing in subsequent rounds which obviated the occasion for such frequent punishment. However, as is clear in Figure 3.4, the impact of antisocial punishment on average payoffs was very strong.

To test the possibility that the net returns to having a punishment option are high when the game is repeated a sufficient number of periods, Gächter, Elke Renner and Martin Sefton (2008) implemented the identical game, but allowed the subjects to interact over 50 periods rather than just 10. They found, as the learning interpretation suggested above had led them to expect, that after the initial rounds, the net benefits to the group with the punishment option significantly exceeded those of the no-punishment

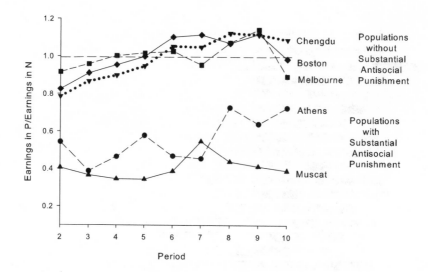

Figure 3.4. Antisocial punishment lowers average payoffs. Shown is the group average earnings in the treatment in which punishment was allowed divided by the average
earnings in the no-punishment treatment. Excepting the end-game effects (lower contributions, greater punishment) subjects in Chengdu, Boston and Melbourne on average
benefited from the opportunity to punish once they achieved a high level of contribution, which then induced little punishment. This did not occur in Athens and Muscat.
Source: Herrmann, Thöni, and Gächter (2008).

group with the difference in net payoffs growing monotonically over time, except for
the final round in which the hapless end-game free-riders were heavily punished (Figure 3.5).

Given that most social dilemma interactions, in neighborhoods, work teams, and the
like, extend over far more than 10 periods, we find the concern that altruistic punishment
lowers group benefits to be misplaced. The experiment of Dreber et al. (2008) does not
constitute evidence for the counterproductive punishment hypothesis for the additional
reason that their two-person game made punishment irrelevant, for one could always
retaliate on a defector simply by withdrawing cooperation, thus obviating the need
for any special kind of punishment. But while the 50-period design of the Gächter
et al. experiment corrects one of the design biases that suggested counterproductive
punishment in the earlier experiment, their design still misses something essential to
altruistic punishment in the real world: it is effective only if it is regarded as legitimate
according to widely held social norms. We model this legitimacy aspect of altruistic
punishment in Chapter 9.

Ertan et al. (2009) designed an ingenious experiment to explore this possibility.
They allowed experimental subjects prior to playing the public goods game to vote on
whether punishment should be allowed and if so, should it be restricted in any manner.
Here is what they found. From their first opportunity to vote, no group ever allowed
punishment of high contributors, most groups eventually voted to allow punishment of

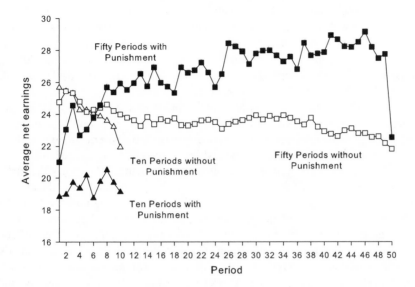

Figure 3.5. The time horizon effect: punishment raises average payoffs in the long run. With a short time horizon (10 periods) punishment promotes cooperation but lowers average payoffs, whereas with a long time horizon (50 periods) punishment increases the level of cooperation and average earnings. Subjects were University of Nottingham students. Source: Gächter, Renner, and Sefton (2008).

low contributors in the baseline treatments, and the result was both high contributions and high efficiency levels. In the laboratory, groups solved their free-rider problems by allowing low contributors alone to be punished. Apparently the determination of the punishment system by majority rule made the punishment not only an incentive but also a signal of group norms.

This experiment suggests a possible explanation of the Herrmann et al. (2008) study of 15 different cultures. Punishment of free-riders, even if they were strangers, was legitimate in Boston, Melbourne, and Chengdu but it was not in Muscat and Athens. We will see in Chapter 6 that ethnographic studies of the punishment of group members is sometimes finely tuned to achieve legitimacy: it is coordinated by gossip and rarely carried out by a single individual. We will also see that in small-scale societies punishment can be highly effective even when it takes the form of ridicule or gossip and it inflicts no material costs on its targets. The importance of the moral signal conveyed by punishment rather than simply the material incentive that it provides is also suggested by experiments.

3.5   Purely Symbolic Punishment Is Effective

People are sensitive to others' evaluation of their moral worth or intentions and will cooperate in social dilemmas when the punishment for free-riding takes the form of criticism by peers rather than a reduction in material payoffs.

To test this idea, Masclet et al. (2003) allowed the subjects in a public goods game to assign "disapproval points" to the other group members after the subjects had been informed about each others' contributions. These disapproval points had no material consequences. They merely indicated the members' evaluation of one another. Allowing for the expression of disapproval raised the contributions to the public good relative to the baseline with no punishment opportunities.

In another experiment, Bochet et al. (2006) compared the usual baseline public goods game with a "chat-room" situation in which four group members communicated with one another through their computer terminals for several minutes before each round, and a "face-to-face" situation in which group members engaged in face-to-face communication. These treatments are often called "cheap talk" by game theorists, because any promises made cannot in any way be enforced. Nevertheless, the experimenters found that both forms of communication increased contributions considerably above the baseline level. Surprisingly, at least to the current authors' generation, chat-room communication was almost as effective in increasing contributions as face-to-face communication, and adding the option of material punishing (i.e., reducing the target's payoffs) increased contributions little more. Specifically, (a) face-to-face, face-to-face with punishment, chat room, and chat room with punishment all induced average contribution rates above 95%, and about 85% in the last of the 10 rounds; (b) punishment alone performed considerably less well, averaging about 70%, and 60% in the last period; (c) the baseline (no communication, no punishment) treatment performed worst of all, starting at 60% cooperation and declining to 20% in the final period, for an average contribution of about 48%.

This is consistent with the results of a public goods with punishment experiment implemented in 18 rural communities in Zimbabwe by Abigail Barr (2001). The game was structured along the above lines, except for the punishment stage, in which there was no option to reduce the payoffs to others. Rather, following the contribution stage, Barr's assistant would stand beside each player in turn and say to the group as a whole, "Player number __, Mr/Mrs __, contributed __. Does anyone have anything to say about that?" A quarter of the participants were criticized for contributing too little ("stingy," "mean," "Now I know why I never get offered food when I drop by your house!"). Five percent were criticized for giving too much ("stupid," "careless with money"). Those who made low contribution and were criticized made larger contributions in subsequent rounds. Moreover, those who contributed a low amount and escaped criticism, but had witnessed the criticism of others who had contributed a similar amount, increased their contributions by even more than those directly criticized. Also, those who had contributed a large amount and were criticized reduced their contribution in subsequent rounds. Where low contributions escaped criticism entirely, contributions fell in subsequent rounds.

Gächter and Fehr (1999) also found that, given some minimal social contact among strangers, making individual contributions publicly observable raises contributions to the public good substantially. Beyond this, Gächter and Fehr asked subjects to fill out questionnaires to measure the strength of their emotional responses toward cooperation and free-riding on the part of others. They show that free-riding elicits extremely strong negative emotions among the other group members. Moreover, in the post-experiment group discussions the other group members verbally insulted the free-riders.

These experiments and those by Falk et al. (2005) and Fudenberg and Pathak (2009) described earlier make two things clear. First, the objective of punishment is not simply behavior modification but punishment per se. And second, the target's positive response to punishment cannot be explained by a desire to maximize payoffs in subsequent play, but as the shirker's attempt to right a wrong in the eyes of fellow group members. Thus the self-interest axiom explains neither the frequency nor the effectiveness of punishment

3.6   People Punish Those Who Hurt Others

People punish not only those who have hurt them, but also those who hurt others. This occurs when the action causing the hurt violates a social norm. Fehr and Fischbacher (2004) studied a *third-party punishment game* with three players, whom we will call Alice, Bob, and Carole. The game between Alice and Bob is a *dictator game*, in which Alice gives a certain amount of money to Bob, who has no say in the matter. In this experiment, Alice was given an endowment of 100 tokens, of which she could transfer any amount to Bob (at the end of the game, the tokens are converted into real money). What differentiates the third-party punishment game from the dictator game is that Carole, the "third party," has an endowment of 50 tokens and observes Alice's transfer. After this Carole can assign punishment points to Alice. Each punishment point assigned to Alice costs Carole one token and Alice incurs a penalty of three tokens. Because punishment is costly, a self-regarding Carole will never punish. However, if there is a sharing norm, Carole may well punish Alice if she gives too little.

In the above experiments Alices were never punished if they transferred 50 or more tokens to Bob. If they transferred fewer than 50 tokens, the punishment was the stronger the less Alice transferred. An Alice who transferred nothing received on average nine punishment points from Carole, so Alice's payoff was reduced by three times this, or 27 tokens. A selfish Alice in this game might still prefer not to give, but in a real-world situation with several Caroles, her cumulative punishment might be sufficient to induce even a selfish Alice to make an equitable gift to Bob.

Engelmann and Fischbacher (2009) studied *indirect reciprocity* and *strategic reputation-building* in an experimental helping game (§4.6). Indirect reciprocity occurs when Carole is likely to punish Alice when Alice has been unfair to Bob, and is likely to reward Alice when Alice has been nice to Bob. Strategic reputation-building occurs when Carole behaves in the above manner only when her actions are seen by others, and hence can help build a reputation for social behavior. Of course, unless there are indirect reciprocators, strategic reputation-building can have no effect. Nevertheless, it is interesting to see that even self-regarding individuals may engage in third-party punishment if they believe that this will induce other-regarding individuals to behave favorably toward them. In their experiment, at any time only half the subjects were capable of building a reputation by having their behavior observed by the group. Engelmann and Fischbacher found that, while non-strategic indirect reciprocity appears to be important, helping behavior was influenced at least as much by strategic considerations. Strategic reciprocators did better than non-strategic indirect reciprocators and, of course, selfish types had the highest payoffs of all. The motives supporting indirect reciprocity when reputation forming is impossible are a form of strong reciprocity, and this experiment shows that people will punish violators of social norms even when they themselves are not directly hurt by the violator. Punishment is thus not simply retaliation in response to personal damages but appears to reflect more general ethical norms (Ule et al. 2009).

3.7   Social Preferences Are Not Irrational

The desire to contribute, to punish shirking, and otherwise to act on the basis of social preferences, like the desire to consume conventional goods and services, can be represented by preferences that conform to standard definitions of rationality (Savage 1954, Hechter and Kanazawa 1997, Gintis 2009a). These preference imply observable trade-offs, depending on the costs, and experiments confirm that the higher the cost of prosocial behavior, the less its frequency.

Many observers of experimental games have interpreted the fact that people sometimes sacrifice material gain in favor of moral sentiment as an indication of irrationality, the term "rationality" being misused as a synonym for "consistent pursuit of self-interest." But subjects appear to be no less rational when deciding to cooperate and punish than when they compare prices to decide what to cook for dinner. This suggests that the preferences that lie behind their social behavior are consistent with the basic axioms of rationality, namely on transitivity (consistency) and completeness.

Andreoni and Miller (2002) tested the "rationality" of prosocial choices by asking 176 subjects to play a version of the dictator game. Recall that in the dictator game, Bob is given a sum of money by the experimenter, and asked to transfer whatever proportion of the money that he wishes to another (anonymous) subject Alice. After Bob makes his decision, the money is transferred, and the game is over. In the Andreoni-Miller version of the game, the cost of giving was varied by the experimenter. Bob is given a sum m, a price p, and is asked to keep an amount π_s, while transferring an amount π_o to Alice, such that $\pi_s + p\pi_o = m$. Thus, for instance, if $m = 40$ and $p = 3$, Bob could keep all 40 for himself or could keep 10 and transfer 10 to Alice, thus satisfying the equation $10 + 3 \times 10 = 40$. This p is the price of generosity. By varying m and p, the experimenters could see if the subjects responded to changes in the price of generosity in the expected way, and thus had "rational preferences."

In this experiment, 75% of the "dictators" gave away some money, showing other-regarding behavior, and the average amount given away was 25.5% when the price $p = 1$ (a dollar-for-dollar transfer), which is about the same as in other dictator games (Forsythe et al. 1994). Moreover, the higher the price of generosity, the less money was given. For instance, when each dollar transferred to the other person cost two dollars ($p = 2$), only 14.1% was given away, and when each dollar transferred cost four dollars, only 3.4% of the dictator's endowment was transferred. Thus the subjects' demand for generosity responded to prices in a way no different from the demand say, for ice cream. Equally important for the status of social preferences as rational, only 18 of the 176 subjects violated the principle of *transitive preferences* that requires, as we saw in Chapter 2, that if an individual prefers A over B and B over C, he then prefers

A over *C*. Moreover, these violations were almost all very minor. Indeed, 98% of the individual choices were consistent with transitive preferences.

Similarly, in a public goods with punishment experiment in which punishment cannot be motivated by self-regarding preferences similar to that of Fehr and Gächter (2000a), Anderson and Putterman (2006) found that the level of altruistic punishment that subjects inflicted on others varied inversely with the cost of punishing.

The fact that other-regarding preferences support price-responsive behaviors conforms to our representation of social preferences as distinct motivations within the framework of transitive preferences rather than some *sui generis* irrational or non-rational mode of behavior requiring a special model of decision-making. The fact that for many experimental subjects virtue is its own reward is perfectly consistent with the fact that, as in the case of people with self-regarding preferences, they would consider the price.

3.8   Culture and Institutions Matter

As experimental evidence accumulated in the 1990's showing that many, perhaps most, individuals are not entirely self-regarding, it appeared natural to wonder if an alternative equally simple representation of human behavior, but one stressing ethical and other-regarding motives, might be universally valid. As the previous century drew to a close we were impressed by how similar were the experimental results coming in from experimental laboratories around the world, from Beijing, Tel Aviv, Pittsburgh, Zurich and Ljubljana. Could *Homo economicus* simply be replaced by *Homo sociologicus*, *Homo altruisticus*, or, as we once suggested, *Homo reciprocans*?

It is too early to say, but we doubt that such a universal model will prove viable. More recent experimental results are consistent with the view that the social preferences that become salient in a population depend critically on the manner in which a people's institutions and livelihood frame social interactions and shape the process of social learning. An expected result, confirmed by a growing body of international comparative evidence, is substantial cross-cultural differences in the nature and extent of social preferences.

We have already (§3.4) discussed the remarkable differences across recent subject pools from around the world in the public goods with punishment game. Here we report ultimatum game experiments in which the subject pool is not, as is usually the case, university students, but instead members of 15 small-scale societies with little contact with markets, governments or modern institutions. With our colleagues, a team of 15 anthropologists and economists, we designed these experiments to explore whether the results reported above are common in societies with quite different cultures and social institutions (Henrich et al. 2004). The 15 societies included hunter-gatherers, herders, and low technology farmers.

Our results strongly affirmed cultural differences in experimental play. Among the Au and Gnau people in Papua New Guinea, ultimatum game offers of more than half the pie were common, Moreover, while even splits were commonly accepted, both higher and lower offers were rejected with about equal frequency. This behavior struck the economists on our team as odd, to say the least. But to the anthropologists it was not surprising in light of the widespread practice of competitive gift giving as a means of establishing status and subordinacy in these and many other New Guinea societies. By contrast, among the Machiguenga in Amazonian Peru, almost three quarters of the offers were a quarter of the pie or less and yet of 70 offers, there was just a single rejection, a pattern strikingly different from the student experiments conducted thus far. However, even among the Machiguenga, the mean offer was 27.5%, far more than would have maximized the proposer's payoffs given the scant likelihood of a rejection.

Analysis of the experiments led us to the following conclusions: behaviors are highly variable across groups, not a single group approximated the behaviors implied by the self-interest axiom, and between-group differences in behavior seemed to reflect differences in the kinds of social interaction experienced in the everyday life of the social group in question.

The evidence for this latter conclusion is quite compelling. For example, the Aché in Paraguay share equally among all group members some kinds of food (meat and honey) acquired through hunting and gathering. In our experiment, most Aché proposers contributed half the pie or more. Similarly, among the Lamalera whale hunters of Indonesia, who hunt in large crews and divide their catch according to strict sharing rules, the proposer's average allocation to the responder was 58% of the pie. Moreover, the Indonesian whale hunters played the game very differently from the Indonesian university students who were the subjects in another set of experiments (Cameron 1999). Indeed, where voluntary public goods provision was customary in real life (for example, the *Harambee* system among the Orma herders in Kenya, whereby individuals contribute resources to build a school or repair a road), contributions in the experimental public goods game were patterned after actual contributions in the actual Harambee system. Those with more cattle contributed more. By contrast, in the ultimatum game, for which there apparently was no everyday life analogue, the wealthy behaved like the other Orma.

It seems likely that the correspondence between the typical livelihood of a group and its customary forms of interaction on the one hand, and the experimental behaviors of its subjects on the other, results from the fact that appropriate behavior is influenced by both custom and livelihood, and these behaviors are then generalized and applied to novel situations such as our experiments.

Evidence that institutions serve as cues for appropriate behaviors comes from ultimatum game experiments with U.S. subjects in which simply naming the game "The Exchange Game," or assigning the role of proposer to those who did well on a current affairs test, resulted in lower offers and a significant reduction in rejections of low offers (Hoffman et al. 1994b). If individuals cared only about their money payoffs, neither manipulation would have changed the game. The fact that significantly less strong reciprocity occurred in the exchange game and the current events test version suggests that social structure affects behavior in ways other than those captured by the money payoffs of the game, in this case by suggesting appropriate behavior (the exchange game) or identifying some individuals as "deserving" (the test manipulation).

Finally, experimental play in the ultimatum game and public goods with punishment game also suggest that institutions may influence behaviors in ways that go beyond the incentives and constraints that they implement. Recall that experimental subjects in the public goods with punishment game readily punish low contributors, despite the fact that in doing so they are adopting a strategy that is dominated in the game's payoffs, meaning that some other strategy would guarantee higher payoffs to the player regardless of what the other players do. Yet the same willingness to adopt a dominated strategy in the interests of the public good is uncommon in the standard public goods game, where there is no punishment option. Our interpretation is that, like institutions in natural settings, by providing the option of reducing the payoffs of others once one knows how much they contributed (the word "punishment" is never used) the game structure conveys information about appropriate behavior and influences beliefs about the actions of others.

Similarly, in the ultimatum game, people in the role of proposer often make an offer that approximately maximizes expected income from the game, the expectation being based on the *ex post* empirically observed rejection behavior of the responders. But, in the role of responder, the very same people rarely maximize expected income, for doing so would entail accepting any positive offer. For example, among the Hadza, hunter-gatherers whom we studied in Tanzania, the mean ultimatum game offer was almost exactly that which maximized expected income, given the empirically observed rejections of low offers. But a quarter of all offers were rejected, and over two fifths of offers of 20% or less were rejected. In this case the social roles created by the game, proposer and responder, apparently cue different behavioral reactions. Among the Hadza, in the role of proposer, considerations of fair treatment are apparently not salient, while in the role of responder, they are.

The study of 15 small-scale societies described here was replicated by using improved methods and a partially overlapping set of small-scale societies with considerably sharpened results (Henrich et al. 2010, Barr et al. 2010).

3.9   Behavior Is Conditioned on Group Membership

In experimental and natural settings, people often behave differently toward others, depending on the organizational, linguistic, ethnic, and religious groups to which they belong. People choose to associate with others who are similar to themselves in some salient respect (Lazarsfeld and Merton 1954, Thibaut and Kelly 1959, Homans 1961). Among the salient characteristics on which this choice operates are racial and ethnic identification, and religion (Berscheid and Walster 1969, Tajfel et al. 1971, Cohen 1977, Kandel 1978, Obot 1988). Conversely, people often seek to avoid interactions with those who are different from themselves.

Those who condition their behavior on the group membership of the other may do this because group membership is thought to provide information about the other's likely behavior. Or group membership may matter because people would like to help or to interact with members of some groups more than others. In the first case the actor's beliefs are involved. In the second case, group-sensitive preferences are at work. Group-sensitive preferences may be other-regarding (valuing the well-being of members of one's own group, for example) or self-regarding preferences (e.g. experiencing anxiety in culturally unfamiliar interactions).

Laboratory experiments (with student subjects) have confirmed the salience of group membership in many settings. In the minimal group experiments initiated by

Henry Tajfel and his colleagues (Tajfel et al. 1971), experimental subjects were assigned to groups on the basis of some trivial distinction (commonly, for example, their preference for paintings by Paul Klee over those of Wassily Kandinsky). In-group favoritism was quite pronounced in these experiments, with Klee-lovers discriminating against and having a low opinion of the Kandinskians, who reciprocated this in-group bias toward the Klee enthusiasts. Later prisoner's dilemma and common pool resource game experiments found higher levels of cooperation when the players are members of the same minimal group than when they are not members of the same group (Kramer and Brewer 1984). However, a series of experiments by Toshio Yamagishi and his associates (Yamagishi et al. 2007) show that experimental subjects' allocations favor in-group members not because of altruistic sentiments toward those who are similar to themselves, but because they expected reciprocation from in-groupers and not from out-groupers.

In contrast to the minimal group experiments favored by psychologists and sociologists, behavioral economists have used the *trust game*, introduced by Berg et al. (1995), generally with experimental subjects drawn from real-world ethnic groups. In this game, Alice is awarded a sum of money and given the opportunity to transfer any amount of it to Bob, knowing that the experimenter will triple the amount transferred (if Alice gives x, Bob receives $3x$). Bob then has the opportunity to return some of this augmented sum to Alice. This ends the game. Alice is sometimes called the "truster" or "investor," and Bob the "trustee."

If Alice cared only about payoffs, and assumed that Bob had the same self-regarding preferences, she would transfer nothing, for she would correctly infer that whatever Bob received would be kept rather than returned. But when the game is played anonymously Alice typically contributes a significant amount, and significant amounts are returned by Bob.

A number of experimenters have implemented the trust game played between subjects who were, while otherwise anonymous, aware of the ethnic, religious, or linguistic identity of their partner. Fershtman et al. (2002) implemented this game in Belgium, played between students at Flemish and Walloon universities. Both Flemish and Walloon Alices make lower offers to outsiders than insiders but offer as much to a partner of unknown insider-outsider status as they do to known insiders. When the same experiment was run in Israel, ultra-orthodox Jews in the role of Alice give more to other ultra-orthodox Jews than to secular partners, but do not discriminate against secular partners by comparison with anonymous partners.

Discrimination against outsiders or in favor of insiders is far from ubiquitous, however. In another study using Belgian subjects, Bouckaert and Dhaene (2004) found no evidence of either type of discrimination in a trust game played by small businessmen of Belgian and Turkish origin. In the experiment just mentioned Yamagishi found that when he redesigned the game so that subjects realized that they could not increase their own payoffs by contributing to their own group, they contributed equally to both groups. Other studies suggest that in some circumstances, in-group favoritism is quite limited or even absent.

In a series of experiments in ethnically and linguistically divided poor neighborhoods of Kampala, Uganda, there was no evidence of favoritism toward coethnics in allocating sums or in choosing partners in a problem-solving task. James Habyarimana and his coauthors (2009) concluded:

> We find no evidence for a commonality of tastes within ethnic groups, or greater degrees of altruism toward coethnics or for an impact of shared ethnicity on the productivity of teams. [Rather]...successful collective action among homogeneous ethic communities...is attributable to the existence of norms and institutions that facilitate the sanctioning of noncontributors.

And here, ethnicity does appear to matter. Norms may dictate ethnic favoritism, and in public settings subjects may fear sanctions were they to not respect these ethnic norms. Remarkably, ethnic favoritism, which was absent in an anonymous dictator game, was evident among some subjects when the dictator's identity was public information. Habyarimana and his coauthors (2009) explained that subjects believed that others would think less of them were they not to favor coethnics.

A series of experiments with subjects drawn from differing ethno-linguistic groups in the highlands of Papua New Guinea (Bernhard et al. 2006, Efferson et al. 2011) provides further evidence on the relevance of group boundaries. We describe these in Chapter 8, as they have a direct bearing on the evolution of what we term parochial altruism modeled there.

Nonetheless, taking account of ethnic, racial and other characteristics of those with whom one interacts appears to be a quite common human trait. We seem quite attuned to noticing and treating as salient the ascriptive markers of group difference. For example, Americans of European and African origin are better at recognizing faces of their own ancestral group, and faces of their own group induce greater activation in the part of the brain associated with face recognition. Elizabeth Phelps et al. (2000) used brain imaging techniques (functional magnetic resonance imaging, fMRI) to study the neural substrates involved in the unconscious evaluation of Black and White social groups. They found that upon exposure to the (unfamiliar) faces of African American males (by comparison to the faces of European Americans), European American subjects exhibited heightened activation of the amygdala, an area of the brain associated with fear processing. Moreover, the extent of amygdala activation was correlated with an indirect (unconscious) measure of racial prejudice (the Implicit Association Test) but not with a direct (conscious) expression of race attitudes. Importantly, these patterns were not obtained when the stimulus faces belonged to familiar and positively regarded individuals (e.g., Martin Luther King Jr., Denzel Washington). Phelps and her coauthors see the

> amygdala activation [as] reflections of social learning within a specific culture at a particular moment in the history of relations between social groups...[the effects of] cultural evaluations of social groups, personal experience with social group members, and one's own group membership. (p. 734)

Due to the acute attention humans give to group boundaries, we might also be called "the parochial species." The forms taken by parochialism today, religious intolerance, racism, xenophobia, vary across cultures and have evolved over time. But the various forms taken may share a common provenance in the evolutionary processes that have made group boundaries salient to people. Like altruism, discriminatory preferences are an evolutionary puzzle, as they often impel people to forgo opportunities for beneficial exchanges and other interactions. We will address this puzzle in Chapter 8.

3.10   People Enjoy Cooperating and Punishing Free-Riders

The most parsimonious and compelling proximate explanation of behavior in the ultimatum game, public goods game, and other social dilemma experiments is that people think that cooperating is the right thing to do and enjoy doing it, and that they dislike unfair treatment and enjoy punishing those who violate norms of fairness. Some studies of collective action in natural settings are consistent with this view. An ethnographic study of people who exposed themselves to mortal risks in support of an agrarian insurgency against an authoritarian regime in El Salvador, for example, identified both ethical and religious commitments and the pleasure of seeking to rectify past injustices as a key motivation (Wood 2003).

Recent studies of brain functioning provide some support for this hedonic view of cooperative behavior. Using positron emission tomography (PET), fMRI, and other techniques, neuroscientists, economists and others have begun to study the activation of the different brain areas of subjects playing experimental games (Fischbacher et al. 2005). There is some evidence, for example, that ultimatum game responders who reject a low offer exhibit heightened activation of the bilateral anterior insula, an area associated with negative emotional states such as anger and disgust (Sanfey et al. 2003). Camerer et al. (2005) comment: "It is irresistible to speculate that the insula is a neural locus of the distaste for inequality and unfair treatment."

Our view that subjects enjoy cooperation is consistent with the results of a series of experiments in which mutual cooperation is associated with elevated activity in one of the reward-related areas of the brain. Rilling et al. (2004) found that mutual cooperation along with a monetary payoff enhances activity in the striatum, the brain area involved in processing rewards resulting from a decision, more than the same payoff resulting from performance of an individual task. Moreover, mutual cooperation with a human partner produces a higher level of striatum activation than does cooperation with a computer partner. De Quervain et al. (2004) studied brain activation of subjects in a social dilemma who had the opportunity to punish a partner who had abused their trust. Among those punishing trust violators, they found enhanced activity in the dorsal striatum. Moreover, those who inflicted more punishment exhibited higher levels of activation than did those punishing less. A related study by Tania Singer found that male subjects (but not female) experienced pleasure, evidenced by activation in a reward processing part of the brain, the nucleus accumbens, rather than empathy, while observing pain inflicted on a partner who had defected in response to a cooperative offer by the subject in a sequential prisoner's dilemma (Singer 2005).

The above studies do not suggest that cooperating and punishing defectors is innate. Some foods that evoke disgust in one culture are delicacies in others. Cross-cultural experimental evidence is consistent with the view that behaviors in social interactions that trigger aversive reactions likewise vary from one society to another. Our inference from these studies concerns the proximate causes of behavior, not its evolutionary origins.

The field of neuroeconomics is still in its infancy and our understanding may be substantially modified by subsequent work. But the evidence available to date suggests that the brain processes the punishment of defectors and the achievement of mutual cooperation much as it processes other pleasurable behaviors. If this view is correct, altruistic cooperation and the altruistic punishment of defectors need not be explained by constraints on behavior but rather by their status as objectives, pursued by reward-seeking individuals and thus an aspect of individual preferences. This does not mean that ethical values are unimportant. Quite the contrary, the experimental evidence that norm violators are punished supports Trivers' (1971) notion that behavior is often motivated by what he termed moralistic aggression, an interpretation strengthened by the fact that altruistic punishment is directed not only toward those who harmed the punisher but also toward those who have harmed others.

3.11   Social Preferences in Laboratory and Natural Settings

Of course, experimental results in the laboratory would not be very interesting if they did not reflect real-life behavior. There is some evidence that they do or, to put it behaviorally, the experimental results have *external validity*. Edward Glaeser et al. (2000) explored whether experimental subjects who trusted others in the trust game also behaved in a trusting manner with their own personal belongings, for example, lending their bike to a friend. The authors found that experimental behavior was a quite good predictor of behavior outside the lab, while the usual measures of trust, based on survey questions, provided virtually no information.

Similarly, Dean Karlan (2005) used a trust game and a public goods game to predict the probability that loans by a Peruvian microfinance lender would be repaid. He found that individuals who were "trustworthy" in the experiment were less likely to default. Also, Nava Ashraf et al. (2006) studied Philippino women, identifying through a baseline survey those women who exhibited a lower time discount rate. These women were significantly more likely to open a savings account, and after 12 months, average savings balances increased by 81 percentage points for those clients assigned to a treatment group based on their laboratory performance, relative to those assigned to the control group. In a similar vein, Fehr and Goette (2007) found that in a group of bicycle messenger workers in Zürich, those who exhibited less *loss aversion* in a laboratory experiment exploring the subjects' preferences over lotteries, namely those for whom the subjective expected value of a gain of a Swiss franc exceeded the subjective expected cost of the loss of a Swiss franc, also exhibited less loss aversion when faced with real-life wage rate changes. Meier and Sprenger (2010) found that people who display present bias in a laboratory setting are more likely to assume credit card debts.

Moreover, Jeffrey Carpenter and Erika Seki (2011) found that Japanese shrimp fishermen who contributed more in a public goods experiment were more likely to be members of cooperatives that shared costs and catch among many boats than to fish under the usual private boat arrangements. A similar pattern was found among fishermen in the Brazilian northeast, where some fish offshore in large crews whose success depends on cooperation and coordination, while others exploit inland waters, fishing singly. The ocean fishers were significantly more generous in a public goods game, ultimatum game and dictator game than the inland fishers (Leibbrandt et al. 2010).

A better test of the external validity of experiments would include a behavior-based measure of how cooperative the individuals were, not simply whether they took part in a cooperation-sensitive production process. The Brazilian fishers provide just such a test. Shrimp are caught in large plastic bucketlike contraptions. Holes are cut in the bottom of the traps to allow the immature shrimp to escape, thereby preserving the stock for future catches. Smaller holes catch more shrimp but compromise the future stock. The fishermen thus face a real-world social dilemma: the present value of expected income of any given shrimper would be greatest if he cut only small holes in his own traps while others cut large holes in theirs. Small trap holes are a form of defection, and just as in the public goods game the small trap hole defection is the dominant strategy for a self-regarding individual: whatever the others do, a self-regarding shrimper would cut small holes. But a shrimper might resist the temptation to defect if he were both public spirited toward the other fishers and sufficiently patient to value the future lost opportunities that larger holes would entail. Fehr and Leibbrandt implemented both a public goods game and an experimental measure of impatience with the shrimpers. They found that both patience and cooperativeness in the public goods game predicted significantly larger trap holes (Fehr and Leibbrandt 2010). The effects, controlling for a large number of other possible influences on hole size, are substantial. A shrimper whose experimentally measured patience and cooperativeness is a standard deviation greater than the mean is predicted to cut holes in his traps that are half a standard deviation larger than the mean.

Additional evidence of external validity comes from a set of experiments and field studies with 49 groups of herders of the Bale Oromo people in Ethiopia who were engaged in forest commons management. Devesh Rustagi and his coauthors implemented public goods experiments with a total of 679 herders. They also studied the success of the herders' cooperative forest projects. The most common behavioral type in the experiments, constituting a bit more than a third of the subjects, were "conditional cooperators" who responded positively to higher contributions by others. Controlling for a large number of other influences on the success of the forest projects, the authors found that groups with more conditional cooperators were significantly more successful, in terms of number of new trees planted, than groups with fewer conditional cooperators. This was in part because members of groups with more conditional cooperators spent significantly more time monitoring the use of the forest by others. As in the case of the Brazilian shrimpers, the effects of group composition were large and statistically significant. A 10% increase in the fraction of experimentally identified conditional cooperators in a group was associated with an increase in trees planted or time spent monitoring of about 3% (Rustagi et al. 2010).

But these examples of correspondence between experimental and real-world behavior are hardly decisive. Consider, for example, the dictator game, in which one subject (the Dictator) is assigned an endowment of money and asked to allocate some portion of it (including none) to a passive recipient. Typically more than 60% of subjects allocate a positive sum to the recipient, which on average is about a fifth of the endowment. But we would be sadly mistaken if we inferred from this that 60% of individuals would spontaneously transfer funds to anonymous passers-by, or even that the same subjects would offer a fifth of the bills in their wallet to a homeless person asking for help. Subjects who reported that they had never given to a charity allocated 60% of their endowment to a named charity in a lab experiment (Benz and Meier 2008). Thus there are counter-examples to the above evidence of experimental validity. A more subtle problem with the studies of experimental validity is the low bar that is implicit in most of these tests. Merely a positive, statistically significant correlation between experimental play and real behavior is taken as evidence for validity. A more demanding test would ask whether the effect size or covariance is what one would expect from a valid measure.

Validity concerns arise from four aspects of human behavioral experiments that do not arise in most well-designed natural science experiments (Levitt and List 2007). First, experimental subjects typically know they are under a researcher's microscope, possibly inducing different behaviors than would occur under total anonymity or under the scrutiny of neighbors, family or workmates. Second, in experiments, interactions with other subjects are typically anonymous and without opportunities for ongoing face to face communication, unlike many social interactions. Third, subject pools may be quite different from the real-world populations of interest, in part due to the process of recruitment and self-selection. Finally, many of the experiments that provide evidence for the salience of social preferences are deliberately structured as strategic interactions like the ultimatum game that give scope for ethical or other-regarding behavior that may be absent in competitive markets and other important real-world settings.

It is not clear whether these four aspects of behavioral experiments induce the greater expression of social preferences in the lab or the opposite. For example, the fact that in most cases subjects are paid a show-up fee to participate in an experiment might attract the more materially oriented while the fact that most subjects are students may bias the results in other ways. Available evidence, however, suggests that the students volunteering for experiments are not more prosocial than those who do not, and that if anything university students are more likely to be self-regarding than older non-students (Fehr and List 2004, Carpenter et al. 2005, Cardenas 2005, Sutter and Kocher 2007, Bellemare et al. 2008, Falk et al. 2010, Burks et al. 2011). Moreover, studies typically find that older subjects exhibit at least as much prosociality as college-age subjects (Sutter and Kocher 2007, Bellemare et al. 2008). We report on several studies supporting this conclusion in §A9.

While warranting caution in generalizing the details of experimental behavior to the real world, none of these validity concerns is sufficient to dismiss the experimental evidence that social preferences are important behavioral motivations. This especially is the case when experiments identify motives that allow a consistent explanation of the otherwise anomalous real-world examples of self-sacrifice and generosity in wage setting, voting, and tax compliance mentioned in Chapter 2.

3.12   Competing Explanations

Nevertheless, the fact that subjects who had never contributed to a charity gave some of their endowment to an anonymous other in the dictator game is a reminder that one can never extrapolate directly from the laboratory to behavior in natural settings. But much stronger doubts have been raised against the experimental evidence. Some have suggested that the importance of social preferences is vastly overstated and distorted by questionable experimental design, especially not properly incentivizing subjects and not giving them sufficient time to learn the proper money-maximizing behavior. In their prominent critique of the experimental findings presented in this chapter, Kenneth Binmore and Avner Shaked (2010) maintain that the allocation that would be a Nash equilibrium were the self-interest axiom true is attained in "most games with money payoffs that have a unique Nash equilibrium, provided that the payoffs are sufficiently large and the subjects have ample time for trial-and-error learning. In spite of much rhetoric to the contrary, the one-shot prisoner's dilemma is a case in point." But the experimental evidence suggests otherwise.

In the case of the one-shot ultimatum game (Slonim and Roth 1998) and the gift exchange game (Fehr and Tougareva 1995), other-regarding behavior remains even at high stakes and for experienced players, and there is to our knowledge no experimental evidence that indicates otherwise. Other experiments agreeing with the above are Roth et al. (1991), Hoffman et al. (1994a), Straub and Murnighan (1995), and Cameron (1999). The high-stakes version of the prisoner's dilemma with a long learning period mentioned by Binmore and Shaked has not been experimentally implemented, to the best of our knowledge. The supporting evidence Binmore and Shaked cite, Ledyard (1995) and Sally (1995), in fact provide no evidence for their assertions. Ledyard reports that cooperation unravels in the repeated public goods game when punishment is not allowed. This is true, but we already have seen that this not due to players "learning" the Nash equilibrium, but rather to cooperators' reactions to the free-riding of other subjects. Moreover, the study of the sequential prisoner's dilemma described in §2.2 illustrates that a large fraction of subjects strictly prefer cooperating to defecting in the one-shot prisoner's dilemma, and especially strongly so when they are guaranteed that their partner will cooperate (Kiyonari et al. 2000). In addition, Kollock (1998) allows subjects to rank possible outcomes in the game, and shows that subjects strongly prefer the outcome of mutual cooperation. These results suggest that defection in the one-shot prisoner's dilemma is often the result of aversion to betrayal rather than selfishness (Bohnet et al. 2008). In short, Binmore and Shaked's generalization that subjects play the Nash equilibrium for payoff-maximizers in simple games when this equilibrium is unique, the subjects are experienced, and the stakes are sufficiently high does not have empirical support.

It is worth noting that even if the degree of other-regarding behavior were to be less where the stakes were higher, as we have seen was the case in the experiments of Andreoni and Miller (2002), this would not indicate the absence of social preferences, but rather that subjects are less likely to perform an action when it becomes more costly to do so. The fact that we would eat less ice cream at $10 a cone than at $3 a cone is not evidence against the hypothesis that we love ice cream. It indicates only that we have a limited budget and ice cream competes for a share of our purchases with other things we like.

Are there other plausible interpretations of cooperative behavior in the various games we have analyzed above? One might suggest that subjects simply do not understand the games, and cooperate by mistake. This is surely true for some subjects in some games, but as generalization it is not very plausible, because most of the games are extremely simple and experimenters generally require subjects to exhibit understanding before permitting them to participate. Moreover, if failure to understand were the problem and the self-interest axiom were true, subjects who play several ultimatum games in succession with different partners, for instance, should eventually learn to accept any positive offer, which they do not (Slonim and Roth 1998, List and Cherry 2000).

Another possibility is that because the anonymous, non-repeated face-to-face interactions are not a part of everyday life, we should expect subjects to confuse the experimental environment with a repeated interaction and, for example, in the ultimatum game, to reject low offers in order to establish a reputation for hard bargaining.

But we do not believe that this argument is correct. Of course experimental subjects bring to the laboratory the moral sensibility and practical knowledge that their personal experiences and received cultural wisdom have conveyed. We have seen this in the sharing behavior of the Lamelera whale hunters, the Orma herders, and the Aché hunters in our own cross-cultural experiments. But the confusion of a one-shot with a repeated interaction, or adhering to a maxim that says "act the same way in anonymous one-shots as in real-life repeated interactions," is not likely to be among these received wisdoms. We are very capable of distinguishing individuals with whom we are likely to have many future interactions from those with whom future interactions are less likely. Indeed, the sharp end-game drop off in contributions exhibited in Figures 3.5 and 4.4 show that experimental subjects are very sensitive to this distinction, cooperating much more if they expect frequent future interactions than if future interactions will not occur (Keser and van Winden 2000, Gächter and Falk 2002).

Other data support the notion that responders reject positive offers, not because they are confused or falsely believe they can establish a reputation for hard bargaining thereby, but simply because they want to punish an unfair proposer. For instance, in a variant of the game in which a rejection leads to the responder getting nothing but allows the proposer to keep the share he suggested for himself, responders rarely reject offers, and proposers make considerably smaller (but still positive) offers (Bolton and Zwick 1995).

A quite different concern about the experimental evidence is the ubiquity of *framing effects*, which are payoff-irrelevant facts that affect behavior. Most individuals are strongly influenced by the cues of appropriate behavior offered by the situation in which an action is taken (Ross and Nisbett 1991), and there is no reason to think that experiments are immune to this context-dependent aspect of individual behavior. We have already seen that naming the game (e.g., the "exchange game") matters. Another example: Andreoni (1995) shows that, when a public goods game is framed as an "individual investment game" in which subjects can invest in their private accounts, even though this imposes a cost on the other players, subjects exhibit little cooperation. Given that the actual payoffs to the game are the same whether the experimenter stresses the gains to social cooperation or the gains to personal investment, but the level of cooperation is equally affected, the preference for cooperation appears to be a fragile commitment easily manipulated by the experimenter.

However, it would be very odd if other-regarding preferences, such as for fairness, reciprocity, or honesty, were not sensitive to framing affects. The reason is that the ethical values an individual applies to a given situation depend on how the individual conceptualizes the social norms appropriate in that situation, and this conceptualization is subject to experimenter manipulation. The fact, then, that the experimenter can find a set of conditions under which subjects behave selfishly is not an argument against the importance of other-regarding preferences.

A final critique of the experimental evidence for the ubiquitous nature of social preferences is that other-regarding and moral preferences are confused expressions of a desire to maintain a good reputation in the eyes of others. In recognition of H. L. Mencken, we will call this the "somebody may be looking" critique. Note that the critique is not that establishing a reputation in the game may be a way of gaining higher payoffs in some later interactions, as one's behavior in the game is anonymous. Rather, the somebody may be looking contention is that people are very concerned about the way they are evaluated by others, independent of any material reward or punishment they might receive by being judged. This is of course true. As we have already seen, Masclet et al. (2003) showed that considerable cooperation could be induced in a public goods game where punishment consisted merely of being assigned "negative points" for free-riding. Similarly, Rege and Telle (2004) showed that having participants in a public goods game write their contributions on an announcement board in full view of the other participants increased contributions markedly, even though the subjects were unlikely ever to meet again.

Perhaps the most dramatic effect of this type is the tendency of subjects in perfectly anonymous settings to respond to the presence of "imaginary" viewers, as revealed by the so-called eye-spot experiments. For instance, Bateson et al. (2006) studied contributions to an "honor box" for the use of tea, coffee, and milk in the common kitchen of the 48 members of the Division of Psychology at the University of Newcastle over a period of 10 weeks. In alternating weeks, they placed a picture of flowers and a picture of a person's eyes looking straight at the viewer above the note to contribute to the honor box. They found that on average, people paid 2.76 times as much under the eye-spot condition than under the flowers condition. The experimenters conclude that this evidence, which is supported by other researchers (Haley and Fessler 2005, Burnham and Hare 2007), suggests that "the self-interested motive of reputation maintenance may be sufficient to explain cooperation in the absence of direct return" (p. 413).

The conclusion is a non-sequitur. It is incorrect to infer from the fact that people act more generously when there appear to be witnesses that people exhibit other-regarding preferences only when they believe, consciously or otherwise, that they are being observed. The above evidence is completely consistent with our view that individuals have moral values that they uphold for their own sake, although their self-assessment as moral beings is highly sensitive to how they fare in the eyes of others. The idea goes back to Adam Smith (2000[1759]).

Nature, when she formed man for society, endowed him with an original desire to please and an original aversion to offend his brethren. She
rendered their approbation most flattering and most agreeable to him *for
its own sake*, and their disapprobation most mortifying and most offensive
(Part III Section I, Paragraph 13, italics added).

The most likely source of this heightened sensitivity to the opinion of others was
investigated long ago by the sociologist Charles Horton Cooley (1902), who coined the
term "looking-glass self" to describe the dynamic whereby individual psychic well-
being depends on self-esteem, and self-esteem is the product of being esteemed by
others with whom one shares a moral community. According to Cooley, and after
him the sociologist George Herbert Mead (1967[1934]), we strive to please others not
only for reputation (material reward in either present or future), but also because our
self-esteem depends on others' evaluation of us.

There have been several interpretations of the looking-glass self as a model of
self-esteem. The one best supported by the evidence (Leung and Martin 2003) is
the internalization-of-norms model according to which we internalize norms that provide for us moral and prosocial preferences, and our self-esteem depends on meeting
moral and prosocial expectations. While some individuals are capable of maintaining
high self-esteem from personal self-assessment, most individuals are acutely dependent
upon the positive evaluation of their behavior by others. The looking-glass self is thus
an amalgam of personal self-assessment and the assessment of others.

It is entirely plausible, therefore, that even the subconscious neural cues of being
watched in the eye-spot experiments would lead many individuals (those dependent
upon the evaluation of others for self-esteem) to increase their other-regarding behavior.
This, however, in no way supports the notion that experimental evidence for social
preferences is spurious.

However one interprets the eye-spot phenomenon in dictator game experiments,
there is no indication that eyespots have any efficacy in social situations in which, unlike
the dictator game, there are strategic interactions among participants. For example, in
an eye-spot experiment using the trust game, the presence or absence of eyespots has
no statistical effect on the behavior of the subjects (Schneider and Fehr 2010).

Many economists, biologists and others will assert, as they have for at least a century, that altruism beyond one's immediate family members is highly exceptional and
ephemeral. The experimental evidence of the last two decades tells strongly against
this view. But the belief that self-interest is unrivaled among human motives has never
depended on empirical tests. Rather it has appeared self-evident because the evolution
of the human species by a process of natural selection was bound to produce a selfish
animal. In the absence of a plausible evolutionary explanation of the origin of altruistic
preferences (excepting close genealogical kin), the self-interest axiom was commonly
accepted by default. But, as we will see, the idea that selfish genes must produce selfish
individuals is false.

4

The Sociobiology of Human Cooperation

Like successful Chicago gangsters, our genes have survived, in some cases for millions of years, in a highly competitive world. This entitles us to expect certain qualities in our genes. I shall argue that a predominant quality to be expected in a successful gene is ruthless selfishness. This gene for selfishness will usually give rise to selfishness in individual behavior.

Richard Dawkins, *The Selfish Gene* (1976) p. 2

Selfish and contentious people will not cohere, and without coherence, nothing can be effected. A tribe possessing... a greater number of courageous, sympathetic and faithful members, who were always ready to warn each other of danger, to aid and defend each other... would spread and be victorious over other tribes... Thus the social and moral qualities would tend slowly to advance and be diffused throughout the world.

Charles Darwin, *The Descent of Man* (1998[1873]) Ch. 5, pp. 134–135

Humans are cooperative. But our genes, like Richard Dawkins' Chicago gangsters, are selfish. Can selfish genes produce altruistic people? We think they can.

In light of what we know about other animals and about human evolution, how could the preferences documented in the previous chapter have become common among humans? Recall that by definition (Chapter 2), behaving altruistically helps others but reduces an individual's fitness or material payoff. Given the tendency of people to copy the successful and the fact that natural selection favors the more fit, how did our altruistic preferences overcome the cultural and biological evolutionary handicaps entailed by the reduced payoffs that they elicited?

To answer this question we draw on a remarkable ensemble of papers that revolutionized our understanding of the biology of social behaviors. Dugatkin (2006) is an introduction to the lives and contributions of the leading biologists of social behavior from Kropotkin at the turn of the 20th century to the present. Valuable syntheses of this literature are presented in Queller (1985), Dugatkin (1997), Frank (1998), Keller (1999), Kerr and Godfrey-Smith (2002), Rousset (2004), McElreath and Boyd (2006), Lehmann and Keller (2006), Fletcher and Zwick (2006), Nowak (2006), Levin (2009) and Sigmund (2010).

The first of these seminal works is William Hamilton's "The Genetical Evolution of Social Behavior," published in 1964, and his subsequent work, which introduced the concept of inclusive fitness that is central to our explanation of human cooperation. Hamilton's focus on the importance of the social structure of populations framed thinking about the evolution of altruism for an entire generation. Hamilton did not invent the idea of inclusive fitness (as Haldane's quip about his eight drowning cousins attests) but his 1964 paper formalized and greatly expanded its reach.

The central importance of social structure was picked up and expanded into a new biological approach to social behavior by Edward O. Wilson in his massively influential *The Insect Societies* (1971) and *Sociobiology: The New Synthesis* (1975). In 1970, George Price provided an ingenious method for the analysis of selection processes operating at multiple levels, providing a way to study the evolution of social behavior in group-structured populations. The method was quickly embraced by Hamilton, and we use it extensively in our explanation of cooperation in humans.

This was soon followed by Robert Trivers' "The Evolution of Reciprocal Altruism" (1971), initiating one of the most vibrant research paradigms in animal behavior to this day, and suggesting some of the distinctive features of human behavior. Two years later Luigi Luca Cavalli-Sforza and Marcus Feldman published "Cultural versus Biological Inheritance" (1973a), initiating the modeling of gene-culture coevolution, the second concept underpinning our explanation of the origins and distinctive nature of cooperation among humans.

Almost simultaneously, in 1973, John Maynard Smith and Price published "The Logic of Animal Conflict." This paper launched the field of evolutionary game theory, applied this theory to the dynamics of animal behavior, and thus provided an analytical technique essential to our reasoning in the pages that follow. This cornucopia for the science of social behavior was capped off just 16 years after Hamilton's initial contribution by his collaboration with Robert Axelrod, "The Evolution of Cooperation" (1981), in which Trivers' insights were formalized using evolutionary game theory and then deployed along with Hamilton's inclusive fitness to provide a convincing explanation of the initial emergence of dyadic cooperative behaviors in a population of erstwhile uncooperative animals.

These models are all logically and mathematically coherent, but are distinguished by two aspects of their empirical adequacy. The first is whether they explain the forms of human cooperativeness that we observe in experiments and in natural settings. The second is whether the key mechanisms of the models could have operated over the long sweep of the human past in such a way as to favor the evolution of the distinctive cooperative behaviors we observe in humans. On both grounds we find that William Hamilton's concept of inclusive fitness provides the most adequate starting point.

In the next section we introduce what we consider to be the most plausible approach, a Hamilton-inspired model of inclusive fitness based on group differentiation and competition, clarifying what is meant by multi-level selection. In §4.1 we explain how multi-level selection works, and in the next section we distinguish between a strong form of multi-level selection, in which group competition offsets the selective pressures operating against altruistic members within a group, and a weak form, in which group competition selects among stable within-group equilibria, meaning that within-group selection pressures against altruistic members are absent, as a result favoring groups with a higher level of cooperation. We then turn to the Trivers-inspired models of self-interested helping, first (§4.4) describing the basic model of repeated dyadic interactions and then extending this model to situations in which there are many potential cooperators (§4.5) and in which helping is rewarded indirectly by third parties (§4.6). We then

(§4.7) introduce models in which helping others enhances one's fitness or other payoffs because it is a credible signal of the individual's otherwise unobservable characteristics as a potential mate, ally, or opponent.

In §4.8 we point out that all of the models surveyed here work because those who provide help to others are more likely than by chance to receive help from others. The models differ in the processes that account for this behavioral assortment benefiting those providing help. In part for this reason, the models also differ in the proximate motives likely to account for helping behavior, providing further clues, which we consider in the concluding section, to the puzzle of how human cooperation evolved.

4.1   Inclusive Fitness and Human Cooperation

Hamilton's rule for the evolutionary success of altruism (Hamilton 1964) states that conferring a fitness benefit b on another individual at a direct fitness cost to oneself of c will be favored by natural selection if

$$rb > c, \qquad (4.1)$$

where r is the genetic relatedness between the actor and the beneficiary (one half for siblings, a quarter for nieces and nephews, an eighth for cousins and so on). The coefficient of genetic relatedness between the helper and the beneficiary, r, is Hamilton's measure of social structure. It will vary from a value of close to zero when most interactions are among total strangers to close to one half when most interactions are among siblings or parents and their offspring. According to Hamilton's rule, helping another person increases the inclusive fitness of the actor by an amount $rb - c > 0$, which if positive means that the population frequency of a hypothetical altruistic allele accounting for the helping behavior will increase. Rowthorn (2006) offers a clear explanation of how Hamilton's rule works when applied to siblings. The mathematical symbols for this and subsequent chapters are summarized in the table at the end of the chapter.

But Hamilton's insight is far more general. His rule captures the key mechanism common to all models of the evolution of altruism, namely that an altruistic allele cannot proliferate if its bearers are no more likely to receive help from those with whom they interact than would occur by chance. All successful models of the evolution of altruistic behaviors share this positive assortment feature, including not only those stressing preferential interaction among siblings or other close genetic family members but also models of group competition for reproductive success. Rousset (2002) clarifies the common features of family-based and group-based assortment. A group may be a tribe, sect, language community, or other ensemble of individuals in more frequent social interaction than with outsiders. In so-called *group selection* models, bearers of an altruistic allele benefit from their many interactions with other altruistic individuals that occur when most interactions are within groups and when the altruists are concentrated in some groups and the non-altruists in others. Following Hamilton we apply the term inclusive fitness to all models in which positive assortment allows the proliferation of an altruistic trait.

While sharing the common feature of genetic assortment and relatedness among those who interact, the two variants of inclusive fitness, based people's interactions being primarily with members of their tribe or band or members of their family, differ sociologically, that is, in the reasons for the positive assortment. They also differ in the forms of behavior likely to be supported—a willingness to sacrifice for close family members but not others in the first case, and to die for one's group and to kill outsiders in the second, for example. Because these differences will emerge as important in our account of the nature and evolution of human cooperation, to avoid confusion we will use the term *kin-based selection* models to mean mutual helping relations among close family members, so that kin-based selection is exactly "kin selection" as originally defined by John Maynard Smith in his influential "Group Selection and Kin Selection": "the evolution of characteristics which favor the survival of close relatives of the affected individual" (1964, p. 1145).

Where, by contrast, the main source of nonrandom interactions in a population is the reproductive isolation of groups larger than families, and where the main selective pressures operating on individuals are competition for group survival, we refer to *group selection* or *multi-level selection* (the two terms are synonymous). As with the term kin selection, the term group selection may be confusing, as it is sometimes thought to refer not simply to the importance of group membership in an individual- or gene-based evolutionary process, but instead to define the unique unit of selection, so that a group selection model would be simply a model of competition among groups, with selection not operating on genes or individuals. Because our models always concern the relative fitness of individuals, we prefer the term multi-level selection.

Kin-based selection and multi-level selection are examples of Hamilton's concept of inclusive fitness in that both take account of the direct effects of one's actions on the evolutionary success of a trait as well as the indirect effects that arise when family structure or group structure results in individuals being more likely than by chance to interact with those bearing the identical trait. Our "kin-based selection" is not synonymous with inclusive fitness selection but rather, along with group selection, is a special case of inclusive fitness selection. Because we are interested in the distinctive aspects of human cooperation, we prefer not to equate kin and inclusive fitness, as is sometimes done, because as a practical matter, the term kin is still widely used in biology and understood by nonbiologists to mean close genealogical relatives, so it would be confusing to use the term kin selection to explain human cooperation that extends considerably beyond the family and includes even total strangers.

Helping close family members is one of the most prominent forms of human cooperation, and is often altruistic. But because one of the distinctive aspects of human cooperation is that it extends far beyond the immediate family, we treat kin-based altruism only in passing. Recalling that helping another is altruistic only if the actor would gain higher fitness by declining to help, we note that not all behaviors considered as examples of kin-based altruism are altruistic. The fitness cost of helping one's genetic relatives may be more than offset by one's own resulting direct fitness gains, in which case helping is not altruistic (the cost, c, in this case would be negative). This is likely to be the case if the relatives in question are one's children or grandchildren and are thus directly counted in one's fitness. But it is less likely to be the case for other equally close relatives, such as siblings or parents.

Examples of kin-based altruism are preferential helping of close kin, which is widely observed in the care of offspring in many animals, and among humans in such diverse aspects of behavior as food-sharing (Case et al. 2000, Gurven et al. 2002), homicide (Daly and Wilson 1988), and migrants' remittances (Bowles and Posel 2005). However, some cooperative behaviors among male chimpanzees, female bonobos, and some other animals are related weakly, if at all, to kin status (Gerloff et al. 1999, Mitani 2006, Silk 2006). About chimpanzees, Linda Vigilant et al. (2001) write: "Kinship may explain cooperative behaviors directed against other communities, but is unlikely to explain the high levels of affiliation and cooperation seen for males within community interactions."

Even for intra-household allocations among humans, kin-based altruism is far from an adequate explanation of helping behaviors. In some studies of food sharing in small-scale societies, kin-altruism effects appear to be very modest or virtually absent (Kaplan and Hill 1985, Gurven et al. 2000a, Kaplan and Hill 1985, Smith et al. 2002). In modern societies important aspects of intergenerational inheritance patterns do not conform to the expectations of the inclusive fitness model in that the spouse, who is typically genetically unrelated or only distantly so, frequently gets a very substantial bequest, and children typically receive equal shares irrespective of their age, health status and other correlates of their reproductive value. Our study (with Dorrit Posel) of migrant workers' remittances of a portion of their urban wages to their rural families of origin in South Africa (Bowles and Posel 2005) shows that less than a third of the remittances sent home can be attributed to the relatedness of the migrant to the members of the household of origin.

But as we have said, the primary weakness of kin-based altruism is not that it fails to explain altruism among close family members, but rather that it fails to explain the forms of human cooperation extending considerably beyond the family and even to virtual strangers. The key insight for the study of the distinctively human cooperation captured by Hamilton's rule is that if altruism is to proliferate among people who are not closely related, the ratio of benefits to costs must be substantial. Thus to explain how quite costly forms of altruism could proliferate when interactions are among people with very modest degrees of genetic relatedness we will need to show that the group benefits of some forms of altruism may indeed be substantial. We will see in subsequent chapters that this indeed was the case where groups competed for survival both against one another and against nature.

Our explanation of the evolution of human social preferences hinges on three facts. First, group living is essential to human survival. Second, groups differ in their evolutionary success, some expanding and dividing many times, while other groups are absorbed into more successful groups or pass out of existence in warfare or during environmental crises. Third, groups in which altruistic and other social preferences are common tend to cooperate, and cooperative groups tend to prevail in the frequent intergroup competition and to survive the severe environmental crises that (as we will see in Chapter 6) characterized the early human condition.

Differential group success therefore plays a central role in the evolution of human behaviors and institutions, members of less successful groups copying the more successful or being eliminated by them. Examples of this process include the peopling of many parts of the world by individuals of European ancestry and the associated spread of European customs and institutions in the past half millennium, and the spread of agriculture and its associated novel systems of social organization and behavior from the Middle East to Europe beginning 11 millennia ago.

The fact that more cooperative groups tended to survive and expand explains two key facts. The first is that altruistic individuals among our ancestors enjoyed enhanced reproductive success, resulting in the spread of altruism as a distinctive human trait. The second is that our altruistic dispositions motivate us to care about and help not only close family but even those related to us only distantly or not at all, as long as we share common group membership.

The idea that the group-structured nature of populations and group competition would strongly affect evolution has long been recognized not only by sociologists and historians (Parsons 1964, Tilly 1981) but also by biologists (Lewontin 1965,1970, Wilson 1977, Alexander 1979, Durham 1991, Dunbar 1993, Laland and Feldman 2004). But until recently, most biologists have concluded that group-level effects that would favor the spread of genes contributing to altruistic behavior cannot offset the effects of individual within-group selection operating against altruists, except where special circumstances heighten and sustain genetic differences between groups relative to differences within the group (Williams 1966, Crow and Kimura 1970, Boorman and Levitt 1973, Maynard Smith 1976). The reason is that the speed of an evolutionary process is proportional to the differences on which it works, so in order for between-group selection to outrun within-group selection, between-group differences must be substantial. But gene flow due to group exogamy and other reasons for migration are thought to preclude this.

However, beginning with Charles Darwin, whose position is clear from the opening quote of this chapter, a number of evolutionary thinkers have suggested that human evolution might provide an exception to this negative assessment of the force of group level, or as we call it, multi-level selection. Hamilton (1975) summarized Darwin's view as follows: "He saw that such traits [as]...courage and self-sacrifice...would naturally be counter-selected within a social group, whereas in competition between groups the groups with the most of such qualities would be the ones best fitted to survive and increase" (p. 117).

In *The Causes of Evolution*, Haldane (1932) had already provided a plausible mechanism for how this might come about. He suggested that in a population of small endogamous "tribes," an altruistic trait might evolve because the "tribe splitting" that occurs when successful groups reach a certain size would by chance create a few successor groups with a very high frequency of altruists, reducing within-group differences and increasing between-group differences, a process very similar to that we will model in Chapters 7 and 8. The modest size of typical human groups during most of our evolution thus could play a crucial role in the chance occurrence of one or more groups with a high fraction of altruists, which would then, as Darwin said, "spread and be victorious over other tribes." Haldane concluded: "evolution in large random-mating populations...is not representative of evolution in general, and perhaps gives a false impression of the events occurring in less numerous species...Our ancestors were mostly rather rare creatures." Hamilton (1975) took up Haldane's suggestion, adding that if the allocation of members to successor groups following "tribe splitting" was not random but was rather what he called "associative," between-group differences would be even greater and multi-level selection pressures would be further enhanced.

More recent research also suggests that impediments to multi-level selection may be less general than was once thought (Uyenoyama and Feldman 1980, Harpending and Rogers 1987). A number of writers have pointed out that multi-level selection may be of considerably greater importance among humans than among other animals given the advanced level of human cognitive and linguistic capabilities and consequent capacity to maintain group boundaries and to formulate general rules of behavior for large groups, and the resulting substantial influence of cultural inheritance on human behavior (Cavalli-Sforza and Feldman 1973, Alexander 1987, Boyd and Richerson 1985, 1990, Sober and Wilson 1994, Boehm 1997).

Among the consequences of these distinctive human capacities are the suppression of within-group phenotypic differences through egalitarianism, coinsurance, consensus decision making and conformist cultural transmission. The reduction in within-group differences slows down the selection against altruistic individuals. Insider biases and individual preferences to interact with like individuals lead to large between-group differences in behavior and, to a lesser but not negligible extent, in genotypes too, as we will see. These insider biases result in frequent between-group conflicts as well as high levels of positive assortment in interactions both within and between groups. Other animals do some of these things, but none does all of them on a human scale. All of these aspects of human social life enhance the force of between-group selection relative to within-group selection. A result, if we are correct, was the evolution this cooperative species.

A rather different interpretation of human altruism and its evolution is that, on closer inspection, most apparently altruistic forms of helping are just self-interest with a long time horizon. This approach takes Trivers' reciprocal altruism as its starting point and shows how, when interactions are frequently repeated, individuals may enhance their fitness by a mutualistic form of helping based on the expectation of reciprocation in the future. Variants of this approach developed in models of indirect reciprocity and costly signaling show that helping others may be repaid not only by the targets of one's help but also by others wishing preferentially to be associated with the helpful.

A schema of these various explanations of human cooperation is shown in Figure 4.1, the main distinction being between Hamilton's inclusive fitness approach in which helping behaviors that are genuinely altruistic can evolve and Trivers' approach in which helping behaviors are not altruistic because they enhance the fitness of the actor (in an equilibrium population of Trivers' reciprocal altruistic helpers, as we will see in §4.2, §4.3, and §4.4, switching to not helping would result in lower fitness). Trivers' contribution was to show that seemingly altruistic behaviors may evolve precisely because they are not in fact altruistic, reminiscent of the accounts given by Tocqueville's Americans. Trivers term "reciprocal altruism" for these behaviors is obviously a misnomer.

4.2   Modeling Multi-level Selection

The multi-level selection model works because members of predominantly altruistic groups have above-average fitness and thus contribute disproportionately to the next generation. Here we apply multi-level selection to a process of genetic transmission, but

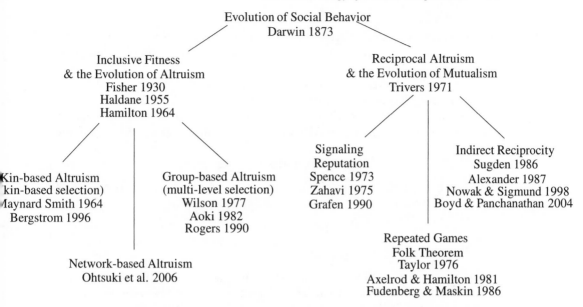

Figure 4.1. Models explaining cooperation in human society.

the same model applies to any process of selection based on the differential replication of traits over time. To see how it works, consider a single altruistic behavior that is the expression of an "altruistic allele," the quotation marks being a reminder that altruistic behaviors are unlikely to be the expression of a single allele.

Thus, we consider a trait that may (A) or may not (N) be present in each individual in a large population that is subdivided into a number of reproductively somewhat isolated groups, commonly known as *demes*. Suppose altruistic behavior costs the individual c and confers a total benefit of b on a randomly selected other member of the group, where c and b are both measured in units of fitness, and $b > c > 0$. It follows that a member in a group composed entirely of A's has an expected payoff of the amount $b - c > 0$ greater than a member of a group composed of all N's. In any mixed group, however, the expected payoff to A's will be lower than that of the N's by an amount c. These payoffs are the same as in Figure 3.1, so the interaction is a prisoner's dilemma.

Let $p_{ij} = 1$ indicate that individual i in group j is an A, and $p_{ij} = 0$ if i is an N. Let p represent the fraction of A's in the population at the start of a given time period, and let p' be the fraction of A's at the start of the next period. Define w_{ij} as the expected fitness of an individual of type i in group j and let

$$w_{ij} = \beta_o + p_j \beta_g + p_{ij} \beta_i \qquad (4.2)$$

where β_g and β_i are respectively the effects on w_{ij} of variations in p_j (the frequency of the A allele in the group) and p_{ij} (the presence of the A allele in individual i), and β_o is a baseline replication rate based on factors not considered here. In equation 4.2 the two effects, between- and within-group selection, are separable, so that the size of the group effect on an individual is independent of whether the individual is altruistic or not, and the individual effect of being an altruist is independent of the frequency of altruists in the group. The assumption that the two effects are separable is unrealistic, but it allows an illuminating simplification.

Price (1972) showed that in this case the change in the frequency of altruists in the population, $\Delta p \equiv p' - p$, can be partitioned into additive between-group and within-group effects (Frank, 1997 provides a clear explication of the Price equation). We derive the Price equation in §A10, where we show that the partition can be written as

$$w\Delta p = \beta_G \text{var}(p_j) + \beta_i \overline{\text{var}}(p_{ij}), \tag{4.3}$$

where w is the population-wide average fitness, which we normalize to unity, as we assume the population size is constant, and $\overline{\text{var}}(p_{ij})$ is given by

$$\overline{\text{var}}(p_{ij}) = \sum_j f_j \text{var}(p_{ij}), \tag{4.4}$$

where f_j is the fraction of the population in group j, and $\text{var}(p_{ij})$ is the genetic variance in group j. The terms $\text{var}(p_j)$ and $\overline{\text{var}}(p_{ij})$ respectively are the between-deme genetic variance and weighted average within-deme genetic variance (the weights f_j, based on group size). The coefficient β_G is the effect of variation in p_j on the average fitness of members of deme j (that is, on w_j), which is determined as follows. If we sum (4.2) over the individuals in a group and divide by group size, we see that

$$w_j = \beta_o + p_j(\beta_g + \beta_i). \tag{4.5}$$

So

$$\beta_G \equiv \frac{dw_j}{dp_j} = \beta_i + \beta_g. \tag{4.6}$$

Recall that a behavior is altruistic if adopting it, hypothetically switching from an N to an A, lowers one's expected fitness while increasing the average fitness of members of one's group. Our definition of altruism thus maps neatly onto the terms of the Price equation, and we are interested in the cases where $\beta_G > 0$ (altruism is group-beneficial) and $\beta_i < 0$ (the individual who switched from N ($p_{ij} = 0$) to A ($p_{ij} = 1$) would as a result have lower fitness).

The separability assumption now allows us to represent equation 4.3 in terms of the payoffs: $\beta_i = -c$ and $\beta_g = b$. Thus using this information, equation 4.6, and recalling that $w = 1$, equation 4.3 can be written

$$\Delta p = (b - c)\text{var}(p_j) - c\overline{\text{var}}(p_{ij}). \tag{4.7}$$

The first term captures the group effect, which is positive, by the definition of altruism, while the second represents the effect of within-group selection, which is negative, also by the definition of altruism. Setting aside degenerate cases such as zero variances, it follows that the frequency of the trait will be stationary (i.e., $\Delta p = 0$) where the two terms in equation 4.7 are of equal absolute magnitude (assuming that the β's and variances making up these terms are themselves stationary). Because the second term is negative, the frequency of the A trait within all groups will fall over time. But as

$b - c$ is positive, this tendency will be offset by the decline in the size of groups with low frequencies of the trait and the expansion of groups with many altruists.

Let us define the *variance ratio* F_{ST} as the ratio of the between-group variance in the fraction of altruists to the total population variance, which is the within-group plus the between-group variance of the fraction of altruists, or

$$F_{ST} = \frac{\text{var}(p_j)}{\overline{\text{var}(p_{ij})} + \text{var}(p_j)}. \tag{4.8}$$

The variance ratio is thus a population-wide measure of the degree of nonrandomness in who interacts with whom, resulting from the tendency of altruists to find themselves disproportionately in groups with many other altruists. The variance ratio F_{ST} is Sewall Wright's *inbreeding coefficient* (Wright 1922), measuring the degree of genetic differentiation among groups.

This ratio measures the difference between the probability of being paired with an altruist conditional on being an altruist, $P(A|A)$, and conditional on being a non-altruist, $P(A|N)$, that arises because the population is group-structured (Crow and Kimura 1970). Thus,

$$F_{ST} = P(A|A) - P(A|N). \tag{4.9}$$

An example illustrating this result is given in §A10. Being "paired with an altruist" means being the recipient of the randomly assigned benefit, b, that altruists confer on fellow group members. This is more likely to occur if there are many A's in one's group. If A's tend to be in groups with many other A's, they enjoy an advantage over N's; i.e., F_{ST} measures the extent of this advantage. Using the definition of F_{ST} (4.8) and rearranging terms in (4.3), we see that the condition for Δp to be zero, so that the fraction of altruists in the population is stationary, is

$$F_{ST} = \frac{c}{b}. \tag{4.10}$$

If $F_{ST} > c/b$, the fraction of altruists may be expected to increase and if $F_{ST} < c/b$, it decreases. Comparing equations 4.10 and 4.1, we see that 4.10 is just Hamilton's rule with F_{ST} the measure of population structure.

Equation 4.10 also indicates the most costly form of altruism that may proliferate by this method. When the variance among group means is zero (so that $F_{ST} = 0$), A's no longer have the advantage of being in groups with disproportionately many A's. In this case multi-level selection is inoperative, so only a costless (that is, non-altruistic) form of group-beneficial behavior could proliferate. By contrast when $\text{var}(p_{ij}) = 0$ for all j, groups are either all A or all N, and one meets only one's own type, independently of the composition of the total population. In this case, within-group selection is absent and between-group selection is the only selective force at work. Thus, the force of multi-level selection will depend on the magnitude of the group benefit relative to the individual cost (b and c) and the degree to which groups differ in their frequency of the trait, relative to the within-group variance of the trait. In Chapter 6 we will use genetic, archeological, and other data to estimate the b's, c's, and F_{ST}'s that are relevant to the evolution of social behavior among early humans.

Figure 4.2 shows how the group structure of the population may overcome the disadvantage of bearing the costs of altruistic behaviors. The figure indicates the variance ratio F_{ST}, namely the difference $P(A|A) - P(A|N)$, which is just sufficient to equate the expected fitness of the two types and thus to maintain a stationary value of p. As is evident from the figure, this is the F_{ST} that satisfies equation 4.10, namely $F_{ST}b = c$. The slope of both expected fitness functions is b and the distance between them is c. How large $P(A|A) - P(A|N)$ must be depends, as we have seen and as the figure makes clear, on the costs and benefits of the altruistic behavior, b and c. It is clear from the figure that for a given level of b (slope of the lines), the greater is the cost of altruism, c (the vertical distance between the lines) the greater must be the degree of positive assortment $P(A|A) - P(A|N)$ in order for altruism to proliferate in the population. In §A10 we provide a numerical example that will clarify how the Price equation and this model based on it work.

The Price equation does not represent a complete dynamical system giving the movements of p. This would require a set of equations giving the movements over time of the between- and within-group variances. It is easy to check, for example, that the variances given in the numerical example in the appendix that render p stationary are not themselves stationary. Because they will be different the next period, the values of b and c that made p stationary in the period under study will not ensure stationarity in subsequent periods. Except in degenerate cases of little interest, equations giving the movement of the relevant variances over time are not attainable. This is the reason that exploring evolutionary processes under the influence of group selection typically requires that we resort (in subsequent chapters) to agent-based computer simulation models.

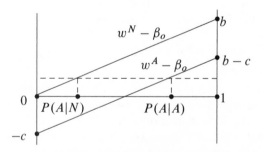

Probability of Being Paired with an A

Figure 4.2. The evolution of an altruistic trait in a group-structured population. The vertical axis measures average population-wide fitnesses of the non-altruists and altruists (w^N and w^A respectively), minus the baseline fitness β_o. If the population structure's variance ratio is such that the difference in the conditional probabilities of being paired with an A, $P(A|A) - P(A|N)$, is as shown, p is stationary, because the expected fitnesses of the two types, $w^A = bP(A|A) - c - \beta_o$ and $w^N = bP(A|N) - \beta_o$, are equal.

4.3   Equilibrium Selection

The above model illustrates what we call *strong multi-level selection*, which occurs when the second term in the Price equation is negative, indicating that those with group-beneficial traits are altruistic and hence would attain higher fitness by abandoning their helping behaviors. But the second term may be zero, so that those who confer benefits on others suffer no disadvantage within groups, while profiting from the group-beneficial effects of their behaviors. When this is the case, we say *weak multi-level selection* is operative. The cooperative traits that may be supported in the equilibria selected by this process are not altruistic, because cooperators would not gain in fitness terms were they to defect. There are two main cases of weak multi-level selection.

The first type of weak multi-level selection occurs when both the A trait and the N trait are evolutionarily stable strategies, so that two stable within-group equilibria exist, one with all N's and the other with all A's, each of which cannot be invaded by a small group of migrants or mutants exhibiting the other type of behavior. This is the case, we will see, when the conditions for the proliferation of cooperation by means of reciprocal altruism, indirect reciprocity or costly signaling obtain. These models provide mechanisms by which a (non-altruistic) cooperative behavior could be stabilized within a population. Note that in this case the second term of the Price equation is zero because if $p_j = 1$ or $p_j = 0$, then $\overline{\text{var}}(p_{ij}) = p_j(1 - p_j) = 0$. This would also be the case, for example, in the repeated game setting studied in the next section, in which both unconditional defection and conditional cooperation are mutual best responses. But here we model the case of weak group selection by extending the above model of a one-shot dyadic interaction between A's and N's. Two stable equilibria could exist in this case, for example if, following an A-N interaction, the A's in the group collectively attempted to punish the N. The A's would then be akin to the strong reciprocators whose preferences were described in the previous chapter. Suppose their attempt to punish the N succeeds with a likelihood equal to the fraction of A's in the population, and if successful, the cost imposed on the N is c_p. Assume each A incurs a cost of k in attempting to punish the N. Then the expected fitness of the A's in group j is

$$w_j^A = p_j b - c - k(1 - p_j) + \beta_o,$$

while the fitness of the N's is

$$w_j^N = p_j b - p_j^2 c_p + \beta_o.$$

These payoffs give the expected fitness functions within a single group illustrated in upper panel of Figure 4.3, for the case where $c_p > c$, so the target of the punishment bears a greater cost than does an A by helping a fellow group member. Note that if $p_j > p_j^*$, which is the value of p such that $w_j^A = w_j^N$, A's will have higher fitness ($b - c$ rather than zero) and thus eventually eliminate the N's, while if the reverse inequality holds, N's will have higher fitness and thus eventually eliminate the A's. A population composed of many groups with this interaction structure could contain some with all A's and some with all N's. But the all A groups would have higher average fitness, and if the total population is constant, the N's would eventually be eliminated. Boyd and Richerson (1985) showed that *conformist cultural transmission,* a tendency to copy the more common behaviors, can have the same effect, giving rise to homogeneous groups among which weak group selection can support the proliferation of an altruistic trait.

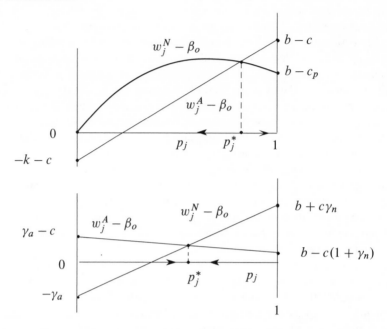

Figure 4.3. Weak multi-level selection. The horizontal axis gives the fraction of A's in the group. In the upper panel p_j^* is an unstable equilibrium and constitutes the boundary between the basin of attraction of the all-N and the all-A equilibria. In the lower panel, where γ_a is the rate at which N's are socialized into A's and γ_n is the rate at which A's revert to N's through imitation (because the N's have higher payoffs), p_j^* is a stable equilibrium. In both cases within-group selection will result in a stationary distribution of A's and N's with no within-group selection operating against the A's. By contrast, Figure 4.2 illustrates the case of strong multi-level selection, in which in the absence of positive assortment, selection within groups results in a reduction in the frequency of A's.

In the second type of weak multi-level selection, cooperative individuals coexist with others in a stable within-group equilibrium and groups differ in the resulting frequency of A's. Multi-level selection works because groups in which the equilibrium number of cooperators is greater produce more offspring than other groups. In this case, at the equilibrium for a particular group, the second term of the right hand side of the price equation is zero because the fitness of the two types within a group must be equal (otherwise it is not an equilibrium) and as a result, the A trait suffers no fitness deficit. An example is in a model of cultural rather than genetic evolution in which non-altruists may turn into altruists, by being socialized through group rituals to behave altruistically, and altruists can revert back to nonaltruists, attracted by the possibility of not paying the cooperation cost c. Equilibrium now occurs when the two movements from altruist to non-altruist and back lead to equal fitness of both phenotypes. This is shown in the lower panel of Figure 4.3, which depicts the model just described. The model on which the bottom panel is based is presented in §A11. We present a more complete model along these lines in Chapter 10.

In the upper panel, depicting the first model in which both cooperation and non-cooperation are evolutionarily stable strategies, $F_{ST} = 1$, reflecting the fact that all of the variance is between groups and none is within, so the second term on the right hand side of Price equation is zero. This, or equivalently condition 4.10, tells us that altruism can proliferate no matter how small is the excess of benefits to others over cost to self. In the lower panel in equilibrium (that is, at p_j^*) $\beta_i = 0$, as there is no within-group selection operating against the A's, the second right hand side term in the Price equation is zero in this case too and equation 4.9 tells us that any positive F_{ST} will be sufficient to promote the spread of altruism.

4.4   Reciprocal Altruism

Trivers' reciprocal altruism, the second workhorse model for the explanation of cooperation by biologists, was proposed independently by economist James Friedman (1971). To see how this works, consider a pair of unrelated individuals from a large population who are randomly paired to play the prisoner's dilemma game repeatedly (§A3). In every period the available actions are to help (H) the other at a cost $c > 0$, thus providing a benefit to the other of $b > c$, where b and c are measured in fitness terms, or not to help (defect D), incurring no cost and providing no benefit. Clearly, each would gain if each helped, each receiving a net gain of $b - c > 0$. But considering just a single period, as we saw in Chapter 2, defecting is what is termed the dominant strategy: a player earns a higher payoff by not helping, no matter what his partner does.

This may not be true if the game is repeated. Suppose the benefits and costs of the interaction are as in Figure 3.1, and the two available strategies for the repeated game are Defect (do not help, with no benefits or costs), or Conditional Cooperation, which involves helping in the first period, and in subsequent periods adopting the strategy played by the other in the previous period (sometimes termed the *nice tit-for-tat* strategy, the "nice" referring to cooperating in the first period). To study whether helping could evolve in this setting we must first determine if helping individuals (those playing nice tit-for-tat) could persist in a population in which they are common. In other words, is helping evolutionarily stable? We will presently ask if tit-for-tat helping could become common if it were originally rare. In other words, is helping evolutionarily accessible?

We explore stability by supposing that virtually all members of the population are tit-for-tat helpers and then ask if a mutant defector could proliferate in this population, eliminating the helpers. If this is not the case, then nice tit-for-tat is termed an *evolutionarily stable strategy* (ESS) and a population of all helpers is termed *uninvadable*. An evolutionarily stable strategy is a best response to itself, in the sense that no other strategy can do better playing against it. Robert Axelrod and William Hamilton (1981) showed that there are conditions under which Conditional Cooperation will be a best response to itself, so that each of two Conditional Cooperators will do better by helping the other as long as the other does the same, and when paired with a Conditional Cooperator, Defect cannot do better than Conditional Cooperation. When these conditions are met, we would expect a large population of randomly paired Conditional Cooperators to persist in cooperating. Mutual Defection in this population would also be evolutionarily stable, because Defect is always the best response to Defect. But at least mutual cooperation supported by tit-for-tat players would also be stable if ever it were to occur.

What are the conditions allowing for the evolutionary stability of tit-for-tat helping? Assuming that after each round of play the interaction will continue for at least one more period with probability δ, the expected duration d of the game is $1/(1 - \delta)$ periods. To see this note that $D = 1 + \delta D$, where the 1 represents the current play, and δD represents the expected number of future plays; that is, with probability δ the interaction continues, and if it does continue to the second round, then its expected duration at that point is D, just as it was at start of the first round. The result follows by solving this equation for D.

In §A6 we show that δ can also be interpreted as a time discount factor (that is, the reciprocal of one plus what economists term the rate of time preference), reflecting an individual's impatience or other reasons for a higher valuation on payoffs nearer to the present in an interaction that is repeated. There we also show how a probability of continuation less than one can be combined with time discounting.

To find the condition under which Conditional Cooperation is a best response to itself, we compare the payoff to a Conditional Cooperator when paired with another Conditional Cooperator, namely $b - c$ per period times the expected duration of the interaction $1/(1 - \delta)$, with what a Defector would get when paired with a Conditional Cooperator; that is, b for the first period and then zero thereafter, given that the tit-for-tat-playing Conditional Cooperator will respond to the defection by defecting in the next and subsequent periods. Thus Conditional Cooperation will be a best response to itself if

$$\frac{b - c}{1 - \delta} > b, \tag{4.11}$$

or, rearranging,

$$\delta > \frac{c}{b}, \tag{4.12}$$

which says that the probability of the interaction continuing must exceed the cost-benefit ratio of the helping action.

When compared to Hamilton's rule (4.1), condition 4.12 makes it clear that the repetition of the interaction (which happens with probability δ) is analogous to genetic relatedness as a support for cooperative behaviors.

If equation 4.12 is satisfied, then in a population composed only of nice tit-for-tat players, the tit-for-tat strategy is not altruistic because adopting it maximizes the expected payoffs of the actor, and defecting would reduce the actors expected payoffs. But remember that mutual defection is also uninvadable, meaning that in a population of defectors, playing tit-for-tat would yield lower payoffs than defecting. In such a population nice tit-for-tat could not be motivated by self-regarding preferences, but instead is a form of strong reciprocity, motivated by altruistic preferences. Moreover, if equation 4.12 is not satisfied, the same conclusion, that nice tit-for-tat is a form of strong reciprocity, holds for any distribution of defectors and tit-for-tat players in the population. This makes it clear that while in some interactions, the one-shot prisoner's dilemma or public goods game, for example, one can denote strategies as either altruistic or not independently of the distribution of behaviors in a population, this is not generally the case.

While mutual defect is also an equilibrium, Axelrod and Hamilton showed that reciprocal altruism can piggyback on kin-based altruism to get started. If the interacting pairs are close family members, for example, and if the continuation probability is sufficiently high, Conditional Cooperators can invade an all-Defector population, thus accounting for the emergence of cooperation when initially rare. Once Conditional Cooperators become prevalent, their payoff advantage no longer requires relatedness among the interacting pairs. Thus the tit-for-tat equilibrium may be both evolutionarily stable and accessible. Reciprocal altruism paired with kin altruism thus provides a simple and elegant example of a mechanism that could account for the emergence and persistence of cooperation among empirically plausible human actors.

Of course, the above argument is hardly definitive because we have not analyzed what happens if there are behavioral or perception errors, and we have not considered invasion by strategies other than Defect. But it turns out that in dyadic interactions, the Conditional Cooperator strategy is quite robust to such adverse conditions, because it has three attractive characteristics: it is nice in the sense that it never defects first, it is punishing in that it does not let an opponent get away with not helping without paying a penalty, and it is forgiving in that if a partner who has defected returns to cooperation, the Conditional Cooperator will return to cooperation as well. However, other strategies with these three characteristics can often outcompete the Conditional Cooperators (Nowak and Sigmund 1993). We will see presently that for interactions of more than two individuals, and in the presence of errors in either behavior or perception of others' behavior, nice tit-for-tat runs into trouble, casting doubt on the robustness of Trivers' approach for explaining cooperation in larger groups.

Many biologists have considered reciprocal altruism to be a common form of cooperation among non-kin in non-human animals. And because cooperation based on reciprocal altruism was thought to be common in the nonhuman animal world, it was natural for biologists and social scientists to accept it as the standard explanation for human cooperation as well. However, there is little evidence of reciprocal altruism in non-human animals. Peter Hammerstein (2003) writes, "After three decades of worldwide research on reciprocal altruism and related phenomena, no more than a modest number of animal examples have been identified." A major impediment is that reciprocal altruism requires that animals act as if future payoffs are not greatly discounted. But non-human animals are extraordinarily impatient (Noe 1990, Clements and Stephens 1995, Connor 1995, Hammerstein 2003, Whitlock et al. 2007, Russell and Wright 2008, Clutton-Brock 2009, Connor 2010). Behaviors that at first appeared to be reciprocal have frequently, on further study, been better explained as simple mutualism in which the benefit to the actor compensates for the cost of the action regardless of the action taken by the other (Dugatkin and Mesterton-Gibbons 1996, Milinski 1996, Stephens et al. 2002).

Non-human primates may eventually provide exceptions to this generalization. There is some evidence (de Waal and Davis 2003) that reciprocity plays a role in alliance formation among macaques and chimpanzees, in the latter among unrelated individuals in high-risk power struggles, both in the wild as well as among captive animals. Capuchin monkeys have been observed experimentally to share more food with a partner whose assistance was needed to acquire the food (de Waal 2000) and chimpanzees to give food to those who groomed them in the past (de Waal 1997).

Among humans the experimental and field evidence for the contribution of repeated interactions to cooperation is overwhelming and well known. An experiment by Gächter et al. (2011) suggests its importance. Four hundred and fifty-six Swiss students were randomly assigned to two roles similar to those of employer and employee in a natural setting. In a gift exchange game setting similar to the one described in §3.1, the "employer" offered a wage, a deduction from his profits, and the "employee" responded with a level of "effort," which was costly to provide. The contrast between two treatments that the experimenters implemented is instructive. In the *Stranger treatment* the pairs were shuffled every period, so that each period was a one-shot interaction for the participants. In the *Partner treatment* the two remained paired over 10 periods. For both treatments the set of 10 periods was itself repeated three times. The dominant strategy for a self-regarding "employee" in the stranger treatment (which, recall, meaning the response giving the highest payoff no matter what the other player does) was to offer one unit of effort, and knowing this the employer's best response was to offer the lowest possible wage. In fact, "employers" made wage offers far more generous than the minimum and employees proved much more than the minimum effort, just as in the Fehr et al. experiment. Figure 4.4 gives the effort responses by "employees" in the two treatments over time.

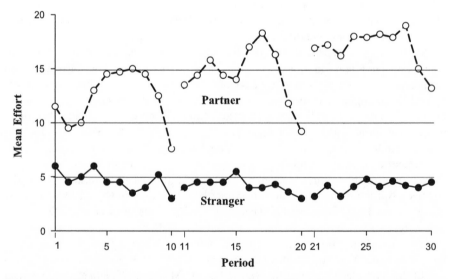

Figure 4.4. Repetition supports cooperation in a gift exchange (wage-effort) experiment. In the Partner treatment the two players play 10 consecutive rounds; in the stranger treatment the pairs are reshuffled after each round. Source: Gächter, Königstein, and Kessler (2011).

Strikingly, the effort offered in the stranger treatment is much higher (four times higher) than would have been optimal for a self-regarding 'employee." But more important for the questions under consideration here, the repeated interaction resulted in much higher levels of effort than the stranger treatment, and except for a dramatic endgame drop-off, effort rose within the three sets of play. The fact that repetition contributed to cooperation and that the subjects readily understood the difference between repeated and non-repeated interactions is evident by the sharp reduction during the last two periods of play. The endgame drop-off cannot be due to learning, as high levels of effort are restored and even exceeded when the second and third set are initiated. The fact that in the last period effort did not fall to the level of the stranger treatment could have occurred because, while repetition engaged the self-regarding motives stressed by the reciprocal altruism model, it also tapped social preferences that the stranger treatment did not evoke.

Among humans in dyadic interactions, reciprocal altruism provides a convincing explanation of at least some of the cooperation we observe (Cooper et al. 1996, Keser and van Winden 2000). Many forms of cooperation in our ancestral past, judging by the practices of foragers in the ethnographic record, had precisely this structure. The sharing of some food in foraging groups does not take the form of the redistribution of food that has been pooled on a groupwide basis, what we term common pot redistribution, but rather is network-based (Kaplan and Gurven 2005). Thus, sharing may take the form of reciprocation in dyadic relationships. In these cases, repeated interactions that reward cooperators with higher fitness or other payoffs make helping a form of mutualism, as in the model of Axelrod and Hamilton (1981).

4.5   Reciprocal Altruism in Large Groups

The plausibility of the model, however, does not extend to large groups in which members sometimes make mistakes. Interactions of this kind are common today and certainly were so in our ancestral past, including such fitness-relevant activities as common defense and predation, sharing information, cooperative hunting and gathering, and sustaining social norms through the punishment of transgressors.

Because reciprocal altruism models are dyadic, how one would extend them to groups with more than two players is not even clear-cut. In this section we consider the most plausible extension. Because tit-for-tat models are based on prisoner's dilemmas, we want a prisoner's dilemma-like interaction, meaning mutual cooperation is beneficial but mutual defect is the dominant strategy, with $n > 2$ players. The public goods game is an example. In the one-shot n-player public goods game, each player has two strategies: Contribute and Defect. Contributing generates a benefit b shared equally by all other members of the group, at a cost $c < b$ to the Contributor. Note that while in §4.1 and 4.2, the benefit of the helping action was conferred with equal probability on all members of the group, including the helper, here the benefit of the Contributor's action goes only to other members of the group. The difference is merely a matter of mathematical convenience. To mimic nice tit-for-tat in this non-dyadic setting we say that individuals cooperate on the first round of a repeated public goods game with $n > 2$

players and on subsequent rounds if a sufficient number of other players contributed on the previous round—we will see what "a sufficient number" means shortly .

All players decide simultaneously whether to contribute or defect, after which the game is over. Clearly, if all members contribute, each earns $b - c > 0$, but each individual has an incentive to defect, in which case his payoff is greater by the amount c than his payoff to contributing, no matter what the other players do. Hence, in a one-shot public goods game, self-regarding agents will all defect.

As in the dyadic case, by repeating the public goods game many times, with a fixed probability of ending after each round, however, cooperation can be sustained under the right conditions. But these conditions are quite stringent. We will show that this game supports cooperative outcomes only if the group is small, the returns to cooperation are high, the behavior of each group member is known with a high degree of accuracy by all of the other group members, errors in execution are infrequent, and group members are very patient and interactions typically endure for many periods.

The reason for the ineffectiveness of reciprocal altruism for groups with several members is simple. In groups of two, a free-rider cannot go undetected because a player's payoff reveals the other player's behavior. Equally important, when one member defects in order to punish a Defector, the punishment is uniquely targeted on the Defector. But, in groups larger than two, a player cannot infer who has defected from the knowledge of his own payoff. Moreover, a retaliatory defection punishes not only the initial defector, but also all other members of the group. Moreover, other group members may not have observed the initial defection and hence may think that a retaliatory defection is a free-riding defection, inviting further retaliatory defections.

Thus the information structure among the players plays a critical role in the viability of the various models. The signals concerning the actions of other players may be *perfect* (completely accurate) or *imperfect* (inaccurate with positive probability). The signals can also be either *public* (the same signal received by all individuals) or *private* (different individuals get different signals, or no signal at all)—see Figure 4.5. As in the previous chapter, we may think of imperfect public signals as caused by *performance errors*, which are then seen by all other players, while private signals are caused by limited scope, in which players observe the behaviors of only a subset of their group members, or perception errors that are not common to all players, so that a player who has cooperated is signaled as having cooperated to some subset of players, and signaled as having defected to the remaining players. Note that with private signals, a player who cooperates in a given period does not know which players, if any, received an inaccurate signal indicating that he defected.

To illustrate the consequences of extending the reciprocal altruism model to groups larger than two, we will develop an *agent-based model*. We explain the structure and logic of agent-based models in §A2.

Here is the structure of our agent-based model. A large population consists of N groups of n members each, and each group plays a public goods game repeatedly d times. We will call this series of d rounds an encounter. At the end of each encounter, players reassort randomly into new groups of size n and carry out another encounter. By cooperating, a player confers a benefit of b on the other members (i.e., a benefit of $b/(n - 1)$ per other member) and a cost c to himself. We generalize the Conditional Cooperator strategy to groups of size $n > 2$ by assuming that there are $n + 1$ possible

	Perfect	Imperfect
Public	Accurate signals received by all	Identical noisy signals received by all
Private	Accurate signals received by some	Different noisy signals received by different people

Figure 4.5. Information structures. Most models of cooperation assume perfect public information, but in all but the simplest human interactions, some critical information is both private and imperfect.

types of players, called t-Cooperators, for $t = 0, \ldots, n$. A t-Cooperator cooperates in the current round provided at least t other players cooperated in the previous round. We call an n-Cooperator, who never cooperates, a Defector, and we call a 0-Cooperator an unconditional Cooperator. On the first round, all players apply the t-criterion as though everyone cooperated in the previous round, so all types cooperate except the n-Cooperator, who defects on all rounds. Finally we assume that a player who attempts to cooperate will accidentally defect with probability $\epsilon > 0$. We call this an *execution error*, and we call ϵ the execution error rate. Note that when $n = 2$, our model reduces to standard conditional cooperation, where the Conditional Cooperator is a 1-Cooperator, universal defect is a 2-Cooperator, and an unconditional cooperator is a 0-Cooperator.

Our central question will be the frequency of cooperation that can be sustained in the long run of this system, for different choices of the benefit b, error rate ϵ, duration of the encounter d, and the group size n. We created a population with 25 groups of size $n = 2, 4, 6, 8, 10, 12, 14$ playing a public goods game repeatedly for 25 periods ($d = 25$), in which by cooperating, an individual contributes b to the other players at a cost of $c = 1$ to himself, where $b = 2$ or $b = 4$. We begin (initialize) the simulation by assigning to each individual a value of t in the range $t = 0, \ldots, n - 1$ with equal probability. The exact initial conditions are unimportant because a small mutation rate ensures that no strategy becomes completely extinct, and in fact the simulation attains its long-run distribution of play, called the model's *stationary distribution*, in the very short time of several hundred periods, as long as some of each type is present from the start.

After each encounter, 5% of individuals are replaced by new individuals, using a Darwinian fitness criterion according to which the probability of reproduction is proportional to the individual's payoff relative to others in the entire population (the replicator dynamic equations describing this process are explained in the appendix). We assume a mutation rate of 2% per newly created individual, which means there is one mutation about every 50 encounters. Also, we assume an execution error rate varying from $\epsilon = 0$ to $\epsilon = 0.1$. To promote cooperation in the face of errors, we assume that an individual who accidentally defected (we assume this fact is known to all group members, so it is public information) cooperates unconditionally on the next two rounds, thus allowing cooperation to be restored (this behavior is known as *contrite*).

As seen in the two upper panes of Figure 4.6, if $n = 2$ and $b/c = 2$, if the error rate is zero, full cooperation results. However, intuitions based on the working of this dyadic case and zero error rates do not extend to larger groups and plausible error rates. Even at a group size of $n = 4$ and an error rate of only 2%, very little cooperation occurs. When $b/c = 4$, we see in the upper right pane of Figure 4.6 that cooperation can be sustained for $n = 4$, but for larger group sizes, and at error rates of 4% or more, very little cooperation results. This shows clearly that reciprocal altruism need not support cooperation in groups of size larger than two unless errors are virtually absent.

These simulations assume a very high probability that the interaction will be continued. Indeed, only in the final period will the interaction not be repeated, so the probability of continuation is $(d - 1)/d$, which is 0.96 in our simulations ($d = 25$). Thus the relevant δ in equation 4.12 is $\delta = 0.96$. This is near its plausible upper limit if a "period" is a year, given human mortality rates, even setting aside other reasons for devaluing the future and terminating interactions, such as myopia and migration. Simulations with more empirically plausible assumptions concerning δ give even more negative results.

But there is even more bad news when it comes to applying this model to real populations. We have assumed that all group members receive the same information indicating the cooperation or defection of each other group member. That is, we assume *public signals*. Moreover, we have assumed that the only kind of error is executional in the sense that an individual tries, but fails to cooperate. It is instructive to move from public to private signals, in which each group member receives an independent signal with a perceptual error rate ϵ as to whether each other member contributed. In this new setting, an individual can have an execution failure rate of ϵ, and in addition, a cooperating individual may be perceived as having defected also with probability ϵ, indepenently, by each other group member (we use the same error rate in both cases for ease of exposition). Our simulations of this situation, illustrated in the two lower panes of Figure 4.6, show that virtually no cooperation is possible for $n > 2$ and $\epsilon \geq 2\%$ when $b/c = 2$, and very little is possible even for $n > 4$ or $\epsilon > 6\%$ when $b/c = 4$.

Students of economic theory may be surprised by these results, because the folk theorem of repeated game theory appears to assure us that for any group size and any error rate, cooperation may be sustained if the discount factor is sufficiently high. In the next chapter we show that this is not the case when we allow information to be private or we require that cooperation be sustained in a stable equilibrium.

Imperfect Public Signaling

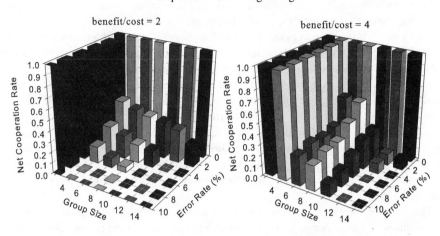

Imperfect Private Signaling

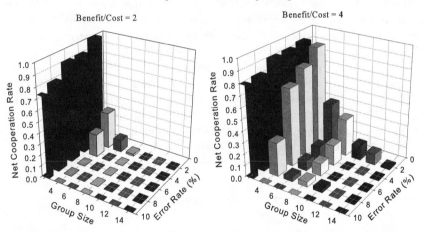

Figure 4.6. Reciprocal altruism in a public goods game: the effects of group size, errors, and information structure. The top two panes show the rate of cooperation in the reciprocal altruism game with public signals, for various group size and error rates. The Net Cooperation Rate is the mean fraction of individuals who attempted to cooperate on a single round. Each encounter lasted 25 game repetitions, so the implicit discount rate is 4%. Each bar represents the average over the final 10,000 periods of 20 independent simulations of 25,000 encounters. The bottom two panes show net cooperation with private signals, using the same parameters.

4.6   Reputation: Indirect Reciprocity

In a sizable group, an individual may interact frequently with a large number of partners, but infrequently with any single one. If the time lag between encounters with a given individual is sufficiently long, unless individuals are infinitely patient and have good memories, the conditions for reciprocal altruism may not hold.

An alternative mechanism of cooperation that addresses this problem is for each individual to keep a mental account of group members who cooperated with their partners in the previous period and those who did not. Let us call an individual who cooperated in the previous period in good standing, and specify that the only way an individual can fall into bad standing is by defecting on a partner who is in good standing. Thus, an individual can always defect when his partner is in bad standing without losing his good standing status. In this more general setting the Conditional Cooperator strategy is replaced by the following standing strategy: cooperate if and only if your current partner is in good standing, except that if you accidentally defected the previous period, cooperate in this period unconditionally, thereby restoring your status as a member in good standing.

This *standing model*, due to the economist Robert Sugden (1986), is an ingenious formalization of the biologist Richard Alexander's (1987) indirect reciprocity notion. As in the case of conditional cooperation, we need to discover the conditions under which the standing strategy is a best response to itself, so that in a population following the standing strategy, no individual has an incentive to defect intentionally. As before, individuals are paired randomly to play with the same payoffs as before. We assume that after each play the game continues with probability δ, with $0 < \delta < 1$, and there is a probability ϵ of accidentally defecting. Suppose all individuals follow the standing strategy, and now consider an individual in good standing. He receives b with probability $1 - \epsilon$, because with probability ϵ his partner fails to deliver the benefit, and he pays c. Then with probability δ, the game is repeated, in which case with probability ϵ he is in bad standing, because he accidentally defected the previous period, and with probability $1 - \epsilon$ he is in good standing. Thus, in a population of individuals who have adopted the standing strategy, the expected value of being in good standing is given by

$$v_g = b(1 - \epsilon) - c + \delta(\epsilon v_b + (1 - \epsilon)v_g),$$

where v_b is the expected value of being in bad standing. This equation says that in the first period the payoff is $b(1-\epsilon)-c$, and if the interaction continues, which occurs with probability δ, the expected payoff from then on is the weighted average of the payoffs to being in bad and good standing, the weights respectively being the probability that the player has mistakenly defected (ϵ) and its complement.

If an individual is in bad standing, he receives b with probability $\epsilon(1 - \epsilon)$, because with probability ϵ his partner is in bad standing and delivers the benefit to restore good standing with probability $1 - \epsilon$, he pays c to restore his good standing, and with probability δ, the game is repeated, in which case with probability ϵ he is in bad standing, because even though he paid c, he mistakenly defected, and with probability $1 - \epsilon$ he is in good standing. Thus, in the same population, the expected payoff of being in bad standing is given by

$$v_b = b\epsilon(1 - \epsilon) - c + \delta(\epsilon v_b + (1 - \epsilon)v_g).$$

If we solve the previous two equations simultaneously for v_g and v_b, we find

$$v_g = \frac{b(1 - \epsilon(1 + \delta)) - c + b\delta\epsilon^2(2 - \epsilon)}{1 - \delta} \tag{4.13}$$

$$v_b = v_g - b(1 - \epsilon)^2. \tag{4.14}$$

The numerator in this expression for v_g is approximately (with an error on the order of ϵ^2) the net expected payoff per period, and $1/(1 - \delta)$ is the expected number of periods in the game. The loss due to the need to punish execution errors is approximately $b\delta\epsilon$ per individual per period, which is not large unless the error rate is quite high. It is a best response to cooperate as long as $v_g \geq b(1 - \epsilon) + \delta v_b$, where the right hand side is the present value of defecting now and hence of falling into bad standing. This inequality simplifies to

$$\frac{b\delta(1 - \epsilon)(1 + \delta(1 - \epsilon)^2 + \epsilon^2)}{1 + \delta} \geq c. \tag{4.15}$$

For any given $\delta < 1$, this inequality is satisfied for sufficiently small error $\epsilon > 0$, as long as $b > c$. Ignoring terms in ϵ^2 or higher because for small error rates they will be very small, the above inequality simplifies to

$$b\delta(1 - \epsilon) > c. \tag{4.16}$$

Note the similarity to Hamilton's rule (4.1), with the degree of relatedness r replaced by the (generally much larger) $\delta(1 - \epsilon)$.

Like the reciprocal altruism model, this result is restricted to dyadic interactions and hence cannot explain many important kinds of cooperation. But Parthik Panchanathan and Richard Boyd (2004) proposed an ingenious use of indirect reciprocity as an adjunct to the n-player public goods game. Suppose a group of size n plays an indirect reciprocity game using the standing strategy with execution error rate $\epsilon \geq 0$ as described above, and also plays a public goods game. They start with the one-shot public goods game, at the end of which they play the indirect reciprocity game, except individuals start out in good standing if and only if they cooperated in the public goods game. At the end of the indirect reciprocity game, they repeat the sequence of a one-shot public goods game followed by an indirect reciprocity game, indefinitely.

To see why this works, suppose the benefit to others and cost to himself in the public goods game are b_g and $c_g < b_g$, while in the indirect reciprocity game, the cost of helping is c and the benefit to the recipient is $b > c$. Panchanathan and Boyd (2004) show that, so long as

$$\frac{b(1 - \epsilon) - c}{1 - \delta} \geq c_g, \tag{4.17}$$

contributing in the public goods game and adopting the standing strategy in the indirect reciprocity game is a best response to itself, so cooperation can be sustained. Parameters favoring this solution are that the cost c_g of cooperating in the public goods game be low, the probability of repeating the indirect reciprocity game δ be near unity, and the net benefit $b(1 - \epsilon) - c$ of cooperating in the indirect reciprocity game be large.

The public goods game has two serious weaknesses that the Panchanathan-Boyd model repairs. First, in some cases it is played very infrequently, as in case of war with other groups, response to famine, and the like. In this case, the probability of repetition in a single time period would be very low, so the cost of defecting would be low as well. Second, as we saw earlier, the only way to punish Defectors in the public goods game is for Cooperators to withdraw their contributions, thus hurting all other players, not only the Defector. The Panchanathan and Boyd solution is for group members to refuse to cooperate in everyday social exchange with Defectors in the public goods game. In this way, punishment of defection becomes targeted, frequent, and costless to the punisher (he avoids the cost of extending help). Everyday social exchange is thus represented as an indirect reciprocity game, with (4.17) being the condition for the game to foster cooperation in the public goods game.

There is a major weakness of this model, however, one that it shares with other indirect reciprocity models: the standing strategy has very demanding informational requirements. Its ability to target defectors makes it an improvement on the repeated game models of the previous section, but this comes at steep price. Each individual must know the current standing of each member of the group, the identity of each member's current partner, and whether each individual cooperated or defected against his current partner, since this information is necessary to ascertain the status of one's partner in the indirect reciprocity game. But real-world dyadic interactions are often private, and hence are unlikely to be directly observed by more than a small number of others, vitiating the model for groups of any significant size. Because in the repeated game models of the previous section punishment is not directed at defectors, they require only that an individual know how many of his current partners defected in the previous period, something that one can infer from one's own payoff.

Especially problematic in the case of indirect reciprocity is the fact that if the dyadic interactions involved are at all complex, it will be virtually impossible for an outsider to ascertain whether an individual's action is or is not a defection. Hence, in many cases, the standing of one's current partner will be subject to considerable error. Equally important, if individuals are entirely self-regarding, they have no reason to report truthfully what they have observed. Though an active area of research, explanations of how private information could be converted to accurate public information in a population of amoral self-regarding individuals have not been presented.

Because the truth-telling that is necessary to convert private to public information cannot be expected in the absence of social preferences and because public information is essential to the empirical plausibility of both the simple reciprocal altruism model and its indirect reciprocity variant, these models do not provide adequate explanations of cooperation among amoral and self-regarding individuals. We return to the problem of converting private to public information at the close of the next chapter, suggesting that the way real societies accomplish this is heavily dependent on the social preferences of those entrusted with the production and distribution of public information.

4.7   Altruism as a Signal of Quality

Another form of mutualistic cooperation is that which results when a cooperative act is a difficult-to-fake signal of some characteristic of the actor, such as strength, skill or bravery, that is otherwise difficult to observe. The basic idea of difficult to fake signaling as a social behavior goes back well over a century to the American economist Thorsten Veblen and his account of how "conspicuous consumption" is a signal of one's wealth that is more readily practiced by the rich, and hence is believable. But its application to biological reasoning is recent.

In the biological models, a cooperative behavior may be favored in selection because it enhances the individual's opportunities for mating and coalition building. This would be the case, for example, if sharing valuable information or incurring dangers in defense of the group were taken by others as an honest signal of the individual's otherwise unobservable traits as a mate or political ally. In this case self-regarding individuals might engage in group-beneficial activities in anticipation of reproductive, political, or other benefits. Cooperative behaviors would thus result in advantageous alliances for those signaling in this manner, and the resulting enhanced fitness or material success would then account for the proliferation of the cooperative behaviors constituting the signal. Models of this process were developed by the economist Michael Spence (1973), initially applied to educational credentials as a signal, and by the biologist Amos Zahavi (1975) to explain helping behavior in Arabian babblers (*Turdoidas squamiceps*). Costly signaling has been proposed as an explanation for some types of food-sharing in human societies, such as providing game that is large and/or difficult to harvest, or providing large quantities of food for consumption at ritual feasts (Boone 1998, Gurven et al. 2000b, Smith and Bliege Bird 2000, Sosis 2000, Hawkes et al. 2001).

Indirect reciprocity and signaling models are similar in that the payback for the individual's cooperative action comes from third parties. Cooperating with those in good standing, in an indirect reciprocity model or sharing the prey of a successful hunt with fellow group members in a signaling model, lead those who have observed these actions, but not necessarily benefited from them, to confer advantages on the actor. The two models differ in a subtle way: in the signaling model the third party responds favorably because the signal is correlated with some desirable but unobservable property of the actor; in the indirect reciprocity model the signal (cooperating with those in good standing) is the desirable property itself. In the case of indirect reciprocity, I want to associate with the hunter who shares his ample prey with other members of the group because I too would like a share of meat. In the signaling model I want to associate with him because the fact that he has lots of meat to share indicates that he is physically able and would be a good mate or coalition partner.

With Eric Alden Smith, we modeled a signaling process as a multi-player public goods game that involves no repeated or assortative interactions, so that non-cooperation would be the dominant strategy if there were no signaling benefits (Gintis et al. 2001). We showed that honest signaling of underlying quality by providing a public good to the rest of the group can be evolutionarily stable, provided that certain plausible conditions hold. The complete absence of such costly signaling by cooperative behavior is also an equilibrium.

A signaling equilibrium, however, does not require that the signal confer benefits on other group members. Antisocial behaviors could perform the same function: beating up one's neighbor can demonstrate physical prowess just as convincingly as bravely defending one's group. If signaling is to be an explanation of group-beneficial behavior, we must explain why group-beneficial signaling is favored over antisocial signaling. There are several possible reasons. It may be that the level of public benefit provided is positively correlated with the individual benefit the signaler provides to those who respond to the signal. For instance, the signaler who defends the group may be more likely to confer a benefit (say, protection) on his partner or allies than the signaler who beats up his neighbor. Group-beneficial signals such as sharing one's prey may attract larger audiences than antisocial signals. Finally, competition among groups for material or fitness resources would favor groups at group-beneficial signaling equilibria over those either at non-signaling equilibria or at antisocial signaling equilibria. Thus, the effects of signaling and group competition on cooperation may be synergistic rather than simply additive. Group competition provides a reason why the signaling that we observe tends to be group beneficial, while signaling theory provides a reason why signaling of any kind may be evolutionarily stable in a within-group dynamic, thus contributing to between-group differences in behavior and, as we will see presently, thereby enhancing the force of group competition (Bergstrom and Lachmann 2001). Where both antisocial and prosocial signalling are evolutionarily stable with groups, the latter can proliferate by means of weak multilevel selection.

4.8   Positive Assortment

In the multi-selection model, as in the kin-based altruism models, the evolution of help-ing behaviors requires that those with a predisposition to help others receive help from those with whom they interact more frequently than would occur by chance. How this *positive assortment* comes about differs from case to case. Eshel and Cavalli-Sforza (1982) provide a glimpse of the variety of causes of assortment: "Kin, deme, niche, and social group structure, neighborhood effect, idiosyncratic behavior, and discrimi-nation in the choice of companions are some of the possible sources of deviation from randomness...critical for understanding the evolutionary stability of social structure."

For the group selection model, we know from equation 4.10 that

$$F_{ST} = P(A|A) - P(A|N) > \frac{c}{b},$$

Hamilton's rule for the degree of positive assortment permitting an altruistic trait to proliferate when rare. This can be seen by returning to Figure 4.2, noting that the same model applies to kin-based selection and using the fact that $P(A|A)$ is the probability that the bearer of an altruistic allele will interact with another bearer of that allele, while $P(A|N)$ is the probability that the bearer of the non-altruistic allele is paired with a bearer of the altruistic allele, so $P(A|A) - P(A|N) = r$.

Surprisingly, a similar expression gives the condition for reciprocal altruism in dyads to evolve even when the process of pairing to interact is random. This has been shown in a number of ways, beginning with Queller (1985) and including Nee (1989) and Fletcher and Zwick (2006). Here, for comparability of notation, we will call the nice tit-for-tat players (i.e., those who conditionally cooperate) A's while the N's unconditionally defect. In this interaction, for groups of substantial size, A's and N's will be paired with an A with approximately the same probability, p. But positive assortment of the A allele and the cooperative phenotype occurs nonetheless. The reason is that tit-for-tat is a conditional strategy, so an N paired with an A will benefit from the partner's cooperation for just one period because the A, a Conditional Cooperator, will switch to defect after the first round. By contrast, the A paired with an A will benefit from the partner's cooperation for as many periods as the interaction endures. The key to the evolutionary success of the Conditional Cooperator in this situation is, as Fletcher and Zwick explain, "there must be sufficient positive assortment between individuals with the altruistic genotype... and the helping phenotypes of others they interact with" (p. 253).

Thus, suppose we observe a large randomly paired population in which the fraction of A's is p, and we count the periods in which an A and an N respectively benefit from the cooperation of a partner, expressed as a fraction of the total periods of interaction for each type. The former will exceed p while the latter will be less than p. The longer the interaction endures, the greater will be the difference in the degree of help received by the A and N genotypes measured by this difference.

It remains to show that the condition for Conditional Cooperator to be an evolutionary stable strategy (ESS) is also just another version of $P(A|A) - P(A|N) > c/b$. Recall that for the case of a repeated prisoner's dilemma, this condition (equation 4.11) is $\delta > c/b$ where δ is the probability of continuation of the interaction at the end of each interaction, and b and c are respectively the benefits and costs of the cooperative act undertaken by the reciprocal altruist. Suppose that the expected total duration of an interaction from initiation to termination is normalized to unity and that opportunities to alter one's action occur at the end of every period, each of which is a fraction, $1 - \delta$, of the expected duration of the interaction. Thus there are $1/(1 - \delta)$ periods in the expected duration, and the probability of continuation at the end of each is δ. We measure the advantageous pairing of the A types by the fraction of the expected total duration of the interaction in which they experience helping from the individual with whom they are paired.

To determine if Conditional Cooperators is an ESS, we study the difference in the number of periods in which an A and an N respectively will experience cooperation from its partner. The duration of cooperation enjoyed by an A is p, because with probability p the A is paired with an A in which case they both cooperate for the expected duration of the interaction, which is 1. The corresponding duration of cooperation enjoyed by an N is $p(1 - \delta)$ because with probability p the N will be paired with an A, who cooperates during the first period, which is a fraction $(1 - \delta)$ of the expected duration, and then defects for all subsequent periods. Letting $P(C|A)$ and $P(C|N)$ represent the expected duration in which an A and an N respectively experience cooperation from its partner, we have $P(C|A) - P(C|N) = 1 - p(1 - \delta)$. Setting $p = 1$ to study the evolutionary stability of the 100% Conditionally Cooperator equilibrium, we therefore have $P(C|A) - P(C|N) = \delta$. Thus δ is a measure of positive assortment given by the difference in the frequency of cooperative actions by one's partner, conditional on one's type. So we can rewrite the condition for Conditionally Cooperate to be an ESS as $\delta = P(C|A) - P(C|N) > c/b$. This demonstrates that the condition for helping behaviors to evolve by repeated interactions is the same as the condition for altruistic cooperation to evolve by means of kin-based selection or multi-level selection.

An ingenious set of papers (Ohtsuki et al. 2006) suggests yet another example of this logic, and one that captures essential aspects of human society. Until now we have studied just two types of social structure: families, meaning kin of recent common descent, and demes, that is, sub-populations within a larger population. But within any group, some individuals are closer to some than to others, and this social proximity should make a difference in evolutionary dynamics. Ohtsuki and his coauthors show that it does.

Suppose his Cooperators and Defectors are arrayed on a network and each plays a public goods game with all of the k "neighbors" with whom they are directly linked. As above, at a cost of c, each cooperative individual contributes an amount b to be shared among its k neighbors, whether they are Cooperators (C) or Defectors (D). Defectors bear no costs and contribute no benefits. Individuals periodically may alter their strategy by adopting a strategy of a neighbor with a probability proportional to the relative fitness of that neighbor. Thus, the individual will adopt C with probability equal to the total payoffs of neighboring C's divided by the total payoffs of all neighbors.

Through extensive simulations using a wide range of network structures, Ohtsuki and his coauthors find that the Cooperators proliferate if $1/k > c/b$ where k is the average number of neighbors (the degree) of the players. This surprising result occurs because by chance there will be one more C in the neighborhood of C's than in the neighborhood of D's independently of the size of the neighborhood. Thus, the smaller the neighborhood, the more different in their compositions are they. The fact that smaller neighborhoods are (relatively) more different one from another than are larger ones arises by a process similar to sampling error, where differences in the means of small samples exceed differences in the means of larger samples. In the simulations by Ohtsuki et al., the probability that any given one of my k neighbors will be a C differs by $1/k$ depending on whether I am a C or a D. Thus, $1/k$ is exactly equal to $P(A|A) - P(A|N)$, affirming the positive assortment logic already demonstrated in the other models. Grafen (2007) and Lehmann et al. (2007) extend the results of Ohtsuki and his coauthors using the inclusive fitness approach adopted here.

Whether this model explains observed forms of human cooperation is open to some question, however. The networks of foraging and other small scale societies are typically quite large, often including virtually all adult members of a group. If average degree (k) of an individual were 20, altruism could not proliferate by this mechanism unless costs did not exceed 5% of the benefits. The average number of exchange partners in the Southern African !Kung coinsurance (so called *hxaro*) networks described in §6.1 is 17, while the families among whom food is shared on a regular basis among the Paraguayan Aché exceeds 10 even for small packages, and 20 for large packages (Kaplan and Hill 1985, Wiessner 2002). Average degree in the coinsurance networks among the Pokot and Himba herders in Africa are much larger than this (Bollig 2006). Thus, in order for a form of altruistic cooperation to be spread by this mechanism, it would have to have truly extraordinary ratios of benefit to cost.

Not surprisingly, positive assortment is also at work in the indirect reciprocity and costly signaling models. In all cases the degree of positive assortment determines the critical cost-benefit ratio for the proliferation of altruism. The differences among the models arise in the way that positive assortment comes about. These results are summarized in Table 4.1.

Model (Citation)	Rule	Interpretation	Reason for Assortment
Kin-based altruism (Maynard Smith 1964)	$r > b/c$, $r =$ average degree of genetic relatedness among interacting individuals	$r =$ difference in the probability that the bearer of an A allele or the bearer of the N allele (resp.) will interact with another bearer of the A allele	Limited dispersal of close relatives
Multi-level selection (Aoki 1982)	$F_{ST} > c/b$; $F_{ST} =$ fraction of variance of A allele that is between demes $= \dfrac{\text{var}(p_j)}{\overline{\text{var}}(p_{ij}) + \text{var}(p_j)}$	$F_{ST} =$ difference arising from the deme structure A in the probability that an N will be paired with an A	Deme structure of population; associative deme fission
Reciprocal altruism (Trivers 1971)	$\delta > c/b$; $\delta =$ probability that the interaction is not terminated at the end of a given period	$\delta = P(C|A) - P(C|N)$ $=$ difference in number interactions in which one's partner cooperates, conditional on strategy A or N when $p = 1$	Cooperative behavior strategically conditioned on partner behavior
Network reciprocity (Ohtsuki, Hauert, Lieberman, and Nowak 2006)	$1/k > c/b$; $k =$ average degree of the network	k is inversely related to the extent of assortment generated by chance on a random network, $1/k$ is thus analogous to F_{ST} (treating each node and its immediate neighbors as a group)	Similar to deme structured population; chance plus small size generates substantial $P(A|A) - P(A|N)$

Table 4.1. Positive assortment, helping, and altruism. Note: in all of the models, helping behavior can evolve because those who help are more likely to receive help than would occur by chance. The models differ in the demographic, sociological, and strategic reasons that account for this positive assortment.

4.9   Mechanisms and Motives

In this chapter we have reviewed the two major biological explanations of cooperation: inclusive fitness in either a kin-based or a multi-level selection model, and reciprocal altruism and its indirect reciprocity and costly signaling variants.

Three of these models, reciprocal altruism, indirect reciprocity, and costly signaling, identify the conditions under which the fitness cost of helping others is more than offset by the corollary fitness benefits for the actor. The evolution of helping behavior is possible by these mechanisms only when these conditions obtain, and when this is the case, by these mechanisms helping is not altruistic, because the actor would suffer reduced fitness by not helping. These models explain how helping behaviors that seem altruistic when considered narrowly, ignoring the effects of helping behaviors on future interactions, may evolve because they are not altruistic when a more comprehensive view of benefits to the actor is taken. Similar reasoning applies to some, but not all, cases of kin-based altruism—for example, helping one's own children.

Our preferred model differs from the others in that, in principle, it could explain the evolution of altruistic behaviors toward fellow group members whether family or not. But its main result (equation 4.10) implies that at least this simplified version of the process is unlikely to pass the test of empirical relevance that we laid down at the start of the chapter. The reason is that evidence from hunter-gatherer groups in the ethnographic record suggests that the degree of genetic differentiation among human ancestral groups, measured by F_{ST}, is unlikely to have been greater than 0.10 and could have been half this number (see Chapter 6). The implication is that for an altruistic trait to have evolved by the process modeled here, the benefits of the altruistic behavior to others would have to have been an order of magnitude greater than the costs to the altruist (and perhaps twice this), suggesting that only rather uncommon forms of altruistic behavior, such as warning calls or sharing food when a fellow group member is on the verge of starvation, could have evolved by this mechanism. But this deliberately simplified model does not include critical aspects of early human social practices, most particularly cooperating to ensure group survival in the face of military or environmental challenges. Where group survival is at stake, the ratio of fitness benefits to the costs of cooperating may indeed be extraordinary. In subsequent chapters we will add these and other empirically grounded features to the model, with a more promising result.

While explaining why humans might have come to behave cooperatively, the models differ in the sociological, strategic and demographic mechanisms accounting for positive assortment and remain silent as to the proximate motives leading humans to engage in helping, and sometimes altruistic, behaviors. We have seen that positive assortment is a common feature of all of these models, so the distinctive character of each must lie in the processes explaining how positive assortment comes about, or in the kinds of social preferences likely to result.

Thus, for example, if kin-based altruism were the main reason for the evolutionary success of helping behaviors, the motives involved in helping would include a love for one's children and other close genetic relatives and a concern for their well-being sufficient to motivate self-sacrifice. Similarly, we would expect that if the sole mechanisms contributing to the evolution of helping behavior were reciprocal altruism, indirect reciprocity or costly signaling, the proximate motives for helping and the cognitive processes activating them would involve individual advantage, accompanied by detailed behavioral bookkeeping about one's fellows. Finally, we will see in subsequent chapters that the most plausible model of multi-level selection involves warfare and other forms of competition among groups. This mechanism would most likely favor feelings of solidarity and generosity toward the members of one's group extending far beyond relatives of recent common descent, accompanied by the lack of such feelings toward members of other groups. A common feature of all of these preferences that might have evolved from these different models is that helping is conditional: on close genetic relatedness, on the likelihood of future interactions, on the possibility of reputation-building or signaling, or on group membership.

The fact that helping behaviors are indeed motivated by this wide range of proximate motives, from maternal love, to enlightened self-interest, to solidarity with one's coethnics or conationals, is consistent with our view that in all likelihood each of the mechanisms we have described here has played a significant role in human evolution, the importance of each depending on the forms of cooperation under consideration and the ecological and social conditions under which ancestral humans interacted. We will see in Chapter 6 that what can be known or reasonably conjectured from genetic, archaeological and other data about these ancestral human conditions suggests that neither helping close family members nor reciprocal altruism provides an adequate account of the emergence of this cooperative species. In subsequent chapters we will show that multi-level selection models based on gene culture coevolution contribute substantially to a convincing explanation.

But before we turn to the Late Pleistocene human condition, we need to make sure we have not sold short the models based on reciprocal altruism. Our analysis in the preceding pages is based on the simplest of models. Over the past two decades economists have made extraordinary advances in repeated game theory, allowing a new generation of models. Do these address the shortcomings of the biologists' reciprocal altruism models concerning large group size, plausible degrees of behavioral or perceptual error and private information?

Symbol	Meaning
b	Benefit
β_o	Baseline replication rate
β_g	Effect of p_j on w_{ij}
β_i	Effect of p_{ij} on w_{ij}
β_G	$= \beta_i + \beta_g$
c	Cost
d	Number of rounds in an encounter
δ	Continuation probability
ϵ	Error rate
f_j	Fraction of total population in group j
F_{ST}	Wright's variance ratio
γ_a	Rate of conversion of N's into A's
γ_n	Rate of conversion of A's into N's
i	Index for individuals
j	Index for groups
k	Average degree of an individual in a network
p	Fraction of altruists in the population
p_j	Fraction of group j who are altruist
p_{ij}	1 if i in group j is altruist, 0 otherwise
r	degree of relatedness
t	Time
v_g	Expected value of being in good standing
v_b	Expected value of being in bad standing
$\overline{\text{var}}(p_{ij})$	The within-group term in Price's equation
w_{ij}	Fitness of individual i in group j
w	Average population-wide fitness
w^A	Average population-wide fitness of altruists
w_j^N	Fitness of nonaltruists in group j
w_j^A	Fitness of altruists in group j
w^N	Average population-wide fitness of nonaltruists
w_j	Average group j fitness
w_{ij}	Fitness of individual i in group j

Table 4.2. Definition of symbols

5

Cooperative Homo economicus

It is not from the benevolence of the butcher, the brewer, or the baker that we
expect our dinner, but from their regard to their own interest.

Adam Smith, *The Wealth of Nations*
(1937[1776]), Book 1, Chapter 2

Two neighbors may agree to drain a meadow, which they possess in common;
because 'tis easy for them to know each others mind; and each must perceive,
that the immediate consequence of his failing in his part, is the abandoning of
the whole project. But 'tis very difficult and indeed impossible, that a thousand
persons shou'd agree in any such action; it being difficult for them to concert so
complicated a design, and still more difficult for them to execute it

David Hume, *Treatise on Human Nature* (1964[1793]), Section vii, p. 304

In contrast to biology, where cooperative behaviors have become a central research
focus only in recent decades, a major goal of economic theory since its inception
two and a half centuries ago has been to explain the mutual benefits provided by a
widespread form of voluntary cooperation, market exchange among self-regarding individuals. This endeavor culminated half a century ago in the fundamental theorem of
welfare economics (Arrow and Debreu 1954, Debreu 1959, Arrow and Hahn 1971),
sustaining Smith's insight that self-regarding behaviors might support socially valued
economic outcomes. In the resulting model of exchange, individuals maximize their
utility given a set of market-determined prices over which they exercise no control.
They thus interact with a list of prices, not with one another. As a result the essential condition for strategic behavior, recognition that the payoffs of each depend on the
actions of others is absent. The reason that individuals are content to interact through
prices alone, and hence have no incentive to engage in strategic personal interactions, is
that all relevant aspects of exchanges are assumed to be covered by *complete contracts*,
enforceable at no cost to the exchanging parties.

A complete contract ensures that any aspect of an exchange in which the parties
have an interest will be explicitly stated in the contract and implemented as specified.
The enforcement of the contract in case of breach is entrusted to a third party, generally
the courts, and is assumed to impose no costs on the injured party. Contracts may be
incomplete because some aspect of the exchange cannot be specified in a sufficiently
precise manner ("fresh fish for sale") or the terms of the agreement cannot be enforced,
such as a worker's promise to "work hard" or, in the case of bankruptcy, a borrower's
promise to repay a loan.

In the past half century, a second major thrust of economic theory has eschewed these implausible complete contracts assumptions and developed models in which the outcomes of exchanges are determined by punishment, threats, and other forms of strategic interaction undertaken by the exchanging parties. Such contracts are thus endogenously enforced, an example being an employer who monitors the performance of an employee, using the promise of promotion and the threat of dismissal to induce the employee to provide high quality services. In the context of social dilemmas, these game-theoretic models refine and extend the insights of Shubik (1959), Trivers (1971), Taylor (1976), and Axelrod and Hamilton (1981) that retaliation against defectors by withdrawal of cooperation may enforce cooperation among self-regarding individuals. This literature culminates in the folk theorems of Fudenberg, Levine, Maskin, and others (Fudenberg and Maskin 1986, Fudenberg et al. 1994). A virtue of these models, in contrast to the older non-strategic paradigm in economics, is that in recognizing that most contracts are incomplete, they describe the real-world interactions among most animals, including humans (Blau 1964, Gintis 1976, Stiglitz 1987, Tirole 1988, Laffont 2000, Bowles and Hammerstein 2003).

But do these game-theoretic models provide an adequate explanation of cooperation among self-regarding individuals? In this chapter, we will show that while the insight that repeated interactions provide opportunities for cooperative individuals to discipline defectors is correct, none of these models is successful. The reason is that even presupposing extraordinary cognitive capacities and levels of patience among the cooperating individuals, there is no reason to believe that a group of more than two individuals would ever discover the cooperative Nash equilibria that the models have identified, and if it were to hit on one, its members would almost certainly abandon it in short order. Except under implausible conditions, the cooperative outcomes identified by these models are neither accessible nor persistent. We term them *evolutionarily irrelevant* Nash equilibria.

5.1   Folk Theorems and Evolutionary Dynamics

All folk theorems are based on a *stage game*, that is, an interaction like the one in Figure 3.1, played an indefinite number of times, with a constant, strictly positive, probability that in each period the game will continue for an additional period (§A3). The restrictions on the stage game tend to be minimal and rather technical, so that the public goods game and other social dilemmas involving costly cooperation fall within the aegis of the major folk theorems (Fudenberg and Maskin 1986, Fudenberg et al. 1994). Players receive signals concerning the cooperate vs. defect behavior of other players in previous periods, and reward or punish other players in such a manner as to render cooperation a self-regarding best response for all players.

With either perfect or public imperfect signals, a folk theorem can be proved, asserting that any feasible allocation of payoffs to a set of amoral self-regarding players that exceeds some minimal amount can be achieved, or approximated as closely as desired, as the equilibrium per-period payoff to the repeated game, for some discount factor strictly less than unity (Fudenberg and Maskin 1986, Fudenberg et al. 1994), and for sufficiently small signal errors.

For example, suppose Alice and Bob, who are amoral and self-regarding, play the prisoner's dilemma shown in Figure 5.1. Of course, in the one-shot game there is only one equilibrium in which both parties defect. However, suppose, as in our discussion of reciprocal altruism in the previous chapter, Alice and Bob play this stage game at times $t = 0, 1, 2, \ldots$ This is then a repeated game, in which the payoff to each is the sum of the payoffs over all periods, where following each period the interaction continues with probability δ, with $0 < \delta < 1$. Recall that we can equally consider δ to be a time discount factor, in which case the expected payoff becomes the present value of a time stream of returns (§A6). A strategy in this game that dictates following one course of action until a certain condition is met and then following a different strategy for the rest of the game is called a *trigger strategy*.

Bob

		C	D
Alice	C	5, 5	$-3, 8$
	D	8, -3	0, 0

Figure 5.1. Alice and Bob play the prisoner's dilemma again.

We can show that the cooperative solution (5,5), which is unattainable in the stage game with self-regarding players, can be attained in the repeated game if δ is sufficiently close to unity, and each player uses the trigger strategy of cooperating as long as the other player cooperates, and defecting forever if the other player defects on one round. We use the fact (see §4.4) that for any discount factor δ with $0 < \delta < 1$, the expected duration of the game in number of rounds is $1/(1 - \delta)$.

Now suppose both players use the trigger strategy. Then, the payoff to each is $5/(1 - \delta)$. Suppose a player tried to do better by using a different strategy. This must involve defecting forever; for once the player defects, his opponent will defect forever, the best response to which is to defect forever. A player who defects receives 8 immediately and zero in each succeeding period. Thus the defect strategy is superior to the cooperate strategy if and only if $5/(1 - \delta) < 8$, or $\delta < 3/8$. Thus, when $\delta > 3/8$, the pair of trigger strategies cannot be invaded by defection.

In fact, there are lots of other equilibria to this game. For instance, consider the following trigger strategy for Alice: alternate $C, D, C, \ldots$ as long as Bob alternates $D, C, D, \ldots$ If Bob deviates from this pattern, defect forever. Suppose Bob plays the complementary strategy: alternate $D, C, D, \ldots$ as long as Alice alternates $C, D, C, \ldots$, and if Alice deviates from this pattern, defect forever. Alice cannot increase her payoffs by deviating from her assigned strategy for δ sufficiently close to unity, and neither can Bob. To see this, note that if it is profitable for Alice to deviate, it will be most profitable for her to defect when called upon to cooperate, in which case she has payoff zero in the first and all succeeding periods, since deviating by cooperating when the strategy calls for defection results in a payoff of -3 on the first round and zero thereafter. Alice's payoff when sticking to the trigger strategy is $-3, 8, -3, 8, \ldots$ To evaluate the expected payoff of this infinite stream of returns, note that Alice gets -3 in the first period, eight in the next period, and then with probability δ^2, she gets to play the game all over again starting two periods from today. Thus, if x is Alice's expected payoff of the game, we have $x = -3 + 8\delta + \delta^2 x$. Solving this, we get $x = (8\delta - 3)/(1 - \delta^2)$. The trigger strategy beats defecting when $x > 0$, which requires that $8\delta - 3 > 0$, or $\delta > 3/8$. Once again, if $\delta > 3/8$, the trigger strategy cannot be beat.

The possible expected per-period payoffs in the repeated game based on this stage game are exhibited in Figure 5.2. The *folk theorem* says in this case that the use of trigger strategies of the kind just illustrated can sustain any point in the shaded region $OABC$ as an equilibrium of the repeated game, provided the continuation probability is sufficiently close to unity. For instance, it is easy to show that to attain point A, Alice can use a trigger strategy in which she plays Cooperate in every period but Bob is permitted to play Defect in seven particular periods out of every 17 (e.g., the first, third, sixth, seventh, twelfth, fourteenth and sixteenth), playing Cooperate in the other 10. If Bob cooperates less frequently than this, Alice pulls the trigger and defects for as long as the game lasts. Bob's trigger strategy is the mirror image of Alice's. If the continuation probability is $\delta = 0.98$, Alice earns zero on average and Bob earns a bit less than seven.

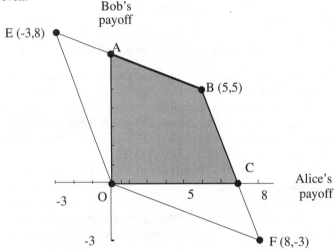

Figure 5.2. The folk theorem. The average per-period payoffs indicated by any point in the shaded region $OABC$ can be sustained in an equilibrium of the repeated game based on the prisoner's dilemma stage game depicted in Figure 5.1.

From this example one suspects that the result may be a little too good to be true, for how would Alice and Bob come to coordinate on this particular pair of trigger strategies? There is an infinite number of other pairs of strategies that would implement the other points along the frontier ABC. Why, for example, would Alice not seek to turn the tables by preemptively adopting Bob's trigger strategy, the best response to which for Bob would be to adopt its complement, implementing point C in the figure, resulting in a reversal of the payoffs at point A.

When we ask how players might actually come to coordinate on an efficient pair of trigger strategies (that is, one on the frontier ABC) or, for that matter, any set of trigger strategies at all other than mutual defect, the theorem is silent. Moreover, when groups are large, the problem is far worse than is suggested by the difficulty that a single pair of individuals, Alice and Bob, might have in coordinating on a set of strategies, for as Hume observes about just this kind of problem in the headquote of this chapter; it is a lot easier to come to a working arrangement among two individuals than among many independent spirits, in the absence of a regulating social institution to which all are committed. To understand just how serious this coordination problem is, we need to consider what happens when the numbers of individuals involved are considerable, and the information each has on the others' actions is subject to error.

5.2   The Folk Theorem with Imperfect Public Information

The argument supporting the folk theorem in the previous section depends critically on the fact that the signal is public and perfect. Errors can have disastrous consequences when trigger strategies are used because a single defection signal causes an immediate collapse of cooperation forever. In this section, we present the folk theorem with imperfect public signals (Fudenberg et al. 1994), which proposes more flexible strategies that are capable of recovering cooperation after a player unintentionally failed to produce the benefit b or did produce the benefit but was incorrectly perceived to have defected. For instance, a hunter may return with no game either because he had bad luck or because he spent the day sleeping under a tree. The signal is imperfect in the sense that it cannot distinguish between the cases of intentional and accidental defection (execution error) or incorrectly reports the individual's behavior (perception error). Table 5.1 shows the mathematical symbols used in this chapter.

We will assume that the total expected benefit produced if all n group members cooperate is nb, but the actual realized benefit is subject to random variations, so group members cannot infer how many members cooperated by observing the actual value of benefit produced in the period. However, each member receives an imperfect public signal with perceptual error that indicates a defect action accurately, but when the member cooperated, indicates a defection with probability $\epsilon > 0$. Full cooperation entails an expected payoff of $b - c$ for each player. The folk theorem in this case asserts that no matter how large the group and however closely we wish to approximate the full cooperation payoff, there is a set of rules for social interaction that achieves this degree of cooperation, provided δ is sufficiently close to unity. Perhaps the most striking aspect of the folk theorem with imperfect public signals is that it is true independent of group size and no matter how imperfect the signal, as long as it predicts defection with better than chance accuracy.

In the previous chapter we found that the n-player reciprocal altruism model can sustain a high level of cooperation only in very small groups. The folk theorem model thus achieves a degree of efficiency that far outstrips the reciprocal altruism model. This superior efficiency, as we shall see, derives from the assumption that punishment can be directed toward the miscreant rather than all players suffering equally through a breakdown in cooperation.

Suppose, then, that a player who is observed to have defected is punished an amount equivalent to losing p in the current period, the punishment being administered by other members of the group, and the costs of punishment being shared equally among the punishers. We assume that the signal indicating that a player carried out his share of the punishment is public and imperfect, indicating with probability ϵ that he failed to punish when in fact he carried out the punishment. If a player is signaled as having failed to punish, he is punished by the others in the same manner and to the same degree as a defector is punished. This model has the property that if Alice is signaled as having failed to punish Bob, then Bob is required to participate in the punishment of Alice. Moreover, if Alice and Bob are both miscreants, each must participate in the punishment of the other. This arrangement may appear bizarre, but there are real-world examples of this, such as a convicted felon paying income taxes that support the costs of his incarceration. Moreover, we could change this assumption without affecting the conclusion, at the expense of a more complicated argument.

Suppose the cost of punishing at level p is αp, where $\alpha > 0$. Because perception errors occur with probability ϵ per individual per period, in a fully cooperative equilibrium, each player will observe an expected number $(n-1)\epsilon$ of defection signals from the other players, which will induce a total punishment of $(n-1)\epsilon p$ of the defectors. Because each punishment is shared among the other $n-1$ players, each member each period will punish the others an expected amount $\epsilon p(n-1)/(n-1) = \epsilon p$, at cost $\alpha \epsilon p$.

For cooperation to be a best response, it must be the case that a player cannot gain by intentionally defecting for one period and then returning to cooperation in all future periods. If π_c is the single-period payoff to cooperating assuming all other players always cooperate, and π_d is the single-period payoff to defecting when all others cooperate, followed by returning to cooperation in the succeeding period, then to maintain cooperation, we must have $\pi_c \geq \pi_d$ assuming, as we do, that if payoffs are identical, the individual cooperates. We have

$$\pi_c = b - c - \alpha \epsilon p - \epsilon p \tag{5.1}$$
$$\pi_d = b - \alpha \epsilon p + p \tag{5.2}$$

where αp is the individual's expected share of the total cost of punishing in a single period. Note that in (5.2), the second term on the right-hand side is the expected cost of punishing others, while the final term is the expected amount of punishment the agent will absorb. In (5.2), the cost c does not occur because the individual defects and hence does not incur this cost, and the cost of being punished becomes p, because defectors are punished with probability one.

We can economize on punishment costs by choosing p to satisfy $\pi_c = \pi_d$, which then gives

$$p = \frac{c}{1-\epsilon}. \tag{5.3}$$

The payoff to cooperating for each player will then be

$$\pi_c = b - c\left(1 + \epsilon\frac{1+\alpha}{1-\epsilon}\right), \tag{5.4}$$

where the second term in the parentheses on the right hand side is the extra cost of punishing due to errors. Note the error-induced inefficiency, $\epsilon c(1+\alpha)/(1-\epsilon)$, goes to zero for infrequent errors, independent of group size. Thus, directed punishment appears to solve the problem of cooperation in large groups.

There is a catch, however. Because punishing costs the punisher, self-regarding players have no incentive to carry out the punishment. Thus, this model does not work assuming self-regarding players. We have seen in Chapter 3 that people avidly punish defectors even at a cost to themselves, providing a solution to this problem, but one that is based on social preferences rather than self-interest. Recall that Panchanathan and Boyd solved the problem by letting the punishment of free riders take the form of withholding help that otherwise would be given to the free rider.

Because the cost of punishing for each individual is $\alpha \epsilon p$ where p is given by (5.3), were social preferences admitted in this model, the cost to such an altruistic punisher would be $\alpha \epsilon c / (1 - \epsilon)$, which is quite small for plausible parameter values. To save the folk theorem, we must thus implement some mechanism to ensure that self-regarding players have an incentive to actually carry out the punishment dictated by the equilibrium. There are potentially many ways to accomplish this, but unfortunately, the proof of the folk theorem does not specify any particular incentive mechanism. This is because the proof is not constructive (Fudenberg et al. 1994). That is, the authors show that an equilibrium with the desired properties exists, but they do not show how to construct one. As a result, in order to explore whether a plausible system of punishment that is incentive compatible for self-regarding agents can be devised, we must construct our own model. This will not be hard to do, and we shall develop the most reasonable model we can devise, but in assessing its plausibility, we must keep in mind there could be some incentive structure of which we are unaware that does not share the limitations of our construction. Here is the best we could devise.

If all individuals cooperate and punish, the expected number of signaled defections will be ϵn. Because $n - 1$ players punish each defection, there will be $\epsilon n(n - 1)$ punishments of defectors, which will then generate another $\epsilon^2 n(n-1)$ defection signals (signals of failure to punish). These new signals of failure to punish engender $\epsilon^2 n(n - 1)^2$ new punishment events. The total number of punishments engendered by one period's failure to cooperate signals is then

$$\epsilon n(n - 1) + \epsilon^2 n(n - 1)^2 + \epsilon^3 n(n - 1^3) + \ldots = (n - 1)\frac{\epsilon n}{1 - (n - 1)\epsilon}$$

Because each individual punishes each miscreant an amount $p/(n-1)$, the total amount of punishment per individual per period will then be

$$\frac{p\epsilon n}{1 - \epsilon(n - 1)} \tag{5.5}$$

provided $\epsilon < 1/n$. We then can write, given (5.3) and (5.4),

$$\pi_c = b - c\left(1 + \epsilon n \frac{1 + \alpha}{(1 - \epsilon(n - 1))}\right). \tag{5.6}$$

Assuming ϵ is considerably smaller than $1/n$, the payoff in this equilibrium is reasonably close to the highest possible equal payoff $b - c$. This is the major message of the folk theorem, although the theorem asserts that there is an incentive structure, doubtless more complicated than ours, that makes the fraction in (5.6) as small as desired for δ near unity. Note that δ does not appear in our formulation. This is because we assume that the punishment of an infraction is confined to a single period, which is not the general case. In particular, for $\epsilon(n-1) > 1$, a more complex argument must be devised. If we confine our attention to groups no larger than about 15 and error rates on the order of about 5%, the condition $\epsilon(n-1) < 1$ will indeed hold.

It is easy to check that for plausible parameter values (we use $\epsilon = 5\%$, $c = 1$, and $\alpha = 1$), the maximum group size with positive payoff is $n = 11$ for $b = 4$, $n = 9$ for $b = 3$, and $n = 6$ for $b = 2$. Moreover, the efficiency of the equilibrium, measured by $\pi_c/(b-c)$, falls below 50% for $n = 8$ when $b = 4$, for $n = 6$ when $b = 3$, and $n = 4$ when $b = 2$. Of course if it is less costly to punish than to be punished ($\alpha < 1$), larger group sizes can be supported while maintaining a significant level of efficiency. For instance, for $\alpha = 1/3$ (that is, it costs the punisher one-third to administer a unit of punishment), when $b = 4$, $b = 3$, and $b = 2$, respectively, we can maintain 50% efficiency with groups of size 10, 8, and 5, respectively. But even this modest piece of good news evaporates if, as is generally the case, information is private.

5.3   The Folk Theorem with Private Information

The case of private signals is more complicated because players cannot coordinate their behavior when a defection is detected. With private signals, some players perceive a defection while others perceive cooperation on the part of the same player, and players do not know what perceptions other players may have formed. If defectors are punished by the withdrawal of cooperation in retaliation, Alice cannot tell if Bob defected to punish an observed defection of player Carole, or because Bob defected intentionally, or even that Bob cooperated but Alice received a defect signal from Bob by mistake. For example, suppose Bob and Alice repeatedly play the prisoner's dilemma depicted in Figure 5.1 with continuation probability δ. We assume the payoffs to Alice and Bob are distributed only at the termination of the game, so Alice cannot use current payoffs to determine whether Bob defected, and vice versa. However, suppose Alice receives a signal that informs her correctly when Bob defects, but with probability $\epsilon > 0$ tells her Bob defected when in fact he cooperated. Suppose Bob has a similar signal informing him of Alice's behavior. To see why private signals cause such a problem, we'll first see how easy it will be if the two signals were public, so Bob always knows when Alice receives a defect signal and Alice always knows when Bob receives a defect signal. Suppose Alice adopts the "one bad signal triggers defect" (OBSTD) strategy of cooperating on all rounds until the game ends or she encounters a defect signal, upon which she defects unconditionally on all future rounds. If Bob adopts the same strategy, we indeed have a Nash equilibrium because, when Alice receives a defect signal, she knows that Bob received the same signal and hence will defect thereafter, the best response to which for Alice is to defect forever as well. This is, of course, the same model as in §5.1, except now errors are possible. We show in §A8 that the resulting Nash equilibrium is fairly efficient when the error rate is small. For instance, with $\delta = 0.9$ and $\epsilon = 0.05$, the expected payoff if both players could precommit to cooperating unconditionally is about 45, while the actual payoff to the Nash equilibrium is about 25, so the efficiency of the Nash equilibrium is about 56%.

Suppose, however, the error signal is private. That is, if Bob cooperates but Alice receives defect signal, Bob does not know that this is the case. One might think that this would make little difference because the OBSTD strategy gives rise to almost the same payoffs. This is indeed the case, as we show in §A8. The problem is that the pair of OBSTD strategies is not a Nash equilibrium of the repeated game! In fact, if Bob plays the OBSTD strategy, Alice's does better to play the "two bad signals trigger defect" (TBSTD) strategy. We show in §A8 that for low error rates, TBSTD has a higher payoff for Alice (and for Bob as well) when played against OBSTD. The original pair of OBSTD strategies thus did not form a Nash equilibrium.

While Alice's TBSTD strategy is better for both Bob and Alice than her OBSTD strategy when played against Bob's OBSTD strategy, TBSTD is not part of a Nash equilibrium. Indeed, if Alice plays TBSTD, then Bob does better by defecting on purpose every other round, because this never induces Alice to defect until she receives a defect signal when Bob actually cooperated. What, then, is a Nash equilibrium with private signals?

Two different sorts of models for dealing with the private signaling case have been offered. In the first, developed in Sekiguchi (1997) and Bhaskar and Obara (2002), players cooperate with probability less than one on the first round and then, in following rounds, they use a trigger strategy in which the first time a player receives a defect signal, he defects forever. To explain the behavior in the first period, and assess the efficiency properties of the equilibrium, assume that from the second period on, Bob and Alice play the prisoner's dilemma depicted in §5.1, which they play repeatedly with continuation probability δ. We show in §A8 that the efficiency of the resulting equilibrium is only about 3%.

There is another approach to constructing Nash equilibria for repeated games with private signals (Piccione 2002, Ely and Välimäki 2002, Mailath and Morris 2006). We will not describe this approach because the resulting Nash equilibria require that players use strictly *mixed strategies* (that is, they randomize over various actions rather than taking a single action) in each period, and there is no reason for players to actually use such mixed strategies, or to conjecture that the other players will use such mixed strategies. We explain why this is so in the next section.

5.4   Evolutionarily Irrelevant Equilibria

The folk theorem provides no reason to believe that players would ever coordinate on one of the equilibria whose existence the theorem demonstrates, or that should this occur by chance the equilibrium would long survive. This is why we say that the resulting equilibria are evolutionarily irrelevant. Nor has there been progress toward supplying a realistic dynamical adjustment process that would render such an equilibrium relevant. It is plausible that individuals are predisposed and able to best respond given full knowledge of the game and the choices of the other players. But when knowledge is imperfect or private and the choices of the other players are not known, surely the most plausible assumption, players will not implement the Nash equilibria whose existence is guaranteed by the folk theorems.

Recent research suggests that the conditions for achieving a Nash equilibrium are quite stringent and rarely satisfied, except in the simplest of cases (Aumann and Brandenburger 1995). The problem with achieving a Nash equilibrium is that individuals may have heterogeneous and incompatible beliefs concerning how other players will behave, and indeed what other players believe concerning one's own behavior. Therefore, individuals may choose best responses to strategies that the other players in fact are not playing, resulting in game play that is far from any Nash equilibrium. It is clear from this research that the conditions required for players to implement a Nash equilibrium in all but the simplest games cannot be deduced from the assumption that the players are rational, i.e., that they choose best responses.

In addition to this general point, if cooperation involves the use of mixed strategies, which is the usual case in repeated game equilibria, then players have no incentive to play their equilibrium strategies at all. A mixed strategy for a player is a probabilistic combination of pure strategies, such as playing heads or tails each with 50% probability in a pennies-matching game. In a Nash equilibrium in mixed strategies, all the pure strategies a player uses with positive probability must have the same payoff against the mixed strategy choices of the other players, or else the player could increase his payoff by dropping a relatively low-payoff strategy. But then it follows that the player has no incentive to play the Nash best response as opposed to any other combination of the strategies used in the Nash best response. Moreover, the other players know this, and thus have no reason to expect a player to choose the Nash best response, and hence have no reason themselves even to restrict the pure strategies they use to those appearing in the Nash equilibrium.

The founders of game theory were poignantly aware of this problem. John Harsanyi, who was awarded the Nobel Prize in economics at the same time as John Nash, offered a very creative resolution in his so-called purification theorem (Harsanyi 1973). Harsanyi showed that in a game with a unique Nash equilibrium, and where this equilibrium is a mixed strategy equilibrium, if there are small random errors in the payoffs, and if a certain technical condition holds, the players will play pure strategies in each period, but on average, the number of times each pure strategy is used approximates the weight of that strategy in the mixed strategy Nash equilibrium. This theorem applies to a number of simple games, but they do not include the repeated games of the form used in the folk theorems, because the required technical condition does not hold in such games (Bhaskar et al. 2004). The upshot of this argument is that the Nash equilibria ensuring efficient cooperation in the public goods game and other social dilemmas are evolutionarily irrelevant. While there are several models in which individuals "learn" over time to play a Nash equilibrium (Fudenberg and Levine 1997, Young 2006), the conditions under which these models apply are limited to simple one-shot games, and hence do not apply to repeated games.

This is not to say that the Nash equilibrium concept is irrelevant in practice. In evolutionary game theory we find that every stable equilibrium of a dynamical system governed by a *monotone dynamic* (one in which higher payoff strategies have higher growth rates than lower payoff strategies), such as the replicator dynamic (Taylor and Jonker 1978), is a Nash equilibrium of the underlying game (Nachbar 1990, Samuelson and Zhang 1992). Here, the analysis runs from the construction of a dynamical system to the analysis of the stable equilibria of such a system, which then must be a Nash equilibrium of the stage game (see §A5). There is no valid inference in the reverse direction: a Nash equilibrium need not be stable in any evolutionary dynamical setting.

Moreover if, as is surely the case in all real-world settings, some signals are private, then trigger and other strategies that require sensitively coordinated responses to defections no longer work because players no longer agree on what happened in the past, and hence cannot coordinate their behavior based on a common understanding of the history of the game. Even in this case, an equilibrium at or near the Pareto frontier for sufficiently patient players can be shown to exist under some conditions (Sekiguchi 1997, Piccione 2002, Ely and Välimäki 2002, Bhaskar and Obara 2002, Mailath and Morris 2006), but we have seen that these equilibria are not very satisfactory. Indeed, if there is a Nash equilibrium with private signals, individuals have no particular incentive to play the strategies that implement the equilibrium, because many other strategies have the same payoffs as the equilibrium payoffs. Moreover, as we have seen, the equilibrium exists only if private signals are very close to being public, so all individuals receive nearly the same signal concerning the behavior of any given group member. When this is not the case, the equilibrium will not exist. Thus, these models apply only to forms of cooperation where all members observe the actions of (nearly) all others with a high level of accuracy.

5.5   Social Norms and Correlated Equilibria

There is an alternative game-theoretic equilibrium concept that does not share the weaknesses associated with the Nash equilibrium described above: the *correlated equilibrium*. A *correlating device* is something that sends out signals, private or public, to the players of a game, indicating which pure strategy each should play. A correlated equilibrium is a situation in which there is a correlating device such that, if all players follow the advice of the correlating device, no player can do better by switching to an alternative strategy.

General arguments support the notion that correlated equilibrium rather than Nash equilibrium is the appropriate equilibrium concept for game theory (Aumann 1987, Vanderschraaf 2001, Gintis 2009a). Assuming players have common knowledge of the game, its rules, and its payoffs, as well as a common belief concerning the probability of the natural events (the so-called moves by Nature) associated with the game, the strategies chosen by rational individuals can then always be modeled as a correlated equilibrium with an appropriate correlating device.

The notion of a correlating device is quite abstract, but one form of correlating device is well known and performs precisely the social function of signaling actions to individuals that, when followed, may lead to a socially efficient outcome. This device is the *social norm* which, like the choreographer in a ballet, is instituted to issue precise instructions that, when followed, produce the desired outcome. For instance, the system of traffic lights in a city's street network instruct drivers when to stop and when to go, and it is normally in the interest of drivers to obey these signals as long as others do so, to avoid accidents.

For a more pertinent example, suppose Alice and Bob repeatedly play the prisoner's dilemma in Figure 5.1. As we have seen, for a sufficiently large continuation probability, a pair of average payoffs anywhere in the quadrilateral $OABC$ of Figure 5.2 can be achieved as a Nash equilibrium. A choreographer could implement a point on the boundary ABC by the judicious choice of instructions to the players. For instance, to achieve the point on AB one third the distance to A, the choreographer could instruct the players to play (5,5) with probability 5/12 and $(-3, 8)$ with probability 7/12. This gives Alice the average payoff 1/3 and Bob the average payoff 27/4, which is indeed the desired result. Now of course there is no reason for the players to obey the Choreographer in a one-shot game, but if the game is repeated, using the logic of the folk theorem where the Choreographer promises to instruct both players to defect forever should one violate the Choreographer's orders, it is a best response for both Bob and Alice to obey the Choreographer.

A cooperative equilibrium supported by social norms is one in which not only is the equilibrium strategy evolutionarily stable, but also the social norms are themselves an evolutionary adaptation, stable against invasion by competing social norms. Sociologists (Durkheim 1933[1902], Parsons and Shils 1951) and anthropologists (Benedict 1934, Boyd and Richerson 1985, Brown 1991) have found that virtually every society has such social norms, and that they are key to understanding strategic interaction. Borrowing a page from sociological theory, we posit that groups have social norms specifying how a game ought to be played and that these norms are identified as social norms by group members. Learning a social norm includes learning that the norm is common knowledge among those who know it, learning what behavior is suggested by the norm, and learning that a large fraction of group members know the norm and follow it.

Social norms do not ensure equilibrium, because error, mutation,migration, deliberate violation of the norm, and other dynamical forces may lead individuals to reject beliefs or behavior fostered by the norm. This may occur because the beliefs might conflict with an individual's personal experience, or its suggested behavior may be rejected as not in the individual's best interest; i.e., the action fostered by a social norm must be a best response to the behaviors of the other group members, given the beliefs engendered by the social norm and the individual's updating. Moreover, social norms cannot be introduced as a *deus ex machina*, as if laid down by a centralized authority, without violating the objective to provide a "bottom-up" theory of cooperation that does not presuppose preexisting institutional forms of cooperation. Social norm are thus discretionary, because any institution that is posited to enforce behavior should itself be modeled within the dynamical system, unless plausible reasons are given for taking a macro-level institution as unproblematically given. Nor are social norms fixed in stone. A group's social norms are themselves subject to change, those groups producing better outcomes for their members sometimes but not always displacing groups with less effective social norms, and changing social and demographic conditions leading to the evolutionary transformation of social norms within groups.

5.6   The Missing Choreographer

The economic theory of cooperation based on repeated games proves the existence of equilibria with socially desirable properties, while leaving the question of how such equilibria are achieved as an afterthought. The theory thus abstracts from problems of stability, convergence, and other aspects of out-of-equilibrium dynamics. The folk theorem shares this defect with the even more celebrated fundamental ("invisible hand") theorem of welfare economics mentioned at the beginning of the chapter, which purports to model decentralized market interactions, but on close inspection requires an extraordinary level of coordination that is not explained, but rather is posited as a *deus ex machina* (Kirman 1989, Ingrao and Israel 1990, Bowles 2004, Gintis 2007).

We have shown, similarly, for the case of cooperation supported by retaliation as in the folk theorem, that highly choreographed coordination on complex strategies capable of deterring defection are supposed to materialize quite without the need for a choreographer. As in the case of the fundamental theorem, the dynamics are thus unspecified, and, if we are correct, impossible to provide without a fundamental change in the underlying theory.

The failure of the models underlying both the folk theorem and the fundamental theorem is hardly surprising, for they sought to explain cooperation among large numbers of self-regarding strangers without recourse to preexisting norms and cooperative institutions, something that most likely never occurred in the history or prehistory of our species. Humans are indeed exceptional among living creatures in the degree and range of cooperation among large numbers of substantially unrelated individuals. The global division of labor and exchange, the modern democratic welfare state, and contemporary warfare alike evidence our distinctiveness. These forms of cooperation emerged historically and are today sustained as a result of the interplay of self-regarding and social preferences operating under the influence of group-level institutions of governance and socialization that favor cooperators, in part by helping to coordinate their actions so as to target transgressions for punishment and thus protect them from exploitation by defectors.

The norms and institutions that have accomplished this evolved over millennia through trial and error. Consider how real-world institutions addressed two of the shoals on which the repeated game models foundered.

First, the private nature of information, as we have seen, makes it virtually impossible to coordinate the targeted punishment of miscreants. In many hunter-gatherer societies the relevant information that would in other societies be private is rendered public by such cooperative customs as eating in public so that violations of sharing norms can be easily detected. Cooperative Japanese shrimp fishermen who pool income across boats deliberately land their catch at an appointed time of day for the same reason (Platteau and Seki 2001). But in most modern societies, where larger numbers are involved, converting private information about transgressions to public information that can provide the basis of punishment often involves civil or criminal trials, elaborate processes that have evolved over centuries and that rely on commonly agreed upon rules of evidence and ethical norms of appropriate behavior. Even with the benefit of these preexisting social preferences, these complex institutions frequently fail to transform the private protestations of innocence and guilt into common knowledge.

Second, here and in the previous chapter we have seen that cooperation often unravels when the withdrawal of cooperation by the civic-minded intending to punish a defector is mistaken by others as itself a violation of a cooperative norm, inviting a spiral of further defections. In virtually all surviving societies with substantial populations, this problem is addressed by the creation of a corps of specialists entrusted with carrying out the more severe of society's punishments. Their uniforms convey the civic purpose of the punishments they mete out, and their professional norms, it is hoped, ensure that the power to punish is not used for personal gain. Like court proceedings, these policing, penal, and related institutions work imperfectly.

Both solutions to the problems of cooperation among self-regarding individuals that we have identified—court proceedings for converting private to public information and specialized professional forces to legitimize the punishments that maintain order—presuppose that jurists, police officers, witnesses and others are committed to upholding other-regarding or ethical standards of behavior. It is difficult to imagine that these institutions could work in the absence of these commitments. The economic models of cooperation that assume pre-existing solutions to these problems thus do not accomplish their goal, namely explaining cooperation among amoral and self-regarding individuals.

Modeling the complex processes that sustain human cooperation is a major challenge of contemporary science. Economic theory, favoring parsimony over realism, has sought to explain cooperation without reference to social preferences, and with a minimalist or fictive description of social institutions. This research trajectory, as we have seen, has produced significant insights. But it may have run its course.

Symbol	Meaning
α	Cost of punishing/Cost of being punished
b	Benefit
c	Cost
δ	Continuation probability
ϵ	Error rate
p	Cost of being punished
π_c	Payoff to cooperating
π_d	Payoff to defecting
n	Group size
t	Time

Table 5.1. Definition of symbols

6

Ancestral Human Society

> [Among] prehistoric men...life was a continual free fight, and beyond the limited and temporary relations of the family, the Hobbesian war of each against all was the normal state of existence.
>
> T. H. Huxley,
> *The Struggle for Existence: A Programme* (1888) p. 163

> The philosophers...have all felt it necessary to go back to the state of nature, but none of them has succeeded in getting there.
>
> J.-J. Rousseau,
> *Discourse on the Origins and Foundations*
> *of Inequality Among Men* (1755) p. 1

Could strong reciprocity, fair-mindedness, and other altruistic and ethical preferences documented in Chapter 3 be the legacy of an evolutionary past in which individuals behaving in these ways had higher fitness than they would have had had they been entirely amoral and self-regarding? Trivers (2007) reasons that "unfair arrangements...may exact a very strong cost in inclusive fitness. In that sense, an attachment to fairness or justice is self-interested" (p. 77). If Trivers is correct, fair-mindedness could have become common among humans if it benefited the individual or close relatives in repeated interactions, allowing fair-minded individuals to gain reputations that advanced their genetic interests. This, indeed, is the explanation of the evolution of fairness norms given by Ken Binmore (2005). The same reasoning may be applied to generosity and punishing those who transgress social norms.

Richard Dawkins (2006) advances exactly this view, having outlined kin-based altruism, reciprocal altruism, indirect reciprocity, and costly signaling as the four models likely to explain the origins of modern human altruism:

> Throughout most of our prehistory, humans lived under conditions that would have strongly favored the evolution of all four...most of your fellow band members would have been kin, more closely related to you than members of other bands...plenty of opportunities for kin altruism to evolve. And...you would tend to meet the same individuals again and again throughout your life—ideal conditions for the evolution of reciprocal altruism. Those were also the ideal conditions for building reputations for altruism and the very same ideal conditions for advertising conspicuous generosity. (p. 220)

Thus, it could be that humans became cooperative because in our ancestral environments we interacted frequently with the same group of close kin, among whom tit-for-tat and other strategies consistent with Trivers' reciprocal altruism were sufficient to support cooperative outcomes. Cooperation, according to this view, emerged as a form of mutualism.

Others, including Leda Cosmides and John Tooby (1992), share this view of the evolutionary origins of social preferences, but in contrast to Trivers hold that in modern settings they are fitness-reducing. Though the cooperation that was extended to family and reciprocating fellow group members enhanced the fitness of cooperators among our ancestors, according to Cosmides and Tooby, in the modern world of more ephemeral social contacts its expression is a maladaptive legacy of the distant evolutionary origins of human motivation. Because our ancestors rarely encountered strangers we just do not sufficiently distinguish, either in lab experiments or in real life, between one-shots and long lasting interactions, treating strangers much as if they were intimates. Dawkins explains it this way: "the lust to be generous and compassionate... is the misfired consequence of ancestral village life" (p. 222).

There is little doubt that reputation-building in repeated interactions and a tendency of close family members to interact frequently contributed to the evolution of cooperation. But we think it unlikely that these mechanisms provide a sufficient explanation. First, as we have seen in Chapter 3, modern humans are perfectly capable of distinguishing between situations in which reputation building and retaliation against free-riding are possible and situations in which they ar not. It is not likely that prosocial behavior in the latter situation is just a mistake. Second, the view that early humans lived in worlds with little contact outside one's family—Dawkins' ideal conditions for self-interested cooperation to flourish—is difficult to square with what is known about the Late Pleistocene and early Holocene. Like Jean-Jacques Rousseau's philosophers, Dawkins, Huxley, and other biologists seem to have jumped on a faulty time machine, and have journeyed to an imaginary ancestral world.

The evidence for a quite different picture of our ancestral condition is necessarily indirect, but convincing. Prehistoric foragers left few archaeological traces and the historical record contains few precontact histories extending over more than half a century. The best we can do is to make inferences from the available data including hunter-gatherer demographics, Late Pleistocene climate records, archaeological evidence on causes of deaths during the Pleistocene, and ethnographic and historical reports as well as genetic evidence from recent foragers.

We will see that neither the likely size of groups, nor the degree of genetic relatedness within groups, nor the typical demography of foraging bands is favorable to the view that Late Pleistocene human cooperation can be adequately explained by kin-based altruism or reciprocal altruism. What is known or can reasonably be inferred about the Late Pleistocene and early Holocene suggests that ancestral humans did not live in small closed groups in which family and self-interest with a long time horizon alone were the cement of society. Rather our ancestors were cosmopolitan, civic-minded, and warlike. They almost certainly benefited from far-flung coinsurance, trading, mating and other social networks, as well as from coalitions and, if successful, warfare with other groups.

In the next section we review the available archaeological and ethnographic evidence suggesting that while isolated groups surely existed, most humans had frequent contact with a substantial number of individuals beyond the immediate family. This conclusion is consistent with data on foragers reviewed in §6.2 on the extent of genetic differentiation among *ethnographic foragers*, by which we mean foragers in the historical and ethnographic record. Had ancestral groups been small and isolated, the extent of between-group genetic differences would have been considerably greater than is observed. We then provide evidence that ancestral humans engaged in frequent and exceptionally lethal intergroup conflicts. In the penultimate section we turn to data suggesting that social order in prestate small-scale societies was sustained in important measure by a process of coordinated peer pressures and punishment, a process that we will model and simulate in Chapter 9.

6.1   Cosmopolitan Ancestors

Were ancestral groups small enough so that, in light of the results of our simulations in Chapter 4, cooperation could be supported by repeated interactions?

The minimal feasible foraging band, Christopher Boehm (2007) reasoned, would include five hunters. The number of adult decision makers then would be triple or more this number, counting women and the elderly. The average band (census) size among the 175 "warm climate, non-equestrian" hunter-gatherer groups identified by Frank Marlowe (2005) as the groups in the ethnographic record most likely to be similar to ancestral humans is 37. Even if we exclude the old and the young, this would be about 12 adult decision makers. In Figure 4.6 we showed that even for groups a half this size reciprocal altruism will evolve only for implausibly low rates of behavioral or perceptual error and extraordinarily high benefit-cost ratios of the altruistic behavior.

But the relevant number for human cooperation is not the average size of the elementary group of foragers. First, seasonal and other aggregations of many bands occurred for purpose of exchange, marital matching, sociality, and defense. Second, most ancestral humans necessarily lived in larger than average groups. For an evolutionary explanation, either cultural or genetic, it is the size of the group that a typical individual lived in that is relevant, not the much smaller average group size. This so-called typical group size may differ substantially from the average group size. Suppose there are two groups, one with 10 members and the other with 100 members. The average group size is 55. But the typical group size, weighting both groups' size by their share of the total population, or $(100 \times 100 + 10 \times 10)/110$, is 92. Another way of seeing this is to note that 100 individuals have 99 neighbors and 10 individuals have nine neighbors, so the average number of neighbors per individual is $(100 \times 99 + 10 \times 9)/110 \approx 91$. Using this concept, we calculated the typical group size for the same warm climate non-equestrian groups in Marlowe's sample. It was an astounding 77, more than twice the average group size. A group of this size would have 40 or more adult decision makers. We think even that this is probably an underestimate, given that during the Late Pleistocene a far greater fraction of hunter-gatherers than today lived in large, partially sedentary villages in the relatively densely populated resource-rich coastal and riverine environments from which they were subsequently expelled by Holocene farmers.

More than limited group size is required for repeated interactions to sustain cooperation: frequent and ongoing interactions are also necessary (equation 4.11). But evidence of extensive contacts outside the group and cataclysmic demographic events make it unlikely that these requirements we met during the Late Pleistocene and early Holocene.

As we saw in Chapter 1, long-distance trade among foraging groups in Africa predates the diaspora of modern humans. Exchange was also common among Australian aboriginal groups:

> Shell, stone, ochre, *pituri* [a narcotic] and wooden tools and weapons all circulated over hundreds of kilometers... shell pendants crossed the continent... A wooden hooked boomerang was seen... at least 1200 km. west of its area of manufacture. (Mulvaney 1976, p. 80)

Aboriginal cultural practices also were exchanged. One, the Molongo ceremony, apparently traveled 1600 kilometers between 1893 and 1918 (Lourandos 1997).

> Exchange often involved seasonal meetings of 1000 or more at which communal food producing activities included... hunting drives [that] sometimes involved a human circle of 20 to 30 kilometers in diameter... These meetings were most often held close to territorial boundaries so as to avoid trespass and therefore further conflict. (Lourandos 1997, p. 65)

Nor were the aboriginal Australians atypical in this respect. Many groups of modern foragers meet in seasonal groupings of quite large aggregations of bands, constituting sometimes many thousands of individuals (Kelly 1995, Binford 2001). Exogamy also promoted contacts with strangers. The average distance between the birthplaces of husbands and wives among hunter-gatherers in tropical areas reported in MacDonald and Hewlett (1999) is 40 kilometers, and much greater for some hunter-gatherers, such as the !Kung (70 kilometers) and Arctic peoples (Fix 1999). Among the ("pure") !Kung groups studied by Harpending and Jenkins (1974) only 58% of the parents of the fertile adult members of the population were born in the same group as their children. These high levels of mobility, also noted in other southern African groups, such as the Hadza (Woodburn 1982), arise in part from the far-flung coinsurance networks, which among the !Kung may include partnerships well over 200 kilometers distant. For example, describing the likely historical patterns of the Dobe !Kung, Howell (2000) writes:

> The pattern of frequent long and short distance migrations, utilizing widespread kinship ties, must be an old pattern, with living groups forming and dissolving, coalescing and splitting to adjust group size to the resources available. While no or few individuals may ever have covered the whole !Kung range during a lifetime, nearly every individual can be expected to travel long distances, living in a number of places and encountering a wide range of other !Kung, even if always in relatively small groups. (p. 11)

Arizona State anthropologist Kim Hill reports (in a personal communication) extensive social interactions among the pre-contact Aché in Paraguay, amounting to several hundred adult contacts over a decade.

In these environments those who failed to distinguish between long-term and short-term or one-shot interactions would be at a significant fitness disadvantage. It seems safe to conclude that all but the most isolated forager groups typically engaged in rela-tionships, both beneficial and hostile, with other groups.

Turning to evidence on cataclysmic demographic events, frequent catastrophic mor-tality due to conflicts, environmental challenges and other causes is the most plausi-ble way to reconcile two pieces of solid evidence about hunter-gatherer demography (Hill and Hurtado 1996). First, human population grew extraordinarily slowly or not at all for the 100,000 years prior to 20,000 years before the present, with estimated growth rates ranging from 0.002% per annum in the earlier period to 0.1% in the later (Bocquet-Appel et al. 2005). Second, population models and data on hunter-gatherer demographics show that they are capable of growth rates in excess of 2% per annum (Birdsell 1957, Hassan 1980, Johansson and Horowitz 1986). The forest Aché, for ex-ample, grew at 2% per annum over the four decades prior to contact (Hill and Hurtado 1996). The two facts—slow long-run growth in total population and high potential growth—are easily reconciled if population crashes were frequent.

Volatile climate must have contributed. Evidence of Late Pleistocene temperature variability based on Greenland ice cores is presented in Figure 6.1. Deep sea cores in the western Mediterranean and other data suggest that the climate variability shown in the figure was a general northern hemisphere phenomenon (Martrat et al. 2004). Even these data (smoothed to 50-year averages to reduce measurement error) indicate that changes in mean temperature as great as eight degrees (C) occurred over time spans as short as two centuries. By way of comparison, the Little Ice Age that devastated parts of early modern Europe experienced a fall in average temperatures of one or two degrees, and the dramatic warming of the last century raised average temperatures by one degree, comparing the unprecedentedly hot 1990s with a century earlier (Mann et al. 1998, McManus et al. 1999).

The high levels of mortality and frequent population crashes and dispersals that probably characterized the Late Pleistocene are unfavorable to the evolution of recip-rocal altruism, even in dyads. Mortality hazard rates of contemporary foragers place an upper limit on the time discount factor of 0.98, even in the absence of myopia, weak-ness of will, and the like (Gurven and Kaplan 2007). The discount factor under these assumptions is one minus the probability of mortality. This purely demographic source of discounting raises doubts about results from repeated game theory that require the discount factor to be arbitrarily close to unity. If older members of the group are criti-cal to the success of cooperation, then the maximal discount factor will be considerably lower.

Moreover, due to frequent group conflicts and extraordinary climatic instability, group longevity was also probably quite limited, so that even if members of a group survived, they were unlikely to remain together over very long periods. Of 14 groups studied in Papua New Guinea over a 50 year period by Soltis et al. (1995), 5 ceased to exist. The expected duration of both the Yanomamo villages reported in Smouse et al. (1981) and of the Gainj groups reported in Long et al. (1987) is about three generations. It is unlikely that groups survived longer than this under the turbulent climatic conditions of the Late Pleistocene.

The only small scale society on which we have adequate long term demographic records, the people of the isolated South Atlantic island Tristan da Cunha, provide a dramatic example (Roberts 1971). Three population crashes occurred in the course of a

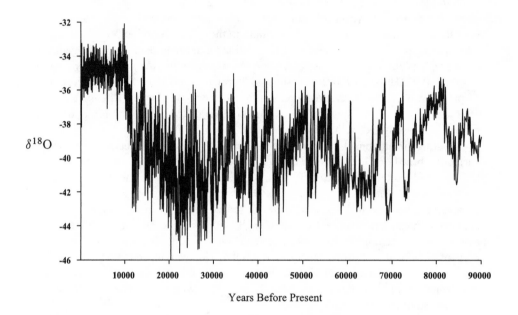

Figure 6.1. Pleistocene temperature variations. Shown are measures of $\delta^{18}O$ taken from Greenland ice cores (from http://www.glaciology.gfy.ku.dk/ngrip/index_eng.htm and described in North Greenland Ice Core Project Members (2004)). Surface temperature scales approximately linearly with the $\delta^{18}O$ signal shown in the figure. Differences in temperature (Centigrade) are about 1.2 times the difference in the signal shown the figure (Johnsen et al. 1992).

century and a half. The first was a conflict-induced fission that resulted in the departure of more than half the population while the second, a seafaring accident, killed all but four of the island's male population. The final crash occurred with the dispersal of the entire population in 1961 due to an eruption of the island's volcano.

Summing up a pattern of demographic instability likely to have been faced by the foraging bands of the Late Pleistocene, Gajdusek (1964) wrote:

> Migrations, murders and suicides, warfare, and massacres, splitting and fragmentation of communities and bands, or amalgamations and sudden mergers of groups, sudden social changes in mating practices and prohibitions and such natural accidents and catastrophes as earthquakes, floods, typhoons, volcanic eruptions, droughts, famines, and plagues all

have a major influence in determining the genetic composition of small groups. (p. 121)

These are hardly conditions under which reciprocal altruism could be expected to flourish (Gintis 2000). Genetic evidence is consistent with this view.

6.2 Genetic Evidence

The extent of genetic differentiation among groups of human foragers is the result of mating practices, selection pressures, reproductive inequalities, migratory patterns, group size, the process of group fission and fusion, and other aspects of population dynamics over the very long run. While contemporary foraging populations are not pristine replicas of ancestral human groups, genetic evidence on foragers nonetheless provides a rare lens with which to study the prehistory of human social and demographic structure. Genetic material collected from foraging populations over the past half-century allows estimates of the degree of genetic distance between groups on scales ranging from elementary foraging bands to meta-populations composed of many ethno-linguistic units. These estimates, taken from Bowles (2006), augmented by more recent data appear in Table 6.1.

Many foraging populations are highly differentiated. Some geographically adjacent groups are as different genetically from one another as are the major ancestral groups of the world. Foraging populations do not appear to be less differentiated genetically than horticultural and more technologically advanced small-scale populations. But our joint work with Stefany Moreno Gamez and Jon Wilkins of the Santa Fe Institute indicates that if ancestral groups indeed had been small and closed, the degree of differentiation among groups predicted by the standard model of equilibrium differentiation would be substantially greater than what we observe (Moreno Gamez et al. 2011). The genetic data thus are more consistent with ancestral groups being of considerable size and with ever-changing composition.

To see how genetic information can provide clues about demographic structure, a little background in population genetics is needed. Equilibrium genetic differentiation among groups balances the effects of small group size and the resulting genetic drift that tends to enhance differentiation on the one hand and between-group migration, tending to reduce it on the other. The equilibrium level of differentiation, denoted F_{ST}^*, is that at which these two effects are exactly offsetting, leading to long-run constancy of the F_{ST} in the absence of exogenous changes in the underlying data. For autosomal genetic markers, assuming that the alleles in question are not subject to selection or mutation and letting m_e and N_e be measures respectively of the rate of migration among groups and group size, we have the following approximation for small m_e (Wright 1935):

$$F_{ST}^* = \frac{1}{1 + 4m_e N_e}. \tag{6.1}$$

The migration and group size terms in the denominator are based on an idealized demographic structure in which group size is constant, the number of expected number of progeny is equal among males and females (who are also equal in number) and migration conforms to the random island model in which migrants are randomly assigned

Population	Index	Value
Indigenous circumpolar Eurasian populations	F_{DT}	0.076
Native Siberian populations	F_{DT}	0.170
Native Siberian populations	F_{DG}	0.114
!Kung demes (southern Africa)	F_{DG}	0.007
Southern African groups	F_{GT}	0.075
Southern African demes (from 18 groups)	F_{DT}	0.081
Aboriginal Australians (14 groups)	F_{GT}	0.042
Kaiadilt-Lardiil groups (Australia)	F_{DT}	0.081
Asmat-Mappi (lowland western New Guinea)	F_{DT}	0.056
Mbuti (Central Africa)-San (southern Africa)	F_{GT}	0.149
Aka (between "villages" in the same group)	F_{DG}	0.042
Aka (between groups)	F_{GT}	0.057
Aka (between "villages" in all groups)	F_{DT}	0.097
Pygmy (9 groups)	F_{DT}	0.052
Pygmy (4 Baka language demes)	F_{DG}	0.061
Aboriginal Australians (10 Arnhem and northern groups)	F_{DT}	0.136
Ainu-Eskimo (Japan-Alaska)	F_{GT}	0.109
Ainu-Chukchi (Japan-eastern Siberia)	F_{GT}	0.075
Eskimo-Chukchi (Alaska-eastern Siberia)	F_{GT}	0.047

Table 6.1. Genetic differentiation among hunter-gatherer populations. Note: F_{DG} measures genetic differentiation among demes (D) in the same etho-linguistic group (G), while F_{GT}, and F_{DT} respectively measure differentiation among groups and demes in a meta-population (T). The mean value is 0.080 (0.041) and the median is 0.075. If within-ethno-linguistic unit estimates (F_{DG}) are excluded, the remaining 15 estimates have a mean of 0.087 (0.038) and a median of 0.076. The first 15 rows are from Bowles (2006). The next two (Pygmy) are from Verdu (2009), the next (Arnhem and northern) are from Walsh et al. (2007), and the final three rows are from Cavalli-Sforza et al. (1994). The Pygmy and Australian data are based on hypervariable microsatellite loci corrected to be comparable with the remainder of the table. These data and the corrections are described in a memo at www.santafe.edu/bowles. F_{ST} estimates between putative ancestral genetic clusters of African hunter-gathers (rather than observed population groups) yield much higher values (Henn et al. 2011).

to groups independent of spatial or other proximity. *Variance effective group size (N_e)* is the number of individuals in a single generation that would result in the same amount of genetic differentiation among groups due to genetic drift, as would occur among the empirical groups under study, given the deviations from the idealized demographic assumptions that are observed in their actual demographic structure. Because by comparison to more realistic assumptions, the idealized demographic structure minimizes the drift-induced genetic differentiation among group, the variance effective group size is less than the observed (so called *census*) size. The *effective migration rate (m_e)* is the fraction of individuals who migrate in the random island model that would have the same effect on between group genetic differentiation as would the observed (nonrandom) patterns of migration among the groups under study. Because nonrandom aspects of observed migration patterns deviate from the random island model in ways that reduce the homogenizing effects of migration, the effective migration rat is less than the observed migration rate.

Under the idealized assumptions above, the observed measures of differentiation are consistent with equilibrium predictions for groups of modest size and migration rates. But it is unlikely that the assumptions underlying equation 6.1 obtained during the Pleistocene. No human societies exhibit these idealized features and the level of genetic differentiation predicted for observed demographic structures is greater than under idealized conditions. Reproductive skew, volatile population dynamics of the type documented above, including rare group extinctions, lineage-based group fission, and nonrandom migration, all must have been common during the Late Pleistocene. Each of these violations of the assumptions of the Wright model reduces either the effective group size or the effective migration rate and thus, from equation (6.1), contributes to elevated equilibrium genetic differentiation among groups. Using data on recent foraging populations to take account of these effects (Moreno Gamez et al. 2011), we found that predictions from the equilibrium model are consistent with the data in Table 6.1 only if group size and migration are substantial, so that the number of migrants per year could have to be double or perhaps even triple the number implied by the calculation based on Wrights idealized assumptions in the previous paragraph. Thus, if observed genetic differentiation reflects a population equilibrium, the data are inconsistent with the common view that our ancestors lived in closed worlds in which social interactions were confined to a small number of relatives or lifelong close associates.

More detailed studies suggest a similar conclusion. Based on the pattern of genetic differentiation among aboriginal Australian groups, for example, Keats (1977) concludes that "local groups traveled large distances and often came into contact with one another for the purposes of trade, which sometimes included exchange of people from each group" (1977, p. 327). Inferences from these genetic data are thus consistent with evidence of both long-distance exchange (McBrearty and Brooks 2000) and hostile conflict (Bowles 2009a) among ancestral groups, and among recent foragers thought to be plausible models of ancestral humans, significant levels of long-distance exchange and migration, occasional large scale seasonal agglomerations, and far-flung coinsurance partnerships (Lourandos 1997, Wiessner 2002, Marlowe 2005).

These data thus are consistent with the above evidence that ancestral conditions were not favorable for the evolution of group-level cooperation by means of reciprocal altruism. The genetic data also support a similarly negative judgment for the adequacy of the kin-based selection model. Members of groups were not very closely related.

Though helping siblings and other close family members would have been supported for plausible benefit-cost ratios, relatedness within typical foraging bands would not support cooperation among band members generally unless the benefit-cost ratio were extraordinarily high. Consider a concrete example of an exceptionally highly related band (of just seven adult members) with two parents and their two sons and wives and one unrelated "outsider." If the spouses are unrelated, the average pairwise degree of genetic relatedness in this group is 0.12. Hamilton's rule (4.1) shows that kin altruism would be supported among group members only if the benefit-cost ratio were to exceed 8 (i.e., the inverse of 0.12).

Moreover, the level of within-group relatedness in this example is far from typical. A survey of band composition in 32 populations of hunter-gatherers (Hill et al. 2010) shows that many members of a band share no recent common ancestor and are related only through marriage. The authors found that among a total of 19,634 within-band pairs of adults in 58 precontact bands of Aché (in Paraguay) the genetic relatedness was $r = 0.054$. The implication is that for altruism toward randomly paired band members to proliferate by Hamilton's rule the benefits would have to be 20 times the costs. The estimates of the fraction of the total genetic variance that is between demes reported in Table 6.1 suggests an average degree of relatedness in demes that would preclude the evolution of altruistic behaviors unless the benefits were an order of magnitude greater than the costs. The genetic data thus make it unlikely that a predisposition of family members to cooperate explains group-level common projects such as hunting, predation and defense, except in cases of extraordinarily high ratios of benefits to costs.

These data also cast further doubt on any explanation relying solely on reciprocal altruism. The reason is that the group census size that we estimated with Moreno Gamez and Wilkins from the observed F_{ST}'s implies a number of adult decision makers that is an order of magnitude larger than the maximum group size for which repeated interactions supported high levels of cooperation in the presence of plausible error rates in the simulations reported in Figures 4.6. The "typical" group census size that we calculated directly in §6.1, namely 77, bears the same conclusion.

Of course the same data present a challenge to any model of the evolution of altruistic cooperation based on positive genetic assortment, including multi-level selection models. In the next chapter, we will see that between-group competition may have provided the necessary extraordinary benefits of group-level cooperation. The main reason why this is so is that conflict among hunter-gatherer groups was common and exceptionally lethal.

6.3   Prehistoric Warfare

Notwithstanding a number of insightful studies (LeBlanc 2003, Burch 2005, Gat 2006), lethal intergroup conflict among hunter-gatherers during the Late Pleistocene and early Holocene remains a controversial and, like the question of altruism itself, ideologically freighted subject, with little agreement on either its extent or its consequences (Keeley 1996, Ferguson 1997).

Among the empirical challenges are the lack of written accounts, the difficulty in making inferences from ethnographic hunter-gatherers about conditions before the domestication of plants and animals and the emergence of states, and the fact that most foragers made little use of fortifications and killed each other with the same weapons that they used to hunt other animals, thus leaving few distinctive archaeological traces other than skeletal remains.

The virtual absence of archaeological evidence of persistent economic and political differentiation between families prior to about 24,000 years ago indicates that the most informative data for understanding Late Pleistocene and early Holocene humans

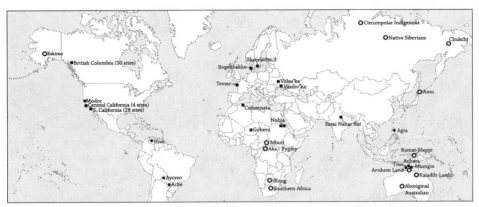

Figure 6.2. Between-group differences. Data sources for archaeological (▪) and ethnographic (●) evidence on warfare and genetic (black open dots) data on between-group differences.

pertain to hunting and gathering populations without formal political structures (chiefs, big men, or states). We exclude populations making substantial use of domesticated plants and animals, namely pastoral, horticultural, agricultural or equestrian hunting populations. As hunter-gatherer populations occupying resource-rich areas in the Late Pleistocene and early Holocene were probably sedentary (at least seasonally), we have included wars involving settled as well as purely mobile populations.

By "wars" we mean events in which coalitions of members of a group seek to inflict bodily harm on one or more members of another group. The term is not ideal for the ambushes, revenge murders, and other kinds of hostilities likely to have occurred between ancestral groups of humans. Most hostile intergroup contact among hunter-gatherers was probably ongoing or intermittent, with occasional casualties, more akin to boundary conflicts among chimpanzees (Manson and Wrangham 1991) than to modern warfare. However "pitched battles" did occur among foragers, as in the conflict between two coalitions of aboriginal Australians involving around 700 combatants (Lourandos 1997).

Using these definitions and selection criteria, we studied all available archaeological and ethnographic sources that present, or are cited as presenting, relevant data (Table 6.2). Of these 34 sources, 14 were found to present data that were unrepresentative (for example, when warfare was primarily with modern agricultural populations), unreliable, or inadequate. In three cases re-estimation of the critical information was possible. Skeletal evidence from sites with fewer than 10 individuals was also excluded. Possible biases in this data set are discussed below. The 8 ethnographic and 15 archaeological sources included both yield results consistent with the view that prehistoric warfare was frequent and lethal, but somewhat less so than estimates based on data in the standard source for these estimates (Keeley 1996). The populations studied appear in Figure 6.2. Details and additional caveats and the data to follow appear in Bowles (2009b).

As with all archaeological data, establishing that the sites that were studied are representative of Late Pleistocene and early Holocene conditions is difficult. Most of the

	Weighted Mean	Arithmetic Mean	Median
Archaeological	0.12	0.14	0.12
Ethnographic	0.16	0.14	0.13–0.15
All	0.14	0.14	0.12

Table 6.2. Fraction of total mortality due to warfare (δ): summary statistics. Note: Complete sources, methods and other details for this and Table 6.3 are in Bowles (2009a) and Bowles (2009b). Weights are the square root of the total number of deaths.

archaeological data are based on evidence of violent death such as spear points embedded in bones. As this evidence comes from burials, it is almost certainly not representative in one respect: simple disposal of the dead (rather than burial) appears to be typical of the archetypal so-called immediate return foraging group (Woodburn 1982). There may be more than accidental bias in the burials studied for signs of violence, given that evidence of violent deaths may be deemed more interesting or worthy of publication than the absence of such evidence. Evidence on given individuals is also incomplete, leading to the opposite bias. Most skeletal remains are never found, and those that are range from intact to fragmentary or poorly preserved, often comprising just a few of the 100 or so bones in an adult human, setting aside the small bones of the hands and feet. The remains of 2185 prehistoric people of present-day California are accessible to researchers in a museum collection that totals only 12,044 bones, excluding hands and feet; more than 90% of the individuals' bones are absent (Tenny 1990).

Moreover, while some osteological evidence is indicative of ongoing intergroup violence (simultaneous burials, severed limbs and other evidence of trophy taking, for example), one cannot always distinguish between deaths due to intergroup violence and those occurring within groups. Other biases may lead to underestimates. Many deaths in warfare do not leave projectile points embedded in bone or the other traces of violent death: "an analysis that included only projectile points embedded in bone would miss over half of the projectiles... and 75% of what was in all probability the actual number of projectile wounds" (Lambert 1997). Studies of arrow wounds treated by U.S. Army surgeons during the Indian Wars found that less than a third of the arrows struck bone (Milner 2005) and that 61% of fatal arrow wounds were to the abdomen (Bill 1862). Finally, fatalities during combat may fall far short of the total effect of warfare when account is taken of the mortality and reduced reproductive success occasioned by the displacement of the surviving losers. Table 6.3 gives the resulting estimates.

Most ethnographic studies of premodern war have concerned populations whose unusually bellicose relations among groups may not reflect conditions of Late Pleistocene hunter-gatherers: horticultural peoples in the highlands of Papua New Guinea and parts of lowland South America, or equestrian hunters or sedentary horticulturalists in North America. Among non-equestrian foragers, detailed accounts provide examples of intergroup conflict of exceptional brutality among Aboriginal Australians, Eskimos and other groups (Morgan 1979[1852], Melbye and Fairgrieve 1994, Burch 2005), but most do not allow quantitative estimates of the resulting mortality. In other groups war is entirely absent from the ethnographic record, but in some of these cases, like the

Site	Years BP	Author (Date)	δ
British Columbia (30 sites)	5500–334	Cybulski (1994)	0.23
Nubia (site 117)	14–12,000	Wendorf (1968)	0.46
Nubia (near site 117)	14-12,000	Wendorf (1968)	0.03
Vasiliv'ka III, Ukraine	11,000	Telegin (1961)	0.21
Volos'ke, Ukraine	"Epipalaeolithic"	Danilenko (1955)	0.22
California (28 sites)	5500–628	Lambert (1997)	0.06
Central California	3500–500	Moratto (1984)	0.05
Sweden (Skateholm I)	6100	Price (1985)	0.07
Central California	2415–1773	Andrushko et al. (2005)	0.08
Sarai Nahar Rai, N India	3140–2854	Sharma (1973)	0.30
Central California (2 sites)	2240–238	Jurmain (2001)	0.04
Gobero, Niger	16,000–8200	Sereno et al. (2008)	0.00
Calumnata, Algeria	8300–7300	Chamla et al. (1970)	0.04
Ilee Teviec, France	6600	Newall et al. (1979)	0.12
Bogebakken, Denmark	6300–5800	Newall et al. (1979)	0.12

Table 6.3. Archaeological evidence on δ, the fraction of adult mortality due to warfare. Note: Before present (BP) indicates before 2008 (Bowles 2009a).

Population, Region	Dates	Author (Date)	δ
Aché, eastern Paraguay[a]	precontact (1970)	Hill and Hurtado (1996)	0.30
Hiwi, Venezuela-Colombia[a]	precontact (1960)	Hill et al. (2007)	0.17
Murngin, NE Australia[ab]	1910–1930	Warner (1931)	0.21
Ayoreo, Bolivia-Paraguay[c]	1920–1979	Bugos (1985)	0.15
Tiwi, N. Australia[c]	1893–1903	Pilling (1968)	0.10
Modoc, N. California[d]	"Aboriginal times"	Ray (1963)	0.13
Casiguran Agta, Philippines[a]	1936–1950	Headland (1989)	0.05
Anbara, N. Australia[abe]	1940–1960	Hiatt (1965)	0.04

Table 6.4. Ethnographic evidence on the fraction (δ) of adult mortality due to warfare. Notes: [a]indicates that the group were foragers; [b]maritime; [c]seasonal forager-horticulturalists; [d]sedentary hunter-gatherers; [e]recently settled. Source: Bowles 2009a, 2009b.

!Kung and other southern African groups this may be the result of recent state interventions (Schapera 1930, Campbell 1986). For eight populations ethnographic studies allow estimates of the deaths due to warfare as a fraction of total mortality (summarized in Table 6.4). As in the case of archaeological studies, selection bias may lead to an exaggeration of the extent of warfare mortality. Moreover, some populations are not entirely representative of foragers during the Late Pleistocene due to the impact of non-hunter-gatherer influences.

The mortality data summarized in Table 6.2 are consistent with what is known about the Late Pleistocene from more indirect data, for example, as we have seen, reconciling the capacity of forager populations to expand rapidly coupled with the virtual absence of population growth until the very end of the Pleistocene. Further, the extraordinary volatility of climate during the Late Pleistocene must have resulted in natural disasters and periodic resource scarcities, known strong predictors of group conflict among hunter-gatherers in the historical record (Ember and Ember 1992), and undoubtedly forced long-distance migrations and occasioned frequent encounters between groups having no established political relations. In light of the climate record Boehm (2000, p. 19) writes that:

> toward the end of the Pleistocene as anatomically modern humans began to emerge, group extinction rates could have risen dramatically as needy bands of well-armed hunters, strangers lacking established patterns of political interaction frequently collided, either locally or in the course of long distance migration.

A statistical analysis of ethnographic evidence is consistent with Boehm's conjecture. Ember and Ember (1992) conclude that a "history of unpredictable natural disasters strongly predicts more war... people, particularly in non-state societies, may try to protect themselves against future disasters by going to war to take resources from enemies."

The impact of the climate variation evident in Figure 6.1 is also suggested in the archaeological record. Commenting on a burial from 12,000 to 14,000 years ago in which almost half of the skeletons indicated a violent death, Wendorf (1968) explained:

> Population pressures may have become too great with the deterioration of Late Pleistocene climate and the effects which this had on the herds of large savanna type animals which were the primary source of food at this time... a few localities which were particularly favorable for fishing would have been repeatedly fought over as sources of food became increasingly scarce. (p. 993)

Archaeological evidence on southern Californian maritime hunter-gatherers over a 7000-year period indicates that violent deaths occurred disproportionately during periods of climatic adversity and resource stress (Lambert 1997).

6.4   The Foundations of Social Order

Social interactions within ancestral groups, we believe, exhibited an interplay of conflict and cooperation not dissimilar from between-group interactions. A difference, however, is that aggression within groups often served to sustain cooperation. The alacrity with which experimental subjects punish defectors and the extent to which people in modern natural settings will go in order to shun, ridicule, humiliate and harm those who violate social norms have their counterparts in small-scale societies. We think that, like intergroup warfare, these forms of peer punishment are both an exemplar of altruistic cooperation and one of the practices that among our ancestors curbed self-aggrandizement and provided a favorable environment for the evolution of other

cooperative behaviors. In subsequent chapters we will explain how warlike predispositions (Chapter 8) and the willingness to bear costs to punish defectors in one's own
group (Chapter 9) could have proliferated in the social and ecological environment of
the Late Pleistocene and early Holocene. But to do this we must, as in the case of
warfare, know the nature of the behaviors in question.

Balikci (1970) reports that among the Netsilik, an isolated hunting people on the
Arctic coast,

> there is a general rule…according to which all able bodied men should
> contribute to hunting, and the returns of the hunt should be shared accord-
> ing to established custom. Any activity in exception to this rule was bound
> to provoke criticism, various forms of conflict, and frequently social os-
> tracism. Lazy hunters were barely tolerated by the community. They were
> the objects of back biting and ostracism until the opportunity came for an
> open quarrel. Stingy men…were treated similarly. (pp. 176-177)

In like fashion, Richard Lee (1979) describes the moral world of the !Kung in
southern Africa:

> The most serious accusations one !Kung can level against another are the
> charge of stinginess and the charge of arrogance. To be stingy, or far-
> hearted, is to hoard one's goods jealously and secretively, guarding them
> "like a hyena." The corrective for this is to make the hoarder give "till it
> hurts"; that is to make him give generously and without stint until everyone
> can see that he is truly cleaned out. In order to ensure compliance with
> this cardinal rule the !Kung browbeat each other constantly to be more
> generous and not to hoard. (p. 458)

Deriving quantitative generalizations from these accounts is difficult. Most of the
lethal violence documented by Lee concerns such problems as adultery, not stinginess.
And in contrast to the reports of Lee and Balikci, Endicott (1988, p. 118) reports the
horror expressed by a Batek informant at the thought of exiling a member whose laziness had caused some resentment.

But there is no reason to doubt the thrust of their observations, that those who
violate a social norm by hoarding or slacking would be in for a rough time. Christopher
Boehm's (2011) survey of social control methods in what he calls "Pleistocene-style"
hunter-gatherer populations shows just how rough it can get. Among the 300 or so
forager societies described in ethnographies, he selected those likely to match the social
and environmental conditions of Late Pleistocene humans. This involved eliminating
mounted hunters, bands dependent on religious missions or that had extensive trade
with farmers, or had engaged for centuries in the fur trade, or that made significant use
of stored food. He then scoured all available accounts for evidence of transgressions of
social norms, and how they were addressed in these small groups lacking both police
and courts of law. Stealing and murder were condemned in all of the societies, and
"failure to share" was considered a violation of a norm in 43 of the 53 societies studied,
the same number that condemned "beating someone." "Bullying" was frowned on in
34 of the societies. In most societies, the common response to these transgressions was

distancing, shunning, ridicule, shaming and gossip. In 20 of the societies expulsion from the group occurred, and in a striking 34 of the populations, assassination of the culprit by the entire group was practiced. Boehm's conclusion: "yesterday's hunter-gatherers were well equipped to identify free-riders, suppress their behavior, and—if they couldn't intimidate them enough to keep them under fairly good control—get rid of them."

The only quantitative investigation of social order in a pre-state society of which we are aware is a remarkable study by Polly Wiessner (2005). During 1974 and 1996/7, she recorded 308 three- to four-hour time blocks of conversations among the Ju/'hoansi (!Kung) of the Dobe-/Kae/kae area in northwest Botswana. In the 1970's, the Ju/'hoansi obtained virtually all of their subsistence through hunting and gathering. By the 1990s their society had been transformed, with government rations, wages, the sale of crafts, and old age pensions occupying a substantial role in their subsistence. Of the conversations studied, 56% included criticism of one or more members of the group including harsh criticism in two fifths of the cases and ridicule and mild forms of expression of displeasure in a fifth of the cases. The remaining two fifths of the cases were explicit but not harsh criticism. Only 7% of the conversations included praise. Frequently, targeted behaviors included stinginess, greed or laziness, including reclusive behavior associated with failure to share, big-shot behavior, failure to honor kin obligations, and drunkenness. The intent of criticism was behavior modification. In 69% of the cases the target was either present or within earshot. In 21% of the cases the target was absent but his close relatives were present. The remaining cases involved coalition building for punishment at a later date.

Wiessner recounts one of these episodes: "In 1974 a highly respected leader and one of the few cattle owners was accused of big-shot behavior and failure to share meat. After suffering extensive criticism in silence, he noted that one of his cows was behaving dangerously, slaughtered it, and distributed the meat widely." Another "big-shot" was initially subjected to ridicule, but when this proved ineffective, harsh criticism followed along with a refusal to share meat with the offender, who eventually left the group for a period. A disruptive woman was ostracized from the group and subsequently died, after which her family was welcomed back into good standing. In one case criticism aimed at expulsion of a segment of the group led to its relocation at a new camp nine kilometers distant, after which friendly relations were resumed.

The content and targeting of these conversations did not differ between the 1970s and 1990s. Men and women initiated criticism about equally, but men were overwhelmingly the targets of criticism because they more frequently engaged in big-shot or disruptive behaviors. High-status ("strong") group members engaged in more criticism than others, and were as likely to be targeted as "weak" members. The most respected figure in the camp (the *n!ore kxao*) tended to refrain from criticism, thereby facilitating reconciliation, so as to avoid the loss of a group member.

Four aspects of social order among the Ju/'hoansi are important in what follows. First, though Wiessner stresses the many ways that the Ju/'hoansi reduce the costs of maintaining order, those engaging in norm enforcement bore costs in the form of disrupted patterns of sharing. In 3% of the cases violent brawls resulted. Second, most of the criticisms were carried out by coalitions (three or more persons) rather than individuals, and this was true in virtually all of the cases where the target had threatened community stability or harmony. As a result, the costs of engaging in punishment of norm transgressors was relatively low as long as the number of altruistic punishers was sufficiently great. In Chapter 9 we will explain how this kind of coalitional punishment of transgressors may have evolved.

Third, the punishment of those who refrained from punishing was entirely absent: "I have not observed any second order punishment in all of my years working with the Ju/'hoansi." Fourth, Wiessner finds no evidence that punishing norm transgressors is a signal of otherwise unobservable quality as a mate, coalition partner, or competitor. Single reproductive-age individuals are the least likely to punish, contrary to the predictions of the signaling model. Moreover, while mediation ability is highly valued, those who punished frequently or harshly were not sought out as coalition partners but were considered to be *tchi n!ai*, "angry, sharp or biting things," and were told to desist.

The other study of the maintenance of order in a pre-state society that has guided our attempts to model the evolution of cooperation concerns ostracism among the Pathan Hill tribes, an acephalous, egalitarian kinship-based people in Afghanistan. Niloufer Mahdi (1986) writes:

> The most striking use of ostracism among the Pathans is the rejection by the tribe or clan of one of its members whose behavior might lead to a feud. [O]stracism functions... to deter behavior that violates customary legal norms, to punish specific acts that are culturally defined as improper, and to unify the primary reference group on which individuals depend for protection and economic support. (p. 295)

The Pathans "do not recognize permanently established or permanently functioning authority either in the central government or at any level of the tribal structure." Rather, social order is sustained by peer punishment. Ostracism is commonly the fate of those who have violated the *Pukhtunwali* (Code of the Pathans).

> The obligation to the Code is not secured in the first instance by any coercive force. Ask any Pathan why he upholds *Pukhtunwali* and the answer will be because of *izzat* (honor). Obedience to *Pukhtunwali* is freely given. (p. 297)

Similarly, ostracizing those who have violated the Code "becomes the obligation of every Pathan, acting individually or as part of a relevant tribal segment." Punishment of those who violate social norms is itself a norm.

Ostracism, writes Mahdi, may include "avoidance, exclusion from social participation, shunning or derision" (p. 295). If a man has to be avoided, he may not be considered for a matrimonial alliance or invited to participate in a *Jirga* (Council of Elders)." Notably, consistent with what we observed in some experiments described in Chapter 3, the aim of ostracism seems to be punishment, not behavior modification:

> the unique expression of overt verbal disapproval that is practiced is *paighor* (insult or taunt). Its main purpose is to shame the person. It is most commonly applied in those cases where a man has been perceived to have failed in valor or in the discharge of an obligation of honor. *Paighor* is not given with the conscious aim of prompting its object to action, nor

is it calculated to reform. However very often it has precisely that effect. (p. 303)

As in Boehm's survey (1993), punishment may take the lethal forms, such a *badal* (revenge killing) or physical expulsion. As a consequence,

> When a Pathan is exiled from his group his situation becomes untenable.
> He is vulnerable not only to his *dushman* (the one who has targeted him),
> but can be victimized by anyone, without fear of *badal*. (p. 301)

The fact that *badal* applies equally to all members of one's kin group provides strong incentives for discipline to be applied within families, therefore reducing the frequency of more costly between-kin group feuding, as, for instance, in the "community responsibility" model of contract enforcement among early modern European craftsmen (Greif 2002).

As among the !Kung, the egalitarianism of the Pathan peoples is essential to the process of peer punishment, as is the ongoing nature of social interaction:

> neither economic or social status deflects its course...if a man seeking *badal* is weak *vis a vis* his *dushman* he will pass on his obligation to his sons and they in turn to their sons. And if a man is well protected enough to escape *badal* himself, it is extremely doubtful that the protection can be extended to his kin or to successive generations, who would constitute legitimate targets of *badal*. (Mahdi 1986, p. 298)

Like the Ju/'hoansi, the Pathans attempted to minimize the costs of punishment. "To mitigate the disadvantages of *badal*, *Pukhtunwali* makes provision for mediation through a *Jirga* when it appears that honor has been satisfied and it is an opportune time to halt the cycle of violence....Certain conditions such as monetary compensation may be imposed to achieve a balance in the redress of grievances" Mahdi (1986, p. 299).

6.5   The Crucible of Cooperation

It has been conventional since Thomas Hobbes' *Leviathan* to attribute the maintenance of social order to states. But for at least 95% of the time that biologically modern humans have existed, our ancestors somehow fashioned a system of governance that without the assistance of governments avoided the chaos of the Hobbesian state of nature sufficiently to become by far the most enduring of social orders ever. The genetic, archaeological, ethnographic, and demographic data make it quite clear that they did not accomplish this by limiting human interactions to a few close genetic relatives. Nor can the oft-repeated nature of their interactions explain this remarkable accomplishment. Rather we will show in the next three chapters that a particular form of altruism, often hostile toward outsiders and punishing toward insiders who violate norms, coevolved with a set of institutions—sharing food and making war are examples—that at once protected a group's altruistic members and made group-level cooperation the *sine qua non* of survival.

7

The Coevolution of Institutions and Behaviors

> A population can be very successful in spite of a surprising diversion of time and energy into aggressive displays, squabbling and outright fights. The examples range from bumble bees to European nations.
>
> William Hamilton, *The Innate Social Aptitudes of Man* (1975)

Few students of human social dynamics doubt that nations, firms, bands, and other groups are subject to selective pressures. The emergence and diffusion of the centralized, tax-collecting and arms-bearing national state as a form of territorial governance during the past half millennium is an example. The national state became the dominant form of governance because it won wars and induced preemptive emulation among those threatened with military subjugation (Tilly 1975, Bowles and Gintis 1984, Bowles 2004). Similar processes of group competition may explain the evolutionary success of other social arrangements, markets, monogamy, private property, worshiping supernatural beings, social ranking, and sharing the necessities of life among non-kin, for example. These have been ubiquitous over long periods of human history and have emerged and persisted in highly varied environments. Talcott Parsons (1964) termed these arrangements *evolutionary universals*, the most likely explanation of which is that societies adopting them prevailed in competition with other groups. Frederich Hayek (1988) referred to the markets and private property nexus, his "extended order," in a similar vein, attributing its success to cultural group selection.

Group competition and culturally transmitted group differences in institutional structure are central to our explanation of the evolution of cooperative behaviors among humans. We stress intergroup competition for empirical reasons: group conflict and the extinction or subjugation of loser populations have been among the most powerful forces contributing to the emergence, proliferation and persistence of novel human behaviors and institutions (Parsons 1964, Tilly 1981, Bowles 2009b).

Group differences in institutional structure persist over long periods of time due to the nature of institutions as conventions. A *convention* is a common practice that is adhered to by virtually all group members because the relevant behaviors, for example, sharing meat or not engaging in extra-pair copulations, are mutual best responses conditional on the expectation of similar behaviors by most others (Lewis 1969, Young 1995). We do not here model the reasons why the behavior prescribed by the institution is a mutual best response, but plausible accounts are not difficult to provide (Kaplan and Gurven 2005). Individuals who violate conventional norms, as we saw in the previous chapter, may face ostracism, shunning, and other costs (Boehm 1993). The conventional nature of institutions accounts for their long-term persistence and also their occasional rapid demise under the influence of shocks.

The inheritance of group-level institutions results from a cultural transmission process based on learned behaviors. While the tendency to copy behaviors that is common in a population independently of the associated payoffs is a strong influence on learning, we simplify by abstracting from this so-called conformist cultural transmission. Thus in our models when new members of the population mature or immigrate, they adhere to the existing institutions, not because of conformist learning but because this is a best response as long as most others do the same. The resulting behavioral uniformity in adherence to a group's institutions permits us to treat the institution as a group-level characteristic. By contrast, the group-beneficial individual traits in our model are replicated by a standard individual fitness-based mechanism in which altruists are at a selective disadvantage within their groups.

We study institutional evolution in ways analogous to the evolution of individual traits (§2.3). Just as the individuals in our model are the bearers of genes or socially learned individual behaviors, groups are the bearers of institutions, and a successful institution, like the European national state, produces many replicas, while unsuccessful ones pass out of existence without leaving a trace. Replication of institutions may take place when a successful group grows and subdivides, forming two groups, or when a group with unsuccessful institutions succumbs to a military, ecological or other challenge and its vacated site is occupied by colonists from a neighboring group.

The evolutionary mechanisms involved in this account are multi-level selection processes with the novel features that both genetically transmitted influences on individual behaviors and culturally transmitted group-level institutional characteristics are subject to selection. The model is thus an example of a gene-culture evolutionary process introduced in Chapter 2, with institutions playing the role of culturally transmitted niches, constructed environments affecting the processes of selection acting on genetically transmitted traits (Odling-Smee et al. 2003). We will show that these niches may allow a genetically transmitted altruistic predisposition to emerge when rare and then proliferate, and that the resulting altruistic behaviors contribute to the competitive survival of those groups in which these niches have been constructed.

Conventions such as sharing food or information with other group members, consensus decision making, and political practices that prevent dominant males from monopolizing reproduction are examples of *reproductive leveling*, a form of niche construction that, as we will see, contributes to the evolution of altruism. Individual differences in size, health, information, behavior, and other influences on access to scarce resources are typically reflected in differences in reproductive success. Among some other primates (Noe and Sluijter 1995, Pandit and van Schaik 2003) and especially among humans, reproductive leveling attenuates this relationship. Because altruists receive lower payoffs than other group members, they benefit from reproductive leveling because this attenuates the within-group selective pressures working against them.

Across a range of biological entities, from multi-cellular organisms to groups of ancestral humans, evolutionary processes are strongly influenced by reproductive leveling because it suppresses competition and reduces differences in behavior or other phenotypic variance within entities. In a paper studying slime mold (*Dictyostelium discoideum*) Steven Frank (1995) writes: "Evolutionary theory has not explained how competition among lower level units is suppressed in the formation of higher level evolutionary units" (p. 520), adding that "mutual policing and enforcement of reproductive fairness are also required for the evolution of increasing social complexity." John Maynard Smith and Eors Szathmáry note that many of what they term the "major transitions in evolution" share a common feature: "entities that were capable of independent replication before the transition can replicate as part of a larger whole after it" (1997, p. 6). As a result, the constituent entities making up the higher-level units come to share a common fate, with selection pressures working on the higher rather than the lower level units.

Christopher Boehm (1982) was one of the first to apply this idea to human evolution. Among ancestral foragers, he wrote, "group sanction emerged as the most powerful instrument for regulation of individually assertive behaviors, particularly those which obviously disrupted cooperation or disturbed social equilibrium needed for group stability." As a result "a 'political revolution' experienced by Paleolithic humans created the social conditions under which group selection could robustly support genes that were altruistic" (Boehm 1999). Relatedly, Irenaus Eibl-Eibesfeldt (1982) pointed to the importance of "indoctrinability to identify with values, to obey authority, and...ethical sharing" and thought that "through these bonding patterns, groups become so tightly knit that they could act as units of selection."

As a result, group institutions that regulate competition among members become themselves subject to selective pressures. For instance, food sharing beyond the family, which reduces within-group differences in material well-being, attenuates within-group selective pressures operating against individually costly but group-beneficial behaviors. Groups adopting leveling institutions like food sharing, as stressed by Boehm, thereby contribute to the proliferation of group-beneficial individual traits, including altruism, thus improving their advantage when faced with environmental crisis or competition from other groups.

The individual traits that we consider include warning others of danger, acquiring and sharing valuable information, participation in the defense of the group or in predation of others, or the punishment of those who fail to conform to these group-beneficial behaviors Thus, the formally altruistic (individually costly but in-group beneficial) traits that may proliferate under the influence of multi-level selection include behaviors that may be harmful to members of other groups. The processes modeled here might be best described, paraphrasing Laland et al. (2000, p. 224), as demonstrating the evolutionary success of selfish groups rather than generous individuals. Though our definition of altruism (§A1) refers only to in-group interactions, in our model individuals interact with out-group individuals as well: the model works because altruists confer fitness advantages on insiders, while inflicting fitness costs on outsiders. Our references to "group-beneficial" behaviors thus refer exclusively to in-group effects.

In the next chapter we will address three shortcomings of this simple formulation. First, here the altruists act on the basis of two quite different proximate motives, generosity toward fellow group members and hostility toward outsiders. There is no particular reason why this suite of motives and behaviors, which we term "parochial altruism," should be linked, so we will need to ask if this linkage itself could have evolved.

Second, ethnographic studies of hunter-gatherers as well as archaeological evidence make it clear that intergroup relations are not exclusively warlike. Recognizing the importance of mutually beneficial intergroup relations (for example, the coinsurance and trade relations we described in the previous chapter), in the next chapter we adopt a more realistic model in which group members not only inflict harm on their neighbors, but also may benefit from friendly relations with members of other groups

Finally, the frequency and intensity of mortal conflict between groups plays a central role in our explanation. The archaeological and ethnographic data on forager mortality in warfare reviewed in the previous chapter along with the other data which we will use here provide empirical support for our explanation. But we would also like an evolutionary explanation of why war was so frequent among early humans. We take up this task up in the next chapter.

Here we address two questions: what accounts for the evolution of individually costly and in-group beneficial forms of human sociality toward non-kin? And what accounts for the differential success of those common group-level institutional structures such as states, resource sharing, and monogamy which have emerged and proliferated repeatedly and in a wide variety of circumstances during the course of human history? The coevolutionary processes that we model and simulate are based on the idea that the two questions may be more convincingly resolved jointly than singly.

This chapter departs in four ways from the material presented thus far. The first, already mentioned, is our introduction of culturally transmitted group institutions and their analysis in a gene-culture coevolutionary model. Second, we use a group selection model based on selective extinction, and show that it provides a much more plausible account of the evolution of altruism than does the selective emigration model considered in §4.2.

Third, recall that where an altruistic trait has evolved because most fitness-relevant interactions take place within genetically differentiated groups rather than between family members within groups, we say that multi-level selection rather than kin-based selection is the explanation. We have treated these as competing models of the evolution of helping behaviors, but they need not be. Recall that Axelrod and Hamilton (1981) showed that a modest amount of kin-based assortment encouraged a reciprocal altruist behavior (nice tit-for-tat) to emerge when rare and to proliferate. In §7.6 we allow non-random family-based assortment within groups itself to evolve. We show that despite such ingroup kin favoritism being costly (always hunting with your brother may not maximize your returns), it does evolve in the model, and by retarding the within-group selection against the altruistic trait, it greatly expands the parameter space under which competition among groups can promote the evolutionary success of an altruistic trait.

Finally, the plausibility of group selection models is an empirical question, so we put our model to an explicit empirical test. We ask: on the basis of archaeological, genetic, and other data presented in the previous chapter, is it likely that genetic differences among groups were great enough and that the survival advantages of predominantly altruistic groups were a sufficiently powerful evolutionary force that under the conditions that ancestral humans experienced during the Late Pleistocene and early Holocene, so that altruism could have proliferated in the way we suggest? Readers interested in more extensive treatments of the empirical estimates and simulations reported here may wish to consult Bowles (2006, 2007, 2009b) and Bowles et al. (2003). Readers unfamiliar with multi-level selection models may wish to consult §4.2.

7.1   Selective Extinction

Selective extinction can favor the evolution of an altruistic trait when altruists contribute to a group's chance of survival in a military challenge or environmental crisis. Consider a large meta-population of individuals living in partially isolated sub-populations (called demes). We assume that altruists (A's) take an action costing the individual c that confers a benefit b on an individual randomly selected from the n members of the deme. In §4.1 for mathematical convenience we assumed that altruist could never benefit from the helping act. Here there is a small probability ($1/n$) that the altruist himself receives the benefit. Benefiting from one's own helping act may seem fanciful, but it is not: the life you save by serving as a lookout, for example, may be your own.

(1)   Generic price equation:
$$\Delta p = \mathrm{var}(p_j)\beta_G + \overline{\mathrm{var}}(p_{ij})\beta_i$$

(2)   Generic condition for A to increases:
$$\mathrm{var}(p_j)/\overline{\mathrm{var}}(p_{ij}) = F_{ST}/(1 - F_{ST}) > -\beta_i/\beta_G$$

(3)   Effect of A on deme-average fitness
$$\beta_G \equiv dw_j/dp_j = \kappa(dw_j/d\lambda)(d\lambda/dp_j) = 2\kappa\lambda_A$$

(4)   Effect of A on individual fitness:
$$\beta_i \equiv dw_{ij}/dp_j = -(1 - \tau_r)c + b/n + 2\kappa\lambda_A/n$$

(4)   Price's equation for the model:
$$\Delta p = \mathrm{var}(p_j)2\kappa\lambda_A - \overline{\mathrm{var}}(p_{ij})\{(1 - \tau_r)c - (b + 2\kappa\lambda_A)/n\}$$

(5)   Condition for A's to increase:
$$F_{ST}/(1 - F_{ST}) > -\beta_i/\beta_G = \{(1 - \tau_r)c - b/n\}/2\kappa\lambda_A - 1/n$$

(6)   Condition for A's to increase ($n = \infty$):
$$F_{ST}/(1 - F_{ST}) > (1 - \tau_r)c/2\kappa\lambda_A$$

Table 7.1. Summary of model and notation. We assume a constant total population so average fitness is $w = 1$; $\mathrm{var}(p_j) =$ between-group genetic variance; $\overline{\mathrm{var}}(p_{ij}) =$ within-group genetic variance (defined in equation 4.4). Note: b and c are benefits and costs to deme members; $p_j =$ percent of deme j that are A's; and $p =$ percent of meta-population that are A's. In equation (1), $\Delta p =$ between-deme effect + within-deme effect; $F_{ST} =$ between-deme variance/total variance; $\kappa =$ probability of inter-demic contest per generation; $\tau_r =$ extent of reproductive leveling; equation (6) says that $F_{ST}/(1 - F_{ST}) >$ individual cost/group benefits.

The model and notation are summarized in Table 7.1, and the mathematical symbols are displayed in Table 7.5. A's are bearers of a hypothetical "altruistic allele"; those without the allele (N's) do not behave altruistically. Reproduction is asexual. In the absence of reproductive leveling, an A in a group with all A's will on average receive benefits b and hence will expect a number of offspring surviving to reproductive age, that is $b - c$ greater than the fitness of an N in a group of all N's.

We want to determine the conditions under which p, the fraction of A's in the meta-population, will increase. Recall from the Price equation that whether altruism evolves, that is, whether $\Delta p > 0$, depends on the outcome of a race in which the between-deme selection process promoting its spread, namely $\mathrm{var}(p_j)\beta_G$, competes with the within-group selection process tending to eliminate it, namely $\overline{\mathrm{var}}(p_{ij})\beta_i$. For the between-deme effect to exceed the within-deme effect we know from equation 4.3, it must be that

$$\frac{\mathrm{var}(p_j)}{\overline{\mathrm{var}}(p_{ij})} > -\frac{\beta_i}{\beta_G}. \tag{7.1}$$

The right hand side of (7.1) is the negative of the ratio of two fitness effects: $\beta_i \equiv dw_{ij}/dp_{ij}$, the total, direct and indirect, effect on i's fitness of switching from N to A, and $\beta_G \equiv dw_j/dp_j$, the effect on average fitness of members of group j of variations in the fraction group j who are A's. A behavior is altruistic if adopting it lowers one's expected fitness while increasing the average fitness of one's deme (§A1). Given this definition, we are interested in the case where β_i is negative and β_G is positive. The left hand side of (7.1) is a measure of positive assortment arising from the fact that if the fraction of A's in demes differ (i.e., $\mathrm{var}(p_j)$ is positive), then A's are more likely than N's to interact with A's. Because (until §7.6) the within-deme benefits of altruism are randomly distributed among all group members, between-deme differences in the prevalence of A's (i.e. $\mathrm{var}(p_j) > 0$) is the only reason why A's are more likely than N's to benefit from the helping actions of A's.

But if A's are likely to benefit for this reason, they are also more likely to compete over deme-specific resources (Taylor 1992, Wilson et al. 1992). In the selective emigration model of Chapter 4 we allowed the predominantly altruistic demes to grow or to send out migrants without these resource constraints. But here we assume the most stringent form of local density-dependent constraints on reproductive output: sites are saturated so that territorial expansion—gaining a new site at some other group's expense—is required for deme growth. Thus altruism can proliferate only by helping a deme to acquire more territory, not by any of the other ways that members of predominantly altruistic demes might produce more surviving offspring.

Selective extinction may allow the evolution of altruism if predominantly altruistic demes are more likely than other demes to survive between-deme contests and to colonize and repopulate the sites vacated by demes that fail (Aoki 1982). This process is captured by the term β_G, the size of which is the product of three determinants: the frequency of between-deme contests, the fitness effects of prevailing in a contest, and the contribution of altruists to prevailing. In every generation with probability κ each deme engages in a "contest." A contest may be a hostile encounter or an environmental challenge without direct deme interaction. Demes that fail are eliminated and surviving demes repopulate the vacated sites. As we saw in the previous chapter, this "all or nothing" warfare in which losing groups are annihilated is rarely observed and is adopted here for mathematical convenience. Note that our data on the degree of genetic differentiation among groups, the F_{ST}'s that determine the evolutionary impact of group competition, are estimated directly from genetic data and so do not depend in any way on our assumptions about warfare. We adopt a more realistic representation of war in the next chapter.

Demes are the same size (normalized to unity) except that demes that have occupied the site of an eliminated deme are momentarily of size two (and eliminated demes are of size zero). The surviving deme then divides, forming two daughter demes of equal size. Let the probability that the deme survives a contest be λ. Recalling that κ is the probability that a group engages in a conflict in a given generation, the size of deme j next generation is thus one, two or zero with probabilities $1 - \kappa$, $\kappa\lambda$ and $\kappa(1 - \lambda)$, respectively, so expected size is $w_j = 1 - \kappa + 2\kappa\lambda$. The effect of the prevalence of A's on the expected size of the deme next generation, $\beta_G = dw_j/dp_j$, is the likelihood of a contest (κ), times the effect on deme size of surviving or not (2), times the effect of the prevalence of A's on the probability of a deme surviving should a contest occur (λ_A). Thus $\beta_G = 2\kappa\lambda_A$. There is no way to estimate λ_A empirically, so we explore two alternative values: $\lambda_A = 1$ is derived from a model in which all-A and all-N demes (respectively) survive and fail with certainty should a contest occur with a deme half of whose members are A; while if $\lambda_A = 1/2$, an all-A deme survives with probability 3/4 and an all-N deme survives with probability 1/4. These two alternatives are shown in Figure 7.1.

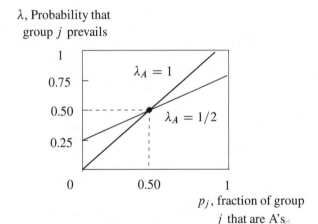

λ, Probability that group j prevails

Figure 7.1. Survival probability for deme j if half of the members of the paired group are A's and p_j is the fraction of members of group j who are altruists (groups are of the same total size).

7.2   Reproductive Leveling

Reproductive leveling reduces the strength of within-group selective pressures against the A's. To see how this works, suppose a particular N were instead an A. In the absence of reproductive leveling and intergroup competition its fitness would be less by an amount c, the cost of the altruistic behavior. But the individual who switched from N to A would also have a $1/n$ chance of garnering the randomly assigned benefit b. Additionally, by switching from N to A, the individual contributes directly to its fitness in another way: by increasing the chance of survival of the deme in a contest and hence its colonization of a new site, in which case, like every member of the surviving deme, its expected fitness will be doubled. This additional direct effect of the switch from N to A is the resulting change in p_j, namely $1/n$, times the effect of variations in p_j on deme-average fitness β_G. Taking account of the effect of the actor's switch from N to A on the composition of the group we therefore have

$$\beta_i \equiv \frac{dw_{ij}}{dp_{ij}} = \frac{\partial w_{ij}}{\partial p_{ij}} + \frac{dp_j}{dp_{ij}}\beta_G = -c + \frac{b}{n} + \frac{2\kappa\lambda_A}{n}. \qquad (7.2)$$

This expression makes it clear that β_i is the total effect of the individual's switch from N to A, not just the partial effect, holding p_j constant. In Chapter 4, β_i was simply $-c$; i.e., the partial effect was the total effect. The reason is that there were no effects on the actor's fitness of a change from N to A because the benefit of the helping action was received by some other member of the group, and there was no group competition for group survival.

Recall that reproductive leveling is a convention, adherence to which is in the interest of each deme member as long as most others follow the convention. Reproductive leveling takes the form of a proportional deduction at rate τ_r of each members' payoffs, the proceeds of which are distributed equally to all members. An example would be "common pot" food sharing in which some fraction of the food available to a group is pooled regardless of who acquired it, and then distributed in equal shares to each member. The effect is to reduce within-deme fitness differences between A's and N's from $-c$ to $-(1 - \tau_r)c$, so taking account of all of the direct and indirect effects of a switch from N to A on the actor's fitness we have

$$\beta_i = -(1 - \tau_r)c + \frac{b}{n} + \frac{2\kappa\lambda_A}{n}. \qquad (7.3)$$

In keeping with our representing the A's as altruistic, we choose parameters such that β_i is negative.

To see how reproductive leveling works, Figure 7.2 reproduces the information in Figure 4.2 but suppresses the baseline fitness, and shows the effect of resource sharing on the payoff differences of the two types. The difference in the probability of interacting with an A, conditional on one's own type, that equalizes expected payoffs is no longer $P(A|A) - P(A|N) = F_{ST}$, as shown by the solid lines in Figure 7.2, but is now given by the dashed lines and is $P(A|A)' - P(A|N)' = F'_{ST} < F_{ST}$. Comparing the two figures one sees that $F^*_{ST} = c/b$ while $F'_{ST} = c(1 - \tau_r)/b$. As a result, were the population structure as in Figure 7.2, the degree of genetic differentiation given by (F_{ST}), and the sharing institution in place ($\tau_r > 0$), then the average fitness of the altruists and non-altruists, w^A and w^N, respectively, satisfies $w^A > w^N$, so p would increase.

Using these values for β_i and β_G in the Price equation, and recalling the definition of F_{ST} (4.8), we rewrite equation 7.1 and find that the A's share of the meta-population will increase if

$$\frac{F_{ST}}{(1 - F_{ST})} > -\frac{\beta_i}{\beta_G} = \frac{(1 - \tau_r)c - b/n}{2\kappa\lambda_A} - \frac{1}{n}. \qquad (7.4)$$

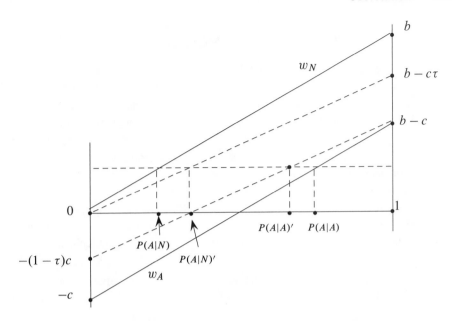

Figure 7.2. Resource sharing reduces the level of positive assortment necessary for the evolution of an altruistic trait. In this figure we have suppressed the baseline fitness term as it has no effect. The average fitnesses of the altruists and non-altruists are w^A and w^N, respectively. The horizontal axis measures the probability of being paired with an A. The dashed payoff functions indicate the effect of within-group resource sharing. For the value of τ_r illustrated here, the altruistic trait will proliferate if $F_{ST} > P(A|A)' - P(A|N)'$ while for $\tau_r = 0$, $F_{ST} > P(A|A) - P(A|N)$ is required. For the case of nonrandom pairing within demes (to be introduced in the simulations reported in §7.6), the analysis is similar, with $b - c\tau_r$ on the right vertical axis replaced by $(1 - \zeta)b$ and $-(1 - \tau_r)c$ on the left axis replaced by $\zeta b - c$, where ζ is the degree of segmentation.

If n is large, this is approximated by the much simpler

$$\frac{F_{ST}}{1 - F_{ST}} > \frac{(1 - \tau_r)c}{2\kappa\lambda_A}. \tag{7.5}$$

This is Hamilton's rule for the evolution of altruism by inclusive fitness. This model thus yields a condition indicating the minimum degree of positive assortment arising from the deme structure of the population necessary to allow altruism to proliferate. To see this, note that Hamilton's rule $r > c = b$ (equation 4.1) can be rewritten as $r/(1 - r) > c/(b - c)$. The left hand term in (7.5) is just $r/(1 - r)$ in Hamilton's rule, while the right hand term is the ratio of individual costs to group-level benefits (analogous to c and $b - c$, respectively, in Hamilton's rule).

We now ask if ancestral humans are likely to have lived under conditions such that equation 7.4 or 7.5 would be satisfied. Table 7.2 is a summary of the main parameters and the estimated range of empirically plausible values.

Parameter Estimated		Range Explored	Comment
Inter-demic genetic differentiation	F_{ST}	0.007–0.17 **0.076**	Genetic markers (recent foragers)
Per-generation probability of a decisive (2,0) contest	κ	**0.28** 0–0.50	Archaeological and ethnographic estimates of mortality in ongoing conflict
Effect of a percentage of altruists on deme survival	λ_A	**0.5, 1**	Arbitrary (see Figure 7.1)
Effective deme size (one generation) (one generation)	n	**32**,∞	Genetic evidence from ethnographic hunter-gatherers (Chapter 7)
Cost to altruist	c	**0.0–0.08**	Depends on behavior under consideration.
Benefits to deme (w/o a contest)	b	**0.05**	As immediately above (virtually no effect)

Table 7.2. Parameter estimates. Note: Benchmark values are in bold. Entries not in bold are alternative values.

7.3   Genetic Differentiation between Groups

Wright (1950, p. 203) speculated that an equilibrium F_{ST} among human groups, namely that which would balance the offsetting effects of migration and genetic drift might be about 0.02, a value that would preclude interdemic competition as an important evolutionary force. For example, in the selective emigration model an F_{ST} of this magnitude would require b to exceed c by a factor of 50 in order for altruism to evolve (equation 4.10). But as we have seen in the previous chapter, most empirical estimates of F_{ST} values are considerably larger.

However, estimates of genetic differentiation at the locus of an allele that is expressed in an altruistic behavior may differ from estimates based on neutral loci (those not under selection) such as those in Table 6.1. First, an altruistic allele would be, by definition, under directional selection. This would be expected to reduce interdemic genetic differentiation at least in the very long run, because in the absence of offsetting effects, the frequency of the A's in the population will eventually go to zero. However this tendency may not work over time scales relevant to human demes. Simulations show that even for very strong selection against the A's and for plausible initial distributions of A's in demes, the F_{ST} rises for tens of generations before declining (Bowles 2006). For moderate selection against the A's, the F_{ST} may rise for more than a hundred generations before falling. Because, as we found in the previous chapter, fission and extinction events that enhance interdemic variance are likely to be an order of magnitude more frequent than this, it appears that high levels of F_{ST} could persist indefinitely. Additional simulations show that exceptionally strong directional selection against the A's ($c = 0.1$) is compatible with the indefinite maintenance of high levels of F_{ST}, even with random rather than Hamilton's "associative" fission of demes.

Second altruists will sometimes be able exclude non-altruists from their demes (Wilson and Dugatkin 1997), resulting in what Eshel and Cavalli-Sforza (1982) called *selective assortment*. In this case, migration might also enhance between-deme variance and reduce within-deme variance (Rogers and Jorde 1987). Here, selective assortment is contingent on past behavior that is itself an observable expression of the altruistic allele. As a result, the only way an N could mimic the A's so as to evade their choosiness would be to adopt the altruistic behavior itself and thus to bear its costs. Thus the instability arising in the case of assortment by "green beards" (Ridley and Grafen 1981) does not arise.

But there is nonetheless an impediment to selective assortment that is sometimes overlooked: exclusion of N's is likely to be costly for the A's, while the associated benefits are shared by all deme members. However, it is not implausible that altruists would undertake some moderate level of N-exclusion as a contribution to the public good. As we have seen, there is ample ethnographic evidence that foragers practice selective assortment when they ostracize or shun individuals who violate behavioral norms. Finally, it is readily shown that a modest amount of selective assortment generates substantial levels of between-deme differences (Bowles 2006).

7.4   Deme Extinction and the Evolution of Altruism

Thus we think that selective assortment is among the processes generating genetic differentiation among groups. But the results, to which we now turn, do not depend in any way on this assessment; they are based on the observed, not hypothetical or assumed, levels of genetic assortment. While the effects of most forms of reproductive leveling cannot be estimated, the degree of within-deme resource sharing is known from empirical studies of the acquisition and consumption of nutrition among foragers. These and the other empirical data mentioned here are summarized in Bowles (2006). On this basis we take $\tau_r = 2/3$ as a plausible benchmark with one third as an alternative value. The appropriate value of n is the number of deme members of a breeding generation (about a third of the census size). Here we take 96 (census) members as a benchmark size, or $n = 32$ members of a single generation. As an alternative, we will also consider very large (strictly, infinite) demes. Plausible values of c and b will depend on the particular altruistic behavior in question. For example, a warning call would have a different b and c than defending the community against hostile neighbors. To facilitate the exploration of a variety of altruistic behaviors, we present results for a given $b = 0.05$ and c varying from 0.00 to 0.08. Equations 7.4 and 7.5 make it clear that for sizable demes b is of little importance. The main contribution of altruistic behavior to fitness arises from group competition, not within-group benefits.

Estimates of the extent of hostile group interactions during the Late Pleistocene and early Holocene surveyed in the previous chapter allow us to estimate κ, the probability that in any given generation a group will engage in a decisive war (in which the loser is eliminated and the winner suffers no losses). Mortality results when a group loses a conflict, occurring with probability $\kappa(1 - \lambda)$. If war does not occur or if the group engages in war but prevails, then all deaths are from other causes. Thus, the fraction of all deaths that are due to war is $\delta = \kappa(1 - \lambda)$. Averaging across groups, $\lambda = 0.5$, so $\kappa = 2\delta$. We use the values of δ in Table 6.2 to estimate κ.

The above parameter estimates are summarized in Table 7.2. They are subject to substantial error given that they are inferences about conditions occurring tens of thousands of years ago for which very little direct evidence is available.

With this caveat in mind, suppose early human demographics and social practices resulted in genetic differentiation at the locus of an altruistic allele that was the magnitude of the median in Table 6.1 (0.075). For the benchmark values of τ_r, n, and λ_A, the solid lines in Figure 7.3 give the combinations of c and κ such that equation 7.4 is satisfied as an equality. More frequent contests or less costly forms of altruism (points above the line) allow altruism to proliferate. Dashed lines do the same for more stringent alternative parameter values. For example, if κ were half of the estimated frequency of warfare based on the morality data in Tables 7.2 to 7.4 (i.e., if $\kappa = 0.14$), and if $c = 0.05$, altruism would proliferate under both survival functions and the benchmark assumptions, but not for very large demes with limited reproductive leveling.

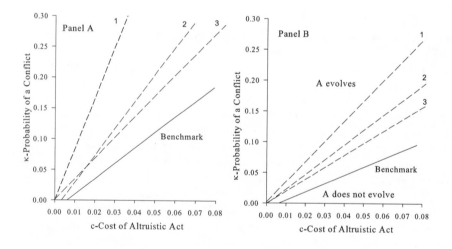

Figure 7.3. Conditions for the evolution of altruism by selective extinction and reproductive leveling. The solid lines are the benchmark values estimated in the text; $n = 32$, $\tau_r = 0.66$. Line 1: $n = \infty$, $\tau_r = 0.33$; line 2: $n = 32$, $\tau_r = 0.33$; line 3: $n = \infty, \tau_r = 0.66$. Points above the each line give combinations of c and κ such that altruism would proliferate according to equations 7.4 and 7.5. Panels A and B (respectively) use $\lambda_A = 0.5$ and $\lambda_A = 1$. For both panels, $b = 0.05$. Similar analysis for each estimate of the genetic differentiation in Table 6.1 is presented in Bowles (2006).

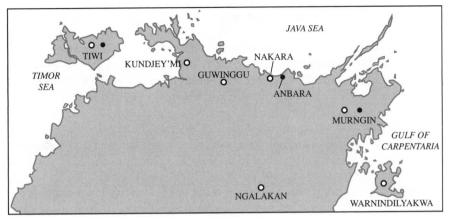

Figure 7.4. Data sources in Arnhem Land, Australia, for ethnographic evidence on warfare (black dots) and genetic differentiation (open dots). The maximum distance between pairs of groups shown is about 600 kilometers. Source: Bowles 2009a and Walsh et al. (2007).

7.5 The Australian Laboratory

To study the evolutionary consequences of warfare under Pleistocene conditions using recent data, one would ideally use estimates of both genetic differentiation and wartime mortality from hunter-gatherer populations living in close proximity with one another but having little contact with farmers or herders. Such groups existed in historical times in Arnhem Land, Australia and have been studied by anthropologists, geneticists, and others. Australia is the continent thought by many to be the best laboratory of likely Pleistocene and early Holocene conditions among foragers (Lourandos 1997). Depictions of warriors and battles in the rock art of Arnhem Land populations date from as early as 10,000 years ago (Tacon and Chippendale 1994). The availability of archaeological, ethnographic and genetic data for this region makes it a remarkable laboratory for this investigation.

To gauge their implications we rearrange equation 7.4 and for simplicity set $b = 0$ to define the critical value c^* as the maximum cost of the altruistic behavior consistent with its proliferating in the population:

$$c^* = 2\kappa\lambda_A \left(\frac{F_{ST}}{1 - F_{ST}} + \frac{1}{n} \right). \tag{7.6}$$

We use data on the extent of wartime mortality in three nearby groups of foragers, the Anbara, Murngin, and Tiwi, along with estimates of genetic differentiation among seven Aboriginal groups, including the Tiwi and the Murngin, in that relatively small area, depicted in Figure 7.4. To decide whether the values of c^* that we calculate using equation 7.6 are "large" or "small," note that $c^* = 0.03$, for example, is a quite substantial cost, one that in the absence of intergroup competition would lead the fraction of altruists in a group to fall from 0.9 to 0.1 in just 150 generations. An illustration more directly related to the question of warfare is the following. Suppose that in every generation a group is engaged in a war with probability $\kappa = 2\delta$ and that an altruistic "warrior" will die with certainty in a lost war and with probability 0.20 in a war in which the group prevails, while non-altruistic members also die with certainty in lost wars but do not die in won wars. These mortality assumptions, of course, are extremely unfavorable for the altruists. Assuming the altruists have no reproductive advantages during peacetime, then $c = 0.26$ or, using the arithmetic mean estimate of from Table 6.2, $c = 0.028$.

To calculate c^* we use an estimated value of $F_{ST} = 0.040$, the lowest of the three estimates for aboriginal Australians and considerably lower than the mean of those for hunter-gather groups generally presented in Table 6.1. The estimates of c^* for these populations, assuming two values of λ_A, make it clear that if groups were as warlike as the Murngin, between-group competition could overcome very strong within-group selection against an altruistic behavior. Even for groups similar to the more peaceful Anbara, quite costly forms of altruism could proliferate by this mechanism ($c^* = 0.015$ for $\lambda_A = 1$).

	Murngin	Tiwi	Anbara
$\lambda_A = 1$	0.066	0.032	0.015
$\lambda_A = 0.5$	0.033	0.016	0.008

Table 7.3. When an altruistic trait can proliferate. Note: Entries are the largest cost c^* for an altruistic trait to proliferate given genetic differentiation and mortality in intergroup hostilities (δ) among three Arnhem Land hunter-gatherer populations. For the Murngin, Tiwi and Anbara, respectively, we estimate (Table 6.4) $\delta = 0.21$, $\delta = 0.10$, and $\delta = 0.04$.

7.6   The Coevolution of Institutions and Altruism

The data in Figure 7.3 and Table 7.3 make it clear that for many populations and for plausible parameter values, genetic differentiation is such that even very infrequent contests would have been sufficient to spread quite costly forms of altruism. The same conclusion holds if group extinctions resulted from a failure of group members to cooperate during environmental crises.

Because the initial spread of altruism among humans could have been propelled by just a few of the vast number of Late Pleistocene demes, the above data and reasoning suggest that selective deme extinction may be part of the account of the evolution of altruism. Figure 7.3 shows that this is likely in the presence of significant levels of reproductive leveling, but much less so in its absence. To see this, compare lines one and three, or line two and the solid benchmark line. This suggests an important role for culturally transmitted practices in creating a niche in which a genetic predisposition to behave altruistically might have evolved, and perhaps accounting for the distinctive aspects of human altruism not found in other species.

But we have not yet modeled the dynamic of genes and group level institutions. Thus far we have posited empirically plausible levels of warfare and reproductive leveling, rather than explained their evolution.

Below and in the next chapter, we will model the coevolution of altruism with these distinctive human institutions. Because this process involves highly complex selection processes operating at two levels—individual and group—in which the magnitude of within-group and between-group selection effects are endogenously determined by the evolution of group-level institutions, the dynamic is not amenable to mathematical analysis using the Price equation, or indeed any other mathematical formulation capable of analytical solution. An agent-based model (§A2), however, is illuminating.

Our objective is to see if the culturally transmitted group-level institutions that support the evolution of the "altruistic allele" could themselves have evolved even if maintaining these institutions imposed costs on the groups adopting them. We will of course consider reproductive leveling. But we first introduce an additional aspect of group social structure, the tendency of like types to interact within groups more frequently than would occur by chance. The resulting nonrandom pairing, sometimes called segmentation, may occur because of a tendency to share residence and thus to interact disproportionately with siblings and other kin by recent common descent, or because people sometimes are able to condition their interactions on the type of the other, based on information about past behavior, for example.

Suppose, then, that in addition to the institution of resource sharing, groups are also segmented, so that rather than the benefit of a given altruist's helping behavior being bestowed by an individual randomly drawn from the group we now let altruists have a higher than chance probability of being the recipient of the help provided by a particular altruist. To see how this works, suppose groups are large. Let $\zeta_j > 0$ be the degree of segmentation in group j, that is, the difference in the conditional probability of an A and an N (in the same group) receiving the benefit of an A's help. Thus the probability of an A in group j getting the benefit is $\zeta_j + (1 - \zeta_j)p_j > p_j$ and the analogous probability for an N is $(1 - \zeta_j)p_j < p_j$. So the expected benefit of the presence of altruists in the group enjoyed by an altruist is no longer $p_j b$ but rather $\{\zeta_j + (1 - \zeta_j)p_j\}b$, and the expected benefit of the non-altruist is only $(1 - \zeta_j)p_j b$. Then, abstracting from reproductive leveling, the expected difference in payoffs between N's and A's in the same group is no longer c, but $c - \zeta_j b$. Segmentation thus reduces the fitness disadvantage of altruists because they are disproportionately likely to benefit from the help of other altruists, while N's are disproportionately likely to not benefit. If $\zeta_j > c/b$, A's will on average do better than N's in group j and as a result the A's will not suffer any reproductive disadvantage. To pose the classical (strong) group-selection problem, we therefore assume $\zeta_j < c/b$. Like resource sharing, segmentation is a convention and is passed on culturally.

Taking account of both segmentation and resource sharing, the difference in the expected payoffs received by N's and A's within a group will now be $(1 - \tau_r)(c - \zeta_j b)$, from which it is clear that both institutions retard the within-group selection against the A's.

The institutions represented by ζ and τ_r differ among groups and they also evolve under the selective pressure resulting from the differential survival of groups. In our simulations, when a conflict occurs, the group with the higher total payoff wins. As in the model presented above, the losing group's members die and the winning group populates the site occupied by the losers with replicas of a random selection of themselves. The new inhabitants of the site adopt the institutions of the winning group from which they descended. Institutions are also subject to stochastic variation, increasing or lowering τ_r and ζ by chance each period. Both segmentation and resource sharing impose costs on the groups adopting them. More segmented groups may fail to capture the benefits of diversity or of economies of scale, and resource sharing may reduce incentives to acquire the resources to be shared. Neither of these costs is modeled formally, but to capture their impact, group average benefits are reduced when larger values of ζ and τ_r are implemented (see the legend of Table 7.4).

With Astrid Hopfensitz and Jung-Kyoo Choi, we simulated an artificial population living in 20 groups (Bowles et al. 2003). We selected an extraordinarily high cost of altruism, $c = 0.1$ and did not allow A's to benefit from their own prosocial actions; that is, $b = 0.2$ is conferred on some other randomly selected group member. Thus within a group, when $\zeta = \tau_r = 0$, A's have 10% fewer offspring than N's, making these simulations a demanding test of our interpretation. These and the other benchmark values of the parameters in the simulations shown in Table 7.4 were chosen on grounds of empirical plausibility. We initiated each simulation with altruists and institutions absent at time zero, to see if they would proliferate if initially rare.

	Benchmark Values	Range Explored
Mean group size ($n = N/g$)	20	7–47
Migration rate (m)	0.2	0.1–0.3
Probability of conflict (κ)	0.25	0.18–0.4
Mutation rate (e)	0.001	0.1–0.000001

Table 7.4. Key parameters for the simulation. Note: Meta-population size is N, and there are g groups; n, m, κ, and e are per generation. Other parameters: benefit $b = 2$, cost $c = 1$; baseline payoffs $= 10$. We varied group size by varying N. For reasons explained in the text, we restricted s to not exceed 0.5 while $\tau_r \in [0, 1]$. The costs imposed by these institutions are $(\zeta^2 + \tau_r^2)/2$, so that each member of a group with both institutions at values commonly observed in our simulations (e.g., $\zeta = 0.2$, $\tau_r = 0.1$) bore a significant "institutional cost" (0.025), or a quarter of the personal cost of the altruistic act itself.

7.7   Simulating Gene-Culture Coevolution

A simulation of this model appears in Figure 7.5. The early rise in p is supported by the chance increase in both ζ and τ_r (between periods 100 and 150). When p, the fraction of the meta-population who are A's, reaches high levels (periods 532 to 588, for example) both ζ and τ_r decline, typically leading to a sharp decline in p. The subsequent rise in ζ or τ_r occurs by chance. This cyclical pattern emerges for the following reason. When the population is evenly divided between A's and N's, many groups are also approximately evenly divided, which means that $\overline{var}(p_{ij}) = p_j(1 - p_j)$ takes its maximum value, so the within-group selection term in the Price equation (4.3) is also at its greatest. As a result, the beneficial effects of retarded within-group selection gained by higher levels of τ_r or ζ are maximized when the population is approximately evenly divided between A's and N's. By like reasoning, when p is well above 0.5, the benefits of the protection of A's offered by the institutions are of less value. But the institutions are costly to bear so when p is high, groups with substantial levels of segmentation or resource sharing are likely to lose conflicts with other groups, and the sites they had occupied are then peopled by the descendants of winners, who typically bear lower levels of these institutional variables. As a result, both ζ and τ_r fall.

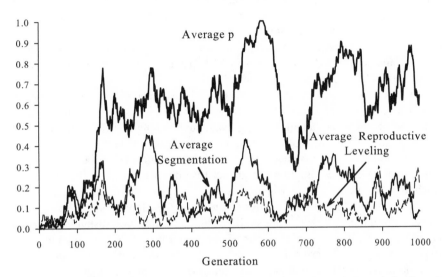

Figure 7.5. The coevolution of leveling, within-group segmentation, and altruism. The figure represents a 1000 generation history of a simulated ethno-linguistic group of about 1200 individuals (census size) using the benchmark parameters from Table 7.2. The population average frequency of altruists is p. Also shown are the average across the 20 groups of the level of reproductive leveling(that is, resource sharing τ_r) and segmentation ζ. Altruism and both group-level institutions are initially rare (set equal to zero). The particular time frame shown was selected because it clearly reveals a dynamic that is observed over long periods in many runs.

We checked to see if the proliferation of the A's could have been the result of the direct fitness benefits to an individual of switching from N to A offsetting the costs in these simulations. This seems possible given the reductions in the effective costs associated with the coevolving levels of resource sharing and segmentation. We found that when these institutions are absent ($\tau_r = 0 = \zeta$), the direct benefits of switching from N to A (associated with increased likelihood of group survival should a conflict occur) were about one eighth of the costs, while when τ_r and ζ are the levels they assumed on average in these simulations, the direct benefits rose to a third of the costs. Thus, the A behavior remained altruistic even under the cost-reducing effects of resource sharing and segmentation.

Could individual-level altruism have evolved if group-level institutions had not co-evolved with it? To answer this question we constrained ζ and τ_r to be zero in all periods. Altruism failed to evolve over a large number of implementations of this treatment. We also investigated whether the institutions would evolve if p, the fraction of altruists in the population, is constrained to zero. They do not, because institutions are costly and where there are no altruists in the population the institutions perform no group-beneficial function, thus leading groups that by chance adopt a high level of sharing or segmentation to lose conflicts in which they are involved.

Finally, we wanted to know how sensitive our simulations are to variations in the key parameters. To do this, we varied group size from seven to 47, and for each size ran 10 simulations of 50,000 generations, with the other parameters at their baseline values. We did this with both institutions constrained to not evolve, with each singly constrained to not evolve, and with neither constrained. We performed the same operation for variations in the migration rate from 0.1 to 0.3, and in the probability of conflict (κ) from 0.18 to 0.51. The results appear in Figure 7.6.

The top panel shows that with both institutions constrained not to evolve ("no institutions"), a group size of 7 individuals per generation, meaning about 21 individuals, roughly the size of a very small foraging band, supports high levels of altruism, but group sizes greater than 8 result in a frequency of altruists of less than 0.3. This is a highly improbable scenario under which altruism could evolve, as a group of this size would surely have a migration rate greater than our benchmark of 0.2. Taking as a benchmark the group size for which $p > 0.5$, we see that with no institutions the critical size is 8, while with both institutions $p > 0.5$ for all group sizes less than 22. The results for the migration rate are similar. With no institutions, sustaining $p > 0.5$ requires a (per-generation) migration rate of not greater than 0.13, but with both institutions free to evolve, the critical migration rate is 0.21. The bottom panel shows that institutions also allow the evolution of high levels of altruism with significantly fewer between-group conflicts. A "vertical" reading of the figure is also illuminating: for example, the bottom panel shows that for $\kappa = 0.3$, p is less than 0.2 without institutions, but is greater than 0.8 with both institutions free to evolve.

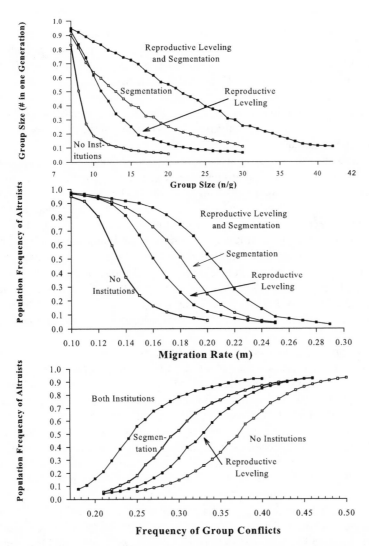

Figure 7.6. Group-level institutions increase the size of the parameter space for which altruistic behaviors are common. Each data point is the population average frequency of altruists over 10 runs of 50,000 periods each for the parameter value indicated on the horizontal axis. Each run began with $p = \tau_r = \zeta = 0$. The curve labeled "No Institutions" gives the results for runs in which τ_r and ζ were constrained to zero; the other curves indicate runs in which one or both of the institutions were free to evolve. The horizontal distance between the curves indicates the enlargement of the parameter space made possible by group level institutions. The vertical distance between the curves shows the impact of institutions on p.

7.8   Levelers and Warriors

We have shown that the between-group genetic differentiation, patterns of group conflict and other conditions under which our model of selective extinction with reproductive leveling could have worked to proliferate altruism are very likely to have existed at least for some early human groups. We have also described a process whereby institutions such as reproductive leveling and within-group segmentation provide an environment within which an individually costly group-beneficial trait may evolve, and in which these institutions proliferate in the population because of their contribution to the evolutionary success of altruism.

Our simulations have shown that if group-level institutions implementing resource sharing or positive assortment within groups are free to evolve, group-level selection processes support the coevolution of altruistic individual behaviors along with these institutions, even where these institutions impose significant costs on the groups adopting them. In the absence of these group-level institutions, however, group-selection pressures support the evolution of altruistic traits only when intergroup conflicts are very frequent, groups are very small, and migration rates are implausibly low. Our simulations also suggest that both altruistic behaviors and reproductive leveling and within-group assortment institutions could have emerged and proliferated from an environment in which they were initially rare. Recall that p, τ_r, and ζ are all set to zero at the beginning of our simulations and all three evolve from this initial condition, as illustrated in Figure 7.5.

Crucial to this process is the fact that food-sharing and other forms of reproductive leveling do not require the preexistence of altruistic preferences: adherence to these conventions is a best response for self-interested individuals. Thus, as we saw in Chapter 4, a norm that prohibits the powerful from monopolizing food supplies could be sustained by the repeated nature of dyadic network interactions or the adverse reputations that violators would suffer. In this dyadic or very small group setting, the conditions outlined in Chapter 4 for the success of reciprocal altruism or indirect reciprocity—frequent ongoing interactions with public and high-quality information—could easily have been met, allowing the initiation of food-sharing, especially in relatively small networks of closely related individuals. Indeed, as we saw in Chapter 1, it seems likely that some kind of food-sharing is a very early development in human behavior, having coevolved with the shift to a diet based on large meat packages. Once established, the norm could persist in larger, less closely related groups, as Axelrod and Hamilton (1981) showed. Its effect, as this chapter has shown, would be to promote the spread of altruistic preferences including the public-spirited punishment of transgressors, thereby stabilizing reproductive leveling even for groups of more substantial size than we have considered here.

Notwithstanding the highly speculative nature of these inferences, it seems possible that the social and physical environments of the Late Pleistocene may fall within the parameter space supporting the coevolutionary trajectories illustrated in Figure 7.6. If so, the multi-level selection model with endogenous institutions may provide at least a partial account of evolution during this critical period of individually altruistic behaviors as well as group-level resource sharing, segmentation, and perhaps other institutions.

The main causal mechanisms of the model—institutionalized resource sharing among non-kin, within-group assortment, and intergroup conflict—suggest a central role for uniquely human cognitive, linguistic and other capacities in this process, perhaps helping to account for the distinctive levels of cooperation among non-kin practiced by humans. The same observation suggests the limited applicability of the model and simulations to most other animals. However, as we have seen, reproductive leveling occurs in some other species, and other forms of within-group variance reduction are also not uniquely human. Moreover, for species in which neighboring groups including unrelated members compete for resources or in which group extinctions are common, a similar model might apply. In these cases individually costly group-beneficial behaviors may contribute by increasing group size, an effect we have not considered here, or in other ways, to the success of the group in avoiding extinctions or in gaining resources from neighboring groups.

Examples include social mammals such as the cooperative mongoose *Suricata suricatta*, for which group extinction rates are inversely correlated with group size and in some years exceed half the groups under observation (Clutton-Brock et al. 1999). Similarly, fire ants (*Solenopsis invicta*) and a large number of other ant species form breeding groups with multiple unrelated queens and practice brood raiding and other forms of hostility toward neighboring groups, with success positively related to group size (Bernasconi and Strassmann 1999). Mortality in intergroup conflict among chimpanzees may be as great as our estimates for humans, with more powerful groups gaining fitness-enhancing territories (Nishida et al. 1985, Manson and Wrangham 1991, Mitani et al. 2010). Whether the levels of cooperation observed in these and other species—cooperative breeding in meerkats or the within-group cooperation of only moderately related male chimps, for example—might be explained in part by the causal mechanisms at work in our model is an interesting question which we have not explored.

Our simulations show that two aspects of the constructed niches that supported the evolution of altruistic individuals, reproductive leveling and within-group segmentation, could have coevolved with altruism. But lethal group conflict also plays a central role in this explanation, and thus far we have not sought to explain either the motives promoting it or the structure of group interactions in which lethal conflict is a likely outcome. This is our next task.

Symbol	Meaning
b	Benefit
c	Cost
β_i	Cost of switching from N to A
β_G	dw_j/dp_j
F_{ST}	Wright's variance ratio
g	Number of groups
i	Index for individuals
j	Index for groups
κ	Probability of inter-demic contest per generation
λ	Probability a deme survives a contest
λ_A	$d\lambda/dp_j$
N	Metapopulation size
n	Group size
p	Fraction of meta-population that are A's
p_j	Fraction of deme j that are A's
p_{ij}	$= 0$ if i is an N, and $= 1$ if i is an A
τ_r	Extent of reproductive leveling
$\overline{\text{var}}(p_{ij})$	Between-group genetic variance
w_j	Mean fitness of group j members
w^A	Mean fitness of Altruists
w^N	Mean fitness of Nonaltruists
ζ	Degree of segmentation
ζ_j	Degree of segmentation in group j

Table 7.5. Definition of symbols

8

Parochialism, Altruism, and War

> Who trusted God was love indeed
> And love Creation's final law
> Tho' Nature, red in tooth and claw
> With ravine, shriek'd against his creed.
>
> Alfred, Lord Tennyson,
> *In memoriam, A.H.H.*
> (1849) Canto 56

For Alfred, Lord Tennyson, love and religious fealty were man's triumph over a violent and recalcitrant Nature. But late 19th century scientists as diverse as Charles Darwin (1998[1873]) and Karl Pearson (1894) recognized war as a powerful evolutionary force that paradoxically might account for social solidarity among humans and altruism toward the fellow members of one's group. The previous chapter confirmed that intergroup conflict may have contributed to the evolution of altruism.

Did Lord Tennyson get it wrong?

> Was love the claw's unwonted child?
> Creation, too, the spawn of strife?
> That creed sustained enduring life
> So let not Nature be defiled.

Though the idea that altruism proliferated among humans by means of war dates back to Darwin (see the headquote in Chapter 4) has not been subjected to systematic investigation. When intergroup conflict has been considered, its extent has simply been assumed, as in most models, rather than estimated, as in the previous chapter. It remains to explain why outgroup hostility and lethal group encounters were common among early humans.

Recent contributions have shown that insider favoritism could evolve if it facilitates generalized exchange (Yamagishi et al. 1999), or supports the higher payoffs that occur when people with similar norms interact (McElreath et al. 2003), or coordinates the efficient selection of particular ways of interacting (Axtell et al. 2001), or improves communication among group members so as to facilitate informal enforcement of prosocial norms (Bowles and Gintis 2004). Related evolutionary explanations of why group boundaries so powerfully influence human behavior are found in Nettle and Dunbar (1997) and Hammond and Axelrod (2006). But the evolution of hostility toward outsiders and other conditions that might account for the distinctly lethal and common nature of human warfare has received little attention.

The importance of insider favoritism in human behavior is well established in experiments, as we saw in Chapter 3. Other evidence demonstrates that individuals often favor fellow group members over "outsiders" in the choice of friends, exchange partners and other associates and in the allocation of valued resources (Brewer and Kramer 1986, McPherson et al. 2001).

We take as emblematic of this evidence a "third-party punishment" experiment with subjects drawn from two nearby, but not recently hostile, linguistic groups in the famously bellicose highlands of Papua New Guinea (Bernhard et al. 2006). Recall that in the third-party punishment game (§3.6) Alice may transfer some of her endowment to Bob, and then an observer (Carole) may devote some of her endowment to punishing Alice, presumably in response to Carole's disapproval of Alice's transfer. In the experiment, all possible combinations of in- and out-group matches were implemented, so all three individuals might be from the same ethnic group, or just the first mover and the third party, or just the recipient and the first mover, or just the third party and the recipient.

First movers among the New Guinean subjects gave more to in-group members, and this was true independently of the level of third-party punishment they anticipated. But significant amounts were given to out-group recipients, too. Stingy first movers were most heavily punished if the first mover was from one group and the recipient and the third party from the other. But third parties also avidly punished ungenerous first movers when all three were from the same group. And third parties also punished first movers from their own group even if the recipient was from the other, and even when both the first mover and the recipient were from a different group.

These results are hardly surprising when one recalls that members of ancestral human groups not only fought one another, they also depended on one another for help in times of need, for information, mates, and trade goods. When we say that altruism is sometimes parochial, we mean that it recognizes group boundaries, not that it always stops at the border. Modeling the evolution of these complex preferences in a way that may reveal how they could have evolved is the task we now set for ourselves.

Intergroup aggression and in-group favoritism are similar to altruism in that each is often costly to the individual actor, who incurs mortal risks in a battle, or in shunning others, forgoes opportunities for beneficial coalitions, mating, coinsurance, and exchange. The struggle for survival of the Norse peoples who settled in Greenland for almost half a millennium prior to their demise around 1400 dramatically illustrates the perils of parochialism. Their hostile relations with the Inuit with whom they uneasily coexisted probably explains why they never learned the boat-building, fishing and hunting strategies that provided the basis for the Inuit survival there even through the Little Ice Age (McGhee 1984).

In a randomly mixed population (that is, in the absence of either positive or negative assortment) neither parochialism nor altruism would seem likely to survive any selection process, whether cultural or genetic, that favors traits with higher payoffs. But parochial altruism could have emerged and proliferated among early modern humans if among our ancestors three conditions held: most altruists were parochial and most parochials were altruistic, most of the parochial altruists were in groups with other parochial altruists, and ancestors lived in environments in which competition for resources favored groups with significant numbers of parochial altruists willing to engage in hostile conflict with outsiders on behalf of their fellow group members. These group benefits could have offset the within-group selection against both parochialism and altruism in a manner similar to that studied for simple altruism in the previous chapter.

Though parochialism and altruism might have coevolved in this way, the evolution of either altruism or parochialism singly seems unlikely. A population of tolerant altruists would not fight their neighbors, while parochialism alone would have prompted frequent hostilities with few willing to risk death on behalf of their group. Thus if we are to explain the etiology of altruism and parochialism it will have to be by a coevolutionary process. But unlike the previous chapter where we studied the joint dynamics of culturally transmitted institutions and genetically transmitted behavioral predispositions, here we explore the coevolution of two genetically transmitted individual traits, parochialism and altruism, each providing the conditions for the evolutionary success of the other, and both jointly explaining why warfare was so frequent and lethal among early humans.

8.1   Parochial Altruism and War

With Jung-Kyoo Choi we modeled a population of foragers who engage in both within- and between-group interactions in which individuals may adopt two types of behavior: altruism and parochialism (Choi and Bowles 2007). A related analytical population genetic model of "belligerence" (our parochialism) and "bravery" (our altruism), with results similar to the simulations reported here, appears in Lehmann and Feldman (2008). There are thus four behavioral types: parochial altruists, tolerant (non-parochial) altruists, parochial non-altruists, and tolerant non-altruists. Parochials (of either type) are hostile toward members of other groups. But only parochial altruists engage in combat, as the non-altruists do not bear personal costs in order to confer benefits on their fellow group members. In the absence of between-group hostilities, tolerant members of a group benefit from intergroup exchange, risk pooling and the kinds of mutually advantageous interactions with other groups mentioned in Chapter 6.

Two types of selection are at work in the model. Within-group selection favors tolerant non-altruists and tends to eliminate parochial altruists (as well as tolerant altruists and parochial non-altruists). By contrast, selective extinction resulting from intergroup conflict may favor parochial altruists. The reason is that if, as it seems, both hostility toward outsiders and a willingness to sacrifice on behalf of other members of one's group are essential to being an effective fighter for the group, then groups with many parochial altruists will tend to win conflicts, and to replace groups with fewer.

In order to clarify the role of war, parochialism and selective extinction, as in the previous chapter, we do not model the other mechanism by which altruism may spread, selective emigration (Rogers 1990). Thus, in contrast to Maynard Smith's haystack model and Wilson's model of trait groups, in the absence of territorial expansion, highly altruistic groups in our model do not contribute more replicas to the next generation (Maynard Smith 1964, Wilson and Dugatkin 1997). Like the model in Chapter 7, our setting is thus quite unfavorable for the evolution of altruism as it is equivalent to models in which local density-dependent selection exactly offsets the group benefits of altruism (Taylor 1992, Wilson et al. 1992).

Parochial altruists do receive a direct benefit if a war occurs, as they share in their group's increased probability of surviving a hostile encounter that results from their status as a "fighter" (relative to the group's likely survival had the individual been of another type). For plausible group sizes and frequencies of conflict, however, this direct benefit is an order of magnitude smaller than the costs. So our parochial altruists are indeed altruistic: they would increase their fitness if they became tolerant non-altruists.

As in the previous chapter, in every generation, at a cost of c, altruists (A's) contribute to a public good whose value (b) is shared equally among the n adult group members. The public good may be any behavior that confers benefits on all group members, excluding predation and defense, which we model separately. Those who are not altruistic (N's) do not contribute. Because we assume that $b > c > b/n$, contributing to the public good raises group-average payoffs but reduces the contributor's payoffs and so is both group-beneficial and altruistic. Not contributing is the dominant strategy, the N's payoffs exceeding the A's by the amount c, regardless of the distribution of A's within the group. Table 8.2 summarizes the mathematical symbols in this chapter.

In every generation members of each group interact with members of another group either cooperatively, enjoying the exchange, coinsurance and other benefits of peaceful interactions described in Chapter 6, or in a hostile manner, as shown in Figure 8.1. In the absence of a group conflict, each tolerant (T) member receives a net benefit from each tolerant member of the paired group resulting from gains from trade or risk pooling. Parochials receive no benefits of this type. As a result, in the absence of war the expected payoff to the T's in a given group exceed that to the P's regardless of the fraction of T's in the group, so T is the dominant strategy. This is why both A's and P's face adverse within-group selection. Payoffs in the absence of group conflict are described in Table 8.1.

	Parochial	*Tolerant*
Altruist	$bf_i^A - c$	$bf_i^A - c + gn_j f_j^T$
Non-altruist	bf_i^A	$bf_i^A + gn_j f_j^T$

Table 8.1. Expected payoffs to four behavioral types in the absence of hostile between-group interactions. Note: The fraction of group i who are altruists is f_i^A. All members receive the benefit of the public good, bf_i^A. Tolerant players of both types receive the benefits of non-hostile group interaction, $gn_j f_j^T$, where g is the benefit of non-hostile group interaction, n_j is the group size of the other group, and f_j^T is the fraction of the other group who are tolerant. For our simulations, benchmark values of the parameters in the table are $c = 0.01$, $b = 0.02$, and $g = 0.001$.

Hostility in an intergroup interaction results if parochial members constitute a sufficiently large fraction of at least one group. Hostility results in war with a probability that is increasing in the imbalance ($|\Delta_{ij}|$) in the number of fighters (parochial altruists) in the two groups. The use of force between the two groups occurs when one is sufficiently likely to win, reflecting the fact that as with other primates, evenly matched human groups seek to avoid costly conflicts (Wilson et al. 2001). The probability that a group survives war is increasing with the number of fighters relative to the number of fighters in the opposing group. If a conflict occurs, a fraction of the members of the losing group are eliminated (the fraction eliminated is a constant times the between-group difference in the fraction of parochial altruists) and replaced by replicas drawn randomly from the winning group. Hostile intergroup interactions in our ancestral past may be more ongoing and less episodic than we model here, but taking account of this would not alter the causal mechanisms of the model.

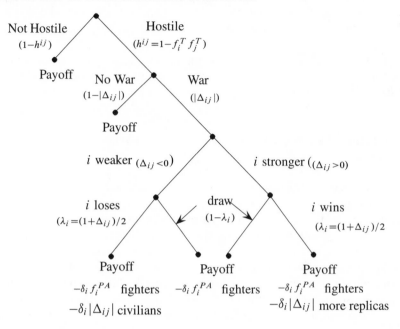

Figure 8.1. Between-group interaction. Notation: f_i^T, f_j^T = the fractions who are tolerant in group i and group j, respectively; $h_{ij} = 1 - f_i^T f_j^T$ = the probability that an interaction between groups i and j will be hostile; f_i^{PA}, f_j^{PA} = the fractions who are parochial altruists in group i and j; $\Delta_{ij} = f_i^{PA} - f_j^{PA}$; $|\Delta_{ij}|$ = probability that a hostile interaction will result in a war; δ_f = the fraction of fighters (PA's) who die ($\delta_f = 0.14$ in our benchmark simulations) and $\delta_c|\Delta_{ij}|$ = fraction of civilian mortality in the losing group ($\delta_c = 2.5$ in our benchmark simulations). Payoff refers to the payoffs to the public goods and peaceful intergroup interactions described in Table 8.1.

The process by which intergenerational transmission of behaviors takes place could be cultural, those with higher payoffs being disproportionately copied by the next generation, or genetic, payoffs measuring reproductive success. In every generation, members of each group are paired randomly to produce offspring, whose expected number is proportional to the parental couple's share of the group's payoffs.

So as not to favor the hypothesized coevolution of parochialism and altruism, which depends on the two behaviors being statistically associated, we assume an intergenerational transmission process with a strong tendency for the behaviors to be separated. Thus we assume no assortment in mating, so a parochial altruist is no more likely to mate with another parochial altruist than would occur by chance, and we also allow complete recombination, so that a parental couple composed of a *PA* and a *TN* will have offspring of all four behavioral types with equal probability. Additionally, this process is modified by mutation: with some probability μ each member's offspring inherits a strategy randomly from the four possible types independently of the parental types. With probability $1 - \mu$ the non-mutational replication described just above takes place. In each generation, with some probability (m), each member migrates to a randomly selected group.

This replication process reflects the assumption that all sites are saturated so that a group's population can grow only if it increases its carrying capacity by territorial aggrandizement.

8.2   The Emergence of Parochial Altruism and War

We used an agent-based computer simulation to explore properties of this model under a range of parameters calibrated to resemble the environment of Late Pleistocene and early Holocene humans.

As in the simulation in the previous chapter, because of the chance elements in the model—which groups meet, who migrates where, whether contests are hostile or not, and if so, who wins—the composition of the simulated population among the four behavioral types is constantly changing. In the simulation, history definitely matters: the distribution of the population in any period is strongly influenced by its distribution in the recent past. But in simulations of the model over a very long period (and very many times) the population spends much more of its time at some compositions than at others, and this is independent of the population composition with which we began the simulation (technically the model is *ergodic*). Figure 8.2 summarizes this stationary distribution. The height of the bars gives the fraction of a very long period in which we observe the indicated pair of population level frequencies of altruists and parochials in the population (we show the fraction of parochial altruists in Figure 8.4).

Over a very long period, the simulated population spends most of the time in states with many parochials and many altruists (the upper-right cluster of bars), or in states with many tolerants and many non-tolerants (the lower-left cluster). States with many altruists and few parochials rarely occur and the same is true of states with many parochial and few altruists. In the former case, near point **b** in the figure, high levels of parochialism in the population sustain a high level of conflict among groups, thereby making between-group selection a formidable evolutionary process and as a result maintaining a substantial fraction of altruists in groups. This replicates the synergy between war and altruism in Chapter 7 (see Figure 7.6). By contrast, when the population is in the states in which tolerant non-altruists are prevalent, few wars occur. As a result the within-group selection pressures against parochials and altruists predominate, and as expected from the payoffs in Table 8.1, this severely limits the population shares of both altruists and parochials.

In this model, parochialism and altruism evolve not because the parochial altruists deliberately associate with like types, but rather because within-group interactions for which cooperation is possible are characterized by positive assortment. This occurs

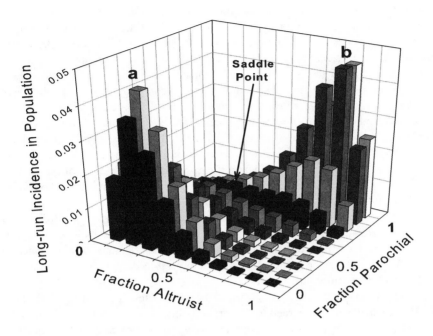

Figure 8.2. Parochial altruist and tolerant non-altruist outcomes occur with high frequency. These frequencies are an approximation of the stationary distribution of the underlying stochastic Markov process implied by our model and have been recovered from a very large number of implementations of the model. The baseline parameters from Table 8.1 are used in this simulation, along with migration and mutation rates $m = 0.3$ and $\mu = 0.005$. The average group size is 26 members per generation.

because parochial altruists are more likely to be in groups with other parochial altruists than under population-wide random matching. Hostile interactions, by contrast, are characterized by negative assortment, because the wars in which most parochial altruists participate (and win) tend to be against groups with larger fractions of the other three types. This is a result of the fact that evenly matched groups tend not to fight. When the number of parochials in the population is sufficient that such hostile conflicts are frequent, the result is to favor the proliferation of both altruists and parochials. Similarly, when tolerant individuals are prevalent in the population they benefit from positive assortment in cooperative interactions because most are in groups that reap benefits from peaceful intergroup relations.

The arrows in Figure 8.3 give the direction of expected movement for a population whose composition is indicated by the root of the arrow. The longer arrows indicate strong selection against parochials in the absence of significant frequencies of altruists and against altruists in the absence of significant frequencies of parochials.

The extent and nature of intergroup relationships are produced endogenously by the model. Thus a comparison of fatalities in war and other aspects of intergroup interactions with available empirical information provides a check on the plausibility of the model and parameters chosen. Tolerant individuals (T's) on average receive benefits from non-hostile interactions with all tolerant members of other groups amounting to 0.016 for all states. These values may be compared to the benefit of 0.02 that each altruist confers on the members of his own group by contributing to the public good. There are few benefits to T's near **b** in Figures 8.2 and 8.3 because at this state most interactions are hostile and even in the peaceful interactions there are few T's in the other group. Near **b**, a group may expect to be engaged in a war every 7.1 generations, the probability of war in each generation being 0.14, if it loses the war, to suffer fatalities equal to about 40% of its population, and if it wins, to suffer fatalities of about 10%, who are all PA's (only fighters die in victorious wars). Thus in the neighborhood of **b**, about 3.6% of the entire population dies in warfare per generation.

This statistic provides the reality check we were looking for: both altruism and parochialism are sustained by levels of intergroup conflict and deaths in warfare considerably below the estimates from archaeological and ethnographic data presented in Chapter 6. We are therefore quite confident that our results do not require implausibly high levels of between-group hostility.

Figure 8.4 illustrates the transition process between states close to **a** and those close to **b**. The fact that neither the fraction who are parochials nor the fraction who are altruists greatly exceeds the fraction who are parochial altruists (they could not, of course be less than the parochial altruist fraction) shows that the parochial and altruist "alleles" though not linked genetically in any way nonetheless come to be highly correlated as a result of the selection pressures in the model.

The two left panels in Figure 8.4 cover the same span of generations in a single simulation and illustrate a transition from a state close to **a** to a state close to **b** in Figures 8.2 and 8.3. Low population frequencies of altruists (A), parochials (P) and parochial altruists (PA) (the darker line in the top panel) for the first 300 generations (top panel) mean that a group's likelihood of engaging in a war is about 5% per generation (bottom panel). A consequence of the infrequency of war is that the within-group peacetime payoffs given in Table 8.1, for which tolerant non-altruism is the dominant strategy, are the main influence on the population dynamic, keeping the fraction of altruists, parochials and parochial altruists at a low level. Then at about generation 33800 a chance upturn in the fraction of parochial altruists results in a sharp increase in the likelihood of war (bottom panel), which in turn sustains and extends the increase in the population frequency of parochial altruists, propelling the population from the tolerant non-altruistic peaceful outcome to the parochial altruist warring outcome. A similar outbreak of peace, tolerance and self-interest is shown in the right two panels.

Figure 8.5 shows the relationship between the population fraction of parochial altruists and the frequency of war. The left panel shows that wars are most frequent when 30% to 80% of the population are parochial altruists. The reason is that at lower frequencies of parochial altruism, hostile group interactions are uncommon while at very high frequencies of parochial altruists hostility is virtually always the case, but imbalances between groups in the number of fighters (required for a war to occur) are uncommon. The right panel shows that the more frequent are wars, the higher is the fraction of population that are parochial altruists.

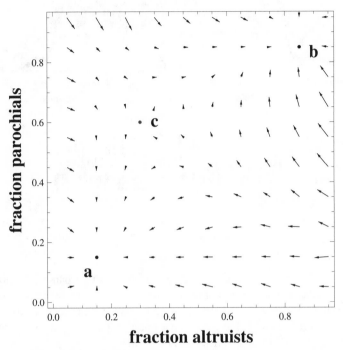

fraction altruists

Figure 8.3. Probabilistic transition dynamics. The parameter values are as before. Each arrow represents the expected change at each state, based on a transition matrix recovered from the underlying Markov process using five million simulations of the model with an initial distribution of types at every state in the state space. The length of the arrows indicates the strength of the selective pressure operating at that point in the state space. Asymptotically stable states occur where both frequencies are approximately 15% (point **a**) and in the neighborhood of the frequencies of A and P equal to (0.95,0.75), point **b**. Point **c** is a saddle (unstable critical point).

In Choi and Bowles (2007) we explored the sensitivity of these results to variations in the parameters. We found that the frequency of parochial altruists and of war varies inversely with group size and the migration rate. This is expected from the Price equation (4.3) because increasing these population structure parameters diminishes the between-group differences in the distribution of types, thereby weakening the effects of selective extinction. The parameters affecting within-group and between-group selection also have the expected effect: war and parochial altruism vary positively with the extent of losses inflicted on losers and inversely with both the benefit from non-hostile interactions (g) and the cost of altruism (c).

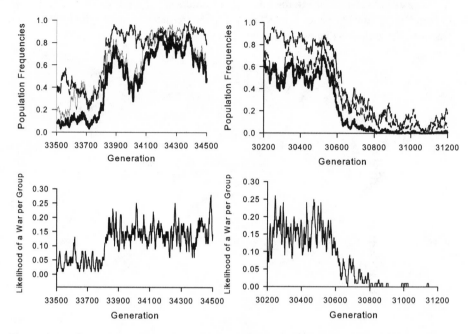

Figure 8.4. Outbreaks of war and peace. In the top two panels, the lowest of the three lines is the critical fraction of the population who are parochial altruists. The two panels on the left show an outbreak of warfare, namely a transition from a state near point **a** in Figure 8.2 and 8.3 to a state near point **b**. The two panels on the right show the reverse transition from a warring to a peaceful state.

8.3   Simulated and Experimental Parochial Altruism

Do recent experiments provide a test of our explanation of the coevolution of parochial altruism and war? It is not immediately clear how experiments can be used to test an evolutionary model. Usually the explanatory framework flows in the other direction: we ask if there is a plausible evolutionary model that would account for the emergence and persistence of the experimentally observed behaviors. The test of the model's plausibility in this framework is that the evolution of the behaviors observed in the experiments is shown to be likely within a parameter set consistent with what is known about the conditions of life of early humans. But a few carefully designed experiments, including some accidental and unfortunate natural experiments, do allow us to reason in the opposite direction; they provide evidence consistent with the evolutionary explanation we have given.

We begin with the experimental third-party punishment experiment in Papua New Guinea mentioned at the beginning of the chapter (Bernhard et al. 2006). If the experimental subject pool comprised the four behavioral types in our evolutionary model,

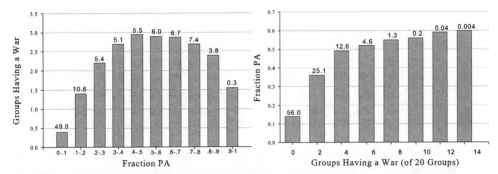

Figure 8.5. Parochial altruists and war. High frequencies of parochial altruists in the population sustain high frequencies of warfare and vice versa. The numbers at the top of each bar indicate the percentage of 50,000 generations in which this fraction of *PA*'s and this many wars occurred.

they well might replicate the results observed. Tolerant altruists would be expected to bear costs in order to give to both insiders and outsiders, and to punish those who violate norms. In view of the importance of mutually beneficial intergroup relations, punishment of norm violators by altruists would include out-group members as well as insiders. But parochial altruists would give preferentially to in-group members and punish those who harm fellow group members more severely than if the victim is not an insider. Our model shows that this spiteful behavior toward outsiders could have evolved by benefiting other group members in hostile intergroup contests. In the experiment the punishment of an outsider increases the relative payoffs of the individual's group, as the cost to the target of punishment is assumed to be three times the cost to the punisher.

Other evolutionary influences may also be suggested by the experiment: it might be thought, for example, that the fact that group members are likely to be more genetically related to insiders than to outsiders would explain group favoritism in giving. But this could not explain giving itself in the non-repeated interactions of the experiment. The reason is that in the experiment the benefit conferred by the gift is fully offset by the cost to the giver (that is, $b = c$ in the terms of equation 4.1) and so could not have evolved by kin-based selection. The reason is that Hamilton's rule in this case would require that for giving not to be inclusive fitness reducing the giver and receiver would have to be genetically identical ($r = 1$), and even then the giving would be simply selectively neutral! Moreover, direct fitness benefits cannot explain the punishment of norm violators, or the more severe punishment of outsiders, assuming the ancestors of these experimental subjects lived in groups of the size typical of our foraging forebears' residential groups.

The Bernhard et al. (2006) experiment shows, then, that the behavioral types observed in the experiment could have been the result of the selective extinction coevolutionary processes we described above, and would be unlikely to have emerged and proliferated if the sole evolutionary process at work had been generosity toward close family members. Among the inclusive fitness-based models, then, it suggests the plausibility of the multi-level selection account.

An alternative account, seemingly more plausible than kin-based altruism, is based on the reciprocal altruism and reputational explanations. It holds that while the game was anonymous, the subjects nonetheless mapped the game onto common experiences in their daily lives and adopted experimental behavior that, in those situations, anticipated reputational benefits, consistent with self-regarding preferences. Another experiment from Papua New Guinea, Efferson et al. (2011), inspired by the model of parochial altruism described above (and initially presented in Choi and Bowles 2007), allows us to test predictions based on this reputation-based explanation against predictions consistent with the group-extinction multi-level selection model presented here.

Efferson and his coauthors implemented a one-shot anonymous trust game among members of two distinct ethnic groups, the Ngenika and Perepka, in which investors and trustees were of either the same or different ethnicities (p. 3.9). Recall that in the trust game an "investor" Alice is given an endowment m, any part m' of which she can transfer to a "trustee" Bob; the experimenter then doubles m' and gives this amount to Bob. Bob can then transfer back any fraction of $2m'$ to Alice. Alice is said to trust Bob if she sends him her whole endowment m. Bob will get $2m$, and if he is trustworthy, he will send back a substantial amount, perhaps half, in which case each will end up with a payoff of m. If Alice does not trust Bob and sends nothing, however, she will still have payoff m, but Bob will have nothing. Finally, if Alice trusts Bob, but Bob is amoral and self-regarding, and hence untrustworthy, then he will keep the whole $2m$, and Alice will have zero payoff.

The experimenters also asked each Alice to indicate the amount of the back transfer from her Bob that she expected based on various hypothetical levels of Alice's initial transfer. As in other experimental trust games, the results contradicted predictions made on the basis of the self-interest axiom: both Alices and Bobs were substantially more generous than would have been the case were the axiom true. Note that we can eliminate kin-based altruism as an explanation because even had both players imagined that they were siblings or parents and children ($r = 0.5$) Hamilton's rule would not predict a transfer by Alice. Alice could infer that the back transfer would in any case be zero, since Bob is just giving away money, so the cost to Bob is exactly equal to the benefit to Alice. So the only incentive for Alice to transfer any amount to Bob would be to enhance Bob's fitness. But because the benefit to Bob is only double the cost to the investor (because m' is doubled) rb cannot exceed c, assuming Bob and alice are not identical twins!.

Of greater interest, however, are the predictions based on the reputation-based explanation and the parochial altruism explanation. Consider Alice's choice. A parochial altruist Alice would act amorally and self-regardingly toward outsiders but not towards insiders. A self-interested and reputation-minded Alice would do exactly the opposite. Thus when playing with coethhics, were the players self-regarding and reputation conscious, their transfers would have varied with their expected payback response of the Bobs, avoiding large transfers that would not be requited so as to not acquire a reputation as one who is easily exploited.

By contrast, when playing with coethnics, a parochial altruist Alice's transfers would be independent of the expected payback. When playing with the outsider, the pattern would be exactly reversed: a parochial altruist Alice's transfers would depend on the expected payback, while the self-interested reputation-oriented Alice's transfers would not, because in dealings with outsiders, the value of a reputation for generosity would be absent or at least less than with insiders.

In the experiment, the expectations of the parochial altruist Alice model were confirmed, and those of the self-interested reputational Alice model contradicted. Similar results hold for the Bobs. For example, if they were self-interested and reputation-conscious, Bob should not make a back transfer that results in his getting a lower pay-off than Alice, while if Bob is a parochial altruist, he would sometimes make such a disadvantageous back transfer. In these and other tests, Bob's behavior also conformed to the predictions of the parochial altruist Bob model and contradicted that of the self-interested reputation-based Bob model.

Quite different evidence concerns the linkage of parochialism and altruism. If, as we think, parochialism and altruism coevolved, each being unviable singly, then we would expect that some proximal causes would be common to both parochialism and altruism. This is exactly what was found from experiments with brain oxytocin, a neuropeptide that has been shown to promote trust and cooperativeness in experiments, and to deter subjects taking advantage of the cooperation of others (De Dreu et al. 2010, 2011). In a series of eight experiments Carsten and his coauthors (De Dreu et al. 2011) found that, by comparison with a placebo, nasally administered oxytocin also heightens in-group bias and in some but not all cases out-group derogation.

Finally, a set of experiments show that both experimental and naturally occurring prosocial behaviors are heightened by warfare or group conflict. While consistent with expectations of our account of the evolution of parochial altruism, this evidence is not a test of our model and simulations, for what we have shown in the model and simulations is not that parochial altruism is heightened during group conflicts, but rather that group conflicts explain its evolutionary success. However, because the evolutionary success of altruism is explained by the behaviors it promotes during times of conflict, we think it likely that group conflicts would stimulate greater altruism.

Evidence to this effect is provided in a study by Gneezy and Fessler (2011). The authors implemented a trust and ultimatum game to a group of adult Israeli citizens not involved in military service before, during, and after the 2006 Israel-Hezbollah war. They found that while before and after war experimental results were statistically indistinguishable, the subjects exhibited stronger social preferences during the war. They found that during the war low ultimatum game offers were much more likely to be rejected and that more generous transfers by Alice to Bob in the trust game were five times more strongly reciprocated during the war than before or after.

Both experimental and natural evidence comes from another study. Maarten Voors and his coauthors (2011) studied the massive indiscriminate killing that took place during the genocidal violence in Burundi and the effects that it had on individuals' altruistic behavior toward neighbors. A total of 300 subjects from 35 randomly selected villages, 26 of which had experienced lethal ethnic violence over the period of Hutu-

Tutsi conflicts during the years 1993–2003, participated in an experiment in which they could allocate money between themselves and another anonymous individual from their village. Controlling for a number of demographic and community differences, those from villages that had been exposed to ethnic violence were much more likely to behave altruistically toward their neighbors in the experiment. The same was true of the individual experience of violence. Those who had themselves been victim of an attack were also more altruistic. The authors provide persuasive reasons to believe that the direction of causation is from intergroup conflict to within-group altruism, and not the other way around. These surprising effects of intergroup violence on experimental behavior were substantial. A standard deviation difference in the number of attacks suffered by a village was associated with almost half a standard deviation increase in altruistic behavior. Exposure to violence was also significantly related to greater participation in community organizations.

A final experiment provides a possible link between group conflict and the evolution of cooperation based not on the fact that altruists, if parochial, are willing fighters but that group conflict stimulates altruistic punishment of free-riding fellow group members. Sääksvuior, Puurtinen and their coauthors (2011) implemented a series of eight-person public goods games with and without a punishment option and in which the payoffs of members of the groups playing these games either depended on the outcome of group competition or were independent of the performance of any other group. Recall that the public goods with punishment game, described in §3.3, is an n-person prisoners dilemma in which members of the group could pay to have the payoffs of other members reduced—that is punish the other member—after having been informed of each member's contributions to the public good. In the treatments with group competition, the groups with the larger contribution to the public good won a prize that was twice the group difference in the level of public contributions. Group competition greatly heightened the punishment of shirking group members where this was possible, so that groups with the punishment option prevailed over groups without it. A fascinating secondary result is that the punishment option greatly reduced the within group variance of payoffs, and hence might be counted among the reproductive leveling mechanisms studied in the previous chapter. The authors conclude: "These results support the importance of intergroup competition in the emergence of costly punishment and human cooperation."

8.4   The Legacy of a Past "Red in Tooth and Claw"

Our approach thus explains *Homo sapiens* as a sometimes warlike species and the status of parochial altruism as a common suite of human behaviors. It also shows that warfare itself may have contributed to the spread of human altruism. We initially recoiled at this unpleasant and surprising conclusion. But the simulations and the data on prehistoric warfare tell a convincing story.

But was warfare necessary in the evolution of human altruism? Could altruism not have evolved in the absence of lethal group conflict, and perhaps taken a tolerant rather than parochial form? The key element in the explanation offered here and in Chapter 7 is that groups with more altruists survive challenges, encroaching on less cooperative groups or even eliminating them. The differential survival of more cooperative groups need not have been the result of warfare. The tumultuous climate of the Late Pleistocene (Figure 6.1) presented groups with extraordinary challenges quite apart from direct confrontations with other groups. If groups with a greater number of altruists were more likely than less cooperative groups to surmount these environmental challenges, they would have had opportunities to occupy the vacated sites of the defunct groups of less altruistic and less cooperative individuals, replicating the process modeled here as the result of warfare. Thus, returning to Darwin and rewriting the head quote of Chapter 4, "the social and moral qualities" could have "advanced and diffused throughout the world" entirely without any tribe being "victorious over other tribes."

While altruism might have evolved in the absence of group conflict by this mechanism, we do not think that it did. The evidence for frequent lethal encounters and the plausibility of the assumption that more cooperative groups would survive these challenges suggests that warfare, no doubt in conjunction with environmental challenges, played a critical role in the evolution of this particular cooperative species. And this evidence that lethal group encounters were a part of the early human condition is compelling.

Although a form of altruism circumscribed by parochialism is in our legacy, it need not be our destiny. The fact that altruism and parochialism may have a common evolutionary origin, whether cultural or genetic, does not mean that the two are inseparable. Examples of tolerant, even anti-parochial, altruism include subjects in some intergroup behavioral experiments, the electoral support in many countries for tax-supported economic aid to the people of poor nations, and the participation of people of all ancestral groups in political movements against racism, including the three young men to whom we have dedicated this book.

Symbol	Meaning
b	Benefit
c	Cost
δ_f	Fraction of fighters who die
δ_c	Fraction of civilian mortality in losing group
Δ_{ij}	$= f_i^{PA} - f_j^{PA}$
f_i^A	Fraction of group i that are altruists
f_j^T	Fraction of group j who are tolerant
f_i^{PA}	Fractions who are parochial altruists in group i
g	Benefit of non-hostile group interaction
h_{ij}	Probability a group interaction will be hostile
i, j	Index for groups
m	Probability of migration
μ	Mutation rate
n	Group size
n_j	Size of group j

Table 8.2. Definition of symbols

9

The Evolution of Strong Reciprocity

> My motive for doing what I am going to do is simply personal revenge. I do not
> expect to accomplish anything by it.... Of course, I would like to get revenge on
> the whole scientific and bureaucratic establishment... but that being impossible,
> I have to content myself with just a little revenge.
>
> Theodore Kaczynski, *Excerpts from the Unabomber's Journal* (1998)

The previous two chapters showed that an unconditional form of altruistic cooperation among members of a group could have evolved under conditions likely to have been experienced by our Late Pleistocene and early Holocene ancestors. But we also know that in experiments and everyday life, altruism is rarely unconditional. In the repeated public goods game, for example, when no other recourse is available, altruistic cooperators react to free-riding by others by withdrawing their contributions. But a cognitively advanced animal can do a lot better than to just walk away. He and his fellow group members can gang up on the defector. And, as we have seen in Chapter 6, this is widely observed in decentralized, non-state, social orders.

Together, a predisposition to cooperate and a willingness to punish defectors is what we have termed strong reciprocity, and it is the combination of the two that is essential to the large-scale cooperation exhibited by our species. Here we show how a willingness to punish those who violate social norms even at personal cost could have evolved.

Punishment reduces the gain to free-riding, and may induce even entirely self-interested individuals to cooperate. Thus groups with more punishers can sustain more cooperation. Such punishment is altruistic so long as a single punisher would have higher payoff by refraining from punishing. Punishment is costly to the punisher and the target alike, but unlike unconditional altruism, the costs to punishers are greatly reduced when they are common. The reason is when punishers are common, the threat of punishment is sufficient to deter free riding, so punishers rarely bear the costs of punishing. As a result, a modest advantage of groups in which cooperation is sustained by the presence of punishers is sufficient to offset the individual cost of punishment.

Thus once strong reciprocators are common in a group, the higher average payoffs of the more cooperative groups in which most strong reciprocators find themselves can readily offset their occasional direct costs of punishing the occasional defection. In the Price equation (4.3) this means that the cost to the individual strong reciprocator, β_i, is small, so that neither the group-level benefits of cooperation nor the between-group differences that make up the between-group selection term $\beta_G \text{var}(p_j)$ need to be very large in order to stabilize the fraction of strong reciprocators in a population. This is roughly the explanation of the evolution that we, along with Robert Boyd and Peter Richerson, offered for the evolution of cooperation (Boyd et al. 2003).

But there are two important problems with this explanation. First, even if punishment sustains high levels of cooperation, it may nonetheless reduce average payoffs to group members if its costs to both the punisher and the target exceed the resulting gains from cooperation (Fehr and Gächter 2000a, Bochet et al. 2006, Cinyabuguma et al. 2006, Herrmann et al. 2008). This problem is exacerbated when punishers target not only shirkers but cooperative group members, as well, as we have seen (Figure 3.3) sometimes occurs in experiments.

Second, the initial emergence of punishment remains a puzzle. In order to survive, punishers must engage in enough punishment of defectors so that the induced cooperation more than offsets the cost of punishing. Rare punishers do not have the benefit of outnumbering their targets, so the cost of punishing a free-rider is substantial. Moreover, they usually bear this cost alone rather than sharing it with other punishers (Boyd and Richerson 1988, 1992, Panchanathan and Boyd 2003, Boyd et al. 2003).

Both problems, however, are artifacts of the unrealistic way that punishment is implemented in existing models, including our own earlier models, and in most experiments. In these models, punishment is an unconditional and uncoordinated individual action automatically triggered by defection. Similarly, in experiments, with few exceptions (Ostrom et al. 1992), individuals cannot coordinate their punishment. But as we saw in Chapter 6, the ethnographic evidence indicates that solitary individuals rarely attempt to punish those who violate social norms. When punishment occurs, it is usually collective, and partly for this reason conveys a message of peer condemnation. Consistent with the anthropological evidence, in behavioral experiments with communication or with a choice of a collective punishment strategy by subjects, punishment is often effective in raising group average payoffs and is rarely aimed at cooperative members (Ertan et al. 2009).

Here, we take account of two empirically grounded features that resolve the above difficulties. First, punishment is coordinated among group members so that it is contingent on the number of others predisposed to participate in the punishment. This is an example of what biologists call "quorum sensing," practiced by bacteria and other organisms (Miller and Bassler 2001, Diggle et al. 2007), in which the bacteria do not become ("turn on") active until there are enough of them to overwhelm the organisms's immune responses. Our Punishers, when they are rare, demur and so bear only the minor cost of signaling their willingness to punish. They thus avoid the cost of punishing when they do not sufficiently outnumber their targets. Second, consistent with the "strength in numbers" and "divide and rule" maxims, punishment is characterized by increasing returns to scale, so the total cost of punishing a particular target declines as the number of punishers increases. Adding these two novel features resolves the problems with previous models. Our model, adapted from Boyd, Gintis, and Bowles (2010), shows that for levels of relatedness consistent with recent genetic data from hunter-gatherer populations (Table 6.1), punishment can proliferate when rare, and when it is common, it increases group-average fitness, but reduces the fitness of the punishers by comparison to their fitness were they not to punish and hence is altruistic. Our agent-based model of the process further illustrates the causal processes accounting for the evolutionary success of contingent punishment motivated by strong reciprocity.

9.1   Coordinated Punishment

Consider a large population in which individuals interact repeatedly in groups of size n. Groups are randomly formed so there is no genetic assortment. Later, we will introduce an empirically plausible degree of genetic assortment among groups. The initial period in the life of a group has three stages. First is a *signaling stage* in which at cost q, punishers can signal their intent to punish any defector (we describe the strategies below). The cost of signaling is high enough that it does not pay to signal and then not to punish. There follows a *cooperation stage*, during which individuals can choose to cooperate or defect. Cooperation costs the cooperator c and benefits each member of the group b/n. As usual, we assume $b > c > b/n$. Were there no punishment option, the interaction would be a public goods game (n-person prisoners' dilemma) in which the dominant strategy would be to not cooperate. Table 9.2 presents the mathematical symbols used in this chapter.

Finally, there is a *punishment stage* in which individuals can coordinate with other punishers to administer punishment. To model the expected cost of punishment for those engaging in punishment against a target, we use a probabalistic version of *Lanchester's law* on the relationship between numbers on opposing sides of a conflict and success in contests (Lanchester 1916, Engel 1954, Hwang 2009). The expected cost of punishing depends on the likely outcome of the encounter with the target. We take account of this aspect of punishment in the following way. Suppose the cost of punishing, k, is borne by a randomly selected member of the party of punishers if and only if the punishing episode is a standoff, a situation in which neither the punishers nor the target "wins" so that both target and punishers bear costs. Suppose further that a standoff occurs with probability $1/n_p$, where n_p is the number of punishers against a lone target. Thus, for instance, a single Punisher against a single target always results in a standoff. The expected cost of joining a party of n_p punishers is thus the probability of a standoff ($1/n_p$) times the expected cost that a member of the punishing party will bear in the case of a standoff (k/n_p), giving expected cost k/n_p^2.

During subsequent periods, there is no signaling stage, as players already know the number of punishers in the group. The cooperation and punishment stages, however, remain, after which the interaction continues to another period with probability δ, so the expected duration of a group is $1/(1-\delta)$ periods. When the interaction ends, the group disbands. When all groups have disbanded, new groups are drawn from the population and the process is repeated.

Population structures like this one, in which groups do not persist forever but rather are created anew periodically by drawing individuals from a larger population, are widely used in models of social evolution, including models of repeated interaction that lead to the evolution of contingent behavior (Axelrod and Hamilton 1981, Nowak and Sigmund 1998b). Such models provide an analytically tractable approximation to more realistic structures in which extensive gene flow among persistent groups causes low relatedness within groups. In the first period of such models individuals have no common history, as they would if we modeled persistent groups, and hence cannot know anything about strategies of other group members. To address this information problem it is standard to introduce a first "information-gathering" period in which individuals may behave differently than in subsequent periods. This is a seemingly unrealistic assumption. But even in the more realistic setting of persistent groups, individuals change, die or leave the group and are replaced by migrants or offspring. This means that actors must in any case deal with situations in which the past behavior of some group members is unknown, analogous to the first period in the present model. The present model represents a worst case for the evolution of punishment because it maximizes the level of uncertainty about the strategies of others and hence maximizes the cost to punishers of determining if a sufficient number are present to warrant punishing.

Individuals have one of two heritable strategies, *Punisher* and *Nonpunisher*. Later we test the robustness of our model by introducing *Liars*, who signal their willingness to punish but then do not, and *Opportunists*, who signal but punish only if their participation is needed to secure a quorum.

During the first period in the life of a group, Punishers signal they are willing to punish, whereas Nonpunishers do not. Next, if at least τ ($0 < \tau < n - 1$) other group members signal, Punishers cooperate with probability $1 - \epsilon$ and defect with probability ϵ, and then punish any individual who did not cooperate. We refer to Punishers with a threshold of τ as τ-Punishers. If fewer than τ other individuals signaled during the first stage, Punishers defect, and do not punish. Nonpunishers do not signal or defect, and do not punish. As a result, they are punished if there are at least $\tau + 1$ Punishers in the group. We assume that the cost to the target of being punished, p, is greater than the net cost of cooperating, $c - b/n$, so, on average, cooperation is the payoff-maximizing action if punishment is anticipated. A fraction ϵ of individuals nonetheless defects, either due to error or because cooperation is more costly for some individuals and so it does pay them to cooperate, even if they expect to be punished. If defectors were punished the last time a defection occurred, both types cooperate with probability $1 - \epsilon$ and defect with probability ϵ. Punishers punish defectors if at least τ other individuals punished the last time a defection occurred.

Nonpunishers are a plausible ancestral state for the evolution of punishment. They do not cooperate or punish, nor do they respond to unverified threats of punishment. However, once they have been punished, they cooperate in subsequent periods in order to avoid more punishment. Note that cooperation is a facultative choice, not an inherited behavior. One might worry that punishment can evolve only when it is linked pleiotropically or in some other way to cooperation. But in our model, after the first period, Punishers and Nonpunishers cooperate under exactly the same conditions, namely the expectation that not doing so will be punished, so the linkage between cooperation and punishment is extremely weak. In Boyd, Gintis, and Bowles (2010), we show that even this weak linkage is not necessary for the evolution of punishment. After the social interaction just described, individuals reproduce at a rate that is proportional to their payoff compared to the population-average payoff, leading to the equations that describe how natural selection changes the frequencies of the two types through time.

Before presenting results based on groups formed for plausible levels of between-group genetic differences, we consider the case of randomly formed groups (i.e., the degree of relatedness of group members is $r = 0$). For most parameter sets, there are

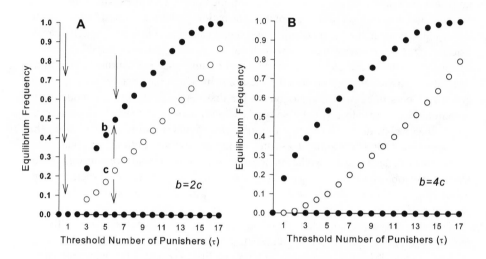

Figure 9.1. Equilibrium frequencies of Punishers for two values of b. For each value of τ the solid dots give locally stable equilibrium frequencies of the punishing type, and the open dots give interior unstable equilibrium frequencies. For Panel A, with $\tau < 3$, the only stable equilibrium is a population without Punishers. For larger τ, there are two stable equilibrium frequencies, zero and a mixed strategy at which Punishers and Nonpunishers coexist. The arrows indicate the effect of natural selection at points above and below the solid and open dots. In these cases, the unstable equilibrium marks the frequency that Punishers must achieve before they are favored by selection. With larger benefits ($b = 4c$) Panel B shows that a punishment strategy with a threshold of one (other) group member can proliferate when rare, attaining an equilibrium population frequency of 10%. Benchmark parameters: $c = 0.01, q = k = p = 1.5c$, $r = 0, a = 2, q = k = p = 1.5c, \epsilon = 0.1, n = 18, T = 25$.

two long-run evolutionary outcomes, illustrated by the solid dots in Figure 9.1, which shows the equilibrium frequency of Punishers as a function of the level of the quorum threshold. For example, panel A shows that if the threshold is 8, then populations with no Punishers or with 60% Punishers are stable equilibria (the solid dots) and that in populations with fewer than 24% Punishers (the open dot) selection will eliminate the Punishers, while in populations with more than 24% Punishers, their numbers will expand to 60% of the population. Technically the open dot gives the boundary of the basin of attraction of the two stable equilibria, much like point **c** in Figure 8.3.

The black dots on the horizontal axis in Figure 9.1 show that if $b = 2c$, for any threshold level, universal non-punishment is stable. When Punishers are rare, they will almost always be alone in a group and thus pay the cost of signaling but do not reap the benefits of cooperation, and thus will have lower fitness than Nonpunishers. The two panels of Figure 9.1 show that Punishers who are willing to punish alone ($\tau = 0$) cannot invade a population of all Nonpunishers because even with $b = 4c$, the benefits from cooperation are not sufficiently large that a single Punisher could recoup the costs of signaling and punishing everyone else in the group. Here, we assume that this "Lone Ranger" condition is not satisfied so that only punishment by two or more Punishers pays. However, the open dot on the horizontal axis of panel B shows that with larger benefits ($b = 4c$) a punishment strategy with a threshold of one (other) group member can proliferate when rare, and the black dot shows that the population will then attain an equilibrium frequency of 10%. We will see that with an empirically estimated degree of genetic assortment, Punishers proliferate when rare for threshold levels between zero and four (Figure 9.2).

Thus for many thresholds mixtures of Punishers and Nonpunishers are also evolutionarily stable. Punishers have a fitness advantage over Nonpunishers only in groups in which there are exactly $\tau + 1$ Punishers. The reason is that in such "threshold groups," each Punisher is necessary to sustain punishment and therefore cooperation. In groups with fewer than $\tau + 1$ Punishers, Punishers pay the cost of signaling, but because they do not punish they, like all group members, enjoy no cooperative benefits. In groups with more than the critical number of Punishers, a Punisher who switched to nonpunishing would enjoy the same payoff from cooperation as other group members without paying the costs of signaling and punishment. This means that in a randomly mixed population selection cannot favor τ-Punishers unless they are in groups in which there are exactly $\tau + 1$ Punishers and the benefits from cooperation are enough to compensate Punishers for the costs of signaling and punishment. Moreover, the advantage enjoyed by Punishers in these critical groups must be large enough to offset the payoff disadvantages suffered by Punishers in groups with fewer or more than the critical numbers of Punishers.

The existence of a stable mixture of Punishers and Nonpunishers depends on the value of the punishment threshold, τ. When the threshold is too low, punishment does not pay even at the threshold, and nonpunishment is the only evolutionarily stable strategy. At higher thresholds, punishment does pay in threshold groups, and this means that punishment may be favored if such groups are sufficiently common. Thus, as the frequency of Punishers in the meta-population increases from zero, the fraction of groups with the threshold number of Punishers increases, and so does the expected fitness of Punishers (Figure 9.2). Once the fraction of threshold groups is high enough, the Punishers' advantage in these groups offsets their disadvantage in all other groups. Then, natural selection will increase the frequency of Punishers. This marks the unstable equilibria (open dots) shown in Figure 9.1 and the leftmost zero intercept, point **c** on the horizontal axis, for each of the functions in Figure 9.2.

Further increases in the metapopulation frequency of Punishers eventually decrease the fraction of threshold groups. When, as a result, the fitness of Punishers and Nonpunishers is equalized, there is a stable *polymorphic (mixed) equilibrium* (Figure 9.1, solid dots, and Figure 9.2, rightmost horizontal axis intersection, point **b** for example). As τ increases, the frequency of Punishers at this polymorphic equilibrium also increases, but the minimum initial frequency of Punishers required for selection to move a population to this equilibrium also increases, making the equilibrium less accessible if Punishers are initially rare.

At the stable polymorphic equilibrium, punishment is not altruistic. The Punisher that switched to Nonpunisher would on average experience no change in payoff. When

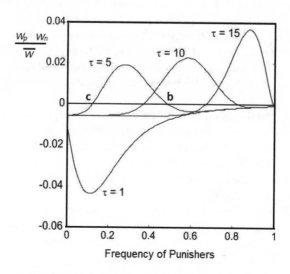

Figure 9.2. The difference in fitness of Punishers (W_P) and Nonpunishers (W_N) as a function of the frequency of Punishers when $b = 2c$. When this difference is positive, Punishers increase in frequency, and when it is negative Punishers decrease in frequency. Equilibria occur when this difference is zero. The equilibrium is stable when the function intersects the horizontal axis from above and unstable otherwise. Thus the zero intersections in this figure correspond to the open and closed interior dots in Figure 9.1, panel A. For example, point **c** in this figure is the interior saddle point when $\tau = 5$, corresponding to the open dot at point **c** in Figure 9.1, panel A, and point **b** is the interior stable equilibrium indicated by the solid dot at point **b** in Figure 9.1, panel A. When $\tau = 1$, punishment at the threshold does not pay for any frequency of Punishers, and thus increasing the frequency of Punishers from zero decreases their relative fitness. For larger values of τ, punishment at the threshold does pay, and thus increasing the frequency of Punishers increases their fitness. This leads to a stable mixed equilibrium at which Punishers and Nonpunishers coexist. Parameters as in Figure 9.1, panel A.

groups are formed at random, averaged over all groups, the long-run benefits of punishment exactly compensate for the costs. However, it is mutually beneficial to the group (Figure 9.3) in that populations with the equilibrium frequency of Punishers have higher average fitness than populations without Punishers.

The results presented so far depend critically on two parameters: the extent of economies of scale in punishment, a, and the cost Punishers have to pay to signal their willingness to punish, q. Considering the first, were we to assume $a = 1$ (constant returns to scale) the total cost of punishing defectors would be independent of the number of Punishers, and much higher frequencies of punishment would be required before

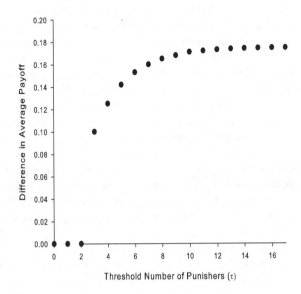

Figure 9.3. Average fitness differences. The difference in average fitness between the mixed equilibrium at which Punishers are present and the monomorphic nonpunishing equilibrium. Whenever the mixed equilibrium exists it has higher average fitness, but near maximum benefit differences occur for relatively low thresholds. Parameters as in Figure 9.1.

punishment would become evolutionarily stable (Boyd et al. 2003). This supports the intuition that increasing returns is crucial, and therefore the notion of coordinated punishment is important.

To determine the minimum cost of signaling, q, necessary to ensure that the signal is honest, we introduced a third strategy, Liar. Liars may benefit by "turning on" the punishment process without paying the costs. During the first period, Liars signal that they are Punishers, incurring the signaling cost, and then cooperate so as to avoid punishment during the first period. However, they do not punish, and therefore avoid the associated costs. In subsequent periods, Liars count the number of other group members that signaled in the first period and cooperate if the number of such signalers is greater than $\tau + 1$. Because Liars never punish, after the first period they behave like Nonpunishers and so receive the Nonpunisher payoff. At equilibrium, Punishers and Nonpunishers have the same fitness, and thus Liars can invade if their expected payoff during the first period is greater than the expected payoff of Nonpunishers during the first period. This determines the minimum cost of signaling, q, which we set so Liars do slightly worse that Nonpunishers. The value of q used in our calculations satisfies this condition for all results presented here.

To explore the effects of genetic assortment, we now drop our assumption that groups are formed at random and assume that the relatedness within groups is $r > 0$, so that individuals are more likely to interact with individuals similar to themselves than expected by chance. Figure 9.4 shows the equilibrium behavior assuming that $r = 0.07$, which is a rough estimate of the average relatedness within human foraging groups (Bowles 2006). For low thresholds ($\tau < 4$), the only stable equilibrium is a mixture of Punishers and Nonpunishers, which means that Punishers invade when rare. And because of the population structure (between-group genetic differences), punishment may also be altruistic at the polymorphic equilibrium. We show in Boyd et al. (2010b) that this result persists when groups are much larger ($n = 72$) and for lower levels of relatedness if the benefit-cost ratio is somewhat higher. However, modest assortment does not allow punishment strategies with higher thresholds to invade populations of Punishers with lower thresholds, so there is no evolutionary process in this model that would ratchet up the threshold levels. Thus, consistent with ethnographic observation, the model predicts that only some individuals will engage in punishment. However, even when $\tau = 3$, meaning that a minimum of 4 out of 18 individuals punish, groups achieve about two thirds of the maximum gains from cooperation attainable with higher thresholds (Figure 9.3).

Unlike many models of the evolution of punishment, this one does not suffer from a "second-order free-rider" problem in which individuals who cooperate but do not punish outcompete the Punishers. To see why, consider a new strategy type, *Contingent Cooperators*, who cooperate during the first period if there are $\tau + 1$ signaling individuals but do not punish. Contingent Cooperators avoid punishment during the first period and otherwise behave like Nonpunishers, and thus have higher fitness than Nonpunishers. As a result, they invade the polymorphic Punisher-Nonpunisher equilibrium, replacing the Nonpunishers. However, because they still respond to punishment, and punishment still benefits Punishers, the population evolves to a stable equilibrium at which Punishers and Contingent Cooperators coexist and that cannot be invaded by other second-order free-riding types. The frequency of Punishers at this new equilibrium is approximately the same as in the original Punisher-Nonpunisher equilibrium.

In our model, the initial proliferation of punishment occurs under plausible levels of group genetic differences and results in persistent and high levels of cooperation. This result depends on the contingent nature of punishment and the existence of increasing returns to punishment. It differs from the model of Hauert et al. (2007), in which the population cycles between periods of cooperation, defection, and opting-out of the interaction entirely, the latter strategy invading the all-defect phase of the cycle and subsequently being invaded by cooperators. Although their model applies to some forms of cooperation, we think that the present model is a more realistic representation of the nature and dynamics of human cooperation (Boyd and Mathew 2007).

9.2   Altruistic Punishment in a Realistic Demography

There are two unrealistic aspects of our model, however: in it the groups are ephemeral, lasting only as long as a single repeated interaction among its members continues, and the degree of genetic assortment is either assumed to be zero or given an exogenously estimated value. Here we use an agent-based computer simulation to explore a more realistic demographic structure in which the degree of genetic assortment is a result rather than an assumption of the model. Here we assume that the meta-population

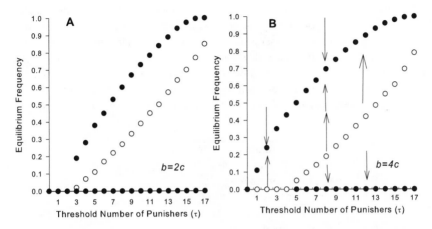

Figure 9.4. The evolution of contingent punishment with an empirically estimated level of genetic assortment.Equilibrium frequencies of Punishers with a threshold level of τ with modest assortment ($r = 0.07$) and two values of b. As in Figure 9.1, for each value of τ, the solid dots give locally stable equilibrium frequencies of the punishing type, and the open dots give unstable equilibrium frequencies. Panel A shows that, as in the case with no assortment, for large enough values of τ there are two equilibria, but Punishers cannot invade and increase when rare. Panel B shows that for $0 < \tau \leq 4$, rare Punishers invade a population of Nonpunishers, and the only stable equilibrium is a mixture of Punishers and Nonpunishers in which cooperation is sustained in most groups. For larger thresholds, there are two stable equilibrium frequencies, zero and a mixed strategy at which Punishers and Nonpunishers coexist. In these cases, the unstable equilibria (open dots) mark the frequency that Punishers must achieve before they are favored by selection. Parameters are as in the previous figures.

is composed of many band-sized sub-populations. The meta-population persists for a great many generations (typically 100,000 or more), and when a subpopulation is formed, it lasts throughout the history of the population unless its size becomes too small to sustain life under Pleistocene conditions. We study only the members of a generation that is currently reproducing, which comprises about a third of the total population. We set the average and minimum group sizes at 30 and 8 reproductive members, respectively. Individual group size and composition change through birth, death, and migration, although we maintain a constant number of groups and a constant total population.

The type of a new group member becomes public information when the individual does or does not signal his type as Punisher, at cost q. We assume behavior is the expression of genetic inheritance and individuals are haploid (an individual has one copy of each gene), but reproduction is diploid (an individual inherits each gene with equal probability from one of two parents). Finally, we assume $\tau = 6$, although, as is clear from Figures 9.1, 9.2, and 9.4, a smaller value would have led Punishers to invade a Nonpunisher population more rapidly.

We assume that in the first period following the group's formation, all Punishers signal their type to all other group members, at a cost q. In succeeding periods, migration, birth, and death will lead to the disappearance of some Punishers and the appearance of other individuals (immigrants and newborns) who we assume are of unknown type. We assume that when the number of known Punishers is τ or fewer, but the number of known Punishers plus individuals of unknown type is greater than τ, the individuals of unknown type who are Punishers signal their willingness to punish, again at cost q.

Variable	Value	Description
a	2	Increasing returns to scale in punishing
b	0.04	Benefits of cooperation
c	0.01	Cost of cooperation
k	0.015	Cost of punishing
p	0.015	Cost of being punished
ρ	0.04	Reproduction rate per period
μ	0.001	Mutation rate
ϵ	0.03	Execution error rate
m	0.003	Migration rate per period
	0.30	Fraction of newborns who migrate to other groups
	250	Number of groups
τ	6	Threshold number of Punishers
n	30	Average group size (members of a reproducing generation)
	8	Minimum Sustainable group size
w_o	0.95	Baseline fitness

Table 9.1. Baseline parameters. Note: These parameters are used in all simulations, unless otherwise noted. Note that n represents the number of members of a reproducing generation. There are 25 periods per generation.

We assume 25 periods occur per generation, so the periods are roughly years. This corresponds to $T = 25$ and $\delta = 0.96$ in the analytical model. Each individual mates and reproduces on average twice per generation, so the per-period reproduction rate is $\rho = 0.04$. The baseline parameters are listed in Table 9.1.

There are 250 groups, giving a total population of 7500 per generation. We assume that 70% of newborns are located in the parental group and 30% are relocated randomly in the population. This implies a total migration rate of $0.3 + 0.003 \times 25 = 37.5\%$ per generation, or 1.5% per period. This allows for partial exogamy plus some random migration. Moreover, we assume that when a group becomes sufficiently small, it is repopulated by additional migration from larger groups and more successful. This repopulation is a form of migration that supplements other forms of migration. Consistent with Pleistocene demographics (Hassan 1973, Bocquet-Appel et al. 2005), we study a population that is not growing, so the death rate is 4% per period. To avoid the artificial situation in which Punishers bear no cost because all individuals cooperate, we assume that with 3% probability, an individual who attempts to cooperate fails, and in fact defects. This means that in a group of 30 at least one defection will occur in a given period with 60% probability.

We start each simulation with only Nonpunishers in the population, so Punishers enter a group only through the random mutation of newborns. We assume offspring mutate at rate 0.001 from the parentally supplied genotype. Whatever the parental type, the mutant is a Nonpunisher with probability 0.97, and is a Punisher with probability 0.03. Thus, in the meta-population of 7500 reproducing members, over 100 generations, there are on average 750 mutants, of which $750 \times 0.03 = 22.5$ are Punishers. We normalize payoffs by a linear transformation so that the payoffs π vary from zero to one. We assume a baseline fitness $w_o = 0.95$ and a selection coefficient $1 - w_o = 0.05$ on π, so that individual fitness is given by $w_o + (1 - w_o)\pi$, normalized so as to maintain a constant population size. We have found that even stronger selection ($w_o = 0.85$) lengthens the expected takeoff time (Punishers are then more disadvantaged when rare), but does not otherwise materially affect our results.

9.3   The Emergence of Strong Reciprocity

Unlike the analytical model, in which we formed groups using a relatedness coefficient, estimated from ethnographic hunter-gatherer populations (Table 6.1), namely $r = 0.07$ or $r = 0$, in the simulation the degree of genetic differentiation among groups is produced by the migration patterns and the distributions of group sizes across groups and over time, reflecting the parameters we have chosen as well as chance, given the random elements in mating and migration. Our strategy therefore is to adopt a parameter set that is both empirically plausible and which in the simulation generates levels of between-group genetic differentiation that are consistent with the estimates in Table 6.1, the mean of which is 0.08. The F_{ST} estimated from the simulation reported in Figure 9.5, for example, is 0.078. The fact that in the simulation quite substantial group size, 30 per generation, and between-group migrations, 37.5% per generation, generate the empirically estimated level of between-group genetic differentiation is consistent with the predictions of our joint work with Moreno Gomez and Wilkins, reported in §6.1. Thus we ensure that we are not implicitly building into the simulation elevated levels of positive assortment that would favor the punishment strategy.

Figure 9.5 shows a single simulation of the evolution of this model over 6000 generations (150,000 periods). The Punisher allele does not go to fixation because Nonpunishers have higher fitness than Punishers in groups in which the fraction of Punishers is far above the quorum threshold $\tau = 6$. The long-run average rate of noncooperation after the emergence and proliferation of Punishers is 15%, one fifth of which is due to behavioral error, with the remainder due to the fraction of Punishers falling below the quorum level in some groups through the migration, birth, and death processes.

To improve our understanding of the takeoff process and the subsequent evolutionary success of the Punisher strategy, we recall two terms, both derived from Price's decomposition of evolutionary processes into additive within-group and between-group selection effects presented in Chapter 4. The first, β_G, is the effect of the fraction of a group that are Punishers on the group average expected fitness, while the second, β_i, is the effect of an individual's own type (Punisher or not) on individual fitness. If β_i

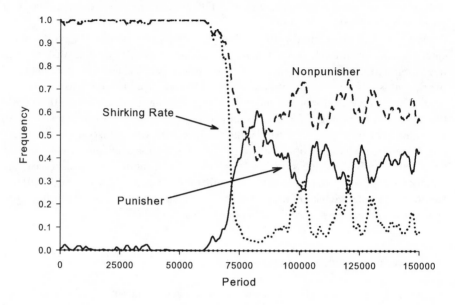

Figure 9.5. The successful invasion of Punishers and stabilization of cooperation. The timing of the takeoff to cooperation, which we define as 20% or less noncooperation, depends on the assumed rate of production of Punishers by the mutation process. In the simulations shown, the mutation rate is $\mu = 0.001$ and 3% of mutants are Punishers. The strength of the selection process is $1 - w_o = 0.05$, and the quorum level is $\tau = 6$ for these simulations. The average F_{ST} was 0.078 and the standard error of the F_{ST} was 0.006 after the 75,000 period.

is negative, then punishing is altruistic, while β_G may be positive if the presence of a large number of Punishers if a group supports a high level of cooperation and hence high fitness for members of the group on average.

Figure 9.6 shows the average movement of these two coefficients in a process of taking off from zero to sustained cooperation. The figure shows only the dynamics after period 30,000, when cooperation is consolidated and Punishers are altruists: the within-group term is negative in most periods. Also, after cooperation is consolidated, the across-group term is positive, indicating that on average, members of groups with a high frequency of Punishers have a fitness advantage over members of groups with few Punishers. The endogenously generated level of genetic differential among groups is such that most Punishers are in such groups and as a result their within-group disadvantage is offset, as described in equation 4.3.

The takeoff of Punishers occurs precisely when most Punishers, by the luck of the draw, are located in *tipping group*, which are groups with just seven Punishers, so that if any one of them were to switch to Nonpunisher, the threshold would not be met, punishing would cease and cooperation would collapse. The *bunching statistic* is the probability that a Punisher is in a group where one individual moving from Nonpunisher to Punisher pushes the group from below to above the quorum level, or moving from Punisher to Nonpunishers pushes the group from above to below the quorum level.

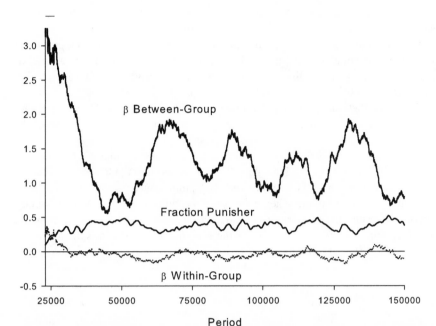

Figure 9.6. Between-group (β_G) and within-group (β_i) coefficients for Punishers. Both β_G and β_i are generally very negative to the takeoff of contingent punishment, after which β_G becomes strongly positive and β_i is negative in most periods, indicating that contingent punishment is altruistic once it has become common, but not during the process of initial proliferation.

This statistic generally shows a rapid, sustained increase during the takeoff period, after which it falls back to a low level when the frequency of Punishers is above 25%.

It is worth mentioning that if we assume there is no quorum, so Punishers always punish, but leave the baseline parameters the same, and even if we favor Punishers by starting the model with a very high level of Punishers (75%), Punishers are driven out by the invasion of Nonpunishers. After about 50,000 periods, the rate of cooperation is invariably close to zero.

We have found that the Punisher type is not altruistic until cooperation is established. The reason for this is that when Punishers are rare, most successful punishing takes place in tipping groups, where a single Punisher defection leads to the collapse of cooperation. When Punishers are well-established in the population, by contrast, most Punishers are in groups above the quorum threshold, where they are clearly altruists (any single Punisher would gain by switching to Nonpunisher).

Note that the same is true if the group is below the quorum: a Punisher would gain from switching to the nonpunishing strategy, although he cannot know that beforehand. When the quorum is more that minimally met, a single Punisher would save both the signaling cost and the cost of participating in punishment by switching to the Nonpunishment strategy. It might therefore be thought that a new type would outcompete the Punishers, in the person of an *Opportunist*, who acts exactly like a Punisher except that he defects in groups that exceed the quorum. However, the strategy of not punishing if the quorum is exceeded, which we call the Opportunist strategy, cannot displace Punishers in a cooperative equilibrium. The reason is that when the ratio of Opportunists to Punishers in the population is high, and if cooperation is widespread, then most cooperative groups will exceed the quorum and will have a high ratio of Opportunists to Punishers. When the Opportunists switch to the nonpunishing strategy, the quorum will no longer be met, and there will be no cooperation. Thus, when Opportunists are plentiful, they will be predominantly in noncooperating groups and their fitness will be low.

We show in Figure 9.7 that Opportunists cannot in fact become established in a population of Nonpunishers and Punishers. The figure shows that Opportunists can do quite well when cooperation is rare, because they punish only when so doing is necessary to attain the quorum, but when cooperation becomes common and they replace Punishers in a group, the Opportunists all defect, and without cooperation, they are replaced by Nonpunishers, who do not pay the signaling costs. It is this that occurs at about period 40,000 in the simulation.

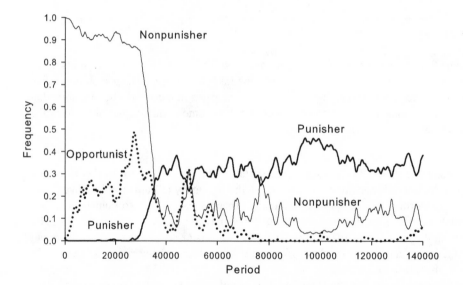

Figure 9.7. The dynamics of Opportunists in a population of Punishers and Nonpunishers. Note that Opportunists do very well in a population of Nonpunishers, but eventually Punishers become established and Opportunists are driven from the population. The values shown represent a single run of the model with the baseline parameters as in Table 9.1.

One could imagine a complex Opportunist-type strategy in which when some but not all Opportunists are needed to support a quorum, they choose equitably among themselves who gets to defect and who remains cooperating with the Punishers. However, such a strategy would need reinforcement against preemptive Opportunists who simply refuse to punish, forcing the sophisticated Opportunists to share all the costs of punishing. This presents a serious second-order free-rider problem that cannot be handled using a quorum-type strategy or any other we have been able to think of. Perhaps Nature has evolved a strategy of this sort in some creature, but it apparently does not exist in humans.

Additional details on the performance of the model are given in Boyd et al. (2010a) and §A12.

9.4   Why Coordinated Punishment Succeeds

The key positive assortment that allows the stabilization of altruistic punishment at high levels in this model is not that the Punisher genotypes are more likely to be in groups with like genotypes. The success of Punishers is due to the fact that quorum sensing results in a genotype-phenotype correlation: when Punisher genotypes are common they are more likely to receive the benefits of cooperative actions by others, whether they are Punisher genotypes or not. As we saw in Chapter 4, such a correlation is necessary for natural selection to favor an altruistic genotype (Queller 1992, Fletcher and Zwick 2006). Our simulations show that this situation is indeed the case. When a state of high-level cooperation is attained, the correlation among groups between the phenotypic trait "fraction cooperated" and the genetic trait "fraction Punisher" becomes strongly positive, taking values between 0.5 and 0.55. In our simulation with much larger groups, average fitness is much higher in groups with substantial fractions of Punishers than in groups where the frequency of Punishers is just above the threshold or below it.

The critical genotype-phenotype correlation is enhanced by that fact that Punishers coordinate their activities. Punishers do not punish unless their frequency in the group is sufficiently high to be cost-effective. This requires truthful communication among group members as to which members have shirked and which have not, as well as how many Punishers will share the costs of punishing. Thus, our model does not solve the problem of sustaining cooperation when information is private, but instead depends on a pre-existing norm of truthful communication.

We have modeled a process of genetic transmission. But were the altruistic punishment trait subject to cultural transmission, as it certainly is in humans, then additional reasons for human exceptionality arise. The process of decay of a state in which virtually all group members are Punishers leading to a takeover of the group by Nonpunishers, one often observed in our simulations, could be slowed or even halted if cultural updating responded not only to payoff differences but also to the frequency of types in the group, so that more common behaviors were preferentially copied. Guzman et al. (2007) demonstrate that conformist cultural transmission of this type supports the evolution of altruistic punishment even for groups of enormous size (over 1000 persons). They also demonstrate that a genetic predisposition to engage conformist updating could coevolve with altruistic punishment in this environment.

9.5   A Decentralized Social Order

As we have seen, a complete account of the evolution of cooperation must explain how shirker-punishing strategies can increase when rare. We saw in Chapter 4 that in their classic work on pairwise reciprocity, Axelrod and Hamilton (1981) showed that with dyadic interactions, a small amount of nonrandom assortment, such as a interaction between weakly related group members, destabilizes noncooperative equilibria but not cooperative equilibria. Here we have proposed that coordination among would-be Punishers might accomplish a similar result allowing the emergence when rare and subsequent proliferation of punishment of shirkers. Our model thus provides an explanation of the emergence and eventual stabilization of environments that may have supported high levels of cooperation among our ancestors living in mobile foraging bands during the Late Pleistocene. We do not know that a human predisposition to strong reciprocity evolved as we have described. But our model and simulations suggest that it could have.

If cooperation did evolve by this route, it is not surprising that, as Cosmides and Tooby (1992) and others have shown, cheater detection is an advanced cognitive capacity of humans. First, humans are capable of inflicting punishment upon transgressors at very low cost to the Punishers. While size, strength, and vigor generally determine the outcome of animal disputes, victory often involving great cost even to the winner, in human societies, through the use of coordination, stealth and deadly weapons, even a small number of attackers can defeat the most formidable single enemy at very low fitness cost to the attackers. Bingham (1999) has correctly stressed the importance of the superior abilities of humans in clubbing and throwing projectiles as compared with other primates, citing Goodall (1964), Plooij (1978) on the relative advantage of humans, and Darlington (1975), Fifer (1987), and Isaac (1987) on the importance of these traits in human evolution. Calvin (1983) argues that humans are exceptional in possessing the same neural machinery for rapid manual-brachial movements that allow for precision stone-throwing.

Our model may also resolve one of the outstanding puzzles raised by behavioral experiments: the fact that while contributing to a public good and punishing those who fail to do so are both altruistic behaviors, subjects are considerably more avid about the latter than the former. As we saw in Chapter 3, the experiments of Ernst Fehr and his collaborators, as well as Fudenberg and Pathak (2009), show that inflicting punishment on norm violators is a strong human motive quite independently of the desire to modify the target's behavior. The fact that some experimental subjects actively take pleasure in punishing transgressors, as indicated by their own accounts and by behavioral neuroscience experiments, could thus be the result of the evolutionary processes we have modeled.

Our model presents a sharp contrast to the repeated game approaches described in Chapters 4 and 5. First, our model is consistent with the empirical facts about forager societies outlined in Chapter 6. Second, unlike the fictive Rube Goldberg strategies invoked by the folk theorem (Chapter 5), the main causal mechanism in our model, the altruistic punishment of norm violators, is widely observed, as we saw in Chapters 3 and 6.

Note that like the models that we criticized in Chapter 5, we have assumed that information is public. All members of a group see the same signals. Equivalently, if signals are not directly observed by all group members, they receive honest reports of the signals from those who did observe them. At the close of Chapter 5 we pointed out that this assumption is difficult to square with the assumption of self-interested behavior, since members will typically have something to gain by misrepresenting the actions taken by others. Modern large-scale societies, we observed, convert private to public information by judicial processes that took centuries to evolve and that presuppose that court officials, jury members, and law enforcement officers adhere to standards of professional conduct that preclude the unrestrained pursuit of self-interest. These models work only if they go beyond self-interest at a critical juncture. This is why the "self-interest with a long time horizon" explanation of seemingly generous acts fails.

The same reasoning applies to our model of the evolution of cooperation by means of the punishment of free-riders. As we have seen, our model requires ethical and other-regarding motives to render the public information assumption plausible. Smaller scale ancestral groups devised other ways to convert private to public information. Gossip, group discussions with all or most members present, and taking meals in public are examples. While we have not explored how this process might have evolved, we think it likely that a norm of truth-telling developed *pari passu* with the punishment of free-riders. This does not mean that individuals were always truthful, but rather that there were effective means of punishing prevaricators and that a reputation for honesty was a valuable resource in early human societies. We do not believe effective collective punishment could have evolved in the absence of a system of information-sharing in which truth-telling was rewarded and lying punished.

We have focused entirely on punishing, saying nothing about why people would contribute to the public good other than that Punishers and Nonpunishers alike contribute when, in light of the likely punishment of shirkers, it is fitness maximizing to do so. But were we to drop the fiction that fitness is explicitly maximized and introduce more empirically plausible proximate motives, how the kind of fitness maximizations we have assumed could occur would be something of a mystery. The benefits of shirking occur now, while the punishment, should it occur, happens later. Humans are too impatient to maximize their fitness, and thus would not correctly weigh the future consequences of shirking even if they were correctly known.

We think that the evolution of the social emotions like shame may be explained not only as a support to the truth-telling essential to making accurate information public, but also in part by their ability enhance the present motivational salience of future punishments and thus to offset what would otherwise be a fitness-reducing myopia of would-be shirkers. In the presence of altruistic punishment by one's fellow group members, individuals with levels of impatience that lead them to shirk when it is not fitness maximizing to do so would improve their fitness were they to be motivated in part by feelings of shame and guilt. Christopher Boehm (2007) calls this process *sanctioning selection*. We will return to it when we address the social emotions in Chapter 11.

Thus individuals who developed the capacity to internalize group-beneficial norms and to feel chastened when punished for violating these norms, as well as groups that devote their socialization practices to this end, would appear to be evolutionarily favored. In the next chapter we show that this is indeed the case.

Symbol	Meaning
a	Increasing returns to scale in punishing
b	Benefits of cooperation
β_G	Between-group coefficient
β_i	Within-group coefficient
c	Cost of cooperation
δ	Time discount factor
ϵ	Execution error rate
k	Cost of punishing
m	Migration rate per period
μ	Mutation rate
n	Average group size (members of a reproducing generation)
n_p	Number of punishers vs. a lone target
p	Cost of being punished
p_j	Frequency of cooperators in group j
q	Cost of signaling willingness to punish
ρ	Reproduction rate per period
r	Time discount rate
τ	Threshold number of Punishers
T	Number of repetitions of stage game
w_o	Baseline fitness

Table 9.2. Definition of symbols

10

Socialization

It is society which, fashioning us in its image, fills us with religious, political and moral beliefs that control our actions.

Émile Durkheim, *Suicide* Ch. 3
(1951[1897]) pp. 211–212

Leges Sine Moribus Vanae
(Laws without morals are empty)

Horace, *Odes* (c. 24–25 BC) *III.24*

In addition to trial and error experimentation, preferences are acquired by genetic predisposition (e.g., a taste for sweets) and by a social learning process termed cultural transmission from our parents, others elders, and our peers (e.g., a taste for rice over potatoes). As we saw in §2.3, genetic and cultural transmission are in many ways similar, a fact that has been exploited by the classic contributions to the modeling of cultural evolution by Cavalli-Sforza and Feldman (1981) and Boyd and Richerson (1985). The main similarity between the genetic and cultural processes that is exploited by these models is the fact that both social learning and genetic inheritance from parents can be represented as the replication of traits over time. Two additional similarities may be mentioned.

First, whether of cultural or genetic origin, the taste for sweets or rice activates the same reward-processing regions of the brain. The taste for sweets is certainly more universal among humans than is the taste for rice. But there is no meaningful sense in which one can say that one is more deeply rooted or fundamental than the other. The genetically transmitted taste for sweets can easily be unlearned (a nauseating experience with sweet food overrides a genetic predisposition to like sweets, for instance). Similarly, culturally learned traits, such as the U.S. Southern culture of honor (Nisbett and Cohen 1996), have physiological correlates, such as elevated testosterone when insulted among males of European origin from the U. S. South (but not the North), much as physical danger elevates adrenaline in virtually all humans.

Second, those who are relatively successful in acquiring material resources tend to produce more copies of their traits in the next generation, whether the process works through their differential success in producing offspring who survive to reproductive age or because of their greater command of resources, more elevated social status, or other reasons for their greater likelihood of being copied as cultural models. In the previous chapters we have specified evolutionary processes in which the frequency of a behavioral type in the population increases if its expected payoff exceeds the average. These so-called payoff-monotone models provide a challenging, if highly simplified, way of posing the puzzle we are addressing, namely, the evolution of preferences that induce people to act in ways that reduce their payoffs by comparison to what they would get if they acted in some other manner. In the models proposed in Chapters 7, 8, and 9, altruistic traits may overcome their within-group payoff disadvantages first, because of the superior payoffs enjoyed by members of groups in which there are many altruists and, second, because groups devise, and culturally transmit over generations, the institutions that mitigate the within-group selection pressures tending to eliminate altruists.

Cultural transmission provides an additional way that the fitness disadvantages of particular preferences might be overcome. In his book *Sick Societies*, Robert Edgerton (1992) catalogues dozens of examples of culture overriding fitness, all, as the title suggests, with unpleasant consequences. Pre-industrial cities provide an example (Knauft 1989). Prior to modern medicine the city was a cultural success, recruiting steady streams of migrants to forsake the countryside for urban living. But it was a biological failure, typically not reproducing its own population even among the urban social elites. A second example is the demographic transition whereby the culturally transmitted preference for smaller families proliferated in many populations despite having apparently reduced fitness (Zei and Cavalli-Sforza 1977, Kaplan et al. 1995, Ihara and Feldman 2004).

But if cultural transmission can induce people to limit their fitness by having small families, or to choose a lethal residential environment, it certainly might also overcome the payoff disadvantages associated with altruistic social preferences. It is this possibility that we explore here. The puzzle, of course, is to explain why humans or any other animal would ever develop the capacity to override fitness concerns, for that capacity itself would seem to be doomed by natural selection.

10.1   Cultural Transmission

Cultural transmission overrides fitness when it causes people to want or feel obliged to do things that result in their having fewer surviving offspring or to reduce their inclusive fitness in other ways. Thus our explanation will involve the proximate causes of behavior, that is to say, preferences. Here, and in the next chapter as well, we depart from the framework of the previous three chapters, which focused entirely on fitness and behavior without exploring the question of motivation. It is not difficult, of course, to associate proximate motives with the kinds of behaviors that we have shown may evolve. Ethically motivated outrage, what Robert Trivers called "moralistic aggression," is a plausible motivation for the strong reciprocators' punishment of defectors in Chapter 9, and group loyalty and out-group hostility could provide the psychological basis for the behaviors studied in Chapters 7 and 8. Our models show that these and other preferences motivating the behaviors in question could have evolved by a fitness-based evolutionary process. Here we seek to understand how altruistic preferences might evolve under the influence of cultural transmission.

We will take account of two facts. First, the phenotypic expression of an individual's genetic inheritance depends on a developmental process that is plastic and open-ended. One expression of this fact is that while human ancestral groups are similar genetically

(Feldman et al. 2003), they differ in important ways in behaviors. We surveyed some of our experimental evidence for this behavioral variability in Chapter 3. This developmental plasticity explains why humans are among the most ubiquitous of species, capable of making a living and surviving in virtually all of the world's environments.

Second, this developmental process is deliberately structured—by elders, teachers, political leaders, and religious figures—to foster certain kinds of development and to thwart others. In many of Edgerton's sick societies, the socialization processes affecting development result in proximate motives leading people to engage in such lethal practices as cigarette smoking or, in the highlands of New Guinea, consuming the brains of deceased relatives (Cavalli-Sforza and Feldman 1981, Durham 1991, Edgerton 1992). In both cases individuals contract a terminal illness with high probability. But in most societies, socialization stresses not only the desirability of behaviors that contribute to one's own well-being, such as moderation, planning ahead, and personal hygiene, but also those that benefit others, such as the altruistic social preferences and character virtues we have identified as common among humans.

In this chapter we analyze the process by which social norms become internalized, that is, taken on as preferences to be sought in their own right rather than constraints on behavior or instrumental means to other ends. Internalization is thus an aspect of cultural transmission that affects preferences rather than beliefs and capacities. The idea of internalized norms is captured in a passage attributed to Abraham Lincoln: "when I do good, I feel good. When I do bad, I feel bad. That is my religion."

Much of the content of cultural transmission can be modeled as information transfer. Members of a group, most often as children, are taught "how to" accomplish particular ends such as acquiring and preparing food or performing music, as in the study of the Central African Aka by Barry Hewlett (1986). We focus instead on the process by which a society's "oughts" become its members "wants," thereby narrowing the hiatus between what Jeremy Bentham famously termed people's "dutys" and their "interests." As a result, we draw upon studies of how values, rather than factual information, are transmitted, such as generosity among the Inuit (Guemple 1988), social solidarity among children on Israeli kibbutzim (Bronfenbrenner 1969), and the control of hostility among children in cross-cultural perspective (Whiting and Whiting 1975). We refer to these "ought" rules of behavior as *norms* and, when they are internalized, as preferences.

Though drawing on a somewhat different mix of social institutions for its accomplishment, the internalization of norms has enough in common with other aspects of cultural transmission that we can draw upon the models of Boyd and Richerson and of Cavalli-Sforza and Feldman. We posit three influences on the cultural transmission of preferences and model how they may interact so as to favor the evolution of other-regarding and ethical preferences. First, we model the *vertical transmission* of traits from parents to offspring. Parental traits that are associated with greater fitness will evolve for the same reason that genes that confer greater fitness enjoy supra-average survival rates. The second is *oblique transmission* to the young from non-parental members of the parents' generation in the myriad of personal interactions with neighbors, teachers, and spiritual leaders by which the young are socialized to internalize particular norms (Cavalli-Sforza and Feldman 1981). Third is payoff-based social learning according to which periodically, over the life course, people compare their behaviors with the behaviors of other individuals, and tend to adopt behaviors of others who appear to be doing relatively well. We take account of the effect of payoffs on the adoption of norms in order to counter the oversocialized concept of the individual according to which socialization simply implants norms in a passive and uncritical target (Wrong 1961, Gintis 1975).

Following Boyd and Richerson (1985), oblique transmission may be conformist, the young tending to adopt the behaviors most common in the parental generation, independently of their payoffs. In this case the resulting dynamic will not be monotonic in either fitness or well-being. If virtually all of the population is altruistic, conformist cultural transmission might overcome the payoff disadvantage suffered by the altruists and allow their persistence in a population. Conformism may also stabilize payoff-reducing behaviors that yield no benefit to others, such as smoking. Indeed, this is the most parsimonious explanation of the long-term persistence of many of the dysfunctional behaviors documented by Edgerton. Conformism may thus contribute to large between-group differences in behavior, with selection against low-payoff behaviors within groups being weak or absent. In the presence of strong conformism, weak group selection (§4.2) may be sufficient to stabilize altruistic preferences.

Conformist cultural transmission may arise for a variety of reasons, ranging from an evolved social learning strategy in which individuals regard the population frequency of a trait as a measure of its desirability, all the way to population-level institutional arrangements for the deliberate socialization of the young, in which the content reflects which types are prevalent in the population. We stress the latter for empirical reasons: most societies devote substantial time and resources to deliberately socializing the young to act in ways that are beneficial to others, and an adequate explanation of social preferences needs to take account of this fact.

Why should the norms that are internalized be altruistic? Linnda Caporeal and her coauthors (Caporael et al. 1989) and Herbert Simon (1990) proposed that altruism might proliferate in a population because it is an inseparable part of an ensemble of culturally transmitted norms that is, on balance, individually advantageous. Simon termed the capacity to internalize such an ensemble of social norms *docility* (literally, "teachability") and explained the evolution of altruistic behaviors as a consequence of the fact that the norms motivating them are linked to other norms that benefit the individual sufficiently to offset the individual costs of altruism. Altruism in this case proliferates in the same way that a genetically transmitted disadvantageous trait may evolve if it is pleiotropically linked to other, advantageous traits and thus may "hitchhike" on their success.

We wish to explore this reasoning and address two aspects in which it is incomplete. First, one needs to address the puzzle of how the capacity to internalize norms evolves. Second, we would like to explain the "pleiotropic analogy" whereby individually costly altruism and individually beneficial other norms are inseparable, with a model in which norms are explicitly cultural, phenotypic expressions of behavior.

These two challenges lead us to model explicitly the interplay between the genetic predisposition to internalize norms and the nature of the norms thereby engendered. In §10.2, we develop a purely phenotypic model in which, as a result of the effectiveness of socialization, a fitness-reducing norm, whether it be smoking or contributing to the public good, may be maintained in a population. Critical to this result is the effectiveness of schools, story telling, and other socialization agents, which in turn depends upon our capacity to internalize norms, and our receptivity to socialization. In §10.3, we therefore model the genetic basis of internalization and give the conditions under which there population equilibrium in which individuals have an "internalization allele" and acquire a fitness-enhancing norm. In §10.4, and §10.5 we reintroduce the fitness-reducing norm of §10.2 into the model of §10.3, and study the conditions under which it can "hitchhike" on the internalization allele to form a stable population equilibrium in which all individuals express both a fitness-enhancing and a fitness-reducing norm. This will turn out to depend critically on the effectiveness of the socialization process compared to the strength of selection against the fitness-reducing norm, much as in the model of §10.2.

Finally, in §10.6 we explain why the individually fitness-reducing norm will generally tend to enhance the average fitness of group members, and hence will be altruistic. This occurs because groups with social norms that enhance the fitness of their members will outcompete groups that foster norms that are both costly to their bearers and of zero or negative fitness benefit to the group. Because the fitness-reducing norm can be maintained in a population (§10.4) weak multi-level selection (§4.2) is sufficient to guarantee this result. This is why, notwithstanding the evidence provided by Edgerton, institutions of socialization tend to favor prosocial preferences.

But developing the capacity to internalize norms is costly to the individual, and sustaining the institutions whereby internalization takes place is costly to society. Why would evolution favor bearing these costs rather than relying on genetic transmission to sustain individually beneficial norms? The answer we propose in §10.7 is an application of the reasoning of Boyd and Richerson (2000), extending the explanation given in Chapter 2: the cultural transmission of preferences allowed humans, exceptionally among animals, to adapt flexibly to rapidly changing circumstances and to modify the results of individual fitness maximization where these are not beneficial on average to members of a group.

10.2   Socialization and the Survival of Fitness-Reducing Norms

Consider a group in which members can either adopt, or not, a certain cultural norm A. We shall call those who adopt the norm A-types, and we call those who do not adopt the norm S-types. Adopting A is costly, in that S-types have fitness 1, as compared with A-types, who have fitness $1 - s$, where $0 < s < 1$ is a fitness loss. The A norm, despite its notation, need not be altruistic; we will later investigate the conditions under which this could be the case. What matters for now is that a person switching from S to A incurs a fitness loss. We assume that in each generation individuals pair off randomly, mate, and have offspring in proportion to their fitness, after which they die. Families pass on their cultural norms to their offspring (we call this *vertical transmission*). Oblique cultural transmission also takes place because the S-type offspring of AS- and SS-families are susceptible to influence by socialization institutions promoting the A norm. As a result, offspring of AA parents are A-types, offspring of SS parents are S-types, and half of the offspring of AS-families (which are the same as SA-families) are A-types, the other half S-types. Table 10.7 summarizes the mathematical symbols used in this chapter.

Socialization occurs when an S offspring encounters a "cultural model" randomly drawn from the population, which occurs once for every member of each generation. If the model is an A, which occurs with probability p, the offspring switches to being an A with a probability $\gamma > 0$.

Combining oblique and vertical transmission, we find that the change in the fraction of A-types in the next generation is given by the familiar replicator equation (see §A5):

$$\Delta p = p(1 - p)\frac{\gamma - s}{1 - sp}, \tag{10.1}$$

where p is the frequency of A's in the population and Δp is its change over some discrete time period. The term $1 - sp$ is the average payoff in the population, γ is the rate of oblique transmission, and $\gamma - s$ is the selective advantage (disadvantage if negative) of the A's over the S's when account is taken of both oblique and vertical transmission. Equation 10.1 illustrates the tension between the differential fitness effects on the evolution of p captured by s that work against the evolution of the A's and the effects of oblique transmission captured by γ, which tend to counteract the selection against A-types. Equation 10.1 shows that when $s = \gamma$, these two effects are exactly offsetting, and the population frequency of A-types will be stationary ($\Delta p = 0$).

Payoff-based updating then occurs. Each group member i observes the fitness and the type of a randomly chosen other member j, and may change to j's type if j's fitness is higher. However, information concerning the difference in fitnesses of the two strategies is imperfect, and individuals' preference functions do not perfectly track fitness, so it is reasonable to assume that the larger the difference in the payoffs, the more likely the individual is to perceive it, and change. Specifically, we assume the probability that an A individual will shift to S is η times the fitness difference of the two types, where $\eta > 0$. The term η represents the power of payoff differences to induce changes in type, and this, naturally will play a big role in our account.

The expected fraction p' of the population that are A's after the above payoff-based updating is the fraction before updating p, minus those A's who switched to S, the latter being the A's who observed an S (a fraction $p(1 - p)$ of the population), multiplied by the probability of a switch taking place in these cases. Thus we have

$$p' = p - \eta sp(1 - p). \tag{10.2}$$

We now combine these three sources of change in the fraction of A-types, adding the changes described in equation 10.2 to those already shown in 10.1, giving

$$\Delta p = p(1 - p)\frac{\gamma - s}{1 - sp} - \eta p(1 - p)s \tag{10.3}$$

The second term on the right hand side represents the influence of payoff-based updating, reducing the frequency of the altruistic norm, in comparison with the vertical and oblique cultural transmission mechanisms, represented by the first term, which may favor this norm or not, depending on whether $\gamma > s$ or $\gamma < s$.

Not surprisingly, the higher the personal cost of altruistic behavior, the more stringent the conditions under which the A norm will emerge, illustrating the tension between socialization institutions and the psychological mechanism of norm internalization on the one hand, and payoff-based updating that induces individuals to shift to higher payoff behaviors, whatever the effect of these behaviors on others and on society as a whole, on the other hand.

This tension is evident from the conditions under which the all-A equilibrium is *globally stable*, meaning that starting from any of the possible states of the population, the population dynamic will move to the all-A equilibrium. In order for this to be the case, the strength of payoff-based updating η must be less than the difference in the size of the oblique transmission and the fitness cost of the A norm, normalized by the latter:

$$\eta < \frac{\gamma - s}{s}. \tag{10.4}$$

However, if

$$\frac{\gamma - s}{s} < \eta < \frac{\gamma - s}{s(1 - s)}, \tag{10.5}$$

both the all S-type equilibrium and the A-type equilibria are locally stable, meaning that there exists a neighborhood of states around these two equilibrium states such that if the equilibrium state is displaced to some state in this neighborhood, the population dynamic will return to the equilibrium. The basin of attraction of the A-type equilibrium, that is, the neighborhood of states from which the dynamic will converge to the all-A equilibrium, shrinks as η increases. Finally, if

$$\eta > \frac{\gamma - s}{s(1 - s)}, \tag{10.6}$$

the all-S equilibrium is globally stable.

Thus if the internalization of norms accomplished by the society's socialization processes (γ) is sufficiently strong relative to the strength of payoff-based updating (η) and the cost of altruism (s), the A norm equilibrium may be stable. In effect, there is a net flow into the A norm at rate γ, the rate of oblique transmission, a net flow out of the A norm due to its fitness cost s, and another flow out because individuals switch from the costly A norm to S behavior by copying the more successful self-regarding individuals, at rate ηs. When the net balance favors a positive flow into the A norm, i.e., when $\gamma > s + s\eta(1 - s)$, the all-A equilibrium is at least locally stable.

10.3   Genes, Culture, and the Internalization of Norms

But why would people, or any animal, internalize norms if taking a norm on board leads one to act in ways that reduce fitness? We will answer this in two steps. Here we explain why the capacity to internalize fitness-enhancing norms, those that correct for human impatience or weakness of will, for example, might evolve even if the capacity to internalize is costly. In the next section we will show that when the capacity to internalize a norm has evolved and societies have developed socialization practices to do this, people will be susceptible to internalizing norms that also reduce fitness, such as the A norm of the previous section. This is what we mean when we say that a fitness-reducing norm can *hitchhike* on a process of norm internalization that has evolved due to the existence of an individually fitness-enhancing norm.

Here we assume that cultural traits are acquired through vertical transmission alone. Oblique transmission and the payoff-based switching of traits, as modeled in §10.2, will be reintroduced in §10.4 and §10.5.

To simplify the analysis we assume that there is one genetic locus that controls the capacity to internalize norms, and that norm internalization is the expression of a single allele, which we will call the "internalization allele" with, as usual, the quotation marks serving as a reminder that this simple genotype-phenotype mapping is a considerable simplification. We will assume that each individual has only one copy at this locus (i.e., genetics are haploid), which is inherited with equal probability from either parent. An alternative diploid model, in which each locus has two alleles, has almost the same properties as the haploid model, but is much more complicated, and is developed in full in Gintis (2003a). Individuals without the allele cannot internalize norms, whereas individuals with the allele are capable of internalization, but whether or not they internalize a norm depends on costs and benefits, as well as the individual's personal history, including which cultural models he has encountered. In this section we assume that an internal norm is fitness enhancing and we derive the conditions under which the allele for internalization of norms is globally stable, and hence can proliferate when rare.

Suppose the norm in question is C (Cleanliness, for instance), which confers fitness $1 + f > 1$, while the normless phenotype, denoted by D (Dirty, perhaps), has baseline fitness 1. There is a genetic locus with two alleles, a and b. Allele a permits the internalization of norms, whereas b does not. We assume that possessing a imposes a fitness cost u, with $0 < u < 1$, on the grounds that there are costly physiological and cognitive prerequisites for the capacity to internalize norms. We assume $(1 + f)(1 - u) > 1$, so the cost of the internalization allele is more than offset by the benefit of the norm C. An individual is now characterized not only by his genes, but by his phenotype (whether he is a C or a D). There are thus three "phenogenotypes," whose fitnesses are shown in Table 10.1.

Individual Phenogenotype	Individual Fitness
aC	$(1 - u)(1 + f)$
aD	$1 - u$
bD	1

Table 10.1. Fitnesses of the three phenogenotypes. Note: Here u is the fitness cost of possessing the internalization allele, and f is the fitness value of possessing the norm C; bC cannot occur because an individual must have a to be able to internalize C.

The rules of gene-culture transmission are as follows. If a familial phenogenotype is xyXY, where x and y can be either a or b, and X and Y can be either C or D, an offspring is equally likely to inherit x or y. An offspring whose genotype is a is equally likely to inherit X or Y. But an offspring of genotype b always has the normless phenotype D. The transition table is shown in Table 10.2, where $\beta \in [0, 1]$ measures the strength of the cultural transmission of C. We assume unbiased cultural transmission ($\beta = 1/2$) unless otherwise stated.

Offspring Phenogenotypic Frequency

Familial Type	aC	aD	bD
aaCC	1		
aaCD	β	$1 - \beta$	
aaDD		1	
abCD	$\beta/2$	$(1 - \beta)/2$	1/2
abDD		1/2	1/2
bbDD			1

Table 10.2. Phenotypic inheritance is controlled by genotype. Note: abCC and bbCC, and bbCD are not listed because bC cannot occur, as an individual must have the a allele to internalize the C norm. Note that $\beta \in [0, 1]$ measures the strength of the cultural transmission of C.

Families are formed, as before, by random pairing, males and females are indistinguishable (i.e., there is recombination but only one sex), and offspring genotypes obey the laws of Mendelian segregation (i.e., an offspring is equally likely to inherit a gene from either parent). A family is characterized by its familial genotype, which is the pattern of genes of the two members, and its familial phenotype, which is the pattern of norms of the two members.

Thus there are three familial genotypes, aa, ab, bb. We assume also that only the phenotypic traits of parents, and not which particular parent expresses them, are relevant to the transmission process. Therefore, there are three familial phenotypes, CC, CD, and DD, and nine familial phenogenotypes, of which only six can occur (because a parent of genotype b must have the D phenotype). The frequencies of the offspring of different familial phenogenotypes are as shown in Table 10.3, where $P(i)$ represents the frequency of parental phenogenotype $i = aC, aD, bD$. For example, the aaCD phenogenotype can occur in two ways: father aC and mother aD, or vice-versa. The probability of each occurrence is $P(aC)P(aD)$. The fitness of this phenogenotype is $(1 - u)^2(1 + f)$ because both parents have the a allele at fitness cost u, and one has the C trait, at fitness gain f. The share of the next generation total population constituted by the offspring of this phenogenotype is thus as given in the second row of Table 10.3.

Phenogenotype	Frequency
aaCC	$P(aC)^2(1 - u)^2(1 + f)^2\beta_o^2$
aaCD	$2P(aC)P(aD)(1 - u)^2(1 + f)\beta_o^2$
aaDD	$P(aD)^2(1 - u)^2\beta_o^2$
abCD	$2P(aC)P(bD)(1 - u)(1 + f)\beta_o^2$
abDD	$2P(aD)P(bD)(1 - u)\beta_o^2$
bbDD	$P(bD)^2\beta_o^2$

Table 10.3. Frequencies of phenogenotypes. Note: β_o is baseline fitness, chosen so the sum of the frequencies is unity; bCC and bCD are not listed, because bC cannot occur.

Equilibrium occurs when the frequency of each phenogenotype is constant from generation to generation. In this case, we need consider only two of the phenogenotypes, say aC and aD, because bC cannot occur, and since the probabilities must add up to unity, we have $P(b\text{D}) = 1 - P(a\text{C}) - P(a\text{D})$. This system has three equilibria, in which the whole population bears a single phenogenotype. These are aC, in which all individuals internalize the fitness-enhancing norm, aD, in which internalization allele is present but the phenotype C is absent, and bD, in which neither the internalization allele nor the norm is present.

Elsewhere (Gintis 2003b) we have proven the following assertions concerning the stability of the various equilibria of this system. The aD equilibrium is unstable, while the aC equilibrium is locally stable, meaning the system will return to this equilibrium starting from nearby states (§A4). The unnormed equilibrium bD is locally stable if $(1 - u)(1 + f) < 2$ and unstable when the opposite inequality holds. Either of two conditions renders the bD equilibrium unstable, in which case aC, in which all individuals internalize the fitness-enhancing norm, will be globally stable, which means the system moves to this equilibrium from any starting point. The first is that $(1 - u)(1 + f) > 2$. The second condition is that the cultural bias transmission coefficient β is sufficiently greater than 1/2. We consider the former condition implausible because it requires that $f > 1$, whereas positive fitness coefficients are rarely so large. However, the latter condition is quite plausible, because it may take only one parent to instill a norm in all offspring with high probability ("Mom taught me to be clean. Dad was always a slob"). Note that biased vertical transmission, $\beta > 1/2$, produces the same effect as oblique transmission, $\gamma > 0$, in the previous section.

10.4   The Internalized Norm as Hitchhiker

We now add a second phenotypic trait with two variants. Internalized norm A is promulgated by the group but imposes fitness cost s, with $0 < s < 1$, on those who adopt it. The normless state, S, is neutral, imposing no fitness cost on those who adopt it. An individual phenotype is then one of SD (internalizes neither norm), SC (internalizes only the fitness-enhancing norm), AD (internalizes only the fitness-reducing norm A), and AC (internalizes both the fitness-enhancing and fitness-reducing norm).

We assume A has the same cultural transmission rules as C: a individuals inherit their phenotypes from their parents, while b individuals always adopt the normless phenotype SD. In addition, there is oblique transmission, as before. There are now two genotypes and four phenotypes, giving rise to five phenogenotypes that can occur, which we denote by aAC, aAD, aSC, aSD, and bSD, and three that cannot occur because b individuals must be normless, i.e., SD. These three are bAC, bAD, and bSC. We represent the frequency of phenogenotype i by $P(i)$, for $i = a\text{AC}, \ldots, \text{SD}$.

As before, families are formed by random pairing and the offspring genotype obeys Mendelian segregation (an offspring is equally likely to inherit a gene from either parent). As above, we assume also that only the phenotypic traits of parents, and not which particular parent expresses them, are relevant to the transmission process. Therefore, there are nine family phenotypes, which can be written as AACC, AACD, AADD, ASCC, ASCD, ASDD, SSCC, SSCD, and SSDD. It follows that there are 27 famil-

Phenogenotype	Frequency
P(aaAACC)	$P(a\text{AC})^2(1-u)^2(1+f)^2(1-s)^2\beta_o^2,$
P(aaAACD)	$2P(a\text{AC})P(a\text{AD})(1-u)^2(1-s)^2(1+f)\beta_o^2,$
P(abASCD)	$2P(2a\text{AC})P(b\text{SD})(1-u)(1+f)(1-s)\beta_o^2,$
P(bbSSDD)	$P(b\text{SD})^2\beta_o^2.$

Table 10.4. Selected phenogenotypic frequencies. Note: β_o is baseline fitness, and is chosen so the sum of the frequencies is unity. To understand this calculation, consider, for instance the abASCD phenogenotype. This can arise in two ways: (1) aAC mother and bSD father or (2) bSD mother and aAC father. In both cases, one parent came from a pool with fitness $(1-s)(1+f)(1-u)$ and the other with fitness 1.

ial phenogenotypes, which we can write as aaAACC,...,bbSSDD, only 14 of which can occur. For instance, aaAACC represents the case where both parents have the internalization allele a, and both parents internalize the fitness-reducing and the fitness-enhancing norm. Similarly, aaAACD represents the case where both parents have the internalization allele a, and both parents internalize the fitness-reducing norm A, but only one internalizes the fitness-enhancing norm C. Finally, abASCD represents the case where one parent carries the internalization norm and the other does not, the former internalizing both the fitness-reducing norm A and the fitness-enhancing norm C. We write the frequency of familial phenogenotype j as $P(j)$, and we assume the population is sufficiently large that we can ignore random drift. For illustrative purposes, a few of the phenogenotypic frequencies are shown in Table 10.4.

The rules of cultural transmission are as before. If the familial phenogenotype is xyXYZW, where x and y are either a or b, X and Y are either A or S, and Z and W are either C or D, an offspring is equally likely to inherit x or y. An a offspring is equally likely to inherit X or Y, and equally likely to inherit Z or W. Offspring of genotype b always have the normless phenotype SD. Oblique cultural transmission occurs when an a individual with S phenotype, genetically capable of internalizing but culturally selfish, adopts the A phenotype in response not to parental socialization but to learning from other A-types in the population. This occurs more frequently the more A-types there are in the population (p) and the more effective are the society's institutions (deliberate or otherwise) for oblique transmission (γ), each aS individual switching at the rate γp, so that the gain in A phenotypes by this mechanism is $\gamma p(1-p)$, where $1-p$ is the frequency of aS-types in the population. Note that oblique transmission in this model is asymmetric: if there are A-types in the population, S-types may learn to become A-types, not the other way around, even if the population is predominantly of the S-type.

We assume both genotypic and phenotypic fitness, as well as their interactions, are multiplicative. Thus, for instance, an aAC individual incurs a fitness cost u from the capacity to internalize, a fitness gain of f from holding norm C, and a fitness loss s from holding the A norm. The individual's resulting fitness is then $(1-u)(1+f)(1-s)$. In the absence of positive assortment, $(1-u)(1+f)(1-s) > 1$ is a necessary condition for the fitness-reducing norm to evolve, so we assume this inequality holds; i.e., the direct individual fitness benefit due to having phenotype C must be sufficient to offset both the cost of having the internalization allele and the cost of expressing the fitness-reducing norm. The fitness of the phenogenotypes that can occur with positive frequency are as shown in Table 10.5.

Phenogenotype	Fitness
aAC	$(1-u)(1-s)(1+f)$
aAD	$(1-u)(1-s)$
aSC	$(1-u)(1+f)$
aSD	$(1-u)$
bSD	1

Table 10.5. Fitnesses of five phenogenotypes.

The fitness of these phenotypes, along with the rules of genetic and cultural transmission given above, allow us to determine for any combination of frequencies of the phenogenotypes in Table 10.5 the change in frequencies that will occur as a result of the combined impact of genetic and cultural transmission. The population is in equilibrium when the frequency of each phenogenotype is constant from generation to generation. We can determine the possible population equilibria using four equations, one each for the constancy of frequency of aAC, aAD, aSC, and aSD, the frequency of bSD being one minus the sum of the other frequencies. These equations show that there are five equilibria, in which the whole population bears a single phenogenotype. These are aAC, in which all individuals internalize both the fitness-reducing and fitness-enhancing norms, aAD, in which only the fitness-reducing norm is internalized, aSC, in which only the fitness-enhancing norm is internalized, aSD, in which individuals carry the allele for internalization of norms, but no norms are in fact internalized, and bSD, in which internalization is absent, and neither the fitness-reducing nor the fitness-enhancing norm is transmitted from parents to offspring. But the aAD and the aSD equilibria are unstable, and hence will not survive an evolutionary process, so we can ignore them.

The analysis of the stability of the remaining equilibria, aAC, aSC, and bSD, is given in Gintis (2003a). The two a equilibria are stable when $s < \gamma$. This inequality expresses the key condition that the fitness-reducing norm cannot be evolutionarily stable unless the effectiveness of oblique transmission is sufficient to overcome the fitness cost of expressing the fitness-reducing norm. Groups with high levels of fitness-reducing norm expression solve the problem of rendering the fitness-reducing norm stable by increasing the effectiveness of oblique transmission so that the new converts to fitness-reducing norms compensate for the lower fitness of A-types.

It is no surprise, therefore, that the aSC equilibrium, in which internalization is possible but the fitness-reducing norm is not internalized, is stable when $\gamma < s$ and unstable when the opposite inequality holds. This reinforces the interpretation presented in the previous paragraph. Moreover, as in the single phenotype case, bSD is unstable if $(1-u)(1+f) > 2$, which is highly unlikely, as we explained above. There are two reasons why the equilibria aSC, aAC, and bSD, all homogeneous populations with a single type, are stable. First, there are positive feedbacks in the oblique transmission process by which individuals are socialized, such that it is inoperative when the internalization gene is absent from the population, and may be powerful enough to offset the fitness disadvantages of the A-types when the internalization gene is universally expressed. This explains why a stable equilibrium population is either all S or all A. Second the bSD ("no internalization, no norms") equilibrium is stable in that a and C are complements, meaning that in the absence of C, a cannot proliferate when rare, and conversely. We have not determined if stable mixed strategy equilibria exist, but for the above reasons we doubt that they could.

This analysis shows that if $s < \gamma$, the fitness-disadvantaged phenotype A coexists in a stable equilibrium with the fitness-enhancing phenotype C. We say that A hitchhikes on C because the fitness value of C renders the internalization allele a evolutionarily viable, and once this allele occurs in high frequency, the normed phenotype A is evolutionarily viable because its fitness cost s is less than the oblique transmission effect γ, which favors A.

10.5   The Gene-Culture Coevolution of a Fitness-Reducing Norm

To simplify the gene-culture interaction, the analysis of the previous section did not include an obvious challenge to the fitness-reducing norm A: when people update their behaviors they not only do so under the influence of schools, elders and the other bearers of oblique transmission, they also pay attention to the payoffs that they and people of different types are receiving, and this must disadvantage the A-types. We now add the payoff-based updating dynamic developed in §10.2 to our gene-culture model, thus allowing individuals to shift from lower to higher payoff strategies, and we show that the result is similar to that of the model developed without genetics in §10.2. In the current context, there are four phenotypes, and only a individuals will copy another phenotype, because they are the only type capable of internalizing a norm, and noninternalizers will not desire to mimic internalizers.

Let XY and WZ be two of the phenotypes AC, AD, SC, SD. We assume an a individual with phenotype XY meets an individual of type WZ with probability p_{WZ}, where p_{WZ} is the fraction of the population with phenotype WZ, and in this case switches to WZ with probability η if that type has higher fitness than XY. Thus, as in §10.2, the parameter η is the a measure of the strength of the tendency to shift from lower to higher payoff phenotypes.

Adding payoff-based cultural updating does not change the single phenogenotype equilibria, because when all equilibria consist of a single phenogenotype, in equilibrium an individual can never meet a distinct phenotype to which he might switch. We find that the aAD and aSD equilibria remain unstable, and payoff-based updating does not affect the conditions for stability of the normless equilibrium bSD. The condition $\gamma > s$ for stability of the fitness-reducing norm equilibrium aAC now becomes

$$\eta < \frac{\gamma - s}{1 - \gamma}\left(\frac{1}{s} - 1\right). \tag{10.7}$$

Note the similarity to the all-A equilibrium conditions (10.4–10.6) in the model without the explicit modeling of genetics. We conclude that a sufficiently strong payoff-based updating process can undermine the stability of the aAC equilibrium, even if the effect of socialization exceeds the fitness cost of the A-type. The condition $s > \gamma$ for stability of the fitness-enhancing norm internalization equilibrium aSC when payoff-based updating is included now becomes

$$\eta > \frac{\gamma - s}{s(1 + \gamma - s)},$$

and this equilibrium is unstable when the reverse inequality holds. Thus in this case, $s > \gamma$ continues to ensure that aSC is stable, but now for sufficiently large η, this equilibrium is stable even when $\gamma > s$.

Adding payoff-based updating changes the stability properties of the model in only one important way: a sufficiently strong payoff-based updating process can render the fitness-enhancing internalized equilibrium aSC, rather than the equilibrium with both norms, aAC, stable. The intuition here is that the fitness-reducing norm A imposes a fitness cost s leading individuals to abandon it. The greater the rate at which this occurs, the larger must be the oblique socialization force γ that replenishes the stock of A-types in the group.

10.6   How Can Internalized Norms Be Altruistic?

As we have seen, internalized norms may reduce the fitness of group members. The reason for the feasibility of antisocial norms is that once the internalization allele has evolved to fixation, there is nothing to prevent group-harmful phenotypic norms from also emerging, provided they are not excessively costly to the individual (s), given the strength of the payoff-based updating process (η). The evolution of these harmful norms directly reduces the overall fitness of the population.

Yet, as Brown (1991) and others have shown, there is a tendency in virtually all populations that persist over long periods for cultural institutions to promote social and eschew antisocial norms, and for A-types to embrace these social norms. The most reasonable explanation for the predominance of socially beneficial norms is weak group selection: societies that promote social norms have higher survival and reproduction rates than societies that do not.

Weak group selection (§4.2) is sufficient for the proliferation of socially beneficial norms as long as the conditions for the stability of the equilibrium with the fitness-reducing norm (10.7) are met. A-types in groups at or near such an equilibrium if A is altruistic will be as fit as other members of their groups and will therefore not suffer adverse within-group selection. But the fitness of all members of groups at or near the altruistic equilibrium will exceed that of members of groups that support group-harmful norms. The evolutionary dynamic is thus an equilibrium selection problem with differential group survival favoring the selection of the altruistic equilibrium.

The question of interest, then, is whether the updating system captured by our vertical, oblique and payoff-based transmission is itself likely to evolve such that the condition for the stability of the altruistic equilibrium (10.7) will be satisfied. If groups with strong systems of oblique transmission (i.e., high levels of γ) were to do poorly for some reason, then (10.7) might not be satisfied in a long-term evolutionary dynamic. Recall that in Chapters 7 and 8 we asked a similar question. Having shown that culturally transmitted reproductive leveling and within-group segmentation practices favor the evolution of a genetically transmitted altruistic predisposition (Chapter 7) and that intergroup hostilities are essential to this process (Chapter 8), we asked if these altruism-favoring conditions themselves could evolve. Here, instead, we explore the coevolution of three distinct aspects of a population: the distributions of its genotypes and phenotypes and the evolution of the process by which individuals update their socially learned traits. The third will require an exploration of the dynamics of γ, the effectiveness of its institutions of socialization, and η, the effect of payoff differences in inducing individuals to switch from altruist to selfish types. As we did in Chapters 7, 8, and 9, we will also determine if an initially rare altruistic trait can proliferate in a reasonable time frame, and if it is sustained in a stochastic environment.

Given the complexity of this task, selection on genes, learned behavior, and two aspects of a society's social learning system operating at both the individual and group level, we are not able to develop an illuminating analytical model, and so, as in previous chapters, we created an agent-based model of society with the following characteristics (the specific assumptions made are not critical, unless otherwise noted). The society consists of 1000 groups, each initially comprising 12 members per generation, or a census size of 36, about the size of a Pleistocene hunter-gatherer group, arranged spatially on a torus (a 50×50 inner-tube-type grid with the opposite edges identified). Each group started with 2% aAC-types, 1% aAD-types, 1% aSC-types, 1% aSD-types, and 95% bSD-types. Table 10.6 summarizes the parameter choices of the simulation. We let $s = 0.03$, $f = 0.06$ and $u = 0.01$, common across all groups, because they represent individual-level costs and benefits unrelated to any group differences in social structure. We take s as constant because we are not concerned with the obvious point that groups with higher s will be disadvantaged. We also fixed the benefit of altruism, corresponding to β_G in §4.2, at 0.05 for all groups; i.e., a group of all A-types has a 5% fitness advantage over a group of all non-altruists.

By contrast, the extent γ of oblique transmission is clearly a socially determined variable, societies with higher γ according more social influence to A-type elders. Similarly the strength of payoff-based updating may vary across groups and over time. Each group initially was randomly assigned a value of γ and a value of η. Random variation in social learning arrangements ("institutional mutation") allowed η and γ to increase or decrease by 1% of their values. The migration rate was set to 25% per generation (very high for a genetic model but reasonable for a cultural model), and the mutation rate was set to 0.01% per generation, and migration was always to a neighboring group, individuals taking their phenotypic traits with them. As in Chapter 7, we assume that institutions are not free goods. In this case a more effective socialization system (greater γ) comes at the price of a larger fitness disadvantage for the A-types. The time they spend teaching altruistic behavior, for example, they cannot be seeking out mating opportunities and caring for their offspring.

We set the cost per A-type of γ to be $s\gamma$; i.e., setting $\gamma = 0.80$ in a group is equivalent to raising the fitness cost to A-types by 0.8s. We found in the simulations that s is inversely related to the long-run value of γ, as one might expect. The level of η, the lure of higher payoffs in motivating the regression from altruism to self-interest, is also socially determined. A-types, whose numbers are reduced by desertion to self-interest when η is substantial, can devote time and energy to reducing the lure of payoffs, teaching, for example, the value of non-material well-being. To reflect his

Simulation Parameter	*Value*
Initial frequency of aAC	2%
Initial frequency of aAD,aSC,aSD	1%
Initial frequency of bSD	95%
Fitness cost of altruism s	0.03
Gain from internalizing fitness-enhancing norms f	0.06
Fitness cost of internalization physiology u	0.01
Initial range of rate of oblique transmission γ	[0,0.9]
Initial range of imitation rate η	[0,0.9]
Initial group size	12
Conflict rate	10%
Cost of γ	$5s$
Cost of η	$5s$
Fitness contribution of A-type to group	0.05
Mutation rate	0.01%
Migration rate	25%
Number of groups	1000

Table 10.6. Parameters for the simulation of the spread of strong reciprocity through weak group selection. $[a, b]$ signifies the initial seeding of the groups with values drawn from the uniform distribution on $[a, b]$. The values of s, f, u, as well as the fitness contribution of A-types and the mutation and migration rates are the same and unchanging for all groups and all generations.

we imposed a cost of $s(1 - \eta)$ on the A-types. Thus setting $\eta = 0.20$ in a group is equivalent to raising the fitness cost to A-types by $0.8s$.

In each generation, for each of the groups, we simulated the theoretical model as described in the previous sections and updated the frequencies of the various types in each group, according to the fitness effect of their A phenotype and the fraction of the group that exhibits this phenotype. Then a randomly selected 25% of individuals in each group migrated randomly to neighboring groups, bringing their phenogenotype with them. Selection among groups takes two forms in this model. First, if group size drops below a minimum (set to one third of initial group size, or four), it is replaced by a copy of the neighboring group that has the highest average fitness of group members. Second, with a small probability for each generation, a group enters into conflict with another randomly chosen group. The group with higher fitness prevails, and members of the losing group copy the group-specific parameters of members of the winning group.

We ran this model many times with varying numbers of generations, and varying the parameters described above. The system always stabilized rapidly, there is virtually no variation in final values across runs, the specific assumptions concerning the parameters move in the intuitively expected direction, and initial conditions were never critical. The parameter values always allow zero altruism to be a stable evolutionary equilibrium, but with as few as 2% initial A-types, altruism always stabilized at a high level. A run with the parameters described above is exhibited in Figure 10.1. There is always strong

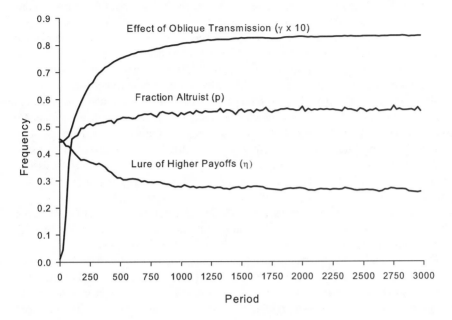

Figure 10.1. The evolution of endogenous parameters. In this simulation, the steady state fraction of Altruists is $p \approx 0.57$, the effect of oblique transmission stabilizes at $\gamma \approx 0.083$, and the rate of switching from A type to N type is $\eta \approx 0.26$.

selection favoring the rate of oblique transmission, unless the cost of maintaining γ at a high level is extremely high (about $10s$). Selection for lower η is also quite strong, so a high cost of reducing it is needed to prevent η from falling to very low levels in the long run.

Figure 10.1 shows the evolution of the endogenous parameters in this simulation. The fraction of A-types increases to about 57% by the end of the run. This value varies between 50% and 75%, depending on the costs, borne by A-types alone, for maintaining a high γ and a low η. It is clear that all three parameters of the model undergo strong selection, γ rising to 0.083 and η falling to 0.26 (γ is multiplied by 10 in the figure).

Migration does not undermine the altruistic equilibrium, because most of the effects occur on the cultural rather than the genetic level, and migrants respond to the social learning environment of their new home.

The simulation thus identifies a wide range of parameter values under which a system of cultural transmission biased toward socialization of the young for altruism and minimizing the lure of material payoffs could itself evolve, and if it did that, these social learning arrangements would support a frequency of altruism in the population.

10.7 The Programmable Brain

Vertical, oblique, and payoff-based updating all affect the internalization of norms. Taking on a general rule of behavior as an objective rather than a constraint or an instrument toward some other end is likely to be costly for two reasons. First, a considerable fraction of the total available time of the members of most societies is spent teaching the young the proper way to behave, rather than providing for the nutritional and other needs of its members. But in addition to the cost of acquiring such a norm ($u > 0$), there is a further cost: the rule will not be ideally suited to all situations, and its internalization deprives the individual of flexibility in dealing with such situations on a case-by-case basis. The parochial preferences that motivate the exclusion of outsiders studied in Chapter 8 ("don't marry outside your religion") is an example of a personally costly general rule of behavior—costly because it reduces the size of the marriage pool.

Why, then, are humans so susceptible to internalizing general rules? If this susceptibility were subject to a purely payoff-based selection process, whether fitness- or payoff-sensitive, one might expect it to be eliminated from any population in which it appeared. What, then, accounts for the extraordinary success of general rules of behavior? An answer that we have found persuasive (Heiner 1985) is that internalizing general rules of behavior may persist in an evolutionary dynamic because it relieves the individual from calculating the costs and benefits in each situation and reduces the likelihood of making costly errors. A similar argument led John Stuart Mill to remark, "Being rational creatures [sailors] go to sea with it [the Nautical Almanac] already calculated; and all rational creatures go out upon the sea of life with their minds made up on the common questions of right and wrong, as well as on many of the far more difficult questions of wise and foolish" (1957[1861], p. 407).

Our models show that cultural transmission and the capacity to internalize norms may coevolve if some of these norms are fitness enhancing for the individuals who adopt them. But if this is the case, what is the evolutionary advantage of taking on the costs of socialization and internalization?

Like those of other animals, our bodies produce the sensations of pleasure and pain in response to the things we experience, and this is what induces our behavior. These hedonic responses that constitute the proximate causes of behavior can be represented as what we in Chapter 3 defined as preferences: reasons for behavior, other than beliefs and capacities, that account for the actions an individual takes in a given situation. These preferences are subject to natural selection, as well as social learning in some animals, and there is some reason to think that, for most animals most of the time, preferences induce behavior approximating that which would result if the individual animal were to deliberately maximize its fitness, at least locally.

Cultural transmission and internalization make humans an exception to this general proposition. Cultural transmission and internalization affect our hedonic responses to situations and induce behaviors that may diverge substantially and systematically from what an individual fitness maximizer would do. As we saw in the introduction to this chapter, individual and even average fitness-reducing behaviors can be successfully promoted by cultural transmission and internalization. But the internalization of culturally transmitted norms can also do better than natural selection in inducing behaviors that enhance fitness. This is true for two reasons.

First, except under special circumstances, individual fitness maximization does not maximize average fitness of the members of a group. The impossibility of altruism evolving by a fitness-monotone dynamic in a random mixing population is a pertinent example. Other examples were studied in Chapters 7 and 9. This being the case, groups that override individual fitness maximizing by means of the cultural transmission of internalized norms may experience higher group average fitness than other groups. These group benefits may offset the costs just mentioned. Indeed, this is one of the key dynamics accounting for the emergence of altruism in the above models, and of social preferences in general.

In our model of socialization, oblique transmission converts a fraction of self-regarding types into altruists. But we did not ask about the proximate motives for the altruists helping others. Does oblique transmission work by teaching children the golden rule or Kant's categorical imperative? By warning them that God may be watching?

These and other cognitive reasons for good behavior are no doubt involved, but the motivation to help others and to act ethically often short-circuits these reflective processes in favor of more visceral influences on behavior such as anger, shame, elation and guilt. To readers who share our horror of road rage and honor killings, the claim that visceral reactions are among the proximate motives for generous, fair-minded and civic actions may seem surprising. But it is true, and we think that a good case can be made that the social emotions evolved precisely because they motivated prosocial actions.

Symbol	Meaning
β	Bias of vertical transmission
β_o	Baseline fitness
η	Imitation rate
f	Fitness gain from C phenotype
γ	Rate of oblique transmission
γ_i	Strength of i's moral standard
λ_i	Strength of i's reciprocity motive
μ_{ij}	Punishment of j by i
ν_i	Strength of i's shame
p	Fraction of A's
π_i	Material payoff to i
s	Fitness cost of A phenotype
u	Fitness cost of a allele
τ_r	Degree of reproductive leveling (effective tax rate)
τ	Quorum threshold level
ζ	Segmentation rate

Table 10.7. Definition of symbols

11

Social Emotions

> This is the gist of human psychology... what the hero does all feel
> that they ought to have done as well. The sophisms of the brain
> cannot resist the mutual aid feeling, because this feeling has been
> nurtured by thousands of years of human social life and hundreds
> of thousands of years of prehuman life in societies.
>
> Pyotr Kropotkin, Mutual Aid Chapter
VIII (1989[1903]) p. 277

> Let's not forget that the little emotions are the great captains of our
> lives and we obey them without realizing it.
>
> Vincent Van Gogh, Letter to his brother
Theo Letter 603 (July 6, 1889)

> The heart has reasons that reason knows nothing about.
>
> Blaise Pascal, Pensées Number
277 (1995[1670])

Social emotions—love, guilt, shame, and others—are responsible for the host of civil and caring acts that enrich our daily lives and render living, working, shopping, traveling among strangers, sustaining social order, even conducting scientific research, feasible and pleasant. Adherence to social norms is underwritten not only by cognitively mediated decisions, but also by emotions (Frank, 1987, 1988; Ekman, 1992; Damasio, 1994; Elster, 1998; Boehm 2007). When Bosman et al. (2001) assayed the feelings of respondents in an ultimatum game, they found that low offers by the proposer provoked anger, contempt and sadness in the respondents, that the intensity of the self-reported emotions predicted the respondents' behavior, stronger emotions inducing rejections of low offers. Interestingly, the introduction of an hour-long "cooling-off" period between the offer and the respondent's choice of an action had no effect on either reported emotions or on the rejection behaviors of the respondents. Recall from Chapter 3 that Sanfey et al. (2003) found that those rejecting low offers in an ultimatum game experienced heightened levels of activation in the brain areas associated with disgust and anger.

One of the most important emotions sustaining cooperation is shame, the feeling of discomfort at having done something wrong not only by one's own norms but also in the eyes of those whose opinions matter to you. Shame differs from guilt in that, while both involve the violation of a norm, the former but not the latter is necessarily induced by others' knowing about the violation and making their displeasure known to the violator.

We will suggest that shame, guilt, and other social emotions may function like pain, in providing personally beneficial guides for action that bypass the explicit cognitive optimizing process that lies at the core of the standard behavioral model in economics and decision theory. Pain is one of the six so-called basic emotions, the others being pleasure, anger, fear, surprise, and disgust. Shame is one of the seven so-called social emotions, of which the others are love, guilt, embarrassment, pride, envy, and jealousy (Plutchik 1980, Ekman 1992). Basic and social emotions are expressed in all human societies, although their expression is affected by cultural conditions. For instance, in all societies one may be angered by an immoral act, or disgusted by an unusual foodstuff, but what counts as immoral or disgusting is, at least to some extent, culturally specific.

Antonio Damasio (1994) calls an emotion a "somatic marker," that is, a bodily response that "forces attention on the negative outcome to which a given action may lead and functions as an automated alarm signal which says: Beware of danger ahead if you choose the option that leads to this outcome... the automated signal protects you against future losses" (p. 173). Emotions thus may contribute to the decision-making process by working with, not against, reason. Damasio continues, analogizing emotions to physical pain: "suffering puts us on notice... it increases the probability that individuals will heed pain signals and act to avert their source or correct their consequences" (p. 264).

To explore the role of guilt and shame in inducing social behaviors we will consider a particular interaction having the structure of a public goods game (§3.2). In the public good setting, contributing too little to the public account may evoke shame if one feels that one has appropriated "too much" to oneself. Because shame is socially induced, being punished when one has contributed little triggers the feeling of having taken too much. In this case, the effect of punishment on behavior may not operate by changing the material incentives facing the individual, that is, by making clear that if he continues to free ride his payoffs will be reduced by the expected punishments in future rounds. Rather it evokes a different evaluation by the individual of the act of taking too much, namely, shame. This is the view expressed by Jon Elster (1998)" "material sanctions themselves are best understood as vehicles of the emotion of contempt, which is the direct trigger of shame" (p. 67). Thus, self-interested actions, per se, may induce guilt, but not shame. If one contributes little and is not punished, one comes to consider these actions as unshameful. If, by contrast, one is punished when one has contributed generously, the emotional reaction may be spite toward the members of one's group. This is one of the reasons why the "antisocial" punishment of high contributors in public goods experiments has such deleterious effects on the level of cooperation in a group.

We assume individuals maximize a utility function that includes five distinct motives: one's individual material payoffs, how much one values the payoffs to others, this depending on both one's unconditional altruism and one's degree of reciprocity, as well as one's sense of guilt or shame in response to one's own and others' actions. To this end, we will amend and extend a utility function derived from the work of Geanakoplos et al. (1989), Levine (1998), Sethi and Somanathan (2001), and Falk and Fischbacher (2006).

In Chapter 3, we presented experimental evidence consistent with the view that punishment not only reduces material payoffs of those who transgress norms, but also may recruit emotions of shame toward the modification of behavior. Indeed, we showed in §3.4 that in some societies many defectors react to being punished by increasing their contribution to the group, even when the punishment does not affect material payoffs, consistent with the shame response, while in other societies they react by counter-punishing contributors, consistent with an anger response. Social emotions in response to sanctions can thus either foster or undermine cooperation. Reacting to sanctions, then, is often not a dispassionate calculation of material costs and benefits, but rather involves the deployment of culturally specific social emotions. In Chapter 9 we showed that the altruistic punishment of shirkers by strong reciprocators can proliferate in a population and sustain high levels of cooperation, but we tacitly assumed that those punished would react prosocially rather than antisocially. Here, we focus on the manner in which social emotions and punishment of miscreants may be synergistic, each enhancing the effects of the other.

We first model the process by which an emotion such as shame may affect behavior in a simple public goods game. We then show that shame and guilt along with internalized ethical norms allow high levels of cooperation to be sustained with minimal levels of costly punishment, resulting in mutually beneficial interactions at limited cost. In §11.2, we ask how prosocial emotions such as shame might have evolved.

11.1   Reciprocity, Shame, and Punishment

Consider two individuals who play a one-shot public goods game in which each has a norm concerning the appropriate amount to contribute to the public project, and each (a) values his own material payoff, (b) may prefer to punish others who contribute insufficiently, (c) feels guilt if he contributes less than the norm; and finally (d) experiences shame if he is sanctioned for having contributed less than the norm. This psychological repertoire captures some of the motives that we think explain cooperation in behavioral experiments. The results that follow for a dyadic interaction generalize to an n-person interaction. A summary of the symbols used in this chapter appears in Table 11.1

In what follows, we represent the two players as i and j, where $j \neq i$. We assume each individual starts with a personal account equal to one unit. Each individual contributes to the public project an amount a_i, $0 \leq a_i \leq 1$, where $i = 1, 2$ refer to the two individuals, and each receives $\chi(a_1 + a_2)$ from the project, where $1/2 < \chi < 1$. Thus, the individuals do best when both cooperate $(a_i, a_j = 1)$, but each has an incentive to defect $(a_i, a_j = 0)$ no matter what the other does. In the absence of punishment, this two-person public goods game thus would be a prisoner's dilemma. But at the end of this cooperation period there is a punishment period, in which each individual is informed of the contribution of the other individual, and each individual may impose a penalty μ on the other individual at a cost

$$c(\mu) = c\frac{\mu^2}{2}. \tag{11.1}$$

This, and the other functional forms below, are chosen for expositional and mathematical convenience.

Letting μ_{ij} be the level of punishment of individual j by individual i, the material payoff to i is then given by

$$\pi_i = 1 - a_i + \chi(a_1 + a_2) - \mu_{ji} - c(\mu_{ij}). \tag{11.2}$$

In (11.2), the first two terms give the amount remaining in i's private account after contributing, the third term is i's reward from the public project, the fourth term is the punishment inflicted by j upon i, and the final term is the cost to i of punishing j.

We assume that the norm is that each should contribute the entire endowment to the public project. The results generalize to the case where the norm is less stringent. Individual i may wish to punish j by reducing j's payoffs, if i is a reciprocator (that is $\lambda_i > 0$) and j contributes less than the entire endowment. To represent the propensity of i to punish j for not contributing sufficiently, we assume that i's valuation of j's payoff is

$$\beta_{ij} = \lambda_i(a_j - 1), \tag{11.3}$$

where we assume $0 < \lambda_i < 1$, so that unless j contributed his entire endowment, i receives a subjective benefit from lowering j's material payoff that is proportional to j's shortfall. The parameter λ_i, $0 < \lambda_i < 1$, is the strength of i's reciprocity motive. The condition that $\lambda_i < 1$ ensures that individual i cannot value j's payoffs negatively more than he values his own positively. Thus should both payoffs increase proportionally, individual i cannot be worse off.

The shame experienced by i is a subjective cost proportional to the product of the degree to which he is punished by j, and the extent to which his contribution falls short of the norm, and is equal to $v_i(1 - a_i)\mu_{ji}$. Thus, punishment triggers shame, which is greater the more the individual has kept for himself rather than contributing to the public project, and the larger is v_i, the susceptibility of individual i to feeling shame. Finally, i may feel guilt simply for having violated his internal standards of moral behavior. We represent this feeling by $-\gamma_i(1 - a_i)$, which is negative for $\gamma_i > 0$ unless i contributes the full amount to the project. The parameter γ_i is i's susceptibility to guilt.

The utility function of i is then given by

$$u_i = \pi_i + \beta_{ij}(1 - a_j + \chi(a_1 + a_2) - \mu_{ij}) - (\gamma_i + v_i\mu_{ji})(1 - a_i). \tag{11.4}$$

The first term is i's material payoffs, which are those from the public project net of his own contribution and minus the cost of being punished by j and the cost of punishing j, from equation 11.2. The second term is (using equation 11.3) i's evaluation of j's material payoffs, which are those from the project net of his own contribution and minus i's punishment of j.

We have not included the cost to j of punishing i, in the material payoffs of j that i takes account of when choosing his contribution level because we think it is unrealistic to imagine that i would seek to reduce j's payoffs by inducing j to bear costs so as to punish i. The third term is the guilt and punishment-induced shame that i experiences when i contributes less than the amount that would maximize the well-being of the two players, namely 1.

Given any level of j's contribution, we can represent individual i's behavior as the joint maximization of two objective functions. The first is, given j's contribution, how much to punish j. The answer is to select μ_{ij} so as to equate the marginal cost of punishment $(dc/d\mu_{ij} = c\mu_{ij})$ with the marginal benefit of punishing j, which is β_{ij}. Given this level of punishment, i will then select the level of contribution that equates the marginal benefits of contributing, which are reduced punishment, guilt and shame, and the marginal costs of contributing, which involve forgoing some of one's endowment and contributing to the material payoffs of j, even though i values these negatively. Note that because the susceptibility to shame and the level of punishment received appear multiplicatively in this last term, punishment and shame are what economists call complements. This means that an increase in the susceptibility to shame increases the marginal effect of punishment on the individual's utility and therefore raises the marginal benefit that i will receive by contributing more. Similarly, an increase in the level of punishment raises the marginal effect of an enhanced susceptibility to shame on the actor's utility. Shame thus enhances what is termed the "punishment technology," the effectiveness of which is measured by the ratio of the utility loss inflicted on the target, including both the subjective costs and the reduction in payoffs from equation 11.2, to the marginal cost to the punisher of undertaking the punishment, which from equation 11.1 is $c\mu_{ij}$. This punishment effectiveness ratio for i's punishment of j is thus

$$\frac{1 + v_j(1 - a_j)}{c(\mu_{ij})},\tag{11.5}$$

from which it is clear that the punishment of j is more effective the more susceptible to shame is j.

Because each individual's valuation of the payoffs of the other depends on the actions the other takes, it is clear that the actions taken by each will be mutually determined. For any given value of j's action, there will be an action—a best response—by i that maximizes his utility as expressed in equation 11.4. The best response function for individual i is shown in Figure 11.1, along with the analogous best response function for j. Their intersection is the mutual best response, and is therefore a Nash equilibrium. In Figure 11.1 we see that because of reciprocity, the best response a_i is an increasing function of a_j, and the a_i schedule shifts up when susceptibility to shame or guilt, or j's degree of reciprocity (v_i, γ_i, λ_j), increases, corresponding to our intuitions concerning the model. There is also a minimal level of susceptibility to shame supporting positive contributions. The minimal level of shame that will induce a positive contribution is increasing in the cost of punishment and decreasing in i's susceptibility to guilt γ_i, j's level of reciprocity λ_j, and the productivity χ of the public project, again confirming our intuitions.

Suppose the level of shame of both individuals were to increase. This is shown in Figure 11.1 by the dashed lines. The result is a displacement of the mutual best response so that both individuals contribute more, and as a result the level of punishment is less. This is the sense in which we mean that because shame enhances the effectiveness of punishment, it economizes on the cost of punishment. When one individual's susceptibility to shame increases the other individual benefits and when this occurs for both, as in Figure 11.1, both benefit. Payoffs therefore are higher in a population that has inculcated a sense of shame in its members, as could be the case, for example,

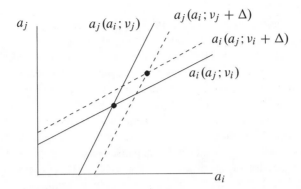

Figure 11.1. Mutual determination of contributions to a public project. The functions slope upwards because the individuals are reciprocators and shift as shown when susceptibility to shame, v, increases, because this enhances the effects of punishment. There is no reason to think that the function would take the linear form shown here.

through the kinds of population-wide internalization of norms studied in the previous chapter.

11.2   The Evolution of Social Emotions

Human behaviors systematically deviate from the model of the self-interested actor, and we think the evidence is strong that social emotions account for much of the discrepancy. But this description of behavior would be more compelling if we understood how social emotions might have evolved, culturally, genetically, or both. There are two puzzles here. First, social emotions are often altruistic, indicating actions benefiting others at a cost to oneself, so that in any dynamic in which the higher payoff trait tends to increase in frequency, social emotions would eventually disappear. We addressed this puzzle in the previous four chapters, showing that by the process of group competition, reproductive leveling, and norm internalization, vertically transmitted altruistic traits may evolve.

The second puzzle concerns social emotions per se. How could it ever be evolutionarily advantageous to bypass one's cognitive decision making capacities and let behavior be influenced by the visceral reactions associated with one's emotions? We addressed a similar question in the previous chapter: internalizing norms may be a way of economizing the costs of calculating benefits and costs in each situation, and of averting costly errors when the calculations go wrong. A related argument, we think, helps explain the evolutionary viability of social emotions.

Humans tend to be impatient, a condition we share with other animals (Stephens et al. 2002). We tend to discount future costs and benefits myopically, that is, more than either a fitness-based or a lifetime welfare-based accounting would require. The mismatch between our impatience and our fitness is in part due to the payoff to patient behaviors that resulted from the extended life histories and prolonged period of learning the skills associated with the distinctive skill-intensive human feeding niche based on hunted and extracted foods. Prior to this period in human history, the importance of the future was more limited and largely concerned the survival of one's offspring. A genetically transmitted disposition to assist one's relatives may have produced a selective degree of patience as a by-product of kin-based selection, resisting stealing food from one's offspring, for example. But even if our genetic development in a cooperative social context has mitigated the extreme short-term benefits of lying, cheating, killing, stealing, and satisfying immediate bodily needs, such as wrath, lust, greed, gluttony, sloth, we nevertheless have a fitness-reducing bias toward behaviors that produce immediate satisfaction at the expense of our long-run well-being.

The internalization of norms and the expression of these norms in a social emotion such as guilt and shame addresses this problem by inducing the individual to place a contemporaneous value on the future consequences of present behavior, rather than relying upon an appropriately discounted accounting of its probable payoffs in the distant future. One may curb one's anger today not because there may be harmful effects next month, but because one would feel guilty now if one violated the norms of respect for others and the dispassionate adjudication of differences. One may punish others for behaving antisocially not because there are future benefits to be gained thereby, but because one is angered at the moment.

Do the social emotions thus function in a manner similar to pain? Complex organisms have the ability to learn to avoid damage. A measure of damage is pain, a highly aversive sensation the organism will attempt to avoid in the future. Yet an organism with complete information, an unlimited capacity to process information, and with a fitness-maximizing way of discounting future costs and benefits would have no use for pain. Such an individual would be able to assess the costs of any damage to itself, would calculate an optimal response to such damage, and would prepare optimally for future occurrences of this damage. The aversive stimulus, pain, could then be strongly distorting of optimal behavior. If you sprain your ankle while fleeing from a lethal predator, you might have a better chance of survival if you could override the pain temporarily. Because pain per se clearly does have adaptive value, it follows that modeling pain presupposes that the individual experiencing pain must have incomplete information and/or a limited capacity to process information, and/or an excessively high rate of discounting future benefits and costs. Are guilt and shame social analogues to pain?

If being socially devalued has fitness costs, and if the amount of guilt or shame that a given action induces is closely correlated with the level of these fitness costs that would otherwise not be taken account of, then the answer is affirmative. The same argument will hold not only for fitness costs, but for any effect, possibly operating through cultural transmission, that reduces the number of replicas an individual will generate.

11.3   The "Great Captains of Our Lives"

Shame and guilt, like pain, dispense with an involved optimization process by means of a simple message: whatever you did, undo it if possible, and do not do it again. Two types of selective advantage thus may account for the evolutionary success of shame and related social emotions. First, social emotions may increase the number of replicas, by either genetic or cultural transmission, of an individual who has incomplete information (e.g., as to how damaging a particular antisocial action is), limited or imperfect information-processing capacity, and/or a tendency to undervalue costs and benefits that accrue in the future. Probably all three conditions conspire to induce people to respond insufficiently to social disapprobation in the absence of social emotions. The visceral reactions associated with these emotions motivate a more adequate response, one that will avert damage to the individual. Of course the role of social emotions in alerting us to negative consequences in the future presupposes that society is organized to impose those costs on norm violators. The social emotions thus may have coevolved with the reciprocity-based emotions motivating punishment of antisocial actions, modeled in the previous chapters.

The second selective advantage favoring the evolution of social emotions refers specifically to shame. The fact that the higher levels of shame among members of a group, the higher (in equilibrium) will be the sum of their payoffs also suggests that shame may evolve through the effects of group competition. As we have seen, where the emotion of shame is common, punishment of antisocial actions will be particularly effective and as a result seldom used. Thus groups in which shame is common can sustain high levels of group cooperation at limited cost and will be more likely to survive environmental, military and other challenges, and thus to populate new sites vacated by groups that failed.

As a result, selective pressures at the group level will also favor religious practices and systems of socialization that support susceptibility to shame for failure to contribute to projects of mutual benefit of the type modeled in the previous two sections.

It is quite likely, then, that the "moralistic aggression" that is involved in the altruistic punishment of miscreants and that motivated the punishment of shirkers in Chapter 9 also created a selective niche favorable to the emergence of shame and other social emotions, or what Christopher Boehm (2007) calls a conscience:

> The human conscience evolved in the Middle to Late Pleistocene as a result of subsistence turning to the hunting of large game. This required...cooperative band-level sharing of meat...bands had to gang up physically against their alphas to ensure efficient meat distribution. This sets the stage for morality to develop as a new, more socially-sensitive type of personal self-control became adaptive for individuals living in these punitive groups. Thus a conscience began to develop biologically. In turn...conscience transformed social control by making punitive sanctioning increasingly moral and also less lethal, as group ostracism and shaming evolved. (Boehm 2007, p. 1)

Combining the model of this chapter and that of Chapter 9, the emergence of shame would have reduced the costs of punishing transgressors incurred by the strong reciprocators. The reason for this is that gossip and ridicule could then suffice where physical, often violent, elimination from the group had been necessary in the absence of shame. The proliferation of strong reciprocators engaging in altruistic punishment that this cost reduction allowed would then have enhanced the advantages of shame.

Thus the moralistic aggression motivating the altruistic punishment of defectors may have coevolved with shame, each providing the conditions favoring the proliferation of the other. The groups in which this occurred initially, perhaps among our foraging ancestors in Africa, would have enjoyed survival advantages over other groups.

Symbol	Meaning
a_i	Individual i' contribution to the project
β_{ij}	Equals $\lambda_i(a_j - 1)$
χ	Each individual receives $\chi(a_1 + a_2)$ from project
γ_i	Individual i's guilt coefficient
i, j	Two players
λ_i	$\lambda_i(a_j - 1)$ is the value i placed on j's contribution
μ_{ij}	Level of punishment of j by i
ν_i	Individual i's shame coefficient
n	Group size
π_i	Material payoff to i

Table 11.1. Definition of symbols

Conclusion: Human Cooperation and Its Evolution

It is true that certain living creatures, as bees and ants, live sociably one with another...and yet have no other direction than their particular judgments and appetites; nor speech, whereby one of them can signify to another what he thinks expedient for the common benefit: and therefore some man may perhaps desire to know why mankind cannot do the same.

Thomas Hobbes, *Leviathan* Chapter 8 (1968[1651]).

Any animal whatever, endowed with well-marked social instincts, the parental and filial affections being here included, would inevitably acquire a moral sense or conscience, as soon as its intellectual powers had become as well developed, or nearly as well developed, as in man.

Charles Darwin, *The Descent of Man* Chapter IV (1998[1873]) pp. 71–72

About 55,000 years ago, a group of hunter-gatherers left Africa and began to move eastward along the shores of the Indian Ocean. They may have originated in the Upper Rift Valley in modern-day Kenya. They could have been the descendants of the cooperative early humans we described at the outset, living 30,000 years earlier at the mouth of the Klassies River far to the south. Wherever they came from, some eventually crossed hundreds of kilometers of open ocean before reaching Australia, just 15,000 years later. We do not know if they encountered or simply bypassed communities of *Homo floresienis*, who persisted in what is now Indonesia almost to the end of the Pleistocene. As they spread northward, they also encountered the Denisovan hominins, who inhabited parts of Asia as recently as 50,000 years ago. Another branch of the African exodus crossed the Levant and somewhat later occupied Europe, then home to the soon-to-be-extinct Neanderthals. Though the possibility of multiple human origins cannot be eliminated, it is now widely thought that the descendants of this small group eventually peopled the entire world and are the ancestors of all living humans (Foley 1996, Klein 1999).

This second great exodus from Africa is remarkable for its speed and eventual spread. One cannot resist speculating about the capacities that made these particular individuals such lethal competitors for the (also large-brained, ornament-wearing and tool-making) Neanderthals or that allowed the construction of oceangoing craft. Some attractive candidates can be ruled out. The physiological innovations allowing for more effective speech, rearrangement of respiratory tract and esophagus, for example, had occurred much earlier. Likewise, the dramatic expansion of hominid brain size had occurred before two million years ago. Richard Klein (2000) suggests a "selectively advantageous mutation" that facilitated the cultural transmission of behaviors as a possible cause.

> Arguably this was the most significant mutation in the human evolutionary series for it produced an organism that could radically alter its behavior without any change in its anatomy and that could cumulate and transmit alterations at a speed that anatomical innovation could never match. (p. 18)

But, as Klein himself points out, the only evidence for such a super-mutation are the facts it is intended to explain (Klein 2000). Whether the source was a single revolutionary innovation or, as many now think (McBrearty and Brooks 2000), the result of a long process of incremental changes, the linguistic capacities and the cultural transmission of norms of social conduct that supported cooperation were a necessary part of the human repertoire that made the peopling of the world possible. These same capabilities must be part of any account of the remarkable success of humans as a species then and since.

12.1   The Origins of Human Cooperation

Humans became a cooperative species because our distinctive livelihoods made cooperation within a group highly beneficial to its members and, exceptionally among animals, we developed the cognitive, linguistic and other capacities to structure our social interactions in ways that allowed altruistic cooperators to proliferate.

Human reliance on the meat of large hunted animals and other high quality, large package-size, and hence high-variance foods meant that our livelihoods were risky, skill-intensive, and characterized by increasing returns to scale. Deploying skills that required years to acquire favored the evolution of large brains, patience, and long lives (Kaplan et al. 2000, Kaplan and Robson 2003). Organizing and sharing the returns to successful hunting additionally favored groups that developed practices of sharing information, food, and other valued resources (Boehm 2000). Moreover, the long period of dependency of human offspring on adults, in part the result of the prolonged learning curve associated with hunting and gathering, meant that there were substantial benefits to cooperative child-rearing practices extending beyond the immediate family. Prolonged juvenile dependency also generated a net food deficit for families with adolescent children, increasing the benefits of food-sharing among unrelated individuals and other forms of social insurance (Kaplan and Gurven 2005). Our experimental evidence, presented in Chapter 3, shows that among today's small-scale societies, those that are especially reliant on big game, like the Lamalera whale hunters that we studied in Indonesia, and those for whom livelihoods require either joint efforts in acquisition or sharing in distribution, are especially likely to exhibit the social preferences that underpin altruistic cooperation.

One of the reasons for the connection between the potential benefits of cooperation and the prevalence of cooperative behaviors that we discovered in our models and simulations is that where the benefits associated with cooperation relative to the costs are substantial, it is more likely that the evolutionary processes of gene-culture coevolution will support populations with large numbers of cooperators, whether altruistic or mutualistic. A high ratio of benefits to costs makes cooperation an evolutionarily likely outcome because, as our models and simulations, for example, Figures 4.6, 9.1, and 9.4 confirmed, in virtually any plausible evolutionary dynamic in which stochastic shocks to payoffs and to behaviors play an important role, the likelihood that a population will develop and maintain cooperative practices is higher, the greater are the net benefits of cooperation.

But the fact that cooperation was group-beneficial in the environments of early humans does not explain why it evolved, for individuals bear the costs of their cooperative behaviors, while it is often others who enjoy the benefits. Thus, the distinctive human livelihood and associated cognitive capacities and longevity are necessary but not sufficient to explain the extent and nature of human cooperation. While benefits of cooperation accruing to the individual cooperator may sometimes offset the costs, this is not likely to have been the case in many situations in which cooperation was essential to our ancestors, including defense, predation and surmounting environmental crises. In these situations involving large numbers of individuals facing their possible demise, people with self-regarding preferences would not cooperate, regardless of their beliefs about what others would do. As a result, for cooperation to be sustained, social preferences would have to motivate at least some of those involved.

The distinctive human capacity for institution-building and cultural transmission of learned behavior allowed social preferences to proliferate. Our ancestors used their capacities to learn from one another and to transmit information to create distinctive social environments. The resulting institutional and cultural niches reduced the costs borne by altruistic cooperators and raised the costs of free-riding. Among these socially constructed environments, three were particularly important: group-structured populations with frequent and lethal intergroup competition, within-group leveling practices such as sharing food and information, and developmental institutions that internalized socially beneficial preferences.

These culturally transmitted institutional environments created a social and biological niche favorable to the evolution of the social preferences on which altruistic cooperation is based. We can only speculate, of course, about the initial appearance and proliferation of these preferences. But their emergence was highly likely for two reasons. The first is that the preferences that constitute strong reciprocity and some other social preferences could appear *de novo* as the result of only a small behavioral modification of either kin-based altruism or reciprocal altruism. In the case of kin-based altruism, those behaving altruistically toward kin may have simply ceased discriminating against the non-kin members of their groups. Likewise, a reciprocal altruist could become a strong reciprocator by simply deleting the proviso that one should condition one's behavior on expectations of future reciprocation.

The second reason why the emergence of social preferences among early humans would be highly likely is the vast number of foraging bands during the Late Pleistocene and earlier. Even if strong reciprocity initially emerged in a very small fraction of the human population, it is highly likely that over tens of thousands of generations and something like 150,000 foraging bands, it would have occurred that the strong reciprocators or other altruistic cooperators were prevalent in one or more such groups at some point. These bands would have done very well in competition with other bands.

We have sought to explain how humans came to develop these exceptional social preferences and the cooperative social practices that supported them, taking the distinctive nature of human ecology, diet, and life course as preexisting. This analytical simplification is almost surely historically inaccurate. The distinctive nature of human livelihoods, the importance of hunted and extracted as opposed to collected foods, apparently does not predate and is not the cause of the emergence of cooperation. Rather, it appears that the two developed in tandem.

Though we have not addressed this question, we think it likely that the models presented here, suitably amended, would illuminate the coevolution of human cooperation along with our distinctive diets, life histories, and livelihoods. The presence on the African savannah of large mammals vulnerable to attack by cognitively advanced predators must have given substantial advantages to the members of groups that developed means of coordinating the hunt and sharing its sporadically acquired prey. Correspondingly, groups that had learned how to cooperate in these ways would have benefited from preferentially targeting large animals, as opposed to food acquired in smaller packages, and thereby enlarging the place of hunted meat in their diet. Winterhalder and Smith (1992) write:

> only with the evolution of reciprocity or exchange-based food transfers did it become economical for individual hunters to target large game. The effective value of a large mammal to a lone forager...probably was not great enough to justify the cost of attempting to pursue and capture it...However, once effective systems of reciprocity or exchange augment the effective value of very large packages to the hunter, such prey items would be more likely to enter the optimal diet. (p. 60)

We think it likely that the distinctive aspects of the human livelihood thus coevolved with the distinctive aspects of our social behavior, most notably cooperation.

Two approaches inspired by standard biological models have constituted the workhorses of our explanation, multi-level selection and gene-culture coevolution. Could it be that altruistic cooperation became common among humans in the absence of these two processes? We think it empirically unlikely. The reason is that the kin-based and reciprocal altruism models, operating alone or in tandem, are peculiarly ill-suited to explain the distinctive aspects of human cooperation, for the reasons given in Chapter 4 and 6.

By contrast, explanations of the emergence and proliferation of cooperative behaviors based on gene-culture coevolution and multi-level selection are quite plausible. First, the models and simulations of our evolutionary past presented in the previous chapters provide strong evidence that in the relevant evolutionary environments, selective pressures based on the positive assortment of behaviors arising from the group-structured nature of human populations could have been a significant influence on human evolution. Second, we have also demonstrated the important contribution to the evolution of social preferences that could have been accomplished by the cultural transmission of empirically well-documented behaviors such as the internalization of norms, within-group leveling, and between-group hostility. Third, the nature of preferences revealed in behavioral experiments and in other observations of human behavior is consistent with the view that genuine altruism, a willingness to sacrifice one's own interest to help others, including those who are not family members, and not simply in return for anticipated reciprocation in the future, provides the proximate explanation of much of human cooperation. These ethical and other-regarding group-beneficial social preferences are the most likely psychological consequence of the gene-culture coevolutionary and multi-level selection processes we have described.

12.2   The Future of Cooperation

Conclusive evidence about the origins of human cooperation will remain elusive given the paucity of the empirical record and the complexity of the dynamical processes involved. As in many problems of historical explanation, perhaps the best that one can hope for is a plausible explanation consistent with the known facts. This is what we have attempted to provide.

The challenge of explaining the origins of human cooperation has led us to the study of the social and environmental conditions of life of mobile foraging bands and other stateless small-scale societies that arguably made up most of human society for most of the history of anatomically modern humans. The same quest has made non-cooperative game theory (which assumes the absence of enforceable contracts) an essential tool. But as Ostrom (1990), Taylor (1996), and other authors have pointed out, most forms of contemporary cooperation are supported by incentives and sanctions based on a mixture of multilateral peer interactions and third-party enforcement, often accomplished by the modern nation-state.

It would thus be wise to resist drawing strong conclusions about cooperation in the 21st century solely on the basis of our thinking about the origins of cooperation in the Late Pleistocene. One may doubt, for example, that lethal intergroup conflict today contributes to the altruism, civic-mindedness or other social preferences that could underpin the more cosmopolitan forms of cooperation required to address global challenges such as climate change and epidemics.

But the fundamental challenges of social living and sustaining a livelihood that our distant ancestors faced are in many respects not fundamentally different from those we face today. Modern states and global markets have provided conditions for mutualistic cooperation among strangers on a massive scale. But altruistic cooperation remains an essential requirement of economic and social life.

The reason is that neither private contract or governmental fiat singly or in combination provides an adequate basis for the governance of modern societies. Social interactions in modern economies are typically at best quasi-contractual. Some aspects of what is being transacted are regulated by complete and readily enforceable contracts, while others are not. Transactions concerning credit, employment, information, and goods and services where quality is difficult to monitor provide examples of quasi-contractual exchanges.

Where contracting is absent or incomplete, the logic of Adam Smith's invisible hand no longer holds. Decentralized markets fail to implement efficient allocations. But governments typically lack the information, and often the motivation, necessary to provide adequate governance where markets fail or are absent.

We now know from laboratory experiments that subjects in marketlike situations with complete contracts tend to behave like the *Homo economicus* of the Adam Smith of *The Wealth of Nations*, but when their contracts are not complete their behavior fortunately resembles more the virtuous citizens of the Adam Smith of *The Theory of Moral Sentiments*. Thus, where the invisible hand fails, the handshake may succeed. Kenneth Arrow wrote (1971)

> In the absence of trust. . . opportunities for mutually beneficial cooperation would have to be foregone. . . norms of social behavior, including ethical and moral codes [may be]. . . reactions of society to compensate for market failures. (p. 22)

Thus, social preferences such as a concern for the well-being of others and for fair procedures remain essential to sustaining society and enhancing the quality of life.

In a world increasingly connected not just by trade in goods but also by the exchange of violence, information, viruses, and emissions, the importance of social preferences in underwriting human cooperation, even survival, may now be greater even than it was among that small group of foragers that began the exodus from Africa 55,000 years ago to spread this particular cooperative species to the far corners of the world.

Appendix

A1 Altruism Defined

In Chapters 1, 2, and 4 we provide two definitions of altruism, one concerning preferences (other-regarding or self-regarding) that motivate behavior and the other based on its fitness effects on the actor and others.

The standard biological definition of altruism concerns not the motives for an action but rather its effects. This definition considers a large population composed of many groups: the behaviors induced by an altruistic genotype increase the expected average fitness of members of the group of which the focal individual is a member, but the focal individual would have higher fitness were he not the bearer of the altruistic genotype. To make this clear, following Kerr et al. (2004), suppose the expected fitness of altruists and non-altruists in a group of m members with j altruists are $w^A(j)$ and $w^N(j)$, respectively. Then our first condition, that the altruistic behavior raises the expected average fitness of members of the group, is that

$$(j+1)w^A(j+1) + (m-(j+1))w^N(j+1) > jW^A(j) + (m-j)w^N(j), \quad \text{(A1)}$$

requiring that the total (and therefore average) fitness of a group with $j+1$ altruists exceed that of a group with only j altruists. The second condition, that switching from an N to an A lowers the actor's fitness, is

$$w^A(j+1) < w^N(j) \quad \text{(A2)}$$

which says that the fitness of an altruist in a group with $j+1$ altruists must be less than the fitness of a non-altruist in a group with just j altruists. These two conditions are respectively conditions four and one of Kerr et al. (2004), which together imply their condition two.

There are two attractive features of this definition. First, it is the most stringent definition possible (other than definitions that preclude the evolution of altruism under any conditions). In the absence of positive assortment altruism cannot evolve under our definition. An alternative definition found in Haldane (1932), Cohen and Eshel (1976), Maynard Smith (1964) and Sober and Wilson (1998) replaces (A2) with the condition that A's have lower fitness than N's, or

$$w^A(j) < w^N(j). \quad \text{(A3)}$$

This is less stringent because it does not preclude that $w^A(j+1) > w^N(j)$, so that an N would increase its fitness by switching to an A. This would be the case if the altruistic act cost c and conferred a benefit b on a randomly selected member of the group, and $b/n > c$. Then condition A3 would hold but condition A2 would not: by switching to A from N, the chance that the benefit would accrue to the actor would more than offset the cost of the behavior. In this case altruism will evolve even under random assortment (Matessi and Jayakar 1976).

The second attractive feature is that the definition maps directly onto the two terms in the Price equation (equation 4.3 and §A10). Recall that β_G is the effect on expected group average fitness of changes in the fraction of altruists in the group and β_i is the effect on the individual's own fitness of a change in the individual's own type (from N to A). Condition A1 requires that $\beta_G > 0$ while condition A2 requires that $\beta_i < 0$, thus defining what we have called in Chapter 4 the strong group selection problem.

Our preference-based definition concerns intentions. Altruistic preferences are those that place a positive value on the beneficial outcomes of one's actions for others, motivating the actor sometimes to bear personal costs so as to help others. Consider a social setting including two individuals, Alice and Bob. A standard if overly simple formulation in economics of Alice being altruistic in this setting is that her utility includes her self-regarding payoffs plus some positive weight on the well-being of Bob. More adequate formulations permit Alice's valuation of the payoffs to Bob to depend on her understanding of Bob's character—his kindness, altruism, nationality, morality or other of Bob's traits that might affect his goodwill toward her or others. Even this more adequate framework in which Alice's valuation of the payoffs to Bob is conditional on what she knows about him—perhaps based on how Bob treated her or others in the past—does not capture the entire range of actions in which Alice bears a cost to help Bob, for these actions include entirely self-regarding motives such as Alice wishing to constitute herself as a generous person (sometimes termed "warm glow" altruism).

The two definitions, fitness-based and preference-based, are not the same, a fact that is hardly surprising, as the latter refers to motives and the former to outcomes, in a situation where unintended consequences are common. If Alice helps Bob because she places a positive weight Bob's payoffs, this could motivate Bob to help Alice, even though this was not the motivation for her beneficence. In this case both Alice and Bob may be altruistic according to the preference-based definition. But if the payoffs under consideration are in fitness terms, as in the fitness-based definition of altruism, and if Bob's actions more than repay Alice's costs in benefiting Bob, then Alice's behavior is biologically self-regarding rather than biologically altruistic. By reciprocating Alice's generosity, however, Bob may be an altruist.

A2   Agent-Based Models

Agent-based modeling is a tool for analyzing complex dynamical systems as a complement to explicit mathematical analysis where the latter is either impossible or uninformative. In these models, the actors are individual agents who share many characteristics, but differ on key characteristics that affect their relative reproductive success, material payoffs or other results that affect the differential replication of distinct types of individuals. The agents operate semi-autonomously, but are linked through a network of structured interactions. The individual characteristics in a complex system evolve through a process of replication, mutation, and finally selection that favors relatively successful individuals. Such dynamics are recursive, meaning that changes in one period become the basis for changes in future periods, and are non-linear, which implies that forces propagate through the system in an uneven and variably dampened or amplified manner, with the implication that they are generally incapable of being expressed as closed-form analytical solutions to sets of equations.

For instance, the individuals may be workers competing for jobs, or males and females interested in finding a good mate, or predators trying to catch prey and prey trying to avoid being caught. Suppose the individuals and their environment undergo mutation and structural change, so that the resulting system is sufficiently complex that it has "emergent properties" that cannot be determined simply by aggregating individual interactions, and the mathematics of the system is too complicated to solve in analytical form. Finally, suppose that the individuals' history of interaction affects their play, and individuals continually adapt by taking on the behaviors of other individuals who have done especially well, in terms of fitness, material gain or some other standard. In such a situation, agent-based modeling is an appropriate tool for investigating the dynamics of the interactive system.

Agent-based modeling is widely used in the natural and behavioral sciences, and the growth in its use has been extremely rapid since the advent of the powerful desktop computer. Such modeling (often called "simulation") lies outside the two standard methods of gaining scientific knowledge: deduction and induction. Deduction means proving theorems, that is, showing that certain mathematical conclusions follow from certain axioms (e.g., the Pythagorian theorem follows from the laws of algebra). Induction means finding lots of evidence and drawing conclusions (e.g., all swans are white). Agent-based modeling is like deduction in that it starts with a rigorously specified computer program, but it is like induction in that it treats the operation of the program as a set of data points from which generalizations can be made. In particular, if a complex system has emergent properties, these can be ascertained by implementing an agent-based model in which these properties are seen and persist over many simulations.

We use agent-based models to study the dynamics of hypothetical populations that are structured to evolve in ways that we think represent long-term human evolution. Using this method, we can generate thousands of artificial histories allowing us to investigate the likely effects of differences in the benefits and costs of cooperative activities, the frequency of group conflict, the structure of a group's socialization practices and other influences.

How do we judge the empirical adequacy of an agent-based model? There are two ways to do this, both of which we have done in the models presented here. First, one can ensure that the parameters chosen are empirically plausible for the populations under study. Thus the simulations reported in Chapters 7–10 use parameters for group size, frequency of between-group migration and conflicts and the like that were estimated (as indicated in Chapter 6, for example) on the basis of available data. One can easily check how much difference variations in the parameters make for the results of the simulation, as we have done in many cases. On the basis of this sensitivity analysis we then spend special attention making sure that the parameters that matter are well estimated. For example Figure 7.6 makes clear that group size and the frequency of conflict are key parameters in the simulation of the evolution of altruism; therefore, we were especially careful in estimating these parameters (Chapter 6).

Second, we can exploit the fact that while the processes under investigation are unknown (that is why we are simulating them), the simulations generate a large number of by-product statistics on aspects of the relevant populations on which we do have some knowledge. Thus we can ask whether the results of the simulation conform to known facts about the populations under study. Thus when we simulate the evolution of parochial altruism (Chapter 8), we ask if the frequency of warfare and the extent of mortality in conflict generated by the model are consistent with what we know from archaeological and ethnographic data (presented in Chapter 6). And in Chapter 10 we ask if the simulations of a population engaged in contingent punishment generate levels of between-group genetic variance that are consistent with the estimates based on actual genetic data from hunter-gatherer populations. In cases where the models have generated implausible by-product statistics, of course, we diagnose the source of the problem and recalibrate the model.

While agent-based modeling is important because many dynamic strategic settings are too complicated to admit standard mathematical analysis, it should not be thought that agent-based models are necessarily second best. The assumptions made to permit explicit analytical solutions are often sufficiently unrealistic (e.g., continuous time, infinite numbers of individuals) that the agent-based model behaves more like the situations we are trying to model than does a tractable analytical model (Durrett and Levin 1994). Nevertheless, agent-based models require extensive experimentation to ensure that results accurately reflect the properties of the system.

The forefather of agent-based modeling in the behavioral sciences was Nobel Prize-winner Thomas Schelling's (1978) study of residential segregation. Schelling did not use a computer simulation or evolutionary updating, but rather simple physical models of social processes. In one of his most famous studies, he used a chess board, each square of which represented a place in which one family could live, and he used pennies and nickels to represent white and black families. He began by placing the coins randomly on the board, and assumed a family would stay put if at least one third of its neighbors were the same type as itself, and otherwise would move to a nearby home that satisfied the one third rule. Schelling showed that in the long run, family relocation is likely to lead to a high degree of segregation, even though obviously each family was perfectly happy in a neighborhood in which it was a minority.

In this case, neighborhood segregation is an emergent property of the system because no individual family wanted this or sought it, and it was not predicted as the logical consequence of the system's initial conditions using some analytical model. We can study residential segregation using Schelling's idea by varying the number of ethnic groups, varying the intensity of preference for uniformity and diversity, and by varying the rules of neighborhood formation and population movement. For instance, Schelling predicted the "tipping" phenomenon often found in residential dynamics: when the fraction of residents of a minority group in a community reaches a certain "tipping point," the community more or less rapidly shifts toward that group becoming a majority.

An evolutionary agent-based model, in addition to a *stage game* representing the interaction of agents, has a replication phase, in which individuals replicate proportional to their success in the stage game, relative to the average in the population. As a result, old individuals disappear, and their offspring inherit their behavior, perhaps with some mutation. In an evolutionary agent-based model, the more successful strategies are permitted to increase in frequency at the expense of the less successful. Thus, evolutionary agent-based models possess the three main characteristics of Darwinian evolution: replication, mutation, and selection according to fitness.

Among the first behavioral science applications of evolutionary agent-based modeling was Joshua Epstein and Robert Axtell's *Growing Artificial Societies* (1997), which produced a wide variety of emergent behaviors from simple rules governing individual behavior inscribed in a "chromosome" that could evolve over time much as DNA, the computer genes being used to represent different strategic behaviors. They modeled migration, environmental externalities, conflict, and even disease transmission in a population of individuals competing for food. More recently, agent-based models of political competition, stock market dynamics and investor strategies, as well as models of parasitism and disease transmission have become standard components of behavioral research (Gintis 2006, 2007a, Miller and Page 2007, Epstein 2007, Farmer and Foley 2010). For a useful overview of the application of such models to various fields in the natural and behavioral sciences, see Tesfatsion and Judd (2006), Gintis (2006, 2007), Miller and Page (2007), Epstein (2007), and Farmer and Foley (2010).

Figure A1 shows the programming structure of a typical evolutionary agent-based model. In the figure, "Game Parameters" refer to the specifics of the stage game being simulated, including the payoffs, the probabilities with which various events occur, and the like. The "Number of Generations" specifies how many rounds of replication you want to take place. This may be as small as 10 or as large as 10,000,000. The "Number of Rounds/Generation" refers to the speed of play as compared to the speed of replication. By the law of large numbers, the more rounds per generation, the more accurately the actual success of individuals reflects the expected payoff of the strategies they represent. "Group All Individuals" captures the matching phase of the simulation, as well as the notion that a strategy in a game reflects a social practice occurring in the population, rather than the carefully thought-out optimizing strategy of classical game theory. Note that in some situations, we will want some structure to this stage of the model. For instance, "neighbors" may meet more frequently than "strangers," or individuals who play similar strategies may meet more frequently than individuals with different strategies.

The "Individuals Replicate" box is worth a diagram of its own, which we present in Figure A2. First we set various parameters, including the rate of mutation of new individuals and the extinction rate of old individuals. We then eliminate the appropriate number of unsuccessful individuals, and make an equal number of copies of the high-success individuals, giving them the same strategies as their replicators, except that we allow some mutation. Success may be measured by fitness (offspring surviving to reproductive age) or by extent to which an individual's behavior is copied (adopted through social learning) by others.

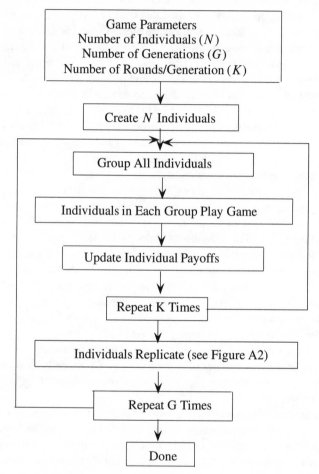

Figure A1. Structure of an evolutionary agent-based simulation.

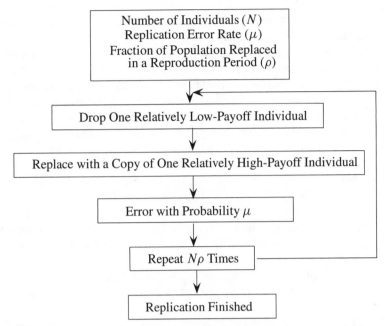

Figure A2. Structure of replication process. In each reproduction period, ρN individuals die and are replaced by copies, possibly mutated, of other agents. More successful individuals have a higher probability of being copied.

A3   Game Theory

Game theory is a mathematical tool for the study of strategic interactions, namely those in which the payoffs of individuals depend on their own actions and the actions taken by others. Gintis (2009b) is a text on the kinds of game theoretic methods used here.

Suppose we have individuals $i = 1, \ldots, n$ involved in a social interaction, each individual i has a set S_i of possible actions available to him, and each individual chooses an action $s_i \in S_i$ independently from the others. To each action profile $(s_1, \ldots, s_n)$ resulting from these choices, each individual i receives a *payoff* $\pi_i(s_1, \ldots, s_n)$. We call the various actions s_i *pure strategies* and we call this social situation a *game in strategic* or *normal form*. This definition extends readily to a *mixed strategy*, where players use probability distributions over their pure strategies.

An example of a game in strategic form is the prisoner's dilemma (§3.1), in which each player $i = 1, 2$ has pure strategy set $S_i = \{H, D\}$, where H stands for help and D stands for defect, and $\pi_1(H, H) = b - c$, $\pi_1(H, D) = -c$, $\pi_1(D, H) = b$, and $\pi_1(D, D) = 0$. The payoffs to player two are $\pi_2(H, H) = b - c$, $\pi_2(H, D) = b$, $\pi_2(D, H) = -c$, and $\pi_2(D, D) = 0$.

Suppose players choose strategies $(s_1, \ldots, s_n)$. We say s_i is a *best response* to the remaining $n - 1$ strategies of the other players if there is no strategy for player i that can give player i a payoff greater than $\pi_i(s_1, \ldots, s_n)$. We say $(s_1, \ldots, s_n)$ is a

Nash equilibrium if every player's choice is a best response to the choices of the other players. In many cases we do not expect players to choose a Nash equilibrium, as for example, in the repeated games described in Chapter 5, but in many games described in this book, it is reasonable to expect individuals to play a Nash equilibrium.

In some games, including the prisoner's dilemma described above, and its extension to an n-player game, the public goods game (§3.2), a player may have a strategy that offers higher payoff than any other strategy, no matter what the other players do. Such a strategy is called *dominant*. A player who has a dominant strategy will play it in any Nash equilibrium, because such a strategy is a best response to any configuration of strategies of the other players. In the one-shot prisoner's dilemma and public goods games, for instance, defecting is a dominant strategy for all players.

In many games, players move more than one time and do not play simultaneously. We represent such games as *extensive form* games, as in Figure 8.1. In this case we use a game tree consisting of nodes connected by branches. Each node represents a point in the game where a particular player gets to move, and each branch emanating from a node represents the various actions that the player has when choosing at that node. At the end of the game tree are terminal nodes where the payoffs to the players are exhibited. For a more complete treatment of extensive form games, consult Gintis (2009b).

Consider a choice of an action at each node of the extensive form game. We say the resulting profile of choices is a Nash equilibrium in that no player can gain by changing his choice at any node where he gets to choose.

Suppose we start with a game as in the previous section, and repeat the game indefinitely, with a probability $1 - \delta > 0$ of terminating the process at the end of each period (§4.5). We then call $\mathcal{G}$ the *stage game* of the repeated game. The payoff to the repeated game is just the sum of the payoffs to the various stages. Note that the payoff is finite, because the process terminates in a finite number of periods with certainty. Note also that we can include a time discount factor in δ, as explained in Chapter 4.

The most important fact about the repeated game based on stage game $\mathcal{G}$ is that it can support cooperative equilibria in situations where $\mathcal{G}$ cannot. Consider, for instance, the prisoner's dilemma (§3.1). The only Nash equilibrium of the stage game has both players defecting, hence earning payoff 0. But suppose the players follow the strategy in the repeated game of cooperating until the first player defects, and then defecting forever. We call this the trigger strategy (§5.1). By following the trigger strategy, the players earn $(b-c)/(1-\delta)$, as analyzed in §4.2. The gain from defecting right away is b, so following the trigger strategy is a Nash equilibrium as long as $(b-c)/(1-\delta) > b$, which reduces to $\delta b > c$.

The evolutionary game models that we use in this book are distinct from classical game theory. The key idea in evolutionary game theory is differential replication rather than best response. The so-called adaptive agents in evolutionary games adopt behaviors in a manner similar to the way people come to have a particular accent or to speak a particular language. Forward-looking payoff-based calculation is not entirely absent (e.g., those aspiring to upward mobility may adopt upper class accents) but conscious optimizing is not the whole story. The answer to "why do you talk like that?" is generally: "because I was born where people talk like that" not "because I considered all the ways of speaking and decided that speaking this way best serves my personal goals." Successful strategies in an evolutionary game are those that make more than the average number of replicas in the next period either because they are favored in the process by which people learn new strategies, or the genotypes expressing the strategies are induced to proliferate by the process of natural selection. The institutional and behavioral characteristics of individuals and societies that we commonly observe are those that have been copied, diffused, in short replicated, while competing rules, beliefs and preferences have suffered extinction, or have been replicated only in marginal niches. The models developed in this book explain why altruistic human behaviors, like strong reciprocity, and the institutional environments, like reproductive leveling, that supported them could have outreplicated alternative behaviors and institutions.

The dramatis personae of evolutionary game models thus are not individuals but behavioral rules, or in population genetic models, the alleles accounting for these behaviors: how they fare is the key, what individuals do—with whom they are matched in a stage game or in an updating opportunity, for example—is important for how this contributes to the success or failure of behavioral rules. Analytical attention is focused on the success or failure of these behavioral rules themselves as they either diffuse and become pervasive in a population or fail to do so and are confined to minor ecological niches or are eliminated.

A final difference is that because evolutionary approaches explicitly model the process by which replication takes place, whether by genetic transmission or updating behaviors by social or individual learning, they allow an explicit analysis of the dynamics by which the distribution of traits in a population changes. Figure 8.3 is an example of such a dynamic. This in turn permits the study of the states of a population that are likely to be often attained, and when attained to persist for long periods. We are thus able to distinguish between the "evolutionarily irrelevant" Nash equilibria (§5.4) on the one hand and population states that will be readily accessed and long enduring, like Talcott Parsons' evolutionary universals introduced at the beginning of Chapter 7.

A4   Dynamical Systems

We will explain two major types of dynamical systems, a continuous time system using differential equations, and a discrete time system using Markov chains. The material presented here is a condensed version of the presentation in Gintis (2009b), to which the reader should refer for additional material and references.

For ease of exposition, suppose our continuous time system has two dimensions, represented by variables x and y, the horizontal and vertical axes of the Cartesian plane. An example is the coevolution of the fraction of altruists and of parochialists in the population depicted in Figures 8.1 and 8.2. The path of the system in time is represented by a pair of functions $x(t)$ and $y(t)$. We assume that the rate of change of the system in the x- and y-directions are functions of the position of the system alone, so we can write

$$\frac{dx(t)}{dt} = f(x, y) \tag{A4}$$

$$\frac{dy(t)}{dt} = g(x, y). \tag{A5}$$

There is a theorem that guarantees that, given an initial time $t = t_0$, if f and g are reasonably well-behaved, there is a unique solution to (A4) and (A5) through $t = t_0$. This is called the path of the dynamical system.

An equilibrium of this dynamical system, also called a critical point or fixed point, or stationary point, is a value (x^*, y^*) such that $f(x^*, y^*) = g(x^*, y^*) = 0$. Note that at an equilibrium, $dx/dt = dy/dt = 0$, so the dynamical system remains forever at (x^*, y^*) once it reaches there. Under what conditions does a dynamical system move toward an equilibrium?

Suppose that, starting from a point (x_0, y_0), the path of the dynamical system approaches (x^*, y^*) as $t \to \infty$; i.e., $\lim_{t\to\infty} x(t) = x^*$ and $\lim_{t\to\infty} y(t) = y^*$. Then we say (x_0, y_0) is in the *basin of attraction* (the set of point starting from which the system moves to the equilibrium point) of the equilibrium (x^*, y^*). If the basin of attraction of an equilibrium is two-dimensional, it must surround the equilibrium, and we say the equilibrium is *locally stable*, or simply stable. If the equilibrium is not stable, it may be either *neutrally stable* or *unstable*. The equilibrium is unstable if, no matter how close a path starts near (but not at) the equilibrium, there is a positive distance d from the equilibrium such that the path eventually is farther than d from the equilibrium, and never gets closer than d thereafter. If the path is neither stable nor unstable, we say it is neutrally stable. In the neighborhood of a neutrally stable equilibrium, paths neither escape nor converge to the equilibrium. They rather trace out paths around the equilibrium.

Very few dynamical systems, even simple ones in two dimensions, can be solved analytically, so the paths $x(t)$ and $y(t)$ cannot be written in closed form. Nevertheless, there are well-developed methods for determining when an equilibrium is stable, unstable, or neutrally stable, using tools from algebra and calculus.

A *finite Markov chain* is a dynamical system that can be in any of n states $s_1, \ldots, s_n$, and if the system is in state i in time period t, it will be in state j in time period $t + 1$ with probability p_{ij}. Of course, for this to make sense, we must have $p_{ij} \geq 0$ for all $i, j = 1, \ldots, n$, and $\sum_{j=1}^{n} p_{ij} = 1$. Statistical estimates of these probabilities, based on thousands of implementations of our model, for example, are the basis of our calculation of the vector field in Figure 8.2 giving the movement of the population among the states indicating various frequencies of altruists and of parochials.

For instance, consider two urns, one filled with 10 red balls and the other with 10 white balls. In each time period, we choose one ball from each urn simultaneously and place each ball in the other urn. Let s_i be the state where the first urn has i red balls, so we start out in state s_{10}. It is easy to write down the transition probabilities if you know a little probability theory, but we will leave this exercise to the reader. It is intuitively obvious that in the long run, there will be an average of 5 white balls in the first urn, and this will be true independent of how many of the 10 white balls were in this urn when we started. When a Markov chain has the property that the average fraction of time in each state in the long run is independent from the starting state, we say the system is *ergodic*, and we call the resulting long-run distribution of probabilities the *stationary distribution* of the Markov chain. The Markov chain represented by our urn problem is thus an ergodic Markov chain. Figure 8.2 gives the stationary distribution of parochials and altruists while Figure 4.6 give the mean levels of net cooperation in the stationary distribution of the agent-based models of cooperation, for varying group sizes and error rates.

We say the states of a Markov chain *communicate* if, for every pair of states, there is a positive probability of moving from the first state to the other and then back. If we write $p_{ij}^{(k)}$ for the probability that the Markov chain moves from state i to state j in k periods, then states i and j communicate if $p_{ij}^{(k)} > 0$ and $p_{ji}^{(m)} > 0$ for some integers k and m. Let i be a state of a Markov chain, and let T_i be the set of integers k such that $p_{ii}^{(k)} > 0$. If the greatest common divisor of the integers in T_i is greater than 1, we say the state i is *periodic*. For instance, consider a Markov chain consisting of 10 points equally spaced on a circle, numbered 1 to 10, and suppose the state can move either clockwise or counterclockwise by one position. Then, every state has period two (meaning the set of states partitions into two subsets and the system is in one set in even-numbered periods and the other subset in odd-numbered periods), because the system can only return to a state in an even number of transitions. If a Markov chain has no periodic states, we say the Markov chain is aperiodic.

Using these definitions, we can state the most important property of finite Markov chains. Suppose every pair of states of a finite aperiodic Markov chain communicate. Then the chain is ergodic. Clearly, this applies to the above urn problem.

An agent-based model is a finite Markov chain because there are a finite number of agents, each can only be in a finite number of states, and if there are parameters in the model (e.g., the current weather), then these are in finite number. Moreover, a computer language can support only a finite number of real numbers without "overflow," so even supposedly "real" numbers are really a finite range of integral fractions. The number of states in the resulting system can be huge, but it is a finite number. Moreover, while it may be quite impractical to calculate the probability of movement from one state to another, the probability itself is perfectly determinate. To ensure that the Markov chain represented by the agent-based model is ergodic, we always allow agents to remain in their current state with positive probability, and mutate to another state with positive probability, however small.

It follows that the ergodic theorem holds for all of the agent-based models used in this book. This means that the long-run behavior of the dynamical systems generated by our agent-based models is independent from the particular initial parameters we have chosen for our illustrative runs. Of course, the ergodic theorem cannot tell us how long it will take to "erase" the effect of our initial conditions, and the number of periods involved could be truly astronomical. Thus, we take the question of how fast a system moves to its stationary distribution to be a very important one,

It may appear that the stationary distribution of an ergodic Markov chain somehow represents a small cluster of nearby "long-run average states," but that is not the case in some Markov chains. For instance, consider the Markov chain with two states s_1 and s_2, where $p_{11} = 0.99$, $p_{12} = 0.01$, $p_{22} = \epsilon$ and $p_{21} = 1 - \epsilon$. If ϵ is a small perturbation, this chain spends almost all its time in state one, but it does spend a positive amount of time, about ϵ periods, on average, in state two. We say a state is *recurrent* if it spends a positive fraction of time in this state in the stationary distribution, so both states in this example are recurrent. However, when it enters state one, it stays there for almost 100 periods, on average, before moving to state two, whereas in state two, it rarely stays for more than one period. We say that a state is *stochastically stable* if, under a small perturbation of size $\epsilon > 0$, the fraction of time it spends in that state is bounded away from zero as $\epsilon \to 0$. Clearly, only state one is stochastically stable in this case. Young (1998) uses finite Markov processes to study the long-term evolution of contracts and other institutions.

A5   The Replicator Dynamic

The most natural dynamic to apply to an evolutionary game is the *replicator dynamic*, which we describe below. Indeed, it can be shown that every equilibrium of an evolutionary game under the replicator dynamic is a Nash equilibrium of the stage game (Nachbar 1990). This shows that the Nash equilibrium criterion remains powerful even without assuming that players are rational (i.e., that they choose best responses) or coordinated.

However, in many cases, Nash equilibria of the stage game are not stable equilibria of the corresponding evolutionary game. For this reason, Maynard Smith developed the stronger notion of an *evolutionarily stable strategy* (ESS) for the case of a two-player stage game $\mathcal{G}$ in which a single population of individuals play against themselves, as in the prisoner's dilemma. A strategy is an ESS if a whole population using that strategy cannot be invaded by a small group playing any other strategy. It is easy to show that an ESS is always a Nash equilibrium, but the converse is false. Indeed, an ESS is always a stable equilibrium of the replicator dynamic (see, for instance, Gintis 2009b), which is not the case in general for a Nash equilibrium.

We here derive the replicator dynamic for an evolutionary game based on the imitation of cultural (phenotypic) traits. The derivation for genetic evolution is similar, but somewhat simpler to derive. Consider a population of individuals who play a game in which each player follows one of n pure strategies s_i for $i = 1, \ldots, n$. For ease of presentation, we will assume $n = 2$, although the argument is perfectly general. The play is repeated in periods $t = 1, 2, \ldots$ Let p^t be the fraction of players playing s_1 in period t, so $1 - p$ is the fraction playing s_2. Suppose the payoff to s_i is $\pi_i^t = \pi_i(p^t)$. We look at a given time t, and assume (perhaps after renumbering) that $\pi_1^t \leq \pi_2^t$.

Suppose in every time period dt, each individual with probability $\alpha dt > 0$ learns the payoff to another randomly chosen other individual and changes to the other's strategy if he perceives that the other's payoff is higher. However, information concerning the difference in the expected payoffs of the two strategies is imperfect, so the larger the difference in the payoffs, the more likely the individual is to perceive it, and change. Specifically, we assume the probability q_{ij}^t that an individual using s_i will shift to s_j is given by

$$q_{ij}^t = \begin{cases} \beta(\pi_j^t - \pi_i^t) & \text{for } \pi_j^t > \pi_i^t \\ 0 & \text{for } \pi_j^t \leq \pi_i^t \end{cases}$$

where β is sufficiently small that $q_{ij} \leq 1$ holds for all i, j. The expected fraction $\mathbf{E}p^{t+dt}$ of the population using s_1 in period $t + dt$ is then given by

$$p^{t+dt} = p^t - \alpha p^t (1 - p^t) \beta (\pi_2^t - \pi_1^t) dt.$$

We can rewrite this as

$$\frac{p^{t+dt} - p^t}{dt} = \alpha\beta p^t(1 - p^t)(\pi_1^t - \pi_2^t)$$

and taking the limit as $t \to 0$ and normalizing so $\alpha\beta = 1$, we get the replicator equation

$$\frac{dp}{dt} = p^t(1 - p^t)(\pi_1^t - \pi_2^t). \tag{A6}$$

There is another common form of this equation, as follows. We define $\bar{\pi}^t = p^t\pi_1^t + (1 - p^t)\pi_2^t$, which is the average return for the whole population. Then

$$\pi_1^t - \bar{\pi}^t = \pi_1^t - \bar{\pi}^t = \pi_1^t - (p^t\pi_1^t + (1 - p^t)\pi_2^t) = (1 - p^t)(\pi_1^t - \pi_2^t).$$

Thus we can rewrite equation A6 as

$$\frac{dp}{dt} = p^t(\pi_1^t - \bar{\pi}^t). \tag{A7}$$

Several points are worth making concerning the replicator dynamic. First, under the replicator dynamic, the frequency of a strategy increases exactly when it has above-average payoff. Second, while a particular strategy can become extinct (e.g., $p = 0$ or $p = 1$), a strategy that is not represented in the population at one point in time will never be represented in the population at any later point in time. So, replicator dynamics abstract from mutation and innovation. A more general system adds a term to the replicator equation expressing the spontaneous emergence of novel replicators.

Book-length treatments on evolutionary game theory are Weibull (1995), Vega-Redondo (2003), and Gintis (2009b). Young (1998), Bowles (2004) and McElreath and Boyd (2006) use evolutionary game theory to study the dynamics of human behavior and institutions. Applications to biology are developed in Nowak (2006).

A6 Continuation Probability and Time Discount Factor

Suppose a game is played in periods $t = 1, 2, \ldots$ such that in each period the game continues for one more period with probability δ, where $0 < \delta < 1$. Suppose a player has payoff π in each period that the game is played, but has a *time discount factor* d, with $0 < d < 1$, such that a payoff π in period t is worth $d^t\pi$ at the start of the game. Note that the discount factor d is related to the rate of time discounting (also termed the rate of time preference) r by $d = 1/(1 + r)$, or equivalently, $r = (1 - d)/d$.

The value v of the game at the beginning of the first period satisfies the equation

$$v = \pi + \delta dv,$$

so, letting $\delta^* = \delta d$, we have

$$v = \frac{\pi}{1 - \delta^*}. \tag{A8}$$

Because the continuation probability δ and the time discount factor d enter multiplicatively in (A8), we can interpret δ^* as an arbitrary combination of continuation probability and time discount factor.

A7   Alternatives to the Standing Model

To investigate the sensitivity of the standing model of §4.6 to informational requirements, suppose that with probability q an individual knows the standing of his partner, and with probability $1 - q$ he has no information concerning the partner's status.
Suppose that an individual following the cooperative strategy who is in good standing
cooperates unless he knows his new partner is in bad standing.

Using this model, and assuming an execution error rate of $\epsilon \geq 0$, we find that the
information requirements for indirect reciprocity being an evolutionary stable strategy
are that the minimum feasible q satisfies

$$q_{\min} > \frac{c}{b}\left(1 + \epsilon\left(1 - \frac{c}{b}\right)\right)$$

(Gintis 2004). This requirement is demanding except perhaps in the smallest groups,
and is not likely to be met in most real-world conditions.

The indirect reciprocity model can be extended to groups of size $n > 2$ in the
obvious fashion, where an individual is in good standing if he cooperated in the previous
period, or when he defected while being in good standing in the previous period in a
group with at least one member in bad standing. But the informational requirements
clearly become prohibitive under normal conditions for larger groups.

Nowak and Sigmund (1998b) addressed the problem of the excessive informational requirements of the standing strategy by investigating an indirect reciprocity
strategy which they term *image-scoring*. Nowak and Sigmund show that the strategy of
cooperating with others who have cooperated in the past, independent of the standing
of the Cooperator's partner, is stable against invasion by Defectors, and weakly stable against invasion by Cooperators once Defectors are eliminated from the population
(i.e., when there are no Defectors in the population, Cooperators and image scorers have
equal payoffs). However, Panchanathan and Boyd (2003) showed that if execution errors, however small, are introduced into the model, cooperation becomes unstable, and
universal defect becomes the only stable equilibrium of the system. Nowak and Sigmund (1998a) use an agent-based model (§A2) to analyze the stability of a somewhat
more complex image-scoring strategy, but Leimar and Hammerstein (2001) show that a
strategy not considered by Nowak and Sigmund, in which one's own image score is low
independent of the image score of the recipient, can invade the image-scoring strategy.
The weakness of image-scoring lies in the fact that in an image-scoring model, there
is no incentive for a self-regarding individual to care about the status of the potential
recipient when deciding whether or not to help.

However, the image-scoring model is considerably less information-demanding
than the standard indirect reciprocity model, so it is useful to investigate conditions
under which it could survive where a standing model would not. Thus, Brandt and Sigmund (2004) show that the robustness of image-scoring dramatically increases when
there are perceptual errors in judging whether an individual has defected. This is because in such circumstances, there is extreme lack of agreement as to who is in good
standing, and hence when a defection is to be considered a reason for falling into bad
standing. Because the image-scoring process does not take into account the status of
the recipient of help, it makes far fewer errors where perceptual errors are frequent.

Brandt and Sigmund (2005) investigated an alternative scenario in which each player i in the indirect reciprocity game knows the status of q_i other players, and the average level of information $q = \sum_i q_i/n$ increases from period to period. For instance, when an individual helps another individual, he may add his new partner to his "circle of friends," and may have a way of retaining information concerning his friends' status in future periods of play. Brandt and Sigmund show that under these conditions, image scoring can resist invasion by Defectors.

A8 The Prisoner's Dilemma with Public and Private Signals

Suppose in §5.3 that the signals are public, and the continuation probability δ and error rate ϵ are such that cooperation can be sustained with the OBSTD ("one bad signal triggers defect") strategies, and if π_r is the expected payoff to playing OBSTD, we must have

$$\pi_r = 5 + (1 - \epsilon)^2 \delta \pi_r. \tag{A9}$$

Here, the first term represents the payoff in the first period assuming mutual cooperation, and the second term reflects the fact that signals with probability $(1 - \epsilon)^2$ neither player receives a defect signal in error, so the game continues another period with probability $(1 - \epsilon)^2 \delta$. Thus we have, in the case of public signals,

$$\pi_r = \frac{5}{1 - \delta(1 - \epsilon)^2}, \tag{A10}$$

and that playing OBSTD beats intentionally defecting, which has expected payoff 8, provided

$$\delta \geq \frac{3}{8(1 - \epsilon)^2}.$$

If the error signal is private, but players still use OBSTD, then (A9) becomes

$$\pi_r = 5 + (1 - \epsilon)^2 \delta \pi_r - 3\delta\epsilon(1 - \epsilon) + 8\delta\epsilon(1 - \epsilon) + \epsilon^2(0). \tag{A11}$$

Here, the first two terms are as before, the third term represents the case that Bob cooperates but Alice receives the defect signal. Bob thus cooperates in the next period when Alice defects, because he does not know that Alice received the defect signal, so Bob receives -3, and both defect in every period after that. The fourth term reflects the case that Alice cooperates but Bob receives the defect signal. The final term is zero because, with a double error, the payoff is zero to each player. Bob thus defects in the next period but Alice cooperates, so Bob's payoff is 8. The expected value of this game, after some algebra, is given by

$$\pi_r = \frac{5(1 + \delta\epsilon(1 - \epsilon))}{1 - \delta(1 - \epsilon)^2}, \tag{A12}$$

which is close to (A10). For instance, if $\delta = 0.9$ and $\epsilon = 0.05$, π_r from (A12) is about 1.5% greater than π_r from (A10).

To see that with private signals, Alice's TBSTD ("two bad signals trigger defect") strategy has higher payoff than OBSTD when played against Bob's OBSTD strategy, we must consider several possible states of the game. Let gg be the state where both players received the good (cooperate) signal in the previous period. In this case each player has payoff 5 for cooperating. Both players in the gg state cooperate, so with probability $(1 - \epsilon)^2$ the next state will also be gg. With probability $\epsilon(1 - \epsilon)$, however, Alice will receive the bad (defect) signal while Bob receives the good signal. We call this state gb. Also with probability $\epsilon(1 - \epsilon)$ Bob will receive the bad (defect) signal while Alice receives the good signal. We call this state bg. Finally, with probability ϵ^2 both players receive the bad signal. We call this state bb. If we write π_s for the expected payoff of the game starting in state s, we then have the equation

$$\pi_{gg} = 5 + \delta[(1 - \epsilon)^2 \pi_{gg} + \epsilon(1 - \epsilon)(\pi_{bg} + \pi_{gb}) + \epsilon^2 \pi_{bb}].$$

In state gb, Alice ignores the defect signal so both players cooperated, with payoff 5. Then with probability $(1 - \epsilon)^2$ both receive the good signal, so the next state will be gg. With probability $\epsilon(1 - \epsilon)$ Alice receives a second bad signal in a row but Bob receives a good signal. We call this state gbb. With probability $\epsilon(1 - \epsilon)$ Alice receives a good signal but Bob receives a bad signal. This is just state bg. Finally, with probability ϵ^2 both players receive the bad signal, which is then the second in a row for Alice. We call this state bbb. We then have the equation

$$\pi_{gb} = 5 + \delta[(1 - \epsilon)^2 \pi_{gg} + \epsilon(1 - \epsilon)(\pi_{gbb} + \pi_{bg}) + \epsilon^2 \pi_{bbb}].$$

We also have

$$\pi_{bg} = -3(1 + \delta)$$
$$\pi_{bb} = -3$$
$$\pi_{gbb} = 5 + 8\delta$$
$$\pi_{bbb} = 0.$$

The first equation follows from the fact that Bob defects unconditionally forever, while Alice ignores the first bad signal. The second equation is the same except Alice only cooperates once. In the third equation, Bob has actually cooperated twice but Alice received two bad signals, so she defects on a cooperating Bob in the second round. The final equation is obvious.

If we solve these six equations simultaneously, we will get a value $\pi_r = \pi_{gg}$ for the original game. The resulting equation for π_r is long and complex, so we won't present it here. Comparing this payoff with (A12), we find that unless ϵ is very large, Alice's TBSTD strategy is better than OBSTD against OBSTD.

To find a Nash equilibrium in the private signal case, following Sekiguchi (1997) and Bhaskar and Obara (2002), suppose players cooperate with probability less than one on the first round and then in following rounds, they use a *trigger strategy* in which the first time a player receives a defect signal, he defects forever. To explain the first period, and assess the efficiency properties of the equilibrium, assume that from the second period on, Bob and Alice play the prisoner's dilemma depicted in §5.1, which they play repeatedly with termination probability $1 - \delta$. Now suppose Bob cooperates on the first round with probability p_o. Suppose Alice cooperates on the first round.

Then if Bob cooperates, Alice's expected value of the game is $5 + (1 - \epsilon)\delta\pi_r$, where π_r is the expected value of the game from the second round on, assuming both players cooperate on each round. The second term represents the probability $(1 - \epsilon)$ that Alice does not accidentally defect, times the probability δ of continuation, times the expected value π_r of the game from the second round on. Thus Alice's expected payoff from cooperating is

$$\pi_c = 5p_o - 3(1 - p_o) + (1 - \epsilon)\delta\pi_r$$

and if she defects, her payoff is

$$\pi_d = 8p_o.$$

To get Alice to cooperate, we must have $\pi_c \geq \pi_d$. Assuming equality, and noting that π_r satisfies $\pi_r = 5 + (1 - \epsilon)^2$, we get the equilibrium probability p_o given by

$$p_o = \frac{3(1 - \delta(1 - \epsilon)^2)}{5\delta(1 - \epsilon)}. \tag{A13}$$

This p_o is a probability, so it must lie between zero and one. We certainly have $p^o > 0$, and we will have $p^o < 1$ provided δ is near unity and $\epsilon < 0.8$. Hence for plausible values of the parameters, a private signal equilibrium exists in this case. The problem is that this equilibrium is extremely inefficient. For instance, with $\delta = 0.90$ and $\epsilon = 0.05$, the efficiency is about 3%. By contrast, as we have seen, in the public signal case with the same parameters, efficiency is over 50%.

A9 Student and Nonstudent Experimental Subjects

Are students who volunteer for experiments more prosocial than the general public? The following studies suggest not.

Bellemare et al. (2008), in an inequity aversion study, write that "extending the subject pool from students only to a more representative population [of Dutch citizens]... generates a distribution with much greater levels of inequity aversion." In other words, students are considerably less inequity averse than the more general Dutch sample studied.

Carpenter et al. (2005) used a dictator game showing that Middlebury College and Kansas City Community College students contributed less than employees at a Kansas City warehouse. Kansas City Community College students offered more in an ultimatum game than warehouse workers, who in turn offered more than Middlebury College students. Workers offered the same amount in the dictator game and the ultimatum game, while students gave much less in the dictator game, consistent with the view that in the ultimatum game workers were not making strategic offers, while students were.

Burks et al. (2011) used a sequential prisoner's dilemma game with subjects drawn from a sample of students on the one hand and professional bicycle messengers on the other, in Switzerland and the United States. The bicycle messengers exhibited more cooperative behavior than the students.

List (2004) studied contributions in a public goods game, finding that the behavior of participants at a sports-card show closely approximated that of students in laboratory experiments such as Andreoni (1988), Isaac et al. (1994), and Fehr and Gächter (2000a).

In the same paper, List found that participants aged 49 years and older cooperated more than college-age students, while middle-aged subjects approximated the behavior of college-age subjects. List also reported that controlling for income, older Florida residents also contributed more in a university fund-raising appeal. In the television game show *Friend or Foe*, a prisoner's dilemma game for big stakes, older players were more likely to cooperate than younger.

Carpenter et al. (2008) used a dictator game with subject-named charity recipients, finding that students gave 25% less than non-students. Students also gave significantly less, controlling for age and other demographics, and older responders gave more, controlling for student status (Carpenter, personal communication). Indeed, 48% of non-students contributed the entire endowment, whereas only 16% of students did.

Cardenas (2005) used a common pool resource game, finding that a sample of students from Colombia were less cooperative, extracting significantly more from the common pool than a sample of Colombian villagers.

Cleave et al. (2010) found that students who volunteered for an experiment were as trustworthy but less trusting than other students from the population from which the experimental subjects were drawn, but who were administered the trust game as a captive audience.

Falk et al. (2010) found that Swiss students who exhibited strong prosocial behavior in an unrelated field donation (contribution to a social fund) were not more likely to participate in experiments than students who did not contribute to the social fund. The experimenters also found that students and the general population were equally trusting in a trust game, but student trustees returned a smaller fraction of what was given to them by investors.

Gächter and Herrmann (2011) found that among Russian rural and urban experimental subjects, nonstudents contributed 18% more than students in a public goods game; 23% of the nonstudents contributed their entire endowment while only 12% of students did so.

A10   The Price Equation

Suppose there are groups $j = 1, \ldots, m$, and let q_j be the fraction of the population in group j. Let w_j be the mean fitness of the members of group j, so $w = \sum_j q_j w_j$ is the mean fitness of the whole population. We use the term fitness here, but as the Price equation is applicable to any system in which traits are differentially replicated over time, we could have used a more general term: number of replicas in the next period. Groups grow from one period to the next in proportion to their relative fitness, so if q_j' is the fraction of the population in group j in the next period, then

$$q_j' = q_j \frac{w_j}{w}.$$

Suppose there is a trait with frequency p_j in group j, so the frequency of the trait in the whole population is $p = \sum_j q_j p_j$. If p_j' and p' are the mean frequency of the trait in group j and the frequency of the trait in the population in the next period, respectively, then $p' = \sum_j q'_j p'_j$, so

$$p' - p = \sum q'_j p'_j - \sum q_j p_j$$
$$= \sum q_j \frac{w_j}{w}(p_j + \Delta p_j) - \sum q_j p_j$$
$$= \sum q_j \left(\frac{w_j}{w} - 1\right) p_j + \sum q_j \frac{w_j}{w} \Delta p_j.$$

Now writing $\Delta p = p' - p$ and multiplying the above expression by w, this becomes

$$w\Delta p = \sum q_j(w_j - w)p_j + \sum q_j w_j \Delta p_j. \tag{A14}$$

Because $\sum q_j w_j = w$ and $\sum q_j = 1$, we have

$$\sum q_j(w_j - w)p = \sum q_j w_j p - wp \sum q_j = qp - qp = 0,$$

Noting that

$$\sum q_j(w_j - w)(p_j - p) \equiv \mathrm{cov}[w_j, p_j]$$

and

$$\sum q_j w_j \Delta p_j \equiv \mathbf{E}[w_j \Delta p_j],$$

we can rewrite (A14) as

$$w\Delta p = \mathrm{cov}[w_j, p_j] + \mathbf{E}[w_j \Delta p_j], \tag{A15}$$

where the covariance and expectations are taken with respect to the population fractions q_j. We interpret (A15) as follows. The trait measured by p will increase in frequency if the left hand side of the equation is positive. Because $w > 0$, this will occur only if the right hand side is positive. If the trait measured by p is altruistic, as in the conventional application of the Price equation, then the first term $\mathrm{cov}[w_j, p_j]$ will be positive, because groups with higher fractions of the trait will have supranormal average fitness of their members. But the second term, $\mathbf{E}[w_j \Delta p_j]$, will be negative, because the altruists are disadvantaged within each group, so their within-group frequency declines, and Δp_j will be negative for all j. The trait will then spread only if the between-group advantage of the high-altruism groups is sufficient to overcome the within-group disadvantage of the altruists.

In Chapter 9 we apply the above equation to the case of Nonpunishing Cooperators, who may be considered within-group parasites rather than altruists, because they free ride on the punishment meted out by strong reciprocators against selfish individuals. In this case, the term $\beta_G = \mathrm{cov}[w_j, p_j]$ may be negative, because groups with higher fractions of Cooperators may have been invaded by selfish individuals and hence have below average fitness, unless the fraction of Cooperators is very high. Within groups the situation is inverted. As long as there is a sufficient number of strong reciprocators and sufficiently few selfish individuals, the term $\beta_i = \mathbf{E}[w_j \Delta p_j]$ will be positive, because the Cooperators are advantaged within each group. The reason is that they are never punished and do not bear the costs of punishing others. As a result, they are advantaged within each group, so their within-group frequency increases. The parasitic trait will then spread as long as the between-group disadvantage of the high Cooperator groups is insufficient to overcome the within-group advantage of the Cooperators. For very high or very low fractions of Cooperators in the population, of course this situation would not obtain. But the accounting of the within- and between-group effects in Figure 4.2 shows that for the simulations we have studied, our interpretation of the parasitic nature of Cooperators is indeed true.

In §4.2, we apply the Price equation to altruism in a social dilemma, where altruists supply a benefit b to other members of the group at a cost c to themselves. In this case, adding (4.2) over all i in group j, of which there are $q_j N$, where N is total population size, and dividing by N, we get

$$q_j w_j = q_j \beta_o + q_j p_j \beta_g + q_j p_j \beta_i. \tag{A16}$$

Adding this equation over all groups and dividing by N gives

$$w = \beta_o + p\beta_g + p\beta_i. \tag{A17}$$

This allows us to rewrite the group effect, the covariance term, in the Price equation above as the between-group variance multiplied by the total derivative of expected group size with respect to the fraction of altruists in a group, namely $\beta_g + \beta_i$:

$$
\begin{aligned}
\text{cov}[w_i, p_i] &= \sum_j q_j (w_j - w)(p_j - p) \\
&= \sum_j q_j (w_j - w) p_j \\
&= \sum_j q_j (p_j - p) p_j (\beta_i + \beta_g) \\
&= \sum_j q_j (p_j - p)^2 (\beta_i + \beta_g) \\
&= \text{var}(p_j)(\beta_i + \beta_g).
\end{aligned}
\tag{A18}
$$

The second equality follows from the fact that $\sum_j q_j (w_j - w)p = 0$ by the definition of w. The third follows by subtracting (A17) from (A16), simplifying, and substituting in the equation. The fourth equation is an algebraic rearrangement. The fifth equation follows from the fact that $\sum_j q_j (p_j - p) = 0$, which follows from the definitions: $\sum_j q_j p_j = p$ and $\sum_j q_j = 1$. More generally, if x and y are random variables and $y = a_o + a_1 x$ is the regression equation of x on y, then $\text{cov}(x, y) = a_1 \text{var}(x)$. To evaluate $\mathbf{E}[w_j \Delta p_j]$, we note that

$$
\begin{aligned}
p_j' - p_j &= \sum_i q_j' p_{ji}' - \sum_i q_j p_{ji} = \sum_i q_j \frac{w_{ji}}{w_j} p_{ji} - \sum_i q_j p_{ji} \\
&= \frac{1}{w_j} \sum_i q_j (w_{ji} - w_j) p_{ji},
\end{aligned}
$$

so

$$E[w_j \Delta p_j] = \sum_i q_j (w_{ji} - w_j) p_{ji} = \beta_j \sum_i q_j (p_{ji} - p_j) p_{ji}$$

$$= \beta_j \overline{\text{var}}(p_{ji}). \tag{A19}$$

Thus, substituting equations A18 and A19 into the Price equation, we have

$$w \Delta p = \text{var}(p_j) \beta_G - \beta_i \overline{\text{var}}(p_{ij}), \tag{A20}$$

where $\overline{\text{var}}(p_{ij})$ is the within-group genetic variance as defined in the text (equation 4.4). Substituting the costs and benefits of the altruistic behavior, defined in Figure 3.1, for the β's in this equation we have

$$w \Delta p = \text{var}(p_j)(b - c) - c \overline{\text{var}}(p_{ij}). \tag{A21}$$

where, as before, w is the population-wide average of the number of replicas (which we normalize to unity).

For an example of using the Price equation, suppose a population is composed of two large groups that in a given period are of equal size, with the fractions of altruists in each, $p_1 = 3/4$ and $p_2 = 1/4$, so $p = 1/2$ (because the groups are the same size, this means, for example, that 3/4 of the A's are in group one, 3/4 of the N's are in group two, and so on). To find the values of b and c such that p will be stationary, we need to equate the average fitness of the two types. Writing w_{ij} for the fitness of type i in group j ($i = A, N$, $j = 1, 2$) and w_i for the population average fitness of type i, and ignoring β_o, we have

$$w_A = p_1 w_{A1} + p_2 w_{A2} = (1 - p_1) w_{N1} + (1 - p_2) w_{N2} = w_N, \tag{A22}$$

or, the average fitness of A's and N's is the weighted average of their respective fitnesses in the two groups, so the condition for p to be stationary is given by

$$w_A = \frac{3}{4} \left(\frac{3}{4} b - c \right) + \frac{1}{4} \left(\frac{1}{4} b - c \right)$$

$$= \frac{1}{4} \left(\frac{3}{4} b \right) + \frac{3}{4} \left(\frac{1}{4} b \right) = w_N. \tag{A23}$$

Solving, we find the values of b and c for which $\Delta p = 0$, namely, $c/b = 1/4$. This means that, given the assumed distribution of A's and N's in the two groups, the population frequency of A's will be stationary if the cost of performing the altruistic act is one fourth the benefit. If we add the further requirement that the size of the total population be constant, so $w_A = 1 = w_N$ and assuming $\beta_o = 0$, we have $b = 8/3$ and $c = 2/3$.

An equivalent method is simply to use equation A21, along with the facts that $\overline{\text{var}}(p_{ij}) = p_j(1 - p_j) = 3/16$ for $j = 1, 2$ and $\text{var}(p_j) = 1/16$, so, using (A21), we have from the Price equation 4.3

$$w \Delta p = (b - c)/16 - 3c/16,$$

which, for $w \neq 0$, gives $c/b = 1/4$ as a condition for $\Delta p = 0$, reproducing the above result.

Further, reproducing the condition for the stationarity of p, given by (4.10), and using the empirical values from the example gives us

$$\frac{c}{b} = F_{ST} \equiv \frac{\text{var}(p_j)}{\overline{\text{var}(p_{ij})} + \text{var}(p_j)} = (1/16)/(3/16 + 1/16) = \frac{1}{4}, \qquad (A24)$$

as we would expect.

Thus, for values of $b > 4c$, the frequency of the altruistic trait will increase, exceeding one half in the next period. This occurs because the relative size of the more altruistic group grows, offsetting the decline in the fraction of altruists in each group.

The proliferation of the group-beneficial but individually costly trait is explained by the group structure of the population, which accounts for the fact that altruists tend to be paired with other altruists more frequently than the population average, despite random pairing within groups. Because a fraction p_1 of all A's are in group one in which the likelihood of being paired with an A is p_1, and analogously for the fraction p_2 of A's in group two, the probability of meeting an altruist conditional on being an altruist is

$$P(A|A) = p_1^2 + p_2^2 = 5/8.$$

Non-altruists meet altruists with probability

$$P(A|N) = (1 - p_1)p_1 + (1 - p_2)p_2 = 3/8.$$

The difference between these two conditional probabilities, $1/4$, is a measure of the degree of positive assortment in this population, and it is the expected advantage enjoyed by the altruistic trait by dint of its favored distribution among groups. Thus, reproducing (4.9) and (4.10), we have an equivalent way of representing (A24):

$$\frac{c}{b} = P(A|A) - P(A|N) = \frac{1}{4}. \qquad (A25)$$

A11   Weak Multi-level Selection

We assume all agents are genetically identical and there is clonal reproduction. We assume also that altruist phenotypes (A's) pass their cultural preference on to their offspring, as do the non-altruists (N's). As this is a cultural model, the term fitness means the number of replicas that an individual will make in the next period, which may be one if the individual retains the status quo trait, or greater if the individual is copied by another, or zero if the individual abandons the trait. The fitness of an N due to material payoffs is now $m_j^N = bp_j$, where p_j is the fraction of A's in group j, and the fitness of an A due to material payoffs (we term this "material fitness") is $m_j^A = bp_j - c$. Suppose w_j^A is the average fitness of A's, including the contribution m_j^A, as well as the net probability that N's switch to A's through socialization and from A's by imitation. Similarly, w_j^N is the average fitness of N's, including the contribution

m_j^N, as well as the net probability that A's switch to N's through imitation. Let γ_a be the rate per non-altruist at which N's are socialized into A's, and let γ_n be the rate per unit of payoff difference per altruist at which A's revert to N's through imitation. Since the payoff difference between A's and N's is $m_j^N - m_j^A = c$, we have

$$w_j^A = bp_j + \gamma_a(1 - p_j) - \gamma_n cp_j - c + \beta_o \qquad (A26)$$

$$w_j^N = bp_j - \gamma_a(1 - p_j) + \gamma_n cp_j + \beta_o \qquad (A27)$$

where β_0 is baseline fitness. There is then an equilibrium when $w_j^A = w_j^N$ with a fraction p_j^* of altruists within the group given by

$$p_j^* = \frac{2\gamma_a - c}{2(\gamma_a + c\gamma_n)}.$$

The average material fitness of a member of group j, which depends only on the material payoffs and not the phenotypic movements, is then

$$p_j^* m_j^A + (1 - p_j^*) m_j^N = \frac{(b - c)(2\gamma_a - c)}{2(\gamma_a + c\gamma_n)} + \beta_0.$$

Because in equilibrium this is greater than β_0 provided $\gamma_a > c/2$, a group with an effective socialization process will have higher mean material fitness than a group without such a process. Therefore any intergroup dynamic that favors wealthier groups will lead to the spread of the socialization process by group selection.

A12 Cooperation and Punishment with Quorum Sensing

We explored the effect on our results of plausible variations in the parameters, reported in the supplementary online materials for Boyd et al. (2010a). We calculated variants of Figures 9.1 to 9.4 to investigate the effect of (a) eliminating economies of scale in punishing (punishment can stabilize in a population only with a very high threshold, thereby making its emergence very unlikely); (b) raising the cost of punishing (reduces the range of parameters under which punishment can evolve); (c) a greater error rate (increases the frequency and cost of punishment, impeding its evolution); (d) variations in the number of periods in the interaction (longer interactions, unsurprisingly, facilitate the evolution of punishment); and (e) raising group size to 72 (very little effect). For the most part, variation among results can be understood as stemming from a trade-off between the first-period costs of inducing Nonpunishers to cooperate and the long-run benefit from the cooperation thereby induced.

Here we report the effect of varying degrees of relatedness (r). As can be seen from Figure A3, for $r = 0.035$, punishment may proliferate when rare only for a low threshold, while for $r = 0.125$, the threshold can be as large as five without preventing the proliferation of punishment when rare.

We subjected the agent-based model of §9.2 to a battery of sensitivity tests. We found that when cooperation is established, the average shirking rate is below 25% even for very high costs of punishing (k), and one standard deviation of the shirking rate in

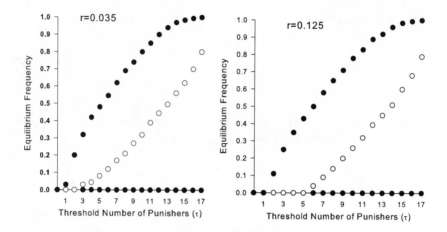

Figure A3. The evolution of continent punishment. In the baseline case in the text, groups are formed at random, so that when Punishers are rare, they are alone in groups and can induce cooperation only if they are willing to act alone. Increasing r, the relatedness among group members, increases the probability that more than one Punisher will be together in groups even when Punishers are rare. Thus for small values of τ, punishment can increase when rare even when r is assumed to 0.035. In each panel the upper curve is the stable equilibrium, while the lower curve indicates the boundary of the basin of attraction of this stable equilibrium. We illustrate the case $b = 2c$.

distinct runs is about 20% of the average. The same approximate picture obtains for variations in group size and the migration rate. We found that the F_{ST} for the population depends on group size as expected from standard population genetics (equation 6.1), and is fairly sensitive to the migration rate, also as is to be expected from standard population genetics.

REFERENCES

Akerlof, George A., "Labor Contracts as Partial Gift Exchange," *Quarterly Journal of Economics* 97,4 (1982):543–569.

Alexander, R. D., *Biology and Human Affairs* (Seattle: University of Washington Press, 1979).

___ , *The Biology of Moral Systems* (New York: Aldine, 1987).

Anderson, Christopher and Louis Putterman, "Do Non-strategic Sanctions Obey the Law of Demand? The Demand for Punishment in the Voluntary Contribution Mechanism," *Games and Economic Behavior* 54,1 (2006):1–24.

Andreoni, James, "Why Free Ride? Strategies and Learning in Public Good Experiments," *Journal of Public Economics* 37 (1988):291–304.

___ , "Impure Altruism and Donations to Public Goods: A Theory of Warm-Glow Giving," *Economic Journal* 100 (1990):464–477.

___ , "Warm-Glow versus Cold-Prickle: The Effects of Positive and Negative Framing on Cooperation in Experiments," *Quarterly Journal of Economics* 110,1 (1995):1–21.

___ and John H. Miller, "Giving According to GARP: An Experimental Test of the Consistency of Preferences for Altruism," *Econometrica* 70,2 (2002):737–753.

___ , Brian Erand, and Jonathan Feinstein, "Tax Compliance," *Journal of Economic Literature* 36,2 (1998):818–860.

Andrushko, V., K. Latham, D. Grady, A. Pastron, and P. Walker, "Bioarchaeological Evidence for Trophy Taking in Pre-historic Central California," *American Journal of Physical Anthropology* 127,375 (2005):375–384.

Aoki, Kenichi, "A Condition for Group Selection to Prevail over Counteracting Individual Selection," *Evolution* 36 (1982):832–842.

Aristotle, *Nichomachean Ethics* (Newburyport, MA: Focus Publishing, 2002[350 BC]).

Arrow, Kenneth J., "Political and Economic Evaluation of Social Effects and Externalities," in M. D. Intriligator (ed.), *Frontiers of Quantitative Economics* (Amsterdam: North Holland, 1971) pp. 3–23.

___ and Frank Hahn, *General Competitive Analysis* (San Francisco: Holden-Day, 1971).

___ and Gérard Debreu, "Existence of an Equilibrium for a Competitive Economy," *Econometrica* 22,3 (1954):265–290.

Ashraf, Nava, Dean S. Karlan, and Wesley Yin, "Tying Odysseus to the Mast: Evidence from a Commitment Savings Product in the Philippines," *Quarterly Journal of Economics* 121,2 (2006):635–672.

Aumann, Robert J., "Correlated Equilibrium and an Expression of Bayesian Rationality," *Econometrica* 55 (1987):1–18.

___ and Adam Brandenburger, "Epistemic Conditions for Nash Equilibrium," *Econometrica* 65,5 (1995):1161–1180.

Axelrod, Robert, *The Evolution of Cooperation* (New York: Basic Books, 1984).

___ and William D. Hamilton, "The Evolution of Cooperation," *Science* 211 (1981):1390–1396.

Axtell, Robert L., Joshua M. Epstein, and H. Peyton Young, "The Emergence of Classes in a Multi-agent Bargaining Model," in Steven Durlauf and H. Peyton Young (eds.), *Social Dynamics* (Cambridge: MIT Press, 2001) pp. 191–211.

Balikci, Asen, *The Netsilik Eskimo* (New York: Natural History Press, 1970).

Barr, Abigail, "Social Dilemmas, Shame Based Sanctions, and Shamelessness: Experimental Results from Rural Zimbabwe," (2001) Working Paper, Oxford University.

Bateson, Melissa, Daniel Nettle, and Gilbert Roberts, "Cues of Being Watched Enhance Cooperation in a Real-World Setting," *Biology Letters* 2 (2006):412–414.

Bellemare, Charles, Sabine Kröger, and Arthur van Soest, "Measuring Inequity Aversion in a Heterogeneous Population Using Experimental Decisions and Subjective Probabilities," *Econometrica* 76,4 (2008):815–839.

Benedict, Ruth, *Patterns of Culture* (Boston: Houghton Mifflin, 1934).

Bentham, Jeremy, *Introduction to the Principles of Morals and Legislation* (New York: Nabu Press, 2010[1789]).

Benz, Matthias and Stephan Meier, "Do People Behave in Experiments as in the Field? Evidence from Donations," *Experimental Economics* 11 (2008):268–281.

Berg, Joyce, John Dickhaut, and Kevin McCabe, "Trust, Reciprocity, and Social History," *Games and Economic Behavior* 10 (1995):122–142.

Bergstrom, Carl T. and Michael Lachmann, "Alarm Calls as Costly Signals of Antipredator Vigilance: The Watchful Babbler Game," *Animal Behaviour* 61 (2001):535–543.

Bergstrom, Ted, "Economics in a Family Way," *Journal of Economic Literature* 34 (1996):1903–1934.

Bernasconi, Giorgina and Joan E. Strassmann, "Cooperation among Unrelated Individuals: The Ant Foundress Case," *Trends in Ecology and Evolution* 14,12 (1999):477–482.

Bernhard, Helen, Ernst Fehr, and Urs Fischbacher, "Group Affiliation and Altrusitic Norm Enforcement," *Nature* 442 (2006):912–915.

Berscheid, E. and E. Walster, *Interpersonal Attraction* (Reading, MA: Addison, 1969).

Bewley, Truman F., *Why Wages Don't Fall during a Recession* (Cambridge: Cambridge University Press, 2000).

Bhaskar, V. and Ichiro Obara, "Belief-Based Equilibria: The Repeated Prisoner's Dilemma with Private Monitoring," *Journal of Economic Theory* 102 (2002):40–69.

___ , George J. Mailath, and Stephen Morris, "Purification in the Infinitely Repeated Prisoner's Dilemma," *Review of Economic Dynamics* 11,3 (2004):515–528.

Bill, J. H., "Notes on Arrow Wounds," *American Journal of Medical Science* 88 (1862):365–387.

Binford, Lewis, *Constructing Frames of Reference: An Analytical Method for Archaeological Theory Using Hunter-Gatherer and Environmental Data Sets* (Berkeley: University of California Press, 2001).

Bingham, Paul M., "Human Uniqueness: A General Theory," *Quarterly Review of Biology* 74,2 (1999):133–169.

Binmore, Kenneth G., *Natural Justice* (Oxford: Oxford University Press, 2005).

___ and Avner Shaked, "Experimental Economics: Where Next?" *Journal of Economic Behavior and Organization* 73 (2010):87–100.

Birdsell, J. B., "Some Population Problems Involving Pleistocene Man," *Cold Spring Harbor Symposium on Quantitative Biology* 22 (1957):47–69.

Blau, Peter, *Exchange and Power in Social Life* (New York: John Wiley, 1964).

Blinder, Alan S. and Don H. Choi, "A Shred of Evidence on Theories of Wage Stickiness," *Quarterly Journal of Economics* 105,4 (2000):1003–1015.

Bochet, Olivier, Talbot Page, and Louis Putterman, "Communication and Punishment in Voluntary Contribution Experiments," *Journal of Economic Behavior and Organization* 60,1 (2006):11–26.

Bocquet-Appel, Jean-Pierre, Pierre-Yvre Demars, Lorette Noiret, and Dmitry Dobrowsky, "Estimates of Upper Palaeolithic Meta-population Size in Europe from Archaeological Data," *Journal of Archaeological Science* 32 (2005):1656–1668.

Boehm, Christopher, "The Evolutionary Development of Morality as an Effect of Dominance Behavior and Conflict Interference," *Journal of Social and Biological Structures* 5 (1982):413–421.

——, "Egalitarian Behavior and Reverse Dominance Hierarchy," *Current Anthropology* 34,3 (1993):227–254.

——, "Impact of the Human Egalitarian Syndrome on Darwinian Selection," *American Naturalist* 150 (Supplement) (1997):S100–S121.

——, "The Natural Selection of Altruistic Traits," *Human Nature* 10,3 (1999):205–252.

——, *Hierarchy in the Forest: The Evolution of Egalitarian Behavior* (Cambridge, MA: Harvard University Press, 2000).

——, "Conscience Origins, Sanctioning Selection, and the Evolution of Altruism in Homo Sapiens," (2007) Department of Anthropology, University of Southern California.

——, *Moral Origins: Social Selection and the Evolution of Virtue, Altruism, and Shame* (New York: Basic Books, 2011).

Boesch, Christophe, "Cooperative Hunting in Wild Chimpanzees," *Animal Behavior* 48 (1984):653–667.

Bohnet, I., F. Greig, Benedikt Herrmann, and Richard Zeckhauser, "Betrayal Aversion," *American Economic Review* 98 (2008): 294–310.

Bollig, M., *Risk Management in a Hazardous Environment* (New York: Springer, 2006).

Bolton, Gary E. and Rami Zwick, "Anonymity versus Punishment in Ultimatum Games," *Games and Economic Behavior* 10 (1995):95–121.

Bonner, John Tyler, *The Evolution of Culture in Animals* (Princeton: Princeton University Press, 1984).

Boone, James L., "The Evolution of Magnanimity: When Is It Better to Give than to Receive?" *Human Nature* 9 (1998):1–21.

Boorman, Scott A. and Paul Levitt, "Group Selection on the Boundary of a Stable Population," *Theoretical Population Biology* 4 (1973):85–128.

Bosman, Ronald, Joep Sonnemans, and Marcel Zeelenberg, "Emotions, Rejections, and Cooling Off in the Ultimatum Game," (2001) Working Paper, University of Amsterdam.

Bouckaert, J. and G. Dhaene, "Inter-Ethnic Trust and Reciprocity: Results of an Experiment with Small Business Entrepreneurs," *European Journal of Political Economy* 20,4 (2004):869–886.

Bowles, Samuel, "Economic Institutions as Ecological Niches," *Behavior and Brain Sciences* 23,1 (2000):148–149.

——, *Microeconomics: Behavior, Institutions, and Evolution* (Princeton: Princeton University Press, 2004).

——, "Group Competition, Reproductive Leveling, and the Evolution of Human Altruism," *Science* 314 (2006):1569–1572.

— , "Genetic Differentiation among Hunter Gatherer Groups," (2007) Santa Fe Institute.

— , "Did Warfare among Ancestral Hunter-Gatherer Groups Affect the Evolution of Human Social Behaviors," *Science* 324 (2009a):1293–1298.

— , "Did Warfare among Ancestral Hunter-Gatherer Groups Affect the Evolution of Human Social Behaviors," *Science* 324 (2009b). Supporting Online Material.

— and Dorrit Posel, "Genetic Relatedness Predicts South African Migrant Workers' Remittances to Their Families," *Nature* 434,17 (2005):380–383.

— and Herbert Gintis, "State and Class in European Feudalism," in Charles Bright and Susan Harding (eds.), *Statemaking and Social Movements: Essays in History and Theory* (Ann Arbor: University of Michigan Press, 1984).

— and — , "The Origins of Human Cooperation," in Peter Hammerstein (ed.), *Genetic and Cultural Origins of Cooperation* (Cambridge, MA: MIT Press, 2004).

— and Peter Hammerstein, "Does Market Theory Apply to Biology?" in Peter Hammerstein (ed.), *Genetic and Cultural Evolution of Cooperation* (Cambridge, MA: MIT Press, 2003) pp. 153–165.

— , Jung-kyoo Choi, and Astrid Hopfensitz, "The Co-evolution of Individual Behaviors and Social Institutions," *Journal of Theoretical Biology* 223 (2003):135–147.

Boyd, Robert and Peter J. Richerson, *Culture and the Evolutionary Process* (Chicago: University of Chicago Press, 1985).

— and — , "The Evolution of Reciprocity in Sizable Groups," *Journal of Theoretical Biology* 132 (1988):337–356.

— and — , "Group Selection among Alternative Evolutionarily Stable Strategies," *Journal of Theoretical Biology* 145 (1990):331–342.

— and — , "Punishment Allows the Evolution of Cooperation (or Anything Else) in Sizeable Groups," *Ethology and Sociobiology* 113 (1992):171–195.

— and — , "The Pleistocene and the Origins of Human Culture: Built for Speed," *Perspectives in Ethology* 13 (2000):1–45.

— and Sarah Mathew, "A Narrow Road to Cooperation," *Science* 316 (2007):1858–1859.

— , Herbert Gintis, and Samuel Bowles, "Coordinated Punishment of Defectors Sustains Cooperation and Can Proliferate When Rare," *Science* 328 (2010a):617–620.

— , — , and — , "Supporting Online Material," (2010b) Submitted to Science.

— , — , — , and Peter J. Richerson, "Evolution of Altruistic Punishment," *Proceedings of the National Academy of Sciences* 100,6 (2003):3531–3535.

Brandt, Hannelore and Karl Sigmund, "The Logic of Reprobation: Assessment and Action Rules for Indirect Reciprocation," *Journal of Theoretical Biology* 231 (2004):475–486.

— and — , "Indirect Reciprocity, Image Scoring, and Moral Hazard," *Proceedings of the National Academy of Sciences* 102,7 (2005):2666–2670.

Brennan, Geoffrey and Philip Pettit, *The Economy of Esteem: An Essay on Civil and Political Society* (New York: Oxford University Press, 2004).

Brewer, Marilyn B. and Roderick M. Kramer, "Choice Behavior in Social Dilemmas: Effects of Social Identity, Group Size, and Decision Framing," *Journal of Personality and Social Psychology* 50,543 (1986):543–549.

Bronfenbrenner, Urie, *Children of the Dream* (London: Paladin, 1969).

Brown, Donald E., *Human Universals* (New York: McGraw-Hill, 1991).

Bugos, P. E., "An Evolutionary Ecological Analysis of the Social Organization of the Ayoreo of the Northern Gran Chaco," (1985) Ph.D Dissertation in Anthropology, Northwestern University.

Burch, Ernest S., *Alliance and Conflict: The World System of the Unupiaq Eskimos* (Lincoln: University of Nebraska Press, 2005).

Burks, Stephen V., Jeffrey P. Carpenter, and Eric Verhoogen, "Playing Both Roles in the Trust Game," *Journal of Economic Behavior and Organization* 51 (2003):195–216.

— , — , and Lorenz Götte, "Performance Pay and Worker Cooperation: Evidence from an Artifactual Field Experiment," *Journal of Economic Behavior and Organization* 70,3 (2011):459–469.

Burnham, Terence and Brian Hare, "Engineering Human Cooperation: Does Involuntary Neural Activation Increase Public Goods Contributions?" *Human Nature* 18 (2007):88–108.

Calvin, William H., "A Stone's Throw and Its Launch Window: Timing Precision and Its Implications for Language and Hominid Brains," *Journal of Theoretical Biology* 104 (1983):121–135.

Camerer, Colin, *Behavioral Game Theory: Experiments in Strategic Interaction* (Princeton: Princeton University Press, 2003).

— and Richard H. Thaler, "Ultimatums, Dictators, and Manners," *Journal of Economic Perspectives* 9,2 (1995):209–219.

— , George Loewenstein, and Drazen Prelec, "Neuroeconomics: How Neuroscience Can Inform Economics," *Journal of Economic Literature* 43 (2005):9–64.

Cameron, Lisa A., "Raising the Stakes in the Ultimatum Game: Experimental Evidence from Indonesia," *Economic Inquiry* 37,1 (1999):47–59.

Campbell, C., "Images of War: A Problem in San Rock Art Research," *World Archaeology* 18,2 (1986):255–268.

Caporael, Linnda, Robyn M. Dawes, John M. Orbell, and J. C. van de Kragt, "Selfishness Examined: Cooperation in the Absence of Egoistic Incentives," *Behavioral and Brain Science* 12,4 (1989):683–738.

Cardenas, Juan Camilo, "Groups, Commons and Regulation: Experiments with Villagers and Students in Columbia," in Bina Agarwal and Alessandro Vercelli (eds.), *Psychology, Rationality, and Economic Behavior: Challenging Standard Assumptions* (New York: Palgrave MacMillan in Association with International Economics Association, 2005).

Carpenter, Jeffrey P. and Erika Seki, "Do Social Preferences Increase Productivity? Field Experimental Evidence from Fishermen in Toyama Bay," *Economic Inquiry* (in press).

— , Cristina Connolly, and Caitlin Myers, "Altruistic Behavior in a Representative Dictator Experiment," *Experimental Economics* 11,3 (2008):282–298.

— , Stephen V. Burks, and Eric Verhoogen, "Comparing Student Workers: The Effects of Social Framing on Behavior in Distribution Games," *Research in Experimental Economics* 1 (2005):261–290.

Case, Anne, I-Fen Lin, and Sarah McLanahan, "How Hungry Is the Selfish Gene?" *Economic Journal* 110 (2000):781–804.

Cavalli-Sforza, Luigi Luca and Marcus W. Feldman, "Cultural versus Biological Inheritance: Phenotype Transmission from Parents to Children," *American Journal of Human Genetics* 25 (1973a):618–637.

— and — , "Models for Cultural Inheritance: Within Group Variation," *Theoretical Population Biology* 42,4 (1973b):42–55.

— and — , *Cultural Transmission and Evolution* (Princeton: Princeton University Press, 1981).

— and — , "Theory and Observation in Cultural Transmission," *Science* 218 (1982):19–27.

— , Paolo Menozzi, and Alberto Piazza, *The History and Geography of Human Genes* (Princeton: Princeton University Press, 1994).

Chamla, M.-C., "Les Hommes Epipaleolitiques de Columnata: Etude Anthropologique," *Memoires du Centre de Recherches Anthropologiques, Prehistoriques, et Ethnographiques* 15,1 (1970):1–117.

Choi, Jung-kyoo and Samuel Bowles, "The Coevolution of Parochial Altruism and War," *Science* 318,26 (2007):636–640.

Cinyabuguma, Matthias, Talbot Page, and Louis Putterman, "Can Second-Order Punishment Deter Perverse Punishment?" *Experimental Economics* 9 (2006):265–279.

Clark, Kenneth and Martin Sefton, "The Sequential Prisoner's Dilemma: Evidence on Reciprocation," *Economic Journal* 111,468 (2001):51–68.

Cleave, Blair, Nikos S. Nikiforakis, and Robert Slonim, "Is There Selection Bias in Laboratory Experiments?" (2010) University of Melbourne Department of Economics Working Paper No. 1106.

Clements, Kevin C. and David W. Stephens, "Testing Models of Non-kin Cooperation: Mutualism and the Prisoner's Dilemma," *Animal Behaviour* 50 (1995):527–535.

Clutton-Brock, T. H., "Breeding Together: Kin Selection and Mutualism in Cooperative Vertebrates," *Science* 296 (2002):69–72.

— , "Cooperation between Non-kin in Animal Societies," *Nature* 462 (2009):51–57.

— , D. Gaynor, G. M. McIlrath, A. D. C. Maccoll, R. Kansky, P. Chadwick, M. Manser, J. D. Skinner, and P. N. M Brotherton., "Predation, Group Size, and Mortality in a Cooperative Mongoose, *Suricata suricatta*," *Journal of Animal Ecology* 68 (1999):672–683.

Cohen, Dan and Ilan Eshel, "On the Founder Effect and the Evolution of Altruistic Traits," *Theoretical Population Biology* 10 (1976):276–302.

Cohen, J. M., "Sources of Peer Group Homogeneity," *Sociology of Education* 15,4 (1977):227–241.

Confucius, *The Analects* (New York: Random House, 1938). Arthur Waley (Tr.).

Connor, Richard C., "The Benefits of Mutualism: a Conceptual Framework," *Biological Reviews* 70 (1995):427–457.

— , "Cooperation beyond the Diad: On Simple Models and a Complex Society," *Philosophical Transactions of the Royal Society of London B* 365 (2010):2687–2697.

Cookson, R., "Framing Effects in Public Goods Experiments," *Experimental Economics* 3 (2000):55–79.

Cooley, Charles Horton, *Human Nature and the Social Order* (New York: Charles Scribner's Sons, 1902).

Cooper, Russell, Douglas V. DeJong, Robert Forsythe, and Thomas W. Ross, "Cooperation without Reputation: Experimental Evidence from Prisoner's Dilemma Games," *Games and Economic Behavior* 12 (1996):187–218.

Cosmides, Leda and John Tooby, "Cognitive Adaptations for Social Exchange," in Jerome H. Barkow, Leda Cosmides, and John Tooby (eds.), *The Adapted Mind: Evolutionary Psychology and the Generation of Culture* (New York: Oxford University Press, 1992) pp. 163–228.

Crow, James F. and Motoo Kimura, *An Introduction to Population Genetic Theory* (New York: Harper & Row, 1970).

Cybulski, Jerome, "Culture Change, Demographic History and Health and Disease on the Northwest Coast," in Clark Spencer Larsen and George Milner (eds.), *In the Wake of Contact: Biological Responses to Conquest* (New York: Wiley-Liss, 1994) pp. 75–85.

Daly, Martin and Margo Wilson, *Homicide* (New York: Aldine de Gruyter, 1988).

Damasio, Antonio R., *Descartes' Error: Emotion, Reason, and the Human Brain* (New York: Avon Books, 1994).

Danilenko, V. N., "Voloshskiy Epipaleoliticheskiy Mogil'nik (Epipalaeolothic Burial Ground at Volos'ke)," *Sovietskaya Etnografia* 3,54 (1955):54–61.

Darlington, P. J., "Group Selection, Altruism, Reinforcement and Throwing in Human Evolution," *Proceedings of the National Academy of Sciences* 72 (1975):3748–3752.

Darwin, Charles, *The Origin of Species by Means of Natural Selection, 6th Edition* (London: John Murray, 1872).

___ , *The Descent of Man* (Amherst: Prometheus Books, 1998[1873]).

Dawes, Robyn M., "Social Dilemmas," *Annual Review of Psychology* 31 (1980):169–193.

Dawkins, Richard, *The Selfish Gene* (Oxford: Oxford University Press, 1976).

___ , *The Extended Phenotype: The Gene as the Unit of Selection* (Oxford: Freeman, 1982).

___ , *The God Delusion* (Boston and New York: Houghton Mifflin, 2006).

De Dreu, Carsten K. W., Lindred L. Greer, Gerben A. Van Kleef, Shaul Shalvi, and Michel J. J. Handgraaf, "Oxytocin Promotes Human Ethnocentrism," *PNAS* 108,4 (2011):1262–1266.

___ , ___ , Michel J. J. Handgraaf, Shaul Shalvi, Gerben A. Van Kleef, and Jatthijs Baas, "The Neuropeptide Oxytocin Regulates Parochial Altruism in Intergroup Conflict among Humans," *Science* 328 (2010):1408–1411.

de Quervain, Dominique J.-F., Urs Fischbacher, Valerie Treyer, Melanie Schellhammer, Ulrich Schnyder, Alfred Buck, and Ernst Fehr, "The Neural Basis of Altruistic Punishment," *Science* 305 (2004):1254–1258.

de Tocqueville, Alexis, *Democracy in America*, Volume II (New York: Vintage, 1958).

de Waal, Frans, *Good Natured: The Origins of Right and Wrong in Humans and Other Animals* (Cambridge, MA: Harvard University Press, 1997).

___ , "Payment for Labour in Monkeys," *Nature* 404 (2000):563.

___ and Jason Davis, "Capuchin Cognitive Ecology: Cooperation Based on Projected Returns," *Neuropsychologia* 41 (2003):221–228.

Debreu, Gérard, *Theory of Value* (New York: John Wiley & Sons, 1959).

Diggle, S. P., Andy Gardner, Stuart A. West, and A. Griffin, "Evolutionary Theory of Bacterial Quorum Sensing: When Is a Signal Not a Signal?" *Philosophical Transactions of the Royal Society of London B* 362 (2007):1241–1249.

Dreber, Anna, David G. Rand, Drew Fudenberg, and Martin A. Nowak, "Winners Don't Punish," *Nature* 452 (2008):348–351.

Dugatkin, Lee Alan, *Cooperation among Animals* (New York: Oxford University Press, 1997).

___ , *The Altruism Equation* (Princeton: Princeton University Press, 2006).

___ and Mike Mesterton-Gibbons, "Cooperation among Unrelated Individuals: Reciprocal Altruism, Byproduct Mutualism, and Group Selection in Fishes," *Biosystems* 37 (1996):19–30.

Dunbar, Robin M., "Coevolution of Neocortical Size, Group Size and Language in Humans," *Behavioral and Brain Sciences* 16,4 (1993):681–735.

Durham, William H., *Coevolution: Genes, Culture, and Human Diversity* (Stanford: Stanford University Press, 1991).

Durkheim, Emile, *The Division of Labor in Society* (New York: The Free Press, 1933[1902]).

___ , *Suicide, a Study in Sociology* (New York: Free Press, 1951[1897]).

Durrett, Richard and Simon A. Levin, "The Importance of Being Discrete (and Spatial)," *Theoretical Population Biology* 46 (1994):363–394.

Edda, "Havamal," in D. E. Martin Clarke (ed.), *The Havamal, with Selections from other Poems in the Edda, Illustrating the Wisdom of the North in Heathen Times* (Cambridge: Cambridge University Press, 1923).

Edgerton, Robert B., *Sick Societies: Challenging the Myth of Primitive Harmony* (New York: Free Press, 1992).

Edgeworth, Francis Ysidro, *Mathematical Psychics: An Essay on the Application of Mathematics to the Moral Sciences* (London: Kegan Paul, 1881).

Efferson, Charles, Helen Bernhard, Urs Fischbacher, and Ernst Fehr, "Ultimate Origins of Human Prosocial Behaviour: An Empirical Test," *Nature* (2011).

Eibl-Eibesfeldt, I., "Warfare, Man's Indoctrinability and Group Selection," *Journal of Comparative Ethnology* 60,3 (1982):177–198.

Ekman, Paul, "An Argument for Basic Emotions," *Cognition and Emotion* 6 (1992):169–200.

Elster, Jon, "Emotions and Economic Theory," *Journal of Economic Perspectives* 36 (1998):47–74.

Ely, Jeffrey C. and Juuso Välimäki, "A Robust Folk Theorem for the Prisoner's Dilemma," *Journal of Economic Theory* 102 (2002):84–105.

Ember, Carol and Melvin Ember, "Resource Unpredictability, Mistrust, and War," *Journal of Conflict Resolution* 32,2 (1992):242–262.

Endicott, Kirk, "Property, Power and Conflict among the Batek of Malaysia," in T. Ingold, D. Riches, and James Woodburn (eds.), *Hunters and Gatherers* (New York: St. Martin's Press, 1988) pp. 110–127.

Engel, J. H., "A Verification of Lanchester's Law," *Operations Research* 2 (1954):163–171.

Engelmann, Dirk and Urs Fischbacher, "Indirect Reciprocity and Strategic Reputation Building in an Experimental Helping Game," *Games and Economic Behavior* 67 (2009):399–407.

Epstein, Joshua, *Generative Social Science: Studies in Agent-Based Computational Modeling* (Princeton: Princeton University Press, 2007).

— and Robert Axtell, *Growing Artificial Societies: Social Science from the Bottom Up* (Cambridge, MA: MIT Press, 1997).

Ertan, Arhan, Talbot Page, and Louis Putterman, "Who to Punish? Individual Decisions and Majority Rule in the Solution of Free Rider Problems," *European Economic Review* 3 (2009):495–511.

Eshel, Ilan and Luigi Luca Cavalli-Sforza, "Assortment of Encounters and Evolution of Cooperativeness," *Proceedings of the National Academy of Sciences* 79 (1982):1331–1335.

— and Marcus W. Feldman, "Initial Increase of New Mutants and Some Continuity Properties of ESS in Two Locus Systems," *American Naturalist* 124 (1984):631–640.

— , — , and Aviv Bergman, "Long-Term Evolution, Short-Term Evolution, and Population Genetic Theory," *Journal of Theoretical Biology* 191 (1998):391–396.

Falk, Armin and James J. Heckman, "Lab Experiments Are a Major Source of Knowledge in the Social Sciences," *Science* 326 (2009):535–538.

— and Urs Fischbacher, "A Theory of Reciprocity," *Games and Economic Behavior* 54,2 (2006):293–315.

— , Ernst Fehr, and Urs Fischbacher, "Driving Forces behind Informal Sanctions," *Econometrica* 73,6 (2005):2017–2030.

— , Stephan Meier, and Christian Zehnder, "Did We Overestimate the Role of Social Preferences? The Case of Self-Selected Student Samples," (2010) Department of Economics, University of Bonn.

Farmer, Doyne and Duncan Foley, "The Economy Needs Agent-Based Modelling," *Nature* 460,7256 (2010):685–686.

Fehr, Ernst and Andreas Leibbrandt, "Cooperativeness and Impatience in the Tragedy of the Commons," (2010) University of Zurich.

____ and E. Tougareva, "Do Competitive Markets with High Stakes Remove Reciprocal Fairness? Experimental Evidence from Russia," (1995) Working Paper, Institute for Empirical Economic Research, University of Zurich.

____ and John A. List, "The Hidden Costs and Returns of Incentives: Trust and Trustworthiness among CEOs," *Journal of the European Economics Association* 2,5 (2004):743–771.

____ and Lorenz Goette, "Do Workers Work More If Wages Are High? Evidence from a Randomized Field Experiment," *American Economic Review* 97,1 (2007):298–317.

____ and Simon Gächter, "Cooperation and Punishment," *American Economic Review* 90,4 (2000a):980–994.

____ and ____ , "Fairness and Retaliation: The Economics of Reciprocity," *Journal of Economic Perspectives* 14,3 (2000b):159–181.

____ and ____ , "Altruistic Punishment in Humans," *Nature* 415 (2002):137–140.

____ and Urs Fischbacher, "Why Social Preferences Matter: The Impact of Nonselfish Motives on Competition, Cooperation, and Incentives," *Economic Journal* 112 (2002):C1–C33.

____ and ____ , "Third Party Punishment and Social Norms," *Evolution & Human Behavior* 25 (2004):63–87.

____ , Georg Kirchsteiger, and Arno Riedl, "Does Fairness Prevent Market Clearing?" *Quarterly Journal of Economics* 108,2 (1993):437–459.

____ , Lorenz Goette, and Christian Zehnder, "A Behavioral Account of the Labor Market: The Role of Fairness Concerns," *Annual Review of Economics* 1 (2009):355–384.

____ , Simon Gächter, and Georg Kirchsteiger, "Reciprocity as a Contract Enforcement Device: Experimental Evidence," *Econometrica* 65,4 (1997):833–860.

____ , Urs Fischbacher, and Simon Gächter, "Strong Reciprocity, Human Cooperation and the Enforcement of Social Norms," *Human Nature* 13,1 (2002):1–25.

Feldman, Marcus W., Richard C. Lewontin, and Mary-Claire King, "A Genetic Melting Pot," *Nature* 424 (2003):374.

Ferguson, Brian, "Violence and War in Prehistory," in Debra L. Martin and David W. Frayer (eds.), *Troubled Times: Violence and Warfare in the Past* (Amsterdam: Gordon and Breach, 1997) pp. 321–354.

Fershtman, Chaim, Uri Gneezy, and Frank Verboven, "Discrimination and Nepotism: The Efficiency of the Anonymity Rule," (2002(Eitan Berglas School of Economics, Tel Aviv University.

Field, Alexander J., *Altruistically Inclined? The Behavioral Sciences, Evolutionary Theory, and the Origins of Reciprocity* (Ann Arbor: University of Michigan Press, 2004).

Fifer, F. C., "The Adoption of Bipedalism by the Hominids: A New Hypothesis," *Human Evolution* 2 (1987):135–47.

Fischbacher, Urs and Simon Gächter, "Social Preferences, Beliefs, and the Dynamics of Free-Riding in Public Good Experiments," *American Economic Review* 100 (2010):541–556.

____ , Ernst Fehr, and Michael Kosfeld, "Neuroeconomic Foundations of Trust and Social Preferences: Initial Evidence," *American Economic Review* 95,2 (2005):346–351.

Fix, Alan, *Migration and Colonization in Human Microevolution* (Cambridge: Cambridge University Press, 1999).

Fletcher, Jeffrey A. and Martin Zwick, "Unifying the Theories of Inclusive Fitness and Reciprocal Altruism," *American Naturalist* 168,2 (2006):252–262.

Foley, Robert A., "An Evolutionary and Chronological Framework for Human Social Behavior," *Proceedings of the British Academy* 88 (1996):95–117.

Fong, Christina M., "Social Preferences, Self-Interest, and the Demand for Redistribution," *Journal of Public Economics* 82,2 (2001):225–246.

—, Samuel Bowles, and Herbert Gintis, "Reciprocity and the Welfare State," in Herbert Gintis, Samuel Bowles, Robert Boyd, and Ernst Fehr (eds.), *Moral Sentiments and Material Interests: On the Foundations of Cooperation in Economic Life* (Cambridge, MA: MIT Press, 2005).

Forsythe, Robert, Joel Horowitz, N. E. Savin, and Martin Sefton, "Replicability, Fairness and Pay in Experiments with Simple Bargaining Games," *Games and Economic Behavior* 6,3 (1994):347–369.

Frank, Steven A., "Mutual Policing and Repression of Competition in the Evolution of Cooperative Groups," *Nature* 377 (1995):520–522.

—, "The Price Equation, Fisher's Fundamental Theorem, Kin Selection, and Causal Analysis," *Evolution* 51,6 (1997):1712–1729.

—, *Foundations of Social Evolution* (Princeton: Princeton University Press, 1998).

Friedman, James W., "A Non-cooperative Equilibrium for Supergames," *Review of Economic Studies* 38,113 (1971):1–12.

Fudenberg, Drew and David K. Levine, *The Theory of Learning in Games* (Cambridge, MA: MIT Press, 1997).

— and Eric Maskin, "The Folk Theorem in Repeated Games with Discounting or with Incomplete Information," *Econometrica* 54,3 (1986):533–554.

— and Parag A. Pathak, "Unobserved Punishment Supports Cooperation," *Journal of Public Economics* 94,1–2 (2009):78–86.

—, David K. Levine, and Eric Maskin, "The Folk Theorem with Imperfect Public Information," *Econometrica* 62 (1994):997–1039.

Gächter, Simon and Armin Falk, "Reputation and Reciprocity: Consequences for the Labour Relation," *Scandinavian Journal of Economics* 104,1 (2002):1–26.

— and Benedikt Herrmann, "The Limits of Self-Governance when Cooperators get Punished: Experimental Evidence from Urban and Rural Russia," *European Economic Review* (2011).

— and Ernst Fehr, "Collective Action as a Social Exchange," *Journal of Economic Behavior and Organization* 39,4 (1999):341–369.

—, Elke Renner, and Martin Sefton, "The Long-run Benefits of Punishment," *Science* 322 (2008):1510.

—, Esther Kessler, and Manfred Königstein, "Do Incentives Destroy Voluntary Cooperation?" (2011. University of Nottingham.

Gadagkar, Raghavendra, "On Testing the Role of Genetic Asymmetries Created by Haplodiploidy in the Evolution of Eusociality in the Hymenoptera," *Journal of Genetics* 70,1 (1991):1–31.

Gajdusek, D. C., "Factors Governing the Genetics of Primative Human Populations," *Cold Spring Harbor Symposium on Quantitative Biology* 29 (1964):121–135.

Gat, Azar, *War in Human Civilization* (Oxford: Oxford University Press, 2006).

Geanakoplos, John, David Pearce, and Ennio Stacchetti, "Psychological Games and Sequential Rationality," *Games and Economic Behavior* 1 (1989):60–79.

Gerloff, Ulrike, Bianka Hartung, Barbara Fruth, Gottfried Hohmann, and Diethard Tautz, "Intracommunity Relationships, Dispersal Pattern, and Paternity Success in a Wild Living Community of Bonobos (Pan paniscus) Determined from DNA Analysis of Faecal Samples," *Proceedings of the Royal Society of London B* 266 (1999):1189–1195.

Gilens, Martin, *Why Americans Hate Welfare* (Chicago: University of Chicago Press, 1999).

Gintis, Herbert, "Welfare Economics and Individual Development: A Reply to Talcott Parsons," *Quarterly Journal of Economics* 89,2 (1975):291–302.

___ , "The Nature of the Labor Exchange and the Theory of Capitalist Production," *Review of Radical Political Economics* 8,2 (1976):36–54.

___ , "Strong Reciprocity and Human Sociality," *Journal of Theoretical Biology* 206 (2000):169–179.

___ , "The Hitchhiker's Guide to Altruism: Genes, Culture, and the Internalization of Norms," *Journal of Theoretical Biology* 220,4 (2003a):407–418.

___ , "Solving the Puzzle of Human Prosociality," *Rationality and Society* 15,2 (2003b):155–187.

___ , "Modeling Cooperation among Self-Interested Agents: A Critique," *Journal of Socio-Economics* 33,6 (2004):697–717.

___ , "The Emergence of a Price System from Decentralized Bilateral Exchange," *Contributions to Theoretical Economics* 6,1,13 (2006). Available at www.bepress.com/bejte/contributions/vol6/iss1/art13.

___ , "The Dynamics of General Equilibrium," *Economic Journal* 117 (2007):1289–1309.

___ , *The Bounds of Reason: Game Theory and the Unification of the Behavioral Sciences* (Princeton: Princeton University Press, 2009a).

___ , *Game Theory Evolving* Second Edition (Princeton: Princeton University Press, 2009b).

___ , Eric Alden Smith, and Samuel Bowles, "Costly Signaling and Cooperation," *Journal of Theoretical Biology* 213 (2001):103–119.

Glaeser, Edward L., David Laibson, Jose A. Scheinkman, and Christine L. Soutter, "Measuring Trust," *Quarterly Journal of Economics* 65 (2000):622–846.

Gneezy, Ayelet and Daniel M. T. Fessler, "War Increases Cooperation-Promoting Punishments and Rewards," (2011. Rady School of Management, UC San Diego.

Goodall, Jane, "Tool-using and Aimed Throwing in a Community of Free-Living Chimpanzees," *Nature* 201 (1964):1264–1266.

Gould, Stephen Jay, *The Structure of Evolutionary Theory* (Cambridge, Massachusetts: The Belknap Press of Harvard University Press, 2002).

Grafen, Alan, "Natural Selection, Kin Selection, and Group Selection," in John R. Krebs and Nicholas B. Davies (eds.), *Behavioural Ecology: An Evolutionary Approach* (Sunderland, MA: Sinauer, 1984).

___ , "Modeling in Behavioral Ecology," in John R. Krebs and Nicholas B. Davies (eds.), *Behavioral Ecology: An Evolutionary Approach* (Oxford: Blackwell Scientific Publications, 1991) pp. 5–31.

___ , "An Inclusive Fitness Analysis of Altruism on a Cyclical Network," *Journal of Evolutionary Biology* 20 (2007):2278–2283.

Greif, Avner, "Institutions and Impersonal Exchange: From Communal to Individual Responsibility," *Journal of Institutional and Theoretical Economics* 158,1 (2002):168–204.

Guemple, Lee, "Teaching Social Relations to Inuit Children," in *Hunters and Gatherers 2: Property, Power and Ideology* (Oxford: Berg Publishers Limited, 1988) pp. 131–149.

Gurven, Michael and Hillard Kaplan, "Longevity among Hunter Gatherers: A Cross-Cultural Examination," *Population and Development Review* 33,2 (2007):321–365.

___ , Kim Hill, and Hillard Kaplan, "From Forest to Reservation: Transitions in Food Sharing among the Ache of Paraguay," *Journal of Anthropological Research* 58 (2002):93–120.

___ , ___ , ___ , Ana Magdalena Hurtado, and R. Lyles, "Food Transfers among Hiwi Foragers of Venezuela," *Human Ecology* 28 (2000a):171–218.

— , Wesley Allen-Arave, Kim Hill, and Ana Magdalena Hurtado, "'It's a Wonderful Life': Signaling Generosity among the Ache of Paraguay," *Evolution and Human Behavior* 21 (2000b):263–282.

Güth, Werner, R. Schmittberger, and B. Schwarze, "An Experimental Analysis of Ultimatum Bargaining," *Journal of Economic Behavior and Organization* 3 (1982):367–388.

Guzman, R. A., Carlos Rodriguez Sickert, and Robert Rowthorn, "When in Rome Do as the Romans Do: The Coevolution of Altruistic Punishment, Conformist Learning, and Cooperation," *Evolution and Human Behavior* 28 (2007):112–117.

Habyarimana, J., M. Humphreys, D. Posner, and J. Weinstein, *Coethnicity: Diversity and the Dilemmas of Collective Action* (New York: Russell Sage, 2009).

Hagoromo Society, *Born to Die: The Cherry Blossom Squadrons* (Los Angeles: Ohara, 1973).

Haldane, J. B. S., *The Causes of Evolution* (London: Longmans, Green & Co., 1932).

— , "Population Genetics," *New Biology* 18 (1955):34–51.

Haley, Kevin J. and Daniel M. T. Fessler, "Nobody's Watching? Subtle Cues Affect Generosity in an Anonymous Economic Game," *Evolution & Human Behavior* 26 (2005):245–256.

Hamilton, William D., "The Genetical Evolution of Social Behavior, I & II," *Journal of Theoretical Biology* 7 (1964):1–16,17–52.

— , "Innate Social Aptitudes of Man: An Approach from Evolutionary Genetics," in Robin Fox (ed.), *Biosocial Anthropology* (New York: John Wiley & Sons, 1975) pp. 115–132.

— , *Narrow Roads of Gene Land* (Oxford: Oxford University Press, 1998).

Hammerstein, Peter, "Darwinian Adaptation, Population Genetics and the Streetcar Theory of Evolution," *Journal of Mathematical Biology* 34 (1996):511–532.

— , "Why Is Reciprocity So Rare in Social Animals?" in Peter Hammerstein (ed.), *Genetic and Cultural Evolution of Cooperation* (Cambridge, MA: MIT Press, 2003) pp. 83–93.

Hammond, R. and Robert Axelrod, "Evolution of Contingent Altruism When Cooperation is Expensive," *Theoretical Population Biology* 69 (2006):333–338.

Hansen, Daniel G., "Individual Responses to a Group Incentive," *Industrial and Labor Relations Review* 51,1 (1997):37–49.

Hardin, Garrett, "The Tragedy of the Commons," *Science* 162 (1968):1243–1248.

Harpending, Henry and Alan R. Rogers, "On Wright's Mechanism for Intergroup Selection," *Journal of Theoretical Biology* 127 (1987):51–61.

Harpending, Henry C. and T. Jenkins, "!Kung Population Structure," in James F. Crow and C. Denniston (eds.), *Genetic Distance* (New York: Plenum, 1974).

Harsanyi, John C., "Games with Randomly Disturbed Payoffs: A New Rationale for Mixed-Strategy Equilibrium Points," *International Journal of Game Theory* 2 (1973):1–23.

Hassan, Fekri A., "Determination of the Size, Density, and Growth Rate of Hunting-Gathering Populations," in Steven Polgar (ed.), *Population, Ecology, and Social Evolution* (The Hague: Mouton, 1973) pp. 27–52.

— , "The Growth and Regulation of Human Population in Prehistoric Times," in Mark Nathan Cohen, Roy S. Malpass, and Harold G. Klein (eds.), *Biosocial Mechanisms of Population Regulation* (New Haven: Yale University Press, 1980).

Hauert, Christoph, Arne Traulsen, Hannelore Brandt, and Martin A. Nowak, "Via Freedom to Coercion: The Emergence of Costly Punishment," *Science* 316 (2007):1905–1907.

Hawkes, Kristin, J. F. O'Connell, and N. G. Blurton Jones, "Hadza Meat Sharing," *Evolution and Human Behavior* 22 (2001):113–142.

Hayashi, N., Elinor Ostrom, James M. Walker, and Toshio Yamagishi, "Reciprocity, Trust, and the Sense of Control: A Cross-Societal Study," *Rationality and Society* 11 (1999):27–46.

Hayek, F. A., *The Fatal Conceit* (Chicago: University of Chicago Press, 1988).

Headland, T. N., "Population Decline in a Philippine Negrito Hunter-Gatherer Society," *American Journal of Human Biology* 1 (1989):59–72.

Hechter, Michael and Satoshi Kanazawa, "Sociological Rational Choice," *Annual Review of Sociology* 23 (1997):199–214.

Heiner, Ronald A., "The Origin of Predictable Behavior: Further Modeling and Applications," *American Economic Review* 75,2 (1985):391–396.

Henn, Brenna, Christopher Gignoux, Matthew Jobin, et al., "Hunter Gatherer Genomic Diversity Suggests a Southern African Origin for Modern Humans," *Proceedings of the National Academy of Sciences* in press (2011).

Henrich, Joseph, "Does Culture Matter in Economic Behavior? Ultimatum Game Bargaining among the Machiguenga of the Peruvian Amazon," *American Economic Review* 90,4 (2000).

__ and Richard McElreath, "The Evolution of Cultural Evolution," *Evolutionary Anthropology* 12,3 (2003):123–135.

__ , Jean Ensminger, Richard McElreath, and Abigail Barr et al., "Markets, Religion, Community Size, and the Evolution of Fairness and Punishment," *Science* 327 (2010):1480–1484.

__ , Robert Boyd, Samuel Bowles, Colin Camerer, Ernst Fehr, and Herbert Gintis, *Foundations of Human Sociality: Economic Experiments and Ethnographic Evidence from Fifteen Small-Scale Societies* (Oxford: Oxford University Press, 2004).

Herrmann, Benedikt, Christian Thöni, and Simon Gächter, "Anti-Social Punishment across Societies," *Science* 319 (2008):1362–1367.

Hewlett, Barry S. and Luigi Luca Cavalli-Sforza, "Cultural transmission among Aka Pygmies," *American Anthropologist* 88,4 (1986):922–934.

Hiatt, L. R., *Kinship and Conflict: A Study of an Aboriginal Community in Northern Arnhem Land* (Canberra: Australian National University, 1965).

Hill, Kim, Ana Magdalena Hurtado, and Robert S. Walker, "High Adult Mortality among Hiwi Hunter-Gatherers: Implications for Human Evolution," *Journal of Human Evolution* 52,443 (2007):443–454.

__ and __ , *Aché Life History: The Ecology and Demography of a Foraging People* (New York: Aldine de Gruyter, 1996).

__ , Robert S. Walker, Miran Bozicevic, James Eder, T. N. Headland, Barry S. Hewlett, Ana Magdalena Hurtado, Frank W. Marlowe, Polly Wiessner, and Brian Wood, "Unique Human Social Structure Indicated by Coresidence Patterns in Hunter-Gatherer Societies," (2010. Arizona State University.

Hobbes, Thomas, *Leviathan* (New York: Penguin, 1968[1651]). Edited by C. B. MacPherson.

Hobsbawm, Eric, "Mass-Producing Traditions: Europe, 1870-1914," in Eric Hobsbawm and Terence Ranger (eds.), *The Invention of Tradition* (Cambridge: Cambridge University Press, 1983) pp. 263–307.

Hoffman, Elizabeth, Kevin McCabe, and Vernon L. Smith, "On Expectations and the Monetary Stakes in Ultimatum Games," *International Journal of Game Theory* 7 (1994a):289–302.

__ , __ , K. Shachat, and Vernon L. Smith, "Preference, Property Rights and Anonymity in Bargaining Games," *Games and Economic Behavior* 7 (1994b):346–380.

Homans, George, *Social Behavior: Its Elementary Forms* (New York: Harcourt Brace, 1961).

Howell, D., *The Demography of the Dobe !Kung*, 2nd Edition (Hawthorne: Aldine de Gruyter, 2000).

Hrdy, Sarah Blaffer, *Mother Nature: Maternal Instincts and How They Shape the Human Species* (New York: Ballantine, 2000).

___ , *Mothers and Others: The Evolutionary Origins of Mutual Understanding* (New York: Belknap, 2009).

Hume, David, *Treatise on Human Nature* (Aalen Darmstadt: Scientia Verlag, 1964[1739]). Philosophical Works.

Huxley, Julian S., "Evolution, Cultural and Biological," *Yearbook of Anthropology* (1955):2–25.

Huxley, Thomas, "The Struggle for Existence: A Programme," *Nineteenth Century* 23 (1888):163–165.

Hwang, Sung-Ha, "Large Groups May Alleviate Collective Action Problems," (2009. University of Massachusetts.

Ihara, Y. and Marcus W. Feldman, "Cultural Niche Construction and the Evolution of Small Family Size," *Theoretical Population Biology* 65,1 (2004):105–111.

Ingrao, Bruna and Giorgio Israel, *The Invisible Hand: Economic Equilibrium in the History of Science* (Cambridge, MA: MIT Press, 1990).

Isaac, B., "Throwing and Human Evolution," *African Archaeological Review* 5 (1987):3–17.

Isaac, R. Mark, James M. Walker, and Arlington W. Williams, "Group Size and Voluntary Provision of Public Goods: Experimental Evidence Utilizing Large Groups," *Journal of Public Economics* 54 (1994):1–36.

Jablonka, Eva and Marion J. Lamb, *Epigenetic Inheritance and Evolution: The Lamarckian Case* (Oxford: Oxford University Press, 1995).

James, William, "Great Men, Great Thoughts, and the Environment," *Atlantic Monthly* 46 (1880):441–459.

Johansson, S. Ryan and S. R. Horowitz, "Estimating Mortality in Skeletal Populations: Influence of the Growth Rate on the Interpretation of Levels and Trends during the Transition to Agriculture," *American Journal of Physical Anthropology* 71 (1986):233–250.

Johnsen, S. J., W. Dansgaard, and J. W. C. White, "The Origin of Arctic Precipitation under Present and Glacial Conditions," *Tellus* B41 (1992):452–468.

Jurmain, Robert, "Paleo-Epidemiological Patterns of Trauma in a Prehistoric Population from Central California," *American Journal of Physical Anthropology* 115,13 (2001):113–23.

Kaczynski, Theodore, "Excerpts from Unabomber's Journal," *New York Times* www.nytimes.com/1998/04/29/us/excerpts-from-unabomber-s-journal.html (1998).

Kahneman, Daniel, Jack L. Knetsch, and Richard H. Thaler, "Fairness as a Constraint on Profit Seeking: Entitlements in the Market," *American Economic Review* 76,4 (1986):728–741.

Kandel, Denise, "Homophily, Selection and Socialization in Adolescent Friendships," *American Journal of Sociology* 84,2 (1978):427–436.

Kaplan, Hillard and Arthur Robson, "The Evolution of Human Longevity and Intelligence in Hunter-Gatherer Economies," *American Economic Review* 93 (2003):150–169.

___ and Kim Hill, "Food Sharing among Ache Foragers: Tests of Explanatory Hypotheses," *Current Anthropology* 26,2 (1985):223–246.

___ and Michael Gurven, "The Natural History of Human Food Sharing and Cooperation: A Review and a New Multi-Individual Approach to the Negotiation of Norms," in Herbert Gintis, Samuel Bowles, Robert Boyd, and Ernst Fehr (eds.), *The Moral Sentiments: Origins, Evidence, and Policy* (Cambridge, MA: MIT Press, 2005) pp. 75–114.

___ , Jane Lancaster, J. A. Block, and S. E. Johnson, "Fertility and Fitness among Albuquerque Men: A Competitive Labor Market Theory," in Robin M. Dunbar (ed.), *Human Reproductive Decisions* (New York: St. Martins Press, 1995).

___ , Kim Hill, Jane Lancaster, and Ana Magdalena Hurtado, "A Theory of Human Life History Evolution: Diet, Intelligence, and Longevity," *Evolutionary Anthropology* 9 (2000):156–185.

Kappeler, P. K. and Carel P. van Schaik, *Cooperation in Primates and Humans* (Berlin: Springer, 2006).

Karlan, Dean S., "Using Experimental Economics to Measure Social Capital and Predict Real Financial Decisions," *American Economic Review* 95,5 (2005):1688–1699.

Keats, B., "Genetic Structure of the Indigenous Populations in Australia and New Guinea," *Journal of Human Evolution* 6 (1977):319–339.

Keeley, L., *War before Civilization* (New York: Oxford University Press, 1996).

Keller, Laurent, *Levels of Selection in Evolution* (Princeton: Princeton University Press, 1999).

Kelly, Robert L., *The Foraging Spectrum: Diversity in Hunter-Gatherer Lifeways* (Washington, DC: The Smithsonian Institution, 1995).

Kennedy, Donald, Colin Norman, and Elizabeth Pennisi, "What We Don't Know," *Science* 309,5731 (2005):75,93.

Kerr, Benjamin and Peter Godfrey-Smith, "Individualist and Multi-level Perspectives on Selection in Structured Populations," *Biology and Philosophy* 17 (2002):477–517.

— , — , and Marcus W. Feldman, "What Is Altruism?" *Trends in Ecology and Evolution* 19 (2004):135–140.

Keser, Claudia and Frans van Winden, "Conditional Cooperation and Voluntary Contributions to Public Goods," *Scandinavian Journal of Economics* 102,1 (2000):23–39.

Kirman, Alan, "The Intrinsic Limits of Modern Economic Theory: The Emperor Has No Clothes," *Economic Journal* 99,395 (1989):126–139.

Kiyonari, Toko, Shigehito Tanida, and Toshio Yamagishi, "Social Exchange and Reciprocity: Confusion or a Heuristic?" *Evolution and Human Behavior* 21 (2000):411–427.

Klein, Richard G., *The Human Career: Human Biological and Cultural Origins* (Chicago: University of Chicago Press, 1999).

— , "Archaeology and the Evolution of Human Behavior," *Evolutionary Anthropology* 9 (2000):17–36.

Knauft, Bruce, "Sociality versus Self-Interest in Human Evolution," *Behavioral and Brain Sciences* 12,4 (1989):12–13.

Knez, Marc and Duncan Simester, "Firm-Wide Incentives and Mutual Monitoring at Continental Airlines," *Journal of Labor Economics* 19,4 (2001):743–772.

Kollock, Peter, "Transforming Social Dilemmas: Group Identity and Cooperation," in Peter Danielson (ed.), *Modeling Rational and Moral Agents* (Oxford: Oxford University Press, 1998) pp. 186–210.

Kramer, Roderick M. and Marilyn B. Brewer, "Effects of Group Identity on Resource Use in a Simulated Commons Dilemma," *Journal of Personality and Social Psychology* 46,5 (1984):1044–1057.

Kropotkin, Pyotr, *Mutual Aid: A Factor in Evolution* (New York: Black Rose Books, 1989[1903]).

Kummer, Hans, *In Quest of the Sacred Baboon* (Princeton: Princeton University Press, 1995).

Laffont, Jean Jacques, *Incentives and Political Economy* (Oxford: Oxford University Press, 2000).

Laland, Kevin N. and Marcus W. Feldman, *Niche Construction* (Princeton: Princeton University Press, 2004).

— , F. John Odling-Smee, and Marcus W. Feldman, "Group Selection: A Niche Construction Perspective," *Journal of Consciousness Studies* 7,1/2 (2000):221–224.

Lambert, Patricia, "Patterns of Violence in Prehistoric Hunter-Gatherer Societies of Coastal Southern California," in Debra L. Martin and David W. Frayer (eds.), *Troubled Times: Violence and Warfare in the Past* (Amsterdam: Gordon and Breach, 1997) pp. 77–109.

Lanchester, Frederick William, *Aircraft in Warfare—The Dawn of the Fourth Arm* (London: Constable, 1916).

Lazarsfeld, P. F. and R. K. Merton, "Friendship as a Social Process," in M. Berger (ed.), *Freedom and Control in Modern Society* (Princeton: Van Nostrand, 1954).

LeBlanc, Steven A., *Constant Battles* (New York: St. Martins Press, 2003).

Ledyard, J. O., "Public Goods: A Survey of Experimental Research," in John H. Kagel and Alvin E. Roth (eds.), *The Handbook of Experimental Economics* (Princeton: Princeton University Press, 1995) pp. 111–194.

Lee, Richard Borshay, *The !Kung San: Men, Women and Work in a Foraging Society* (Cambridge: Cambridge University Press, 1979).

Lehmann, Laurent and Laurent Keller, "The Evolution of Cooperation and Altruism—A General Framework and a Classification of Models," *Journal of Evolutionary Biology* 19 (2006):1365–1376.

— and Marcus W. Feldman, "War and the Evolution of Belligerence and Bravery," *Proceedings of the Royal Society of London B* 275,1653 (2008):2877–2885.

—, Laurent Keller, and J. T. Sumpter, "The Evolution of Helping and Harming on Graphs: the Return of the Inclusive Fitness Effect," *Journal of Evolutionary Biology* 20 (2007):2284–2295.

Leibbrandt, Andreas, Uri Gneezy, and John A. List, "Ode to the Sea: The Socio-ecological Underpinnings of Social Norms," (2010. University of Chicago, Department of Economics.

Leimar, Olof and Peter Hammerstein, "Evolution of Cooperation through Indirect Reciprocity," *Proceedings of the Royal Society of London B* 268 (2001):745–753.

Leung, King To and John Levi Martin, "The Looking Glass Self: An Empirical Test and Elaboration," *Social Forces* 81,3 (2003):843–879.

Levin, Simon A., *Games, Groups, and the Global Good* (New York: Springer, 2009).

Levine, David K., "Modeling Altruism and Spitefulness in Experiments," *Review of Economic Dynamics* 1,3 (1998):593–622.

Levitt, Steven D. and John A. List, "What Do Laboratory Experiments Measuring Social Preferences Reveal about the Real World?" *Journal of Economic Perspectives* 21,2 (2007):153–174.

Lewis, David, *Conventions: A Philosophical Study* (Cambridge, MA: Harvard University Press, 1969).

Lewontin, Richard C., "Selection in and of Populations," in John Moore (ed.), *Ideas in Modern Biology* (New York: Natural History Press, 1965).

—, "The Units of Selection," in Richard Johnston (ed.), *Annual Review of Ecology and Systematics* (Palo Alto: Annual Review Inc., 1970).

List, John A., "Young, Selfish, and Male: Field Evidence on Social Preferences," *Economic Journal* 114 (2004):121–149.

—, "Friend or Foe? A Natural Experiment of the Prisoner's Dilemma," *Review of Economics and Statistics* 88,3 (2006):463–471.

—, "On the Interpretation of Giving in Dictator Games," *Journal of Political Economy* 115 (2007):482–493.

— and Todd Cherry, "Learning to Accept in Ultimatum Games: Evidence from an Experimental Design that Generates Low Offers," *Experimental Economics* 3,1 (2000):11–29.

Long, Jeffrey, Peter Smouse, and J. J. Wood, "The Allelic Correlation Structure of the Gainj- and Kalam-Speaking People II. The Genetic Distance between Population Subdivisions," *Genetics* 117 (1987):273–283.

Lorenz, Konrad, *On Aggression* (New York: Harcourt, Brace and World, 1963).

Lourandos, Harry, *Continent of Hunter-Gatherers* (Cambridge: Cambridge University Press, 1997).

Lumsden, C. J. and Edward O. Wilson, *Genes, Mind, and Culture: The Coevolutionary Process* (Cambridge, MA: Harvard University Press, 1981).

MacDonald, Douglas and Barry S. Hewlett, "Reproductive Interests and Forager Mobility," *Current Anthropology* 40,4 (1999):501–514.

Mahdi, Niloufer Qasim, "Pukhtunwali: Ostracism and Honor among the Pathan Hill Tribes," *Ethology and Sociobiology* 7 (1986):295–304.

Mailath, George J. and Stephen Morris, "Coordination Failure in Repeated Games with Almost-Public Monitoring," *Theoretical Economics* 1 (2006):311–340.

Mann, Michael, Raymond Bradley, and Malcolm Hughes, "Global-Scale Temperature Patterns and Climate Forcing over the Past Six Centuries," *Nature* 391 (1998):779–787.

Manson, Joseph H. and Richard W. Wrangham, "Intergroup Aggression in Chimpanzees," *Current Anthropology* 32,4 (1991):369–390.

Marlowe, Frank W., "Hunter-Gatherers and Human Evolution," *Evolutionary Anthropology* 14 (2005):54–67.

Martrat, Belen, Joan Grimalt, Constancia Lopez-Martinez, Isabel Cacho, Francisco Sierro, Jose Abel Flores, Rainer Zahn, Miguel Canals, Jason H. Curtis, and David Hodell, "Abrupt Temperature Changes in the Western Mediterranean over the Past 250,000 Years," *Science* 306 (2004):1762–1765.

Masclet, David, Charles Noussair, Steven Tucker, and Marie-Claire Villeval, "Monetary and Nonmonetary Punishment in the Voluntary Contributions Mechanism," *American Economic Review* 93,1 (2003):366–380.

Matessi, C. and Samuel Karlin, "On the Evolution of Altruism by Kin Selection," *PNAS* 81 (1984):1754–1758.

— and Suresh Jayakar, "Conditions for the Evolution of Altruistic Traits," *Theoretical Population Biology* 9 (1976):360–387.

Maynard Smith, John, "Group Selection and Kin Selection," *Nature* 201 (1964):1145–1147.

— , "Sexual Selection and the Handicap Principle," *Journal of Theoretical Biology* 57 (1976):239–242.

— and Eörs Szathmáry, *The Major Transitions in Evolution* (Oxford: Oxford University Press, 1997).

McBrearty, Sally and Alison Brooks, "The Revolution that Wasn't: a New Interpretation of the Origin of Modern Human Behavior," *Journal of Human Evolution* 39 (2000):453–563.

McCabe, Kevin, Vernon L. Smith, and M. LePore, "Intentionality Detection and Mindreading: Why Does Game Form Matter?" *Proceedings of the National Academy of Sciences* 97 (2000):4404–4409.

McElreath, Richard and Robert Boyd, *Mathematical Models of Social Evolution: Guide for the Perplexed* (Chicago: University of Chicago Press, 2006).

— , — , and Peter J. Richerson, "Shared Norms and the Evolution of Ethnic Markers," *Current Anthropology* 44,1 (2003):122–129.

McGhee, Robert, "Contact between Native North Americans and the Medieval Norse: A Review of the Evidence," *American Antiquity* 49,4 (1984):4–26.

McManus, Jerry, Delia Oppo, and James Cullen, "A 0.5 Million-Year Record of Millennial-Scale Climate Variabilty in the North Atlantic," *Science* 283 (1999):971–975.

McPherson, M., L. Smith-Lovin, and J. Cook, "Birds of a Feather: Homophily in Social Networks," *Annual Review of Sociology* 27 (2001):415–444.

Mead, George Herbert, *Mind, Self, and Society* (Chicago: University of Chicago Press, 1967[1934]).

Meier, Stephan and Charles Sprenger, "Stability of Time Preferences," (2010. IZA Discussion Paper 4756.

Melbye, Jerry and Scott Fairgrieve, "A Massacre and Possible Cannibalism in the Canadian Arctic: New Evidence from the Saunaktuc Site (NgTn-1)," *Arctic Anthropology* 31,2 (1994):55–77.

Mencken, H. L., *A Mencken Chrestomathy* (New York: Alfred A. Knopf, 1949).

Milinski, Manfred, "Byproduct Mutualism, Tit-for-Tat Reciprocity and Cooperative Predator Inspection," *Animal Behavior* 51 (1996):458–461.

Mill, John Stuart, "Utilitarianism," in A. I. Melden (ed.), *Ethical Theories 2nd Edition* (Upper Saddle River, NJ: Prentice Hall, 1957[1861]).

Miller, John H. and Scott E. Page, *Complex Adaptive Systems: An Introduction to Computational Models of Social Life* (Princeton: Princeton University Press, 2007).

Miller, Melissa B. and Bonnie L. Bassler, "Quorum Sensing in Bacteria," *Annual Review of Microbiology* 55 (2001):165–199.

Milner, George, "Nineteenth-Century Arrow Wounds and Perceptions of Prehistoric Warfare," *American Antiquity* 70 (2005):144–156.

Milo, R., "Evidence for Hominid Predatation at Klasies River Mouth, South Africa and Its Implications for the Behaviour of Modern Humans," *Journal of Archaeological Science* 25 (1998):99–133.

Mitani, John C., "Reciprocal Exchange in Chimpanzees and Other Primates," in P. K. Kappeler and Carel P. van Schaik (eds.), *Cooperation in Primates and Humans* (Berlin: Springer, 2006) pp. 107–119.

— , David P. Watts, and S. Amsler, "Lethal Intergroup Aggression Leads to Territorial Expansion in Wild Chimpanzees," *Current Biology* 20,12 (2010):R507–R508.

Moore, Jr., Barrington, *Injustice: The Social Bases of Obedience and Revolt* (White Plains: M. E. Sharpe, 1978).

Moratto, M., *California Archaeology* (Orlando: Academic Press, 1984).

Moreno Gamez, Stefany, Jon Wilkins, and Samuel Bowles, "Cosmopolitan Ancestors: Simulations Calibrated with Genetic and Ethnographic Data Show that Prehistoric Populations were not Small and Isolated," (2011. Santa Fe Institute.

Morgan, J., *The Life and Adventures of William Buckley: Thirty-two Years a Wanderer amongst the Aborigines* (Canberra: Australia National University Press, 1979[1852]).

Morris, M. W., W. M. Sim, and V. Girotto, "Distinguishing Sources of Cooperation in the One-round Prisoner's Dilemma: Evidence for Cooperative Decisions Based on the Illusion of Control," *Journal of Experimental Social Psychology* 34 (1998):464–512.

Mulvaney, D. J., "The Chain of Connection: The Material Evidence," in N. Peterson (ed.), *Tribes and Boundaries in Australia* (Canberra: Australian Institute of Aboriginal Studies, 1976) pp. 72–94.

Nachbar, John H., "Evolutionary' Selection Dynamics in Games: Convergence and Limit Properties," *International Journal of Game Theory* 19 (1990):59–89.

Nash, John F., "Equilibrium Points in n-Person Games," *Proceedings of the National Academy of Sciences* 36 (1950):48–49.

Nee, Sean, "Does Hamilton's Rule Describe the Evolution of Reciprocal Altruism?" *Journal of Theoretical Biology* 141 (1989):81–91.

Netting, Robert, *Balancing on an Alp: Ecological Change and Continuity in a Swiss Mountain Community* (Cambridge: Cambridge University Press, 1989).

Nettle, Daniel and Robin M. Dunbar, "Social Markers and the Evolution of Reciprocal Exchange," *Current Anthropology* 38 (1997): 93–99.

Newell, R. R., T. S. Constandse-Westerman, and C. Meikeljohn, "The Skeletal Remains of Mesolithic Man in Western Europe: An Evaluative Catalogue," *Journal of Human Evolution* 8,29 (1979):29–154.

Nikiforakis, Nikos S., "Punishment and Counter-punishment in Public Goods Games: Can We Still Govern Ourselves?" *Journal of Public Economics* 92,1–2 (2008):91–112.

Nisbett, Richard E. and Dov Cohen, *Culture of Honor: The Psychology of Violence in the South* (Boulder, CO: Westview Press, 1996).

Nishida, T., M. Hiraiwa-Hasegawa, T. Hasegawa, and Y. Takahata, "Group Extinction and Female Transfer in Wild Chimpanzees of the Mahale National Park, Tanzania," *Z. Tierpsychol.* 67 (1985):284–301.

Noe, Ronald, "A Veto Game Played by Baboons: A Challenge to the Use of the Prisoner's Dilemma as a Paradigm for Reciprocity and Cooperation," *Animal Behavior* 39 (1990):78–90.

—— and A. A. Sluijter, "Which Adult Male Savanna Baboons Form Coalitions?" *International Journal of Primatology* 16 (1995):77–105.

North Greenland Ice Core Project Members, "High-resolution Record of Northern Hemisphere Climate Extending into the Last Interglacial Period," *Nature* 431 (2004):147–151.

Nowak, Martin A., *Evolutionary Dynamics: Exploring the Equations of Life* (Cambridge, MA: Belknap Press, 2006).

—— and Karl Sigmund, "A Strategy of Win-Stay Lose-Shift that Outperforms Tit-for-Tat in the Prisoner's Dilemma Game," *Nature* 364 (1993):56–58.

—— and —— , "The Dynamics of Indirect Reciprocity," *Journal of Theoretical Biology* 194,4 (1998a):561–574.

—— and —— , "Evolution of Indirect Reciprocity by Image Scoring," *Nature* 393 (1998b):573–577.

Oberholzer-Gee, Felix, Joel Waldfolgel, and Matthew W. White, "Friend or Foe? Cooperation and Learning in High-Stakes Games," *Review of Economics and Statistics* 92,1 (2010):179–187.

Obot, I., "Value Systems in Cross Cultural Contact: The Effect of Perceived Similarity and Stability on Social Evaluation," *International Journal of Intercultural Relations* 12 (1988):363–379.

Odling-Smee, F. John, Kevin N. Laland, and Marcus W. Feldman, *Niche Construction: The Neglected Process in Evolution* (Princeton: Princeton University Press, 2003).

Ohtsuki, Hisashi, Christoph Hauert, Erez Lieberman, and Martin A. Nowak, "A Simple Rule for the Evolution of Cooperation on Graphs and Social Networks," *Nature* 441 (2006):502–505.

Olson, Mancur, *The Logic of Collective Action: Public Goods and the Theory of Groups* (Cambridge: Harvard University Press, 1965).

Oosterbeek, Hessel, Randolph Sloop, and Gus van de Kuilen, "Cultural Differences in Ultimatum Game Experiments: Evidence from a Meta-analysis," *Experimental Economics* 7 (2004):171–188.

Orbell, John M., Robyn M. Dawes, and J. C. van de Kragt, "Organizing Groups for Collective Action," *American Political Science Review* 80 (1986):1171–1185.

Ostrom, Elinor, *Governing the Commons: The Evolution of Institutions for Collective Action* (Cambridge: Cambridge University Press, 1990).

—— , James M. Walker, and Roy Gardner, "Covenants with and without a Sword: Self-Governance Is Possible," *American Political Science Review* 86,2 (1992):404–417.

Page, Talbot, Louis Putterman, and Bulent Unel, "Voluntary Association in Public Goods Experiments: Reciprocity, Mimicry, and Efficiency," *Economic Journal* 115 (2005):1032–1053.

Panchanathan, Karthik and Robert Boyd, "A Tale of Two Defectors: The Importance of Standing for Evolution of Indirect Reciprocity," *Journal of Theoretical Biology* 224 (2003):115–126.

—— and —— , "Indirect Reciprocity Can Stabilize Cooperation without the Second-Order Free Rider Problem," *Nature* 432 (2004):499–502.

Pandit, Sagar and Carel P. van Schaik, "A Model for Leveling Coalitions among Primate Males: toward a Theory of Egalitarianism," *Behavioral Ecology and Sociobiology* 55 (2003):161–168.

Parsons, Talcott, "Evolutionary Universals in Society," *American Sociological Review* 29,3 (1964):339–357.

—— and Edward Shils, *Toward a General Theory of Action* (Cambridge, MA: Harvard University Press, 1951).

Pascal, Blaise, *Pensées* (New York: Penguin, 1995).

Pearson, Karl, "Socialism and Natural Selection," *Fortnightly Review* 56 (1894).

Phelps, Elizabeth, Kevin J. O'Connor, William A. Cunningham, E. Sumie Funayama, Christopher Gatenby, John C. Gore, and Mahzarin R. Banaji, "Performance on Indirect Measures of Race Evaluation Predicts Amygdala Activity," *Journal of Cognitive Neuroscience* 12 (2000):1–10.

Piccione, Michele, "The Repeated Prisoner's Dilemma with Imperfect Private Monitoring," *Journal of Economic Theory* 102 (2002):70–83.

Pilling, A., "Predation and Warfare: Discussion," in Richard Borshay Lee and Irwin DeVore (eds.), *Man, the Hunter* (Chicago: Aldine, 1968) pp. 157–158.

Platteau, Jean-Philippe and Erika Seki, "Community Arrangements to Overcome Market Failure: Pooling Groups in Japanese Fisheries," in Masahiko Aoki and Yujiro Hayami (eds.), *Communities and Markets in Economic Development* (Oxford: Oxford University Press, 2001) pp. 344–402.

Plooij, F. X., "Tool-using during Chimpanzees' Bushpig Hunt," *Carnivore* 1 (1978):103–106.

Plutchik, R., *Emotion: A Psychoevolutionary Synthesis* (New York: Harper & Row, 1980).

Popper, Karl, *Objective Knowledge: An Evolutionary Approach* (Oxford: Clarendon Press, 1979).

Price, Douglas T., "Affluent Foragers of Mesolithic Southern Scandinavia," in Douglas T. Price and James A. Brown (eds.), *Prehistoric Hunter-Gatherers: The Emergence of Cultural Complexity* (Orlando: Academic Press, 1985) pp. 341–363.

Price, G. R., "Extension of Covariance Selection Mathematics," *Annals of Human Genetics* 35 (1972):485–490.

Queller, David C., "Kinship, Reciprocity and Synergism in the Evolution of Social Behaviour," *Nature* 318 (1985):366–367.

—— , "A General Model for Kin Selection," *Evolution* 42,2 (1992):376–380.

Ray, V. F., *Primitive Pragmatists: The Modoc Indians of Northern California* (Seattle: University of Washington Press, 1963).

Rege, Mari and Kjetil Telle, "The Impact of Social Approval and Framing on Cooperation in Public Goods Situations," *Journal of Public Economics* 88 (2004):1625–1644.

Richerson, Peter J. and Robert Boyd, "The Evolution of Ultrasociality," in I. Eibl-Eibesfeldt and F. K. Salter (eds.), *Indoctrinability, Ideology and Warfare* (New York: Berghahn Books, 1998) pp. 71–96.

___ and ___ , *Not by Genes Alone* (Chicago: University of Chicago Press, 2004).

Ridley, Mark and Alan Grafen, "Are Green Beard Genes Outlaws?" *Animal Behaviour* 29,3 (1981):954–955.

Ridley, Matt, *The Origins of Virtue: Human Instincts and the Evolution of Cooperation* (New York: Penguin, 1998).

Rilling, James K., Alan G. Sanfey, Jessica A. Aronson, Leigh E. Nystrom, and Jonathan D. Cohen, "Opposing Bold Responses to Reciprocated and Unreciprocated Altruism in Putative Reward Pathways," *Neuroreport* 15,16 (2004):2539–2543.

Roberts, D. F., "The Demography of Tristan da Cunha," *Population Studies* 25,3 (1971):465–479.

Rogers, Alan R., "Group Selection by Selective Emigration: The Effects of Migration and Kin Structure," *American Naturalist* 135,3 (1990):398–413.

___ and L. B. Jorde, "The Effect of Non-random Migration on Genetic Differences between Populations," *Annals of Human Genetics* 51 (1987):169–176.

Ross, Lee and Richard E. Nisbett, *The Person and the Situation: Perspectives of Social Psychology* (New York: McGraw-Hill, 1991).

Roth, Alvin E., Vesna Prasnikar, Masahiro Okuno-Fujiwara, and Shmuel Zamir, "Bargaining and Market Behavior in Jerusalem, Ljubljana, Pittsburgh, and Tokyo: An Experimental Study," *American Economic Review* 81,5 (1991):1068–1095.

Roughgarden, Joan, *The Genial Gene: Deconstructing Darwinian Selfishness* (Berkeley: University of California Press, 2009).

Rousset, François, "Inbreeding and Relatedness Coefficients: What do they Measure?" *Heredity* 88 (2002):371–380.

___ , *Genetic Structure and Selection in Subdivided Populations* (Princeton: Princeton University Press, 2004).

Rowthorn, Robert, "The Evolution of Altruism between Siblings: Hamilton's Rule Revisited," *Journal of Theoretical Biology* 241,4 (2006):774–790.

Russell, A. F. and J. Wright, "Avian Mobbing: Byproduct Mutualism not Reciprocal Altruism," *Trends in Ecololy and Evolution* 24 (2008):3–5.

Rustagi, Devesh, Stefanie Engel, and Michael Kosfeld, "Conditional Cooperation and Costly Monitoring Explain Success in Forest Commons Management," *Science* 330 (2010):961–965.

Sääksvuir, Lauri, M. Tapio, and Mikael Puurtinen, "Costly Punishment Prevails in Intergroup Conflict," *Proceedings of the Royal Society B* in press (2011).

Sally, David, "Conversation and Cooperation in Social Dilemmas," *Rationality and Society* 7,1 (1995):58–92.

Samuelson, Larry and Jianbo Zhang, "Evolutionary Stability in Asymmetric Games," *Journal of Economic Theory* 57,2 (1992):363–391.

Sanfey, Alan G., James K. Rilling, Jessica A. Aronson, Leigh E. Nystrom, and Jonathan D. Cohen, "The Neural Basis of Economic Decision-Making in the Ultimatum Game," *Science* 300 (2003):1755–1758.

Sato, Kaori, "Distribution and the Cost of Maintaining Common Property Resources," *Journal of Experimental Social Psychology* 23 (1987):19–31.

Savage, Leonard J., *The Foundations of Statistics* (New York: John Wiley & Sons, 1954).

Schapera, I., *The Khoisan Peoples of South Africa* (London: Routledge and Kegan Paul, 1930).

Schelling, Thomas C., *Micromotives and Macrobehavior* (New York: W. W. Norton & Co, 1978).

Schneider, Frédéric and Ernst Fehr, "Eyes Are Watching but Nobody Cares: The Irrelevance of Eye Cues for Strong Reciprocity," *Proceedings of the Royal Society of London B* 277 (2010):1315–1323.

Sekiguchi, Tadashi, "Efficiency in Repeated Prisoner's Dilemma with Private Monitoring," *Journal of Economic Theory* 76 (1997):345–361.

Sereno, Paul, Elena Garcea, Helene Jousse, Christopher Stojanowski, and Jean-Francois Saliege, "Lakeside Cemeteries in the Sahara: 5000 Years of Holocene Population and Environmental Change," *PLoS ONE* 3,1 (2008):1–22.

Sethi, Rajiv and E. Somanathan, "Preference Evolution and Reciprocity," *Journal of Economic Theory* 97 (2001): 273–297.

Sharma, G. R., "Mesolithic Lake Culture in the Ganga Valley," *Proceedings of the Prehistoric Society* 39,129 (1973):129–146.

Shubik, Martin, *Strategy and Market Structure: Competition, Oligopoly, and the Theory of Games* (New York: Wiley, 1959).

Sigg, Hans and Jost Falett, "Experiments on Respect of Possession and Property in Hamadryas Baboons (*Papio hamadryas*)," *Animal Behaviour* 33 (1985):978–984.

Sigmund, Karl, *The Calculus of Selfishness* (Princeton: Princeton University Press, 2010).

Silk, Joan B., "Practicing Hamilton's Rule: Kin Selection in Primate Groups," in P. K. Kappeler and Carel P. van Schaik (eds.), *Cooperation in Primates and Humans* (Berlin: Springer, 2006) pp. 25–46.

Simon, Herbert, "A Mechanism for Social Selection and Successful Altruism," *Science* 250 (1990):1665–1668.

Singer, R. and J. J. Wymer, *The Middle Stone Age at Klasies River Mouth in South Africa* (Chicago: University of Chicago Press, 1982).

Singer, Tania, "The Neuroeconomics of Mind Reading and Empathy," *American Economic Review* (2005):340–345.

Slonim, Robert and Alvin E. Roth, "Learning in High Stakes Ultimatum Games: An Experiment in the Slovak Republic," *Econometrica* 66,3 (1998):569–596.

Smith, Adam, *The Wealth of Nations* (New York: Modern Library, 1937[1776]).

— , *The Theory of Moral Sentiments* (New York: Prometheus, 2000[1759]).

Smith, Eric Alden and Rebecca L. Bliege Bird, "Turtle Hunting and Tombstone Opening: Public Generosity as Costly Signaling," *Evolution and Human Behavior* 21,4 (2000):245–261.

— , — , and Douglas W. Bird, "Risk and Reciprocity in Meriam Food-Sharing," *Evolution and Human Behavior* 23 (2002):297–321.

Smouse, Peter, Virginia Vitzthum, and James Neel, "The Impact of Random and Lineal Fission on the Genetic Divergence of Small Human Groups: A Case Study among the Yanomama," *Genetics* 98 (1981):179–197.

Sober, Elliot and David Sloan Wilson, "Reintroducing Group Selection to the Human Behavioral Sciences," *Behavior and Brain Sciences* 17 (1994): 585–654.

— and — , *Unto Others: The Evolution and Psychology of Unselfish Behavior* (Cambridge, MA: Harvard University Press, 1998).

Soltis, Joseph, Robert Boyd, and Peter J. Richerson, "Can Group-functional Behaviors Evolve by Cultural Group Selection: An Empirical Test," *Current Anthropology* 36,3 (1995):473–483.

Sosis, Richard, "Costly Signaling and Torch Fishing on Ifaluk Atoll," *Evolution and Human Behavior* 21,4 (2000):223–244.

Spence, A. Michael, "Job Market Signaling," *Quarterly Journal of Economics* 90 (1973):225–243.

Stephens, W., C. M. McLinn, and J. R. Stevens, "Discounting and Reciprocity in an Iterated Prisoner's Dilemma," *Science* 298 (2002):2216–2218.

Stern, Jessica, *Terror in the Name of God* (New York: Harper Collins, 2003).

Stiglitz, Joseph, "The Causes and Consequences of the Dependence of Quality on Price," *Journal of Economic Literature* 25 (1987):1–48.

Straub, Paul G. and J. Keith Murnighan, "An Experimental Investigation of Ultimatum Game: Common Knowledge, Fairness, Expectations, and Lowest Acceptable Offers," *Journal of Economic Behavior and Organization* 27 (1995):345–364.

Sugden, Robert, *The Economics of Rights, Co-operation and Welfare* (Oxford: Basil Blackwell, 1986).

Sutter, Mathias and Martin G. Kocher, "Trust and Trustworthiness across Different Age Groups," *Games and Economic Behavior* 59 (2007):364–382.

t. s. eliot , "Tradition and Individual Talent," in *The Sacred Wood: Essays on Poetry and Criticism* (London: Methuen & Co., 1920).

Tacon, P. and C. Chippendale, "Australia's Ancient Warriors: Changing Depictions of Fighting in the Rock Art of Arnhem Land, N.T.," *Cambridge Archaeological Journal* 4 (1994):211–248.

Tajfel, Henri, M. Billig, R. P. Bundy, and Claude Flament, "Social Categorization and Intergroup Behavior," *European Journal of Social Psychology* 1 (1971):149–177.

Taylor, Michael, *Anarchy and Cooperation* (London: John Wiley & Sons, 1976).

___ , "Good Government: On Hierarchy, Social Capital, and the Limitations of Rational Choice Theory," *Journal of Political Philosophy* 4,1 (1996):1–28.

Taylor, Peter, "Altruism in Viscous Populations: An Inclusive Fitness Model," *Evolutionary Ecology* 6 (1992):352–356.

___ and Leo Jonker, "Evolutionarily Stable Strategies and Game Dynamics," *Mathematical Biosciences* 40 (1978):145–156.

Telegin, D., "Vaslivs'kiy Tretiy Nekropol v Nadporojji (The Third Vasilivs'kiy Necropolis in Nadporozhie)," *Arkheologiya* 13 (1961):3–19.

Tenny, J. M., "Trauma among Early Californians," *Human Evolution* 5,4 (1990):397–401.

Tesfatsion, Leigh and Kenneth L. Judd, *Handbook of Computational Economics II: Agent-Based Computational Economics* (Amsterdam: Elsevier/North-Holland, 2006).

Thibaut, J. and H. Kelly, *The Social Psychology of Groups* (New York: Wiley, 1959).

Tilly, Charles, *The Formation of National States in Western Europe* (Princeton: Princeton University Press, 1975).

___ , "Charivaris, Repertoires and Urban Politics," in John M. Merriman (ed.), *French Cities in the Nineteenth Century* (New York: Holmes and Meier, 1981) pp. 73–91.

Tirole, Jean, *The Theory of Industrial Organization* (Cambridge: MIT Press, 1988).

Trivers, Robert L., "The Evolution of Reciprocal Altruism," *Quarterly Review of Biology* 46 (1971):35–57.

___ , "Reciprocal Altruism: 30 Years Later," in P. K. Kappeler and Carel P. van Schaik (eds.), *Cooperation in Primates and Humans: Mechanisms and Evolution* (Berlin: Springer, 2007) pp. 67–85.

Ule, Aljaz, Arthur Schram, Arno Riedl, and Timothy N. Cason, "Indirect Punishment and Generosity toward Strangers," *Science* 326 (2009):1701–1704.

Uyenoyama, Marcy and Marcus W. Feldman, "Theories of Kin and Group Selection: A Population Genetics Approach," *Theoretical Population Biology* 17 (1980):380–414.

Vanderschraaf, Peter, *Learning and Coordination: Inductive Deliberation, Equilibrium, and Conventions* (London: Routledge, 2001).

Veblen, Thorstein, *The Theory of the Leisure Class* (New York: Macmillan, 1899).

Vega-Redondo, Fernando, *Economics and the Theory of Games* (Cambridge: Cambridge University Press, 2003).

Verdu, Paul, Frederic Austerlitz, Arnaud Estoup, Renaud Vitalis, Myriam Georges, Sylvain Thery, Alain Froment, Sylvie Le Bomin, Antoine Gessain, Jean-Marie Hombert, Lolke Van der Veen, Luis Quintana-Murci, Serge Bahuchet, and Evelyne Heyer, "Origins and Genetic Diversity of Pygmy Hunter-Gatherers from Western Central Africa," *Current Biology* 19 (2009):1–7.

Vigilant, Linda, Michael Hofreiter, Heike Siedel, and Christophe Boesch, "Paternity and Relatedness in Wild Chimpanzee Communities," *Proceedings of the National Academy of Sciences* 98,23 (2001):12890–12895.

Voors, Maarten, Eleonora Nillesen, Philip Verwimp, Erwin Bulte, Robert Lensink, and Daan van Soest, "Does Conflict Affect Preferences? Results from Field Experiments in Burundi," *American Economic Review* in press (2011).

Walsh, Simon J., R. John Mitchell, Natalie Watson, and John S. Buckleton, "A Comprehensive Analysis of Microsatellite Diversity in Aboriginal Australians," *Journal of Human Genetics* 52 (2007):712–728.

Warner, W. L., "Murngin Warfare," *Oceania* 1,457 (1931):457–492.

Watabe, M., S. Terai, N. Hayashi, and Toshio Yamagishi, "Cooperation in the One-Shot Prisoner's Dilemma based on Expectations of Reciprocity," *Japanese Journal of Experimental Social Psychology* 36 (1996):183–196.

Weibull, Jörgen W., *Evolutionary Game Theory* (Cambridge, MA: MIT Press, 1995).

Wendorf, F., "Site 117: A Nubian Final Paleolithic Graveyard Near Jebel Sahaba, Sudan," in F. Wendorf (ed.), *The Prehistory of Nubia* (Dallas: Methodist University Press, 1968) pp. 954–998.

Whiting, Beatrice B. and John W. M. Whiting, *Children of Six Cultures: A Psycho-Cultural Analysis* (Cambridge, MA: Harvard University Press, 1975).

Whitlock, M. C., B. H. Davis, and S. Yeaman, "The Costs and Benefits of Resource Sharing: Reciprocity Requires Resource Heterogeneity," *Journal of Evolutionary Biology* 20 (2007):1772–1782.

Wiessner, Polly, "Hunting, Healing and Hxaro Exchange: A Long Term Perspective on !Kung (Hu/'hoansi) Large-Game Hunting," *Evolution and Human Behavior* 23 (2002):407–436.

——, "Norm Enforcement among the Ju/'hoansi Bushmen: A Case of Strong Reciprocity?" *Human Nature* 16,2 (2005):115–145.

Williams, G. C., *Adaptation and Natural Selection: A Critique of Some Current Evolutionary Thought* (Princeton: Princeton University Press, 1966).

Wilson, David Sloan, "Structured Demes and the Evolution of Group-Advantageous Traits," *American Naturalist* 111 (1977):157–185.

—— and Lee Alan Dugatkin, "Group Selection and Assortative Interactions," *American Naturalist* 149,2 (1997):336–351.

__ , G. B. Pollock, and Lee Alan Dugatkin, "Can Altruism Evolve in Purely Viscous Populations?" *Evolutionary Ecology* 6 (1992):331–341.

Wilson, Edward O., *The Insect Societies* (Cambridge, MA: Harvard University Press, 1971).

__ , *Sociobiology: The New Synthesis* (Cambridge, MA: Harvard University Press, 1975).

Wilson, Margo, Marc Hauser, and Richard W. Wrangham, "Does Participation in Intergroup Conflict Depend on Numerical Assessment, Range Location, or Rank for Wild Chimpanzees?" *Animal Behavior* 61 (2001):1203–1216.

Winterhalder, Bruce and Eric Alden Smith, *Evolutionary Ecology and Human Behavior* (New York: Aldine de Gruyter, 1992).

Wood, Elisabeth Jean, *Insurgent Collective Action and Civil War in El Salvador* (Cambridge,: Cambridge University Press, 2003).

Woodburn, James, "Egalitarian Societies," *Man* 17,3 (1982):431–451.

Wright, Robert, *The Moral Animal* (New York: Vintage, 1995).

Wright, Sewall, "Coefficients of Inbreeding and Relationship," *American Naturalist* 56 (1922):330–338.

__ , "Evolution in Populations in Approximate Equilibrium," *Journal of Genetics* 30 (1935):257–266.

__ , "Discussion on Population Genetics and Radiation," *J. Cell. Comp. Physiol.* 235:(Suppl.1) (1950):187–210.

Wrong, Dennis H., "The Oversocialized Conception of Man in Modern Sociology," *American Sociological Review* 26 (1961):183–193.

Yamagishi, Toshio, "The Provision of a Sanctioning System as a Public Good," *Journal of Personality and Social Psychology* 51 (1986):110–116.

__ , "The Provision of a Sanctioning System in the United States and Japan," *Social Psychology Quarterly* 51,3 (1988a):265–271.

__ , "Seriousness of Social Dilemmas and the Provision of a Sanctioning System," *Social Psychology Quarterly* 51,1 (1988b):32–42.

__ , "Group Size and the Provision of a Sanctioning System in a Social Dilemma," in W. B. G. Liebrand, David M. Messick, and H. A. M. Wilke (eds.), *Social Dilemmas: Theoretical Issues and Research Findings* (Oxford: Pergamon Press, 1992) pp. 267–287.

__ , N. Jin, and Toko Kiyonari, "Bounded Generalized Reciprocity: In-Group Boasting and In-Group Favoritism," *Advances in Group Processes* 16 (1999):161–197.

__ , Shigeru Terai, Toko Kiyonari, Nobuhiro Mifune, and Satoshi Kanazawa, "The Social Exchange Heuristic: Managing Errors in Social Exchange," *Rationality and Society* 19,3 (2007):259–291.

Young, H. Peyton, "Conventions," *Journal of Economic Perspectives* 10 (1995):105–122.

__ , *Individual Strategy and Social Structure: An Evolutionary Theory of Institutions* (Princeton: Princeton University Press, 1998).

__ , *Strategic Learning and its Limits* (Oxford: Oxford University Press, 2006).

Zahavi, Amotz, "Mate Selection—A Selection for Handicap," *Journal of Theoretical Biology* 53 (1975):205–214.

Zei, G. and Luigi Luca Cavalli-Sforza, "Education and Birth Control," *Genus* 33 (1977):15–42.

Subject Index

Author Index